Women in France since 1789

EUROPEAN STUDIES SERIES

General Editors: Colin Jones, Richard Overy, Joe Bergin, John Breuilly and Patricia Clavin

Published

Women in France
since 1789
The Meanings of Difference

SUSAN K. FOLEY
Associate Professor,
School of History, Philosophy,
Political Science and International Relations,
Victoria University of Wellington

Principal Fellow,
Department of History,
University of Melbourne

First published 2004 by
PALGRAVE MACMILLAN
Houndmills, Basingstoke, Hampshire RG21 6XS and
175 Fifth Avenue, New York, N.Y. 10010
Companies and representatives throughout the world

PALGRAVE MACMILLAN is the global academic imprint of the Palgrave Macmillan division of St. Martin's Press, LLC and of Palgrave Macmillan Ltd. Macmillan® is a registered trademark in the United States, United Kingdom and other countries. Palgrave is a registered trademark in the European Union and other countries.

ISBN 13: 978-0-333-61993-3

This book is printed on paper suitable for recycling and made from fully managed and sustained forest sources.

A catalogue record for this book is available from the British Library.

A catalog record for this book is available from the Library of Congress.

10 9 8 7 6 5 4 3 2 1
13 12 11 10 09 08 07 06 05 04

Transferred to Digital Printing 2008

For Jeremy and Marcelle

Contents

Preface

What can we know of the lives of women in France over the past 200 years? In *The Second Sex*, published in 1949, Simone de Beauvoir asserted that woman is 'a free and autonomous being like all human creatures', but 'finds herself living in a world where men compel her to assume the status of the Other' (p. 29). This means that we often find it difficult to know the lives of women of the past, more difficult perhaps than to know those of men. But it also means that the lives of women are conditioned by their gendered experience, that they nevertheless live their lives in the society and culture they share with men, and that they have struggled, at least since the French Revolution, to cease to be other and to gain control of their lives through politics. This book seeks to present the lives of women in France since the Revolution appeared to open new possibilities to them but instead sought to enshrine their difference. The book focuses on women's gendered experience, on their lives in society, and on their struggle to gain a place as actors in the world of politics. Above all it focuses on the tension between difference and equality, between women's place in a 'separate sphere' and their engagement with the world of public life and citizenship.

Nineteenth-century French society was distinguished by deep divisions based on class and milieu as well as on gender. The lives of women in this society must be understood in their different contexts, as peasant women, urban working women and elite women. Part I of this book is thus a study of women's lives in these three main contexts. Their gendered experience, however, gives rise to efforts to shape the world through politics, initially on the part of elite women. During the nineteenth century, their efforts must take the form of indirect participation. Part II of this book is thus a study of women's indirect participation in politics as well as of their struggle for direct participation, which we know as feminism.

In the twentieth century, women found themselves called upon to act publicly more and more, even before they obtained the suffrage and even by organisations, like the Catholic Church and fascist parties, which proclaimed that women's primary duties were in the home, as mothers and helpmeets of men. Part III of this book is thus a study of women's increasingly public activity in the first half of the twentieth century. At the same time, the social and economic forces unleashed by modern capitalism tended to blur if not eliminate the differences between rural and urban women, and between working women and elite women. Their lives were of course different, but in the second half of the twentieth century they all partook increasingly of one national culture. Part IV of this book is thus a study of women increasing their sphere of activity and of their increasingly similar lives.

We move in this way from a primarily social interpretation, at a time when women had little voice, to a more political interpretation, at a time nearer our own when women have gained a significant voice and appear to be on the way to gaining yet more chance to speak for themselves. This shift in interpretation corresponds to the shift in women's position, from 'Other' excluded from political action to an increasingly integrated if still 'Other', more and more engaged in politics.

This may seem like an old-fashioned story of continuing progress. It is not, certainly, a story of straightforward and even progress. Poor and especially immigrant women are still left out of the majority culture. Gains have been won and lost. Nevertheless, overall, French women in the twenty-first century have significantly larger spheres of activity available to them for their self-realisation. The story of the shift from social to political is the story of women's increasing control over their own lives.

Acknowledgements

The Faculty of Humanities and Social Sciences at Victoria University of Wellington supported the research for this book most generously with periods of leave and financial grants. Without that support the project would not have been viable and I am most grateful. The Library staff, particularly those in inter-loan services, have been enormously helpful in meeting my needs and it gives me great pleasure to acknowledge their professional expertise and friendly support.

My friends in the History Department (now Programme) at Victoria University of Wellington have acted as sounding boards and critics as well as sources of encouragement. Somehow they knew when to adopt each of those stances. Their friendship has made the writing of this book a pleasure. I also thank colleagues in the History Department of the University of Melbourne for their support and interest in the project. I owe a special debt to Dr Alice Garner for finding me some fabulous things when I needed them. Her wonderful research skills, as well as her practical support and suggestions, have been invaluable.

This book draws on the research and knowledge of the many historians whose work I have enjoyed, and been challenged by, over many years. Those debts are not always explicit, although they have been acknowledged as far as possible in the notes to each chapter. Translations from the French are my own unless otherwise indicated.

Finally, I must acknowledge the special contribution of those close to me, without which this book would never have been completed. The tolerance and love of my family, particularly Jeremy and Marcelle, are constantly treasured. Charlotte and Kerry have been pillars of strength. I thank, in particular, Charles Sowerwine, for his intellectual companionship and generosity, for his heroic editorial interventions, and for his unfailing support.

Introduction: The French Revolution and Gender Politics – Creating a World of Difference

> You have broken the sceptre of despotism, you have pro-
> nounced that beautiful motto that deserves to be inscribed
> on every forehead, and in every heart: *the French are a free
> people*, and every day you continue to allow thirteen million
> slaves to wear the shameful chains of thirteen million despots!
> You have declared equality of rights, and you unjustly deprive
> the gentlest and most useful group amongst you of those
> rights! [...] you have decreed that access to dignities and
> honours will be open without distinction to every talent; and
> you still continue to present insurmountable barriers to ours!
>
> *Requête des dames à l'Assemblée Nationale*, 1789

The 'ladies' who presented this petition to the National Assembly in
late 1789 called on the male legislators to end privileges based on
sex, consistent with their abolition of other forms of discrimination.
They requested the Assembly to confer on women 'the same liberty,
the same advantages, the same rights and the same honours as the
masculine sex'.[1] The National Assembly and the governments that
followed between 1789 and 1799 proved unwilling to do this. Following the coup d'état of Napoleon Bonaparte in 1799, the inequality of
women was officially inscribed in the new legal code, the Code
Napoléon of 1804. Some women embraced the maternal role to
which they were now assigned, but French women emerged from

1

the Revolutionary decade with clear legal and political disadvantages compared to men.

Studies of this transformative Revolutionary period have frequently overlooked the fact that the political changes it instituted worked in different or even contradictory ways for the two sexes. As Joan Landes argued in an influential study of late eighteenth-century politics, the period celebrated for 'enlightenment' and 'revolution' might be considered one of anti-enlightenment and counter-revolution when evaluated from women's perspective.[2] As men gained political rights and saw the prospect of citizenship open before them, women were excluded and thus became less 'equal' than previously to men of their own social group.

The 'modern' woman was born of the shift from Old Regime autocracy to nineteenth-century representative government. She was to inhabit a 'private' sphere created specifically to contain her. The 'modern' man, by contrast, was to inhabit the newly created 'public' sphere of citizenship. A number of historians have argued that this strongly delineated gender order was not accidental: it was an inherent and pivotal feature of the new political world. In the transition to modernity, gender differentiation became one of the features by which the world was perceived and ordered; by which the natural was distinguished from the unnatural, the normal from the abnormal, the normative from the aberrant, the acceptable from the unacceptable. The vision of modernity both reflected and reproduced – socially, culturally and politically – a mental landscape delineated by sexual difference which has had significant consequences for French society, and indeed for Western society, to the present day. The history of women in France in the 'modern' period has been strongly influenced, then, by the circumstances in which modernity itself came into being there. Understanding the process by which the 'modern' world emerged as a gendered world is fundamental to understanding the history of women in modern France, especially the complexities of their struggles to define themselves and be recognised as political subjects of the democratic nation state.

Gender and the challenge to the old political order

During the Old Regime, as the period before the French Revolution of 1789 is often called, few people, male or female, had the right to a say in affairs of State. Old Regime society was a 'corporatist' society in which people's place and entitlements were shaped by their membership of different groups, not by their personal qualities as individuals. Women's status in this society – and men's too – depended more on their social origins than on their sex.

The 'spectacular' nature of Old Regime monarchy, which relied on the public display of royal splendour to assert its legitimacy and power, demanded the visibility of the court. The glamour and conspicuous consumption of the aristocracy, with the royal family at its head, affirmed the social hierarchy and their own place within it. Noble women possessed considerable power in such a society, though never on the same terms as men.[3] The role of King's mistress, for instance, was one of the most influential in the Kingdom. Given that royal marriages were primarily political alliances, the King's 'favourite' had his ear in a way that the Queen often did not. The archetypal Royal Mistress was Madame de Pompadour, lover of Louis XV from 1745 until her death in 1764. She promoted her own favourites to key posts, and acted as a gatekeeper controlling access to the king. She also intervened directly in both domestic affairs and international diplomacy.[4] Queen Marie-Antoinette (1755–1793), wife of Louis XVI, played a similar role and was heavily criticised as a result.

Such women, though few in number, wielded enormous influence: a fact that made them hated rather than admired by unsuccessful claimants to office. Their lifestyles and roles allowed arguments that women exerted an undesirable influence in Old Regime politics. They were held responsible for the supposed 'effeminacy' of the Old Regime and the emasculation of men, who were seen as subject to female whims and political conniving. Female political participation, it followed, was inevitably self-serving and destructive.[5] As Dorinda Outram points out, the fact that women were closely associated with power under the Old Regime meant that the terms in which that regime was condemned had an antifeminine dimension.[6] Attributing power to women in the discredited past also justified defining power as a male prerogative as the new Revolutionary order unfolded.[7]

Ancien régime society valued sociability over domestic privacy, so the social roles of women in the top ranks of that society also gave them considerable influence. The institution of the 'salon', in particular, enabled prominent women to play major roles in the intellectual life of the Old Regime. By the late eighteenth century, salons had been transformed from frivolous social gatherings into centres for the exchange of ideas and the sharing of knowledge.[8]

The salons brought together people of different ranks. They rewarded superiority of intellect, not the superiority of birth that was the foundation of Old Regime social hierarchy. Salons were fundamental to the creation of a new 'public sphere' – a sphere of public debate and social criticism where the King's authority did not reach.[9] Leading *salonnières* like Mme Geoffrin, Mlle de Lespinasse and Mme Necker created physical spaces and intellectual environments in which 'enlightened' ideas could be debated and new ways of organising social and political life was imagined. The male leaders of the French Enlightenment, the *philosophes*, used these female-headed salons to debate and refine their ideas. For this reason, Dena Goodman argues that 'Enlightenment' is best regarded as a collective project of debate and criticism, rather than as a series of great individual works.[10]

Enlightened thinkers were committed to social improvement. They turned to 'nature' as an infallible guide to how people should live. Above all, they sought to identify the characteristics of man and woman in their uncorrupted state, before the impact of 'civilisation'. Defining the appropriate place of women in society was a key theme of Enlightenment writings, because it was integral to defining more rational and progressive ways of organising society.[11] The idea that women and men were inherently different, bound together by ties of complementarity, was one of the most influential (though contentious) claims developed by 'enlightened' theorists. Earlier biological theories had seen male and female bodies as largely similar. But, as Robert Nye puts it, biologists and doctors undertook a 'bio-ethnography' in the 1780–1830 period, cataloguing the attributes identified with each sex.[12] They created complementarity by locating femininity in the reproductive, maternal body. Biology now became destiny for women.[13]

The most significant feature of the complementarity model is that it excluded women from the 'universality' now identified with masculinity. Rather than being an imperfect male, the female now became his opposite. The male was the 'universal' norm; woman was his 'other'. He embodied reason; she embodied emotion. He was an autonomous individual, capable of governing his own behaviour and hence that of others. She needed to be governed. He was defined as capable of participating in a 'social contract' between the governed and those in authority – a model of political life being developed in this period to challenge autocracy – while she was not. Carole Pateman argues that 'social contract' theories of government were premised on a '*fraternal* social contract' despite claiming to be universal: men envisaged sharing political power amongst themselves and maintaining their power over women, who were excluded from the new consensual politics.[14]

The detailed catalogue of gender traits produced by eighteenth-century theorists was couched in the language of science. Doctors like Pierre Roussel, in his *Moral and Physical System of Woman* (1775), confidently pronounced on the social implications of female reproductive biology, although the processes of ovulation and conception would not begin to be understood until the mid-nineteenth century. The project of mapping the landscape of sex and gender traits was designed to tie down those traits and 'anchor' them in the body, but this betrayed the fear that they were inherently unstable. And the instability of sexual identities pointed to an instability in the social identities that sexed beings assumed. This had important implications at a time when new social and political identities – the identities associated with citizenship and representative public authority in particular – were being created.

The determination to 'tie down' the natural world to the 'laws' that human science had 'discovered' was also a response to the anxieties provoked by change in other dimensions of life. Emergent concerns about population decline, as well as about economic change and its impact on the family economy, were to strengthen as the nineteenth century unfolded. As Nye points out, the responses to economic change, like those provoked by political change, were to be justified by reference to biological 'laws' governing the sexes.[15]

In the gendered universe created by eighteenth-century theorists, man's 'natural' sphere was identified as the public world of business and politics, and woman's as the private world, governed by sentiment and emotion. Woman was destined for dependence on man in this model. Yet there was no necessary connection between 'difference' and dependence. It was not inevitable that women construed as domestic should automatically be deprived of the rights of personhood, or even the rights of citizenship. Rather, claiming a natural and logical relationship between 'difference' and dependence was a means of legitimating male power, as new patterns of social relations were created. It also rationalised denying women the right of consent within a new consensual model of politics.[16]

The complementarity model, as Thomas Laqueur has eloquently demonstrated, broke with an earlier conception of the gender order that saw women as similar to men in nature but less perfect.[17] Within that model women were subordinate but their potential to attain men's level was sometimes acknowledged. There was no 'species barrier' between the sexes. That earlier view still lingered in 'enlightened' arguments that differences between men and women, especially in matters like rationality, stemmed from women's inadequate education rather than from 'nature'. Louise d'Epinay insisted, for instance, that 'men and women have the same nature and the same constitution [...] the weakness of our constitution and our organs belongs definitely to our education, and is a consequence of the condition to which we have been assigned in society'. While she noted that it 'would no doubt take several generations to get us [women] back to how nature made us', she argued that, given a different education, women were capable of the same autonomy and the same social functions as men.[18] Other writers attributed women's inequality to men's power over them. Madame Lambert charged: 'Men usurped authority over women by force, rather than by natural right', and the Marquis de Condorcet concurred: 'One searches in vain', he wrote, to justify men's authority over women. 'This inequality has no other origin than the abuse of force.'[19]

The correspondence and published writings of *salonnières* and *philosophes* reveal a wide array of different views on woman's nature and social roles, but Jean-Jacques Rousseau was particularly influential. The Rousseauian social model appealed to many men. It contrasted a private sphere and a new 'bourgeois' public sphere (called 'bourgeois' because it by-passed Old Regime social hierarchies and was open to a broad array of participants). Significantly, too, the biological model of separate and distinct sexes was fully compatible with this social structure, indicating that both emerged from a similar preoccupation with defining and ordering the social universe.[20] But despite making citizenship a male prerogative, it also appealed to many women because it acknowledged the value of their contributions. Rousseau's argument that motherhood was a critically important social function won many female admirers, who embraced his call for them to send their wetnurses home and breastfeed their infants themselves. Ironically, however, Rousseau's four children were deposited in foundling homes at birth.[21]

The separation of 'public' and 'private' spheres associated most clearly with the philosophy of Rousseau not only divided 'political' and 'personal' matters, but also distinguished the behaviours appropriate to each sphere. Sexuality was increasingly defined as inappropriate to public life because it was governed by emotional expressiveness and personal needs, rather than by self-constraint and consideration for the public good. The spectacle of sex – an image that critics associated with the Old Regime, where women were said to have utilised their sexuality for political ends – was to be replaced by sexual privacy, and politics was to be an 'asexual' domain. Since women were commonly identified with sexuality – they were called 'the sex' as though men were not sexed beings – this idea had significant implications for women. It implied that 'woman' and 'public life' did not mix.

This helps to explain why condemnations of 'public' women in the late eighteenth century were often shaped as attacks on their sexuality. The Queen, in particular, was targeted as 'unnatural': she was described as a whore with bisexual proclivities, who committed incest with her seven-year-old son.[22] There was no evidence for these calumnies, but the 'unnaturalness' of female power was evoked by alluding to female sexual disorder. From this perspective, too, it appeared logical that the privatisation of sexuality and the creation of an orderly political sphere could be achieved by the removal of women from public life.

The rational male was presented as capable of governing his own sexual conduct whereas women's sexuality was feared (by men) as uncontrollable.[23] But if women's capacity for sexual enticement was troublesome, men's inability to resist them was also problematic. Rousseau's condemnation of playwrights who gave actresses 'the same power over spectators as they have over lovers' suggests his fear not only of actresses but of women in general.[24] Even before the Revolution, then, arguments for the exclusion of women from the political domain reflected men's fear of their own powerlessness before female sexuality. Men's vulnerability to their sex drive was at the heart of the problem. Rather than drawing the conclusion that lack of self-control should exclude men from public life, however, they resorted to the disqualification of women and thus the removal of anything that might distract men (heterosexual men, at least) from their public responsibilities.

The exclusion of women from public life was also justified by theories that transformed their power of sexual enticement into a socially useful device. Women, for Rousseau and later for his Revolutionary devotees, became the lure by which men could be tamed, and their baser instincts diverted to serve the public good. By raising women to the pedestal, placing them out of reach (and out of competition with men) and transforming them into objects of reverence, men could be urged to 'transcend' 'the baseness of [their] human nature'.

Unsatisfied male desire would be diverted to public service, and the threat of a slide into barbarism and naked self-interest would be averted. The price, again, was female seclusion and the idealisation of the chaste wife.[25]

Men's constant resistance to sharing power with women, and the array of arguments presented to justify it, have led some scholars to conclude that its origins are psychological. Both Carole Pateman and Lynn Hunt have explored the psychodynamics by which masculinity has historically been linked to power over women. They identify the late eighteenth-century shift from monarchical rule to representative politics as a key moment when such tendencies can be glimpsed in operation. Hunt argues that the French revolutionaries operated from within a family dynamic in creating their new model of politics. They could best imagine a new political order by imagining new types of families, because the patriarchal family structure of the day provided a model for hierarchical relationships of power, and because political power had long been explained in familial language. Hunt describes the Revolutionary process of 'imagining' politics in familial terms as the 'family romance' of the French Revolution.[26] In her reading, this imaginative venture of social reconstruction reshaped rather than removed male dominance. Men's power in the post-Revolutionary world was justified by representing them as kindly fathers and loving husbands, and casting those of earlier eras as tyrannical patriarchs.

As Joan Landes has argued, 'public' man could not be imagined without the 'private' woman against whom he defined himself. In her view, 'the bourgeois public [sphere] is essentially, not just contingently, masculinist'.[27] In other words, sexual inequality is integral to the new model of politics, not a historical accident. Other historians have concurred. Karen Offen emphasises men's rejection of an egalitarian model of politics,[28] while Lenard Berlanstein underlines the fact that the new vision of sexual complementarity, defined by the differences inscribed on the body and incorporating the subordination of women, distinguished 'the modern gender order' from its predecessor.[29]

Arguments that the democratic project was inherently 'masculinist' have, however, been challenged. Some historians argue that the picture of female exclusion is exaggerated because it is based on 'discourses' that prescribed how women should live, rather than on evidence of how they actually did live. Carla Hesse has argued, for instance, that women were not silenced and confined to the private sphere during the French Revolution. For one thing, they were more heavily represented amongst the ranks of published authors than they had been under the Old Regime.[30] In Hesse's view, the idea that political power should be based on the consent of reasoning adults allowed women to make a case for their inclusion, as they would do over the next 150 years. Furthermore, the fact that women's exclusion needed to be justified showed that their inclusion was also conceivable. From this perspective, women's exclusion from the new representative forms of politics created by the French Revolution was not due to the inherent 'masculinism' of these political ideas. It emerged gradually through the cut and thrust of Revolutionary power-plays.[31]

While the ranks of published female authors doubled during the Revolutionary period, they rose from only two to four per cent of the total.[32] Besides, women's greater access to the 'Republic of Letters' – the world of print and publishing – was quite compatible with their exclusion from political activity and power-sharing. Nevertheless, Hesse rightly points out that women's exclusion, rather than being a foregone conclusion in 1789, was a constantly negotiated facet of Revolutionary politics. Despite the limitations already inscribed theoretically in the 'modern gender order', many women assumed that they shared with men the rights acquired with the overthrow of the Old Regime. They began to participate with enormous enthusiasm in Revolutionary public life. This appears to have taken many men by surprise. It forced them to articulate the exclusions they took for granted or believed were implicit in Revolutionary doctrines. Perhaps men preferred not to admit that their proclamations of liberty and equality did not apply to women, since they found it necessary to justify at length the contradiction of excluding them. Besides, exclusion was easier to achieve in theory than in practice. A closer examination of women's roles during the French Revolution and of the prescriptions about women by male Revolutionary leaders illustrates an unfolding process of exclusion, both theoretical and political, that was continually contested by women.

Women's roles in Revolutionary politics

The French Revolution 'began' in 1789, although its starting point can be defined in different ways. The contest among the political interest groups came to a head once a meeting of the Estates-General (the body representing each of the three 'estates' that comprised Old Regime society – the clergy, the nobility and the commoners) assembled on King Louis XVI's summons in May of 1789. The Third Estate or Commoners, together with reformist elements in the other two Estates, rapidly gained the upper hand by declaring themselves to be the 'National Assembly', the representatives of 'the nation' against Royal 'despotism'. Popular revolution in support of this challenge erupted on 14 July 1789 with the famous storming of the Bastille, a political prison and symbol of autocratic power. Currents of popular unrest were to superimpose themselves on the power struggles of the political elites, creating an uneasy, discordant and sometimes violent mix over the next decade.[33]

Women participated enthusiastically in Revolutionary politics, producing pamphlets and petitions, and intervening in a variety of political gatherings. They demonstrated their assumption that they had just as much right as men to give their views on political issues and have those views taken seriously. Women's political clubs were active in many towns from 1789, and women participated in a number of mixed popular societies.[34] By 1792, when the sans-culottes movement (comprising urban workers and small shopkeepers) came to the fore in Revolutionary politics, women were actively engaged in attempting to reshape the political sphere and the principles on which it rested.

Female political intervention was sometimes sparked by women's increasingly desperate attempts to feed their families. When the market women of Paris marched to Versailles in October 1789, for instance, to bring the Royal family back to Paris, they were seeking to ensure the King paid attention to the critical food supply issue in the capital. But while women's actions were undoubtedly motivated by subsistence issues on many occasions, their actions were not apolitical. On the contrary, women's responsibility for feeding their families brought them to the fore of protest activities when hunger loomed, but their interventions were clearly marked by political insight: they drew political conclusions from the economic problems they faced. Women's slogans illustrate their linking of political and economic matters: 'Give us bread, but not at the price of liberty' in 1789, or 'Bread and the constitution of 1793' in 1795 when both sustenance and democracy were under attack. Like men, women blamed governments for mismanagement or even for deliberately trying to starve the troublesome masses. Like men, too, some women expressed more sophisticated political ideas than others.[35]

Dominique Godineau identifies three levels of political engagement by women, and her outline provides a useful guide to the array of their activities during the Revolutionary years.[36] The most basic level of female Revolutionary activity was that of the *sans-culottes* women who identified with and promoted the ideals of the popular movement: 'the right to sustenance, egalitarianism, political and economic Terror, and belief in the sovereignty, dignity and happiness of the people'. They turned out in large numbers at crucial moments amongst the crowds that made the 'sovereign people' a major political force in the early 1790s. A second level of political activity involved a group of women who, while not prominent as individuals, participated regularly in clubs and political meetings. They expressed their reactions to political debates in a variety of fashions, and figured as anonymous but noteworthy participants in official reports of public disturbances. Finally, a third level of political activity was represented by prominent militant individuals: those who constantly engaged in Revolutionary political activities like attending clubs and meetings, participating in the key incidents of insurrection that altered the course of the Revolution, or denouncing enemies of the Revolution. They demonstrated a 'sustained revolutionary politics' and their names featured prominently in police reports.

As Godineau argues, 'The militant woman wished to be a citizen, behaved as a citizen, and demanded the rights of a citizen, which would allow her to carry her political struggle to a successful conclusion.'[37] From the time of the calling of the Estates General in 1789, women began to demand redress of their grievances over education, employment, inheritance and the removal of other disadvantages they suffered because of their sex. They also demanded that they be allowed to participate in political decision-making, if not in exactly the same way as men nevertheless as 'female citizens' (*citoyennes*). These appeals aroused men's scorn and anxiety and provoked an outburst of satirical attacks.[38]

The Constitution of 1791 set a property qualification for the suffrage. It thereby distinguished 'active citizens' (able to vote and hold office) from 'passive citizens'. This distinction excluded many men as well as all women from participation in representative government. It reflected an emerging gap between popular notions of citizenship, which were democratic, and those of the political leadership who advocated meritocracy. The assumption of power in 1792 by the Jacobin faction, supported by the Parisian *sans-culottes*, gave rise to a more democratic system. That shift, and its foundation in popular militancy, was captured in the memorable words of Camille Desmoulins: 'the active citizens are those who took the Bastille'.[39] The Constitution of 1793 established universal male suffrage, as well as a radical agenda of direct democracy and social welfare measures. Though not formally entitled to vote in 1793, women joined in when voting was by acclamation, participated in taking the oath to the constitution, and generally refused to be excluded even if their votes did not 'count'.[40] Despite claiming 'We are the Sovereign [People]',[41] however, they were not recognised as such. They were denied the formal rights to debate and to vote, to bear arms and to hold positions of authority in Revolutionary politics. The demands of women militants to be permitted to bear arms, their prominent unofficial roles in weeding out and denouncing traitors, and their role in pressuring men to exert their right of insurrection, can all be viewed as attempts to assert their presence as citizens, if in ways that differed from men's. They might not be able to take up arms and fight in the Revolutionary armies, but they could watch over the 'holy guillotine' to ensure that enemies within France received their just desserts.[42]

Sans-culotte women did not necessarily see their political role as identical to that of men. Some operated within a 'household' model that acknowledged men as representatives of their families in political matters. Women's role was to be the eyes and ears of the Revolution in the markets and the streets, and to form part of the 'sovereign people' in its vigilant pursuit of Revolutionary goals.[43] Women's understanding of their political role may have reflected their family circumstances. Godineau has established that female militants had an age profile different from that of their male counterparts. They were generally either young women without families to care for or women whose children had reached adulthood. Whereas male militants were normally family men in the prime of life, then, women were more likely to engage actively in politics when their lives were not dominated by the duties of motherhood.[44] Furthermore, the most prominent feminist militants were single women struggling to support themselves. A number of them belonged to the 'demimonde' of theatre and public entertainment where male patrons supplemented uncertain incomes.[45] Their economic vulnerability may have provided a significant motivation for claiming the extension of individual 'rights' to women.

The divisions that marked male politics during the Revolution were also evident amongst women. They supported different visions of the Revolution's goals; some opposed it altogether. For both men and women, social position influenced responses to the Revolution. Those with more to lose from political change were more likely to oppose it. Female hostility to the *sans-culottes* and their Jacobin allies in 1793–1794 was demonstrated dramatically by Charlotte Corday's assassination of the Jacobin Jean-Paul Marat. 'All these men who were supposed to give us liberty have destroyed it: they are nothing but executioners [of liberty]', she wrote.[46] Manon Roland's support for the Girondins, political opponents of the Jacobins, was also motivated by a determination to defend an alternative vision of the Revolution. Like many with more privileged social backgrounds, she was enthusiastic about political reform and the creation of a constitutional political system, but dismayed by what she saw as the fanaticism of Jacobins and *sans-culottes*. For Roland and those like her, the Terror represented not the preservation of Revolutionary purity but an attack on justice and liberty.[47]

As Olwen Hufton argues, too, religion became a critical issue dividing women and shaping their responses to the Revolution. In peasant France, she suggests, hostility to the revolutionaries' attack on the Church and, in particular, the attempts to 'dechristianise' France and replace traditional Catholicism with a new cult of Reason, met stubborn resistance from women. Village France did have its radicals, of course, and hostility to the hated feudal system was a powerful stimulus to Revolutionary militancy.[48] 'Goddesses of Reason' were recruited in the villages, just as they were in the cities, to represent the new ideology. Nevertheless, many women were unpersuaded that abandoning their devotion to Mary, the Mother of Jesus made sense. As Hufton points out, rural life offered little proof that the world was rational, and the new goddesses 'commanded no hot line to the deity and could boast no proven record in the alleviation of labor pains or the extermination of weevils'.[49] So women found ways to resist the attacks on their beliefs and the removal of their priests, mainly by a collective refusal to embrace the new practices. Since they had command of the rituals surrounding birth and death, they could continue the secret baptism of babies and the surreptitious burial of the dead, evading new secular practices.[50] In Western France, where Royalism remained strong, noble women like the Marquise de la Rochejacquelin also played major roles in organising and leading counter-revolutionary peasant armies, defending Church and King against godless Republicanism.[51] The strength of support for Catholicism among certain groups of women confirmed male Republican

views that women were 'fanatical' and superstitious, unfit for entry
into the new political order of reasoning individuals. Yet, Jacobinism
had its own kind of fanaticism. And while peasant women reacted to
the Revolution with the insights stemming from their own experiences, educated women were sometimes unnerved by a Jacobin
political language and mythology that associated Republican 'virtue'
with attacks on the family.[52]

Women's place: the battle of ideas during the French Revolution

Women's eruption into public life during the Revolutionary decade
posed a fundamental challenge to the 'modern' political order envisaged in pre-Revolutionary treatises and anticipated by Revolutionary
leaders. Those leaders had not expected the explosion of the 'Sovereign People' onto the political stage either, despite warnings by some
deputies in 1789 that a declaration of 'rights' risked arousing unrealistic popular expectations.[53] But if the claims of the lower orders
needed simply to be deferred, those of women needed to be rejected
definitively. They had to be shown to lie outside the bounds of the
'natural' order on which the new politics rested, and which was
clearly gender-defined.

The term 'feminist' did not exist in 1789. But as the Revolution
unfolded some women began to realise that the new social and political structures did not address women's needs and that it actively
discriminated against them. Women who came to see the Revolution
in these terms produced what would later be described as a 'feminist'
analysis of the changes of this period. They exposed the exclusionary
practices and assumptions underpinning the new political order,
which conferred rights on the 'individual' political subject: an
'individual' defined as male.

Militant women like Théroigne de Méricourt, Olympe de Gouges
and Etta Palm fought for the construction of a new 'Revolutionary'
society that would extend the gains of the revolution to women.[54]
Etta Palm raised the widely debated question of women's position in
marriage: 'What could be more unjust! Our life, our liberty, our
fortune, does not belong to us (sic); emerging from childhood, handed
over to a despot, whom our heart often rejects, the best days of our
lives are spent in distress and tears, while our fortune is exposed to
fraud and debauchery.'[55] By contrasting liberty and despotism she
highlighted the oppression suffered by women in marriage, which

was often described in terms of tyranny or slavery. If the family provided a language for expressing political meanings, politics provided a language for describing the failings of the familial 'Old Regime' and the need for a 'revolution' in domestic life. The best-known attempt to place women's rights on the Revolutionary agenda was Olympe de Gouges' 'Declaration of the Rights of Woman and the Female Citizen'. Modelled explicitly on the 'Declaration of the Rights of Man and the Citizen', this pamphlet made an extended case for 'revolutionising' women's place in the new society. It highlighted the fact that the new order was being created by men and against women, engaging specifically with the underlying gender dynamic of the new political model. The preamble began with a challenge: 'Man, are you capable of being just? It is a woman who poses the question ... Tell me, what gives you the sovereign right to oppress my sex?' It then proceeded to mirror the clauses of the original Declaration, asserting the 'natural, inalienable and sacred rights of woman':

> Woman is born free and remains the equal of man in rights [...] The aim of every political association is the conservation of the natural and imprescriptible rights of Woman and Man [...] The law must be the expression of the general will. All female and male citizens must participate personally, or through their representatives, in its formation; it must be the same for all; all female and male citizens being equal before [the law], women must be admissible to all dignities, positions and public functions.

It concluded with a rallying call to women to demand their own rights: 'Oh women! Women, when will you cease to be blind [?] What advantages have you gained from the Revolution? A more pronounced mistrust, a stronger disdain [...] What are you left with? The proof of man's injustice.'[56] This declaration was an attempt to identify women as a political 'class', a grouping with common purpose and shared interests. In reality, women were no more a unified and coherent political group than men, whose views on the Revolution also differed and who had been divided into active and passive citizens under the Constitution of 1791. Yet, as de Gouges suggested, women had a political interest in common as a category excluded from the ranks of rights-bearing individuals on the basis of their sex.

Her problem in claiming 'rights' for women within the public order of citizenship was partly due to the dilemma of inserting herself into

Revolutionary public discourse. As Dorinda Outram has argued, the public discourse of 'rights' and 'virtue' was not sex-neutral but gendered male.[57] In utilising this discourse women were forced to utilise a 'masculine' configuration of ideas and resonances that sometimes fitted ill with their 'feminine' position in Revolutionary politics. The idea of 'virtue', for instance, assumed a male subject for whom virtue meant giving primacy to public interest over personal interest. The 'virtuous' woman could not speak as a public figure; nor could she demonstrate her 'virtue' by claiming to work in the public interest: a public woman was not a virtuous woman. Yet women had no alternative. They engaged with politics utilising a male-defined discourse or were silent. In de Gouges' case, to be silent was to accept the very exclusion she wished to contest, and to accept the definition of 'virtue' that justified female silence.

Whilst claiming women's entitlement to the 'rights of man', de Gouges simultaneously recognised that they were excluded from that entitlement, because otherwise there would have been no need for her Declaration. Her text wavered between asserting the similarity between the sexes, and emphasising the specificity that necessitated women's representation *as women* in the political sphere. She asserted that woman was a rational and self-directed individual akin to man, and also asserted female specificity as 'the sex superior in beauty as in courage during childbirth'. Woman ought to have the same rights as man, she declared, but also different rights pertaining to her sex and her sexual roles. As Joan Scott has forcefully argued, the 'paradoxical' position of modern feminism was first articulated by Olympe de Gouges at this point. She made a case for that specific category 'woman' – a being defined by her difference from 'man' – to possess the rights pertaining to all who shared a 'universal' human nature. De Gouges both accepted and rejected 'sexual difference' simultaneously.[58]

Responses to women's Revolutionary political activities highlight the extent to which their exclusion was fundamental – for most men – to the new political order. Those responses were complex and must be seen within the context of factional power struggles. The Queen was the archetypal political woman and enemy of the new order, so her execution (on 16 October 1793) is not surprising. De Gouges' monarchist sympathies helped ensure her execution on 3 November 1793: her writings constituted an 'attack on the Sovereignty of the people'.[59] The execution of Manon Roland five days later was due at least in part to her leading role amongst the Girondins. Similarly, the suppression of the most radical women's organisation, the Society of Revolutionary Republican Women, can be interpreted partly as a result of its close alignment with the Jacobins' opponents on the Left, the Hébertists. The Society's zealous pursuit of counter-revolutionaries, its prominent role in disturbances prompted by the food shortages of 1793, and its clashes in the streets with women who refused to wear the Revolutionary cockade, also saw it condemned for undermining public order.

Nevertheless, the terms in which women were condemned demonstrate that more was at stake than political infighting. Their condemnation to death or to silence was explicitly justified by accusations of the 'unnaturalness' of their political engagement: politics was a masculine domain and was to be preserved as such. The Queen, described as 'the scourge and the bloodsucker of the French', was held responsible for the decay of the monarchy by her nefarious effect on Louis XVI.[60] Opponents asserted that her power had been possible only because the King was weak: 'if the fate of France lay one day in the hands of a woman, it is because there was a king who did not have a man's head'.[61] Furthermore, the apparently 'private' crime of which she was also accused, incest with her son, was also a 'political' one: corrupting the body politic.[62]

Olympe de Gouges and Manon Roland were also condemned as 'political women'. Roland not only exemplified an alternative 'liberal' Republicanism but was a female political theorist and leader. De Gouges was not merely a monarchist sympathiser who called for an end to internecine factional struggles, but an outspoken defender of women's political rights. Their executions served, like that of the Queen, to exorcise the demons aroused by the prospect of feminine rule. Jacobin justifications for their executions linked these women to each other, and to the female usurpation of male roles and male power. In the same speech in which he condemned the Queen's illegitimate rule, the Jacobin Deputy Chaumette also singled out Roland and de Gouges:

Remember this haughty wife of a stupid and treacherous husband, la femme Roland, who believed herself fit to govern the Republic and who raced to her doom; remember the impudent Olympe de Gouges who abandoned the cares of her household to interfere in Republican affairs, and whose head fell beneath the avenging blade of the law. Is it up to women to present [legislative] motions? Is it up to women to lead our armies?[63]

Supporting Chaumette's analysis, the official newspaper, the *Moniteur*, explicitly linked the political crimes of these women to their transgression of sexual divisions and their denial of 'nature'. Marie Antoinette 'sacrificed her husband, her children and the country who had adopted her to the ambitious plans of the House of Austria'; Olympe de Gouges 'wanted to be a Statesman, and it seems that the law has punished this conspirator for having forgotten the virtues which are proper to her sex'; Madame Roland 'was a mother, but she sacrificed nature, by wanting to raise herself above it; the desire to be an intellectual [*savante*] caused her to forget the virtues of her sex; this forgetfulness, which is always dangerous, eventually led her to the scaffold'.[64]

Despite these attacks, women could never be entirely removed from public life. The aim was to contain and limit women's public presence. Utilising female images in Revolutionary culture, to represent 'Liberty', 'the Republic' or the Republican virtues, was one way of doing this. Women's exclusion from political roles allowed them to represent political ideals without raising factional and ideological questions. At the same time, their presence as visual metaphors camouflaged their exclusion from political rights and the separation of male and female domains. As far as most Revolutionary men were concerned, women were destined to be mothers in the Republic: a role they regarded as critical to the survival of the Nation, but one premised on women's docility and subjection to men.[65] The female presence in political iconography served as a contained way of allowing or acknowledging women's presence in public life. They could not be shut away, but they could be 'trapped within a picture', as Landes puts it.[66]

Underlying the attacks on these women, then, was the explicit reassertion of men's power over women. Chaumette's outburst against the Society of Revolutionary Republican Women betrayed a deep anxiety: 'Impudent women who want to become men, aren't you well enough provided for? What else do you need?'[67] Robespierre expressed a similar anxiety when he accused the Revolutionary Republican Women of proclaiming 'that men must abandon to women the speaker's rostrum and the seats in the Senate, and that all the masculine Clubs must submit themselves to the authority of revolutionary women presidents'.[68] As Carole Pateman has suggested, if the Revolution overturned the political and psychic structures of patriarchal rule, the gender order by which males controlled females remained firmly entrenched in the minds and politics of many Revolutionaries.[69]

The language of sexuality utilised in many Revolutionary contexts affirmed a new hierarchy dominated by heterosexual masculinity. The charge of sodomy directed at political opponents served to emasculate them, just as the language of rape affirmed the power and political prerogatives of the virile 'Herculean' Revolutionary male of popular iconography.[70] The metaphorical 'rape' of the counter-revolutionary asserted victory by reducing the opponent to a supine and feminised position: an imaginary model of sexual relations hardly compatible with ideas of female equality.[71] Furthermore, the theme of lesbianism in the pornographic pamphlets of the day, especially those directed at the Queen, expressed the charge of political interference in the language of sexuality: the 'tribade' (as lesbians were then called) acted like a man by asserting her own sexual desires. Male revolutionaries used the language of illicit sexual power to condemn the female assumption of male political prerogatives.[72]

According to the Jacobin leaders, the division of sexual spheres was the work of 'nature', inscribed in the bodies of men and women. André Amar spelled this out before the Convention in October 1793 as he called for the closing of women's political clubs. The physiology of men, he argued, showed that 'nature' had designated them for 'public' functions: 'Man is strong, robust, born with great energy, audacity and courage; [...] he is almost exclusively destined for agriculture, commerce, navigation, voyages, war – everything that calls for force, intelligence, capability.'[73] Chaumette likewise argued that women active in the Club movement wanted to make themselves men. 'Since when is it permitted to give up one's sex?', he asked. 'Is it to men that nature confided domestic cares? Has she given us breasts to breast-feed our children?' Only Charlier, who recognised the implications of this line of argument, challenged the Convention: 'Unless you are going to question whether women are part of the human species, can you take away from them this right [to assemble peaceably] which is common to every thinking being?'[74]

The *philosophes'* arguments, which had allowed women to be thought of as a separate and different version of the 'human species', now justified women's exclusion from the 'rights of man'. But Charlier's intervention reminds us that, while the exclusion was attributed to 'nature', it was actually founded in politics: the determination to exclude women from public roles. To 'be a woman' was to find 'public places [...] the galleries [...] the bar of the Senate' out of bounds.[75]

André Amar also relied on the demands of a 'social order' premised upon sexual difference to exclude women from politics:

> The private functions for which women are destined by their very nature are related to the general order of society; this order results from the differences between man and woman. Each sex is called to the kind of occupation which is fitting for it; its action is circumscribed within this circle which it cannot break through, because nature, which has imposed these limits on man, commands imperiously and receives no law.[76]

He did not argue that women were *incapable* of exercising other functions but that they *should not* do so: the aim was to prevent women from *continuing* to act politically. 'Nature' obviously did not command imperiously enough to disabuse women of false understandings of their capacity. It was up to men to compensate by closing women's political clubs and imposing upon them the 'natural' call of domesticity by force.

The Napoleonic settlement

The Jacobins' Revolutionary zealotry, which had taken many of their opponents to the guillotine, finally led surviving opponents to engineer an overthrow of the Jacobin faction in 1794. The Revolution then took a more conservative tack, its leaders utilising the army to repress popular militancy and destroy counter-revolutionary insurgency. Napoleon Bonaparte, one of the Generals called on for these roles, developed a taste for political power, and eventually carried out a coup d'état in November 1799. By 1804, having destroyed the Republic, he was sufficiently powerful to have himself crowned Emperor of France. Napoleon's legacy was to be a mixed one for women, but perhaps most importantly it enshrined in law the inequality of rights founded in the gendered social model of Revolutionary politics.

Napoleon regarded the Civil Code of 1804 as one of his greatest achievements. A portrait of Napoleon that celebrates it shows him as the new Moses. Having laid aside the symbols of his military leadership, he is pictured inscribing the laws on a tablet of stone and being crowned by Father Time. Napoleon himself is reported to have said on Saint Helena: 'My glory is not to have won forty battles, for Waterloo's defeat will blot out the memory of as many victories. But nothing can blot out my Civil Code. That will live eternally.'[77] Napoleon was not the sole author of the Code, or even its main one, but he did play an active role in discussing its provisions, particularly those dealing with civil rights, marriage, divorce and adoption. His impact on sections affecting the status of women was significant.[78] For that reason, feminists since the time of Napoleon himself have associated his name with the legal structures of female dependence and inequality inscribed in the Civil Code, and which were painfully dismantled step by step over two centuries.

The Civil Code systematised an array of legal codes and practices and gave France a single and uniform set of laws. In this sense, at least, it was a great achievement. Prior to its introduction, French law was a hotchpotch of customary law, Roman law, Royal ordinances, and the more than 15,000 new laws passed during the Revolutionary period. The lawyers appointed by Napoleon in 1800 to create a new legal code borrowed elements from all of these precedents, but they also sought to apply the ideas of the day: the principles of reason derived from the Enlightenment and the customary views of the community.[79] The strengths and weaknesses of the Civil Code as it applied to women reflect its patchwork legal origins, as well as the assumptions that guided its creators, not least Bonaparte himself.

The French Revolution claimed to make all 'Frenchmen' equal before the law. But while the Code is frequently hailed for creating an equal system of justice, that verdict takes no account of the legal status of women under the Code. The Revolutionary principles of civil marriage and equal inheritance of property between all legitimate children were retained. Daughters therefore benefited along with sons. In other respects, however, the egalitarian principle was over-ridden, for women, by principles drawn from customary law. These established the legal disability of married women: they were 'covered' by their husbands and therefore had no independent legal existence. Other forms of social inequality may have been removed in the Civil Code, therefore, but a number of distinctions based on sex were confirmed.

The inequalities pertaining to women affected them differently depending on their marital status. An unmarried woman, if she had an income of her own, was the least disadvantaged. But even she was deprived of legal functions by virtue of being female. Her word was not legally of any account whereas the word of any man was. A widow was in a similar position, and her legal relationship with her children also depended upon the conditions laid out in her dead husband's will. He could even exclude her from contact with her children, or at least hand guardianship to a male relative or family council. Married women were the most disadvantaged because in marrying they lost independent legal status. In marrying, a woman undertook to obey her husband, while he undertook to protect her. She could not choose where the couple would reside, and could be forcibly returned to the family home if she absconded. A married woman could not set up a business, exercise a profession or receive income that was free of her husband's control. She could not sue or be sued. Her husband could open her correspondence, forbid her from particular social contacts (though not with her family) and chastise her (unless, in beating her, he created a public disturbance). While there were different ways in which joint marital property could be handled, none gave the wife control over her own property, and some entitled her husband to retain the revenue accrued from managing her assets. Divorce remained legal until 1816, but it was far more restrictive than the Revolutionary law and favoured husbands over wives.[80] From 1816 until 1884, divorce would remain illegal.

The laws of sexual conduct were also defined by sex. A woman who committed adultery could be jailed, while a man could only be prosecuted if he brought a mistress to reside in the family home. He might then receive a fine. He could kill his wife and her lover with impunity if he caught them in the act of adultery, but she had no such leeway. While a father had full parental rights over his legitimate children, illegitimate children were the responsibility of their mother, and legal action to force acknowledgement of paternity and support for the child were illegal. These clauses emphasised the role of marriage as the basis for property transfer, and the need to ensure that property could only pass down the legitimate line. They also echo the personal views of Napoleon that married women should be firmly under the legal control of their husbands – perhaps a reflection of his own inability to keep Josephine under his thumb. Personal elements aside, Napoleon's view that women were primarily a vehicle for producing legal heirs was summed up in his assertion: 'Women and children belong to the man as the tree and its fruits belong to the gardener.'[81]

If Revolutionary equality did little to ensure equal rights for women, then, the Revolution did help to influence the provisions of the Code in fundamental ways. It implemented an Enlightenment view of women that shaped the foundations of French citizenship, and was still being cited as an impediment to women's political representation in the 1990s. The Civil Code defined women according to their relationships with men, asserting the 'legality' of their subordinate position in marriage, whilst making marriage the normative status for women. It was premised upon the model of sexual difference that had guided Revolutionary politics. The Code was to transmit that model to subsequent generations through legal channels, just as cultural models were to transmit it via the norms of social interaction.

The Enlightenment – and the French Revolution which in many ways enacted responses to the Enlightenment – preached universal rights but in fact based those rights on male prerogatives over women. Hence the Revolution formalised the exclusion of women. This political exclusion, and the cultural notion of 'separate spheres' on which it was premised, set the stage for the 'modern' gender order of the nineteenth century. That gender order was effectively implemented only amongst the social elites. It is to them that we now turn.

Part I

The Social Structures of Difference: The Nineteenth-Century Gender Order

1 Elite Women

The social elite that emerged from the Revolutionary period was a mixed group with diverse social origins, often referred to as the 'notability'. The old nobility was still a force to be reckoned with in the early decades of the nineteenth century, although its influence waned thereafter. It was gradually surpassed by a new elite based in principle on 'merit', which in practice meant on wealth and economic power. Some families gained their social promotion through the Revolutionary changes fostering a market economy; others had been promoted by Napoleon, who had created his own nobility to reward his supporters. The political affiliations of the elite were therefore diverse, but they shared a commitment to a society marked by hierarchy and the rule of the few over the many. The women of this diverse elite form the focus of this chapter.

The creation of the modern gender order based on sexual difference, as we have seen, was integral to the creation of a system of representative government which placed power in the hands of a male elite. By envisaging a world marked by sexual difference, with social roles based on 'separate spheres', men of the educated elites created a social model in which public affairs were the domain of men like themselves: men whose wealth enabled them to maintain dependent wives and servants as marks of independence and authority. Women were excluded (as were men of the lower social orders). In the post-Revolutionary world it was the women of these elites whose lives most closely approximated the ideal of sexual 'difference' and the operation of 'separate spheres'. These women invested heavily in the idealised role of maternity, which was pivotal to the Rousseauian model and which underpinned their sense of identity and purpose. The maternal role received greater emphasis in elite culture after the Revolution, even women of the old aristocracy coming to support it. Nevertheless, the maternal ideal placed significant demands on women to narrow their expectations. This is evident in the writings of young women being socialised into the model of 'separate spheres', who often perceived it as restrictive and frustrating. The emphasis on 'social motherhood' by elite women also shows that they attempted to redefine the ideal in ways that provided broader opportunities than the Rousseauian model had encompassed. During the nineteenth century, women increasingly challenged the division between 'separate spheres' that was unsustainable in reality.

Creating 'women'

Simone de Beauvoir wrote in 1949: 'One is not born a woman: one becomes one.'[1] This observation is particularly accurate as far as elite women of the nineteenth century were concerned. From infancy, they were moulded and shaped, constrained and disciplined, so that they would conform as closely as possible to the ideal of femininity being elaborated at that time. Masculinity was also socially defined, but the socialisation of girls was a more intrusive process given that the acceptable options for their lives were more limited. The fundamental goal was not to develop a girl's intrinsic 'self' but to create a being who conformed to a predetermined model. A woman was to live for others, not for herself. She needed to learn to suppress her own will and desires. A girl who grew up anxious for marriage, envisaging a life committed to the happiness of her husband and the raising of children, had truly become a woman.

In the early nineteenth century, doctors regarded children as sexually undifferentiated until about the age of seven, when girls' 'natural' timidity and gentleness began to distinguish them from bold and noisy boys. From the mid-century, however, they claimed to distinguish the 'little woman' in the less developed musculature and particular feminine intelligence (which 'senses rather than understands') of the female infant.[2] This shift in medical perception reflected the increasing pervasiveness of the model of sexual difference, and the role of doctors in delineating the norms of femininity. The assumption of difference meant that the education of elite children varied according to sex. Where boys were groomed for public responsibilities and an expansive view of their future, girls were groomed primarily for domestic responsibilities and to seek fulfilment in the family. Girls were shaped to be 'different' and to lead different lives.

Girls' education was designed to accustom them to their specific and unique social mission, as distinct from the wide-ranging possibilities that were available to men. The conservative politician Joseph de Maistre pointed out to his daughter Constance in 1808:

> Women have created no masterpiece of any kind. They did not produce the *Iliad* or the *Aeneid* [...] or the Panthéon, or Saint Peter's Basilica [...] They did not invent algebra, or telescopes, or spectacles, or the fire pump, or the stocking frame, etc. [but women] create something greater than all that: on their knee the most excellent thing in the world is formed: an honest man and an honest woman [...] This is the greatest masterpiece in the world.[3]

According to De Maistre, the great cultural achievements of Western civilisation were nothing compared to the raising of children. This was the message to be impressed on the minds and hearts of elite girls. Its cultural resonance is illustrated by the fact that this text was used to teach grammar in Mademoiselle Adam's school for girls in Paris in 1846.[4] Storybooks for girls spread the message more widely. Little Aimée, in one popular example from 1869, asked why there were no great women inventors, to be told that women were destined to be the mothers of inventors instead.[5] Significantly, however, by imagining that girls would ask the question about women's inventiveness, the author recognised that they did not naturally assume that their potential and destiny were limited. De Maistre's letter was prompted by Constance's complaint that she was condemned to mediocrity because of her sex. Other evidence also suggests that girls frequently perceived their socialisation as restrictive, and chafed at their limited and predefined lives.

Given their specific destiny, girls were perceived to have little need of intellectual development, and until the late nineteenth century received a patchy education designed to make them suitable companions for their husbands. The broad-ranging education of aristocrat Marie d'Agoult in Latin, French grammar, secular and religious history, geography and elementary mathematics was unusual for the early nineteenth century, as was her later career as a writer and historian (she wrote under the male pseudonym Daniel Stern).[6]

Girls generally received a basic grounding in subjects like history and geography to enable them to converse intelligently on matters of general knowledge. They were also taught a range of 'accomplishments': music, dancing, drawing and one or more languages. The education of Lucile le Verrier during the Second Empire (1852–1870) was typical for the period. Her mother taught her history, geography and recitation, and she had tutors for Italian, English, singing and piano (her piano tutor was the composer César Franck).[7] Lucile's education was intellectually limited, then, despite the fact that her father was a renowned astronomer.

Household management also formed part of the education of the daughters of the elite. The wealthiest employed a housekeeper to supervise the domestic staff, but training in running a home, managing the household budget, and directing the servants was essential for most women. Thrift and careful household management were regarded as domestic virtues. Magazines like the *Journal des Femmes* and an array of household manuals provided sample menus and budgets, patterns for making clothes, and suggestions for arranging rooms and setting the table for dinner parties.[8] The title of Madame Gacon-Dufour's compendium, the 'Complete manual for the mistress of the home and the perfect housewife', set the tone for the endeavour. First published in 1826, it was reprinted many times over the century.[9] Such manuals were integral to the process of 'inventing' domesticity as a lifestyle for elite women.[10] If the home was to be women's domain, their role there needed to occupy their time and have a serious purpose.

In many ways, the content of a girl's education was less important than the shaping of her personality and outlook through the education process. To 'become a woman' was to learn to personify the virtues of femininity, which were not readily compatible with sustained intellectual development. School prize-givings for girls emphasised character over ability: the prize for knowledge at Marie d'Agoult's elite school was a lesser prize than the one for good behaviour. She won the former but not the latter, because she refused to join the Children of Mary, a religious association. Hortense de Beauharnais, by contrast, was rewarded with the higher prize for her 'order, cleanliness, precision, diligence and submission'.[11] In order to be marriageable, a girl required docility and conformity. The key role of the 'mother-educator' was to prepare her daughter to submit to the will and needs of her husband, not to have ideas of her own. As 17-year-old Caroline Brame, a *bourgeoise* from Lille, noted in her diary in 1865:

'I must accustom myself to crushing my will underfoot and learning to do everything with submission and joy.'[12]

The discipline and constraint to which girls were subjected and which they gradually internalised were intended to mould them to social requirements, and in particular, to 'crush their will'. The weak sense of self they thereby acquired produced the malleability that made them desirable as marriage partners.[13] It was essential to their ability to accept male superiority, and hence their own lesser rights and power. However, for many girls such lessons were embedded in a strongly religious framework emphasising spiritual perfection via self-sacrifice and altruism. This could give solace and meaning to the struggle to master the will.[14]

The constraints imposed on girls were both physical and social. Their bodies, first of all, were moulded to the required shape. They were fitted with spinal supports and corsets to cure real or imagined back problems.[15] Doctors attributed these problems to the weakness of their spines, although it is more likely that they were due to the sedentary lives imposed on girls by cumbersome clothing and social restrictions. The educationist Pauline Guizot noted in the 1820s: 'I know of no little girls who if left to themselves would not prefer the noisy, rough games of little boys to the most amusing pretty little object with which we try to entertain them.' Girls therefore had to be discouraged or prevented from playing such games. As she specified, a girl does not 'do a somersault, jump a horse over a high barrier, climb a wall or hang from a tree'.[16] The fact that little girls were dressed in pantaloons for modesty suggests that they were not as sedate as the ideal dictated. Nevertheless, constraining the child's body made it possible to train her to sedentary pursuits like sewing and playing with dolls. Sewing was 'useful', and trained her to be still and quiet. It helped teach her to devote her days to 'useful work'.[17] Playing with dolls made a game of the initiation into domesticity.[18] By the mid-nineteenth century, dolls had been transformed from imitation 'ladies' into imitation 'babies' to be dressed and cared for, thus re-emphasising the young girl's destiny.[19]

Puberty marked the end of childhood and justified further restrictions on girls' activities on both medical and social grounds. In the first half of the nineteenth century, girls reached menarche at 15.5 years on average although those of the elite, with a better diet and therefore a higher body weight, were likely to undergo puberty earlier.[20] Menarche was a 'crisis' and doctors spelled out its dangers: girls' nervous systems were 'fragile', so they ran the risk of epilepsy, hysteria and even insanity if it was not negotiated with care.[21] Menstruation was presented as a recurring time of particular weakness for girls. Mothers were advised to prevent physical and intellectual over-stimulation, to maintain a bland diet, and to keep their daughters 'tranquil'.[22] Puberty was also the critical rite of passage confirming a girl's predestination for motherhood. Menstruation 'announced the future' that awaited the young woman, wrote Dr Bureaud-Rioffrey.[23] This differed significantly from the way puberty was interpreted for boys: for them, it announced a potential rather than a destiny.

The extensive medical literature on female puberty highlights once again the central role played by doctors in shaping perceptions of womanhood in educated circles in the nineteenth century. Given that their understanding of female anatomy and physiology was still poor, this had serious implications for women. The discovery of spontaneous ovulation in 1845 revealed that menstruation was not caused by the phases of the moon or impurities in the blood. However, the functioning of the ovaries remained largely a mystery, and the link between menstruation and pregnancy was only beginning to be understood.[24] Doctors frequently spoke as moralists rather than scientists, therefore, making pronouncements on 'woman', seeking a female 'essence' distinct from its male counterpart, and deducing from it a female lifestyle dictated by 'Nature'.

By adolescence, physical weakness seemed natural among girls of the social elite. Doctors thought them capable of very limited physical effort, despite the fact that peasant and working-class girls laboured long and hard at a similar age.[25] Significantly, girls were defined as 'weak' and prone to 'illness' just as young men of their age were becoming stronger and more self-reliant. Where puberty for boys was associated with the growing possibility of personal independence, for girls it was construed as a shift towards dependence on others. The body's functions were perceived in ways that supported the social order of separate spheres and male domination. In asserting that female nature was characterised by weakness and maternity, then, doctors' increasingly authoritative voices helped to justify a social model marked by 'difference' on medical if not on natural grounds. They confirmed 'scientifically' that women were predestined for a life of dependence, and hence of submission.[26]

The term 'adolescent' was used only of boys. It described the period when boys completed their education and embarked on careers. Girls, however, moved from childhood to young adulthood, the adolescent years forming a 'parenthesis' between puberty and marriage.[27] Preparation for marriage dominated that period. Young women began to attend the round of balls, dinners and musical evenings that completed their social training, and introduced them into the circles in which they might find suitable husbands. Girls also hosted their own 'salons' as training for their role as hostess.[28]

The rules of behaviour at social events were strictly defined in manuals of good conduct. A young woman was instructed not to attract attention; to remain seated by her mother; to dance with anyone who invited her; never to meet a man's gaze directly; to remain within her mother's field of vision; to reply to questions but not to initiate conversation. She would be judged by her silence and good bearing, she was told, not by her brilliant conversation.[29] The ideal young woman was not a strong and self-assured individual, then, but submissive, malleable and modest, with no will of her own. Sometimes the strict rules made socialising onerous rather than enjoyable. Marie Lafarge – later imprisoned for poisoning her husband – wrote: 'my mother had forbidden such a large number of topics of conversation that I could do nothing but be dumb, like the rain and the fine weather which comprised my vocabulary'.[30] However, young women's diaries also describe social events that were great fun. Célestine de Ségur 'had a wonderful time' at a series of balls in the winter of 1847–1848, finally 'dancing almost all the time with M. d'Amaillé', who became her husband.[31] Caroline Brame recalled her first ball, when she was about 15, as a very exciting event:

Ah! where has that day gone, the one I will never forget in my entire life, when I first set foot in a salon filled with flowers and light? It was my first ball and mama took pleasure in my first attempts [at dancing] and in my smiles! When I sat out a dance from exhaustion, I met her eyes which smiled at me and seemed to say: 'Don't worry, I am here!'[32]

Girls were allowed little activity free of the oversight of others, and no well-bred woman went out alone. Their diaries frequently express their sense of physical confinement: a confinement dictated by the need to protect their honour and that of the family. When Caroline Brame and her cousin were allowed to make the brief walk between their houses without a chaperone for the first time, Caroline wrote in her diary: 'We laughed and laughed realising that no-one was behind us, and it seemed to us that everyone was looking at us.'[33] A girl's mother was usually her passport to the outside world, and without a mother her mobility could be particularly limited. Amélie Weiler, whose mother died when she was 20, frequently used metaphors of claustration in her diary, likening her situation to living in a convent, a besieged medieval castle or a prison. Even at age 20 she could not go walking on her own, and her family's straitened circumstances did not allow balls or soirées, about which she could only dream.[34] Similarly Lucile le Verrier, aged 15, chafed at the confinement that resulted from her mother's protracted illness:

> For a little while I was going out, but my walking companion [*promeneuse*, literally 'walker'] has left. At the moment I am living in hope: Mama has engaged another one who arrives in a month's time. I understand that it is a problem for me to go out with a servant: my appearance makes me noticeable; attractive girls face greater dangers than the others. But what can I do? Papa is too busy, Mama does not walk, and nevertheless I have to get some exercise.[35]

Two years later the situation had improved: 'Mama is very well, and, Ida, we go out every day, she, papa and I, on foot! I walk Ida!'[36]

Girls were permitted noticeably less freedom than boys, and they sometimes found this difficult to accept. The difference between Lucile's life and that of her brother in 1869 was only partly explained by the difference in their ages. Urbain was 21 and she only 16, but Lucile's diary frequently expressed frustration at her lot: 'Urbain has been to see another show. He isn't affected like I am by Mama's illness because he goes out where and when he likes.' 'Lucky boys, they can go out even when their mother is ill! They are free!'[37] This freedom was particularly evident in 1873: 'Urbain left on Friday for a wonderful trip with his friend Marcel Bertrand. They are going to visit Italy, Greece, Turkey, Austria. I would willingly take their place.'[38]

Lucile's solution was to live a vivid imaginary life nourished by her reading of history. As 14-year-olds, she and her friend Elisabeth played a game in which they assumed male personae and enacted imaginary adventures based on historical events.[39] This suggests that she struggled to accept her destiny as a woman, which required constraining not only her body, but her aspirations and imagination. Two years later, at 16, her imaginary games may have been abandoned but she had taken refuge in her singing. When singing, she wrote, she imagined herself as one of the 'heroines' of the aria, and made 'exciting voyages in the world of the imagination'.[40]

The need to discipline young girls' imaginations and aspirations explains the many warnings against permitting them to read novels. The imaginary world of the novel was likely to appear too enchanting, contrasting dangerously with the real lives for which they were destined.[41] This message was emphasised in religious manuals for girls, which condemned novels for making women's lives appear monotonous or mediocre.[42] Girls sometimes fought a running battle with their mothers over their reading. If they were lucky, like Marie d'Agoult, they found the bookcase unlocked and happily worked their way through its contents until the key mysteriously disappeared. If they were not, they read only what they were given, or kept up a constant struggle for permission. They read in secret, hurriedly devouring the contents of forbidden books in moments of privacy.[43]

Girls' reactions to the novels they read illustrate why these books were regarded as dangerous. As adults feared, girls embraced the dream of 'romance'. Marie d'Agoult later recorded of her reading: 'I knew from that moment on that perfect happiness lay in seeing a handsome knight at your feet, swearing to love you forever': hardly a good preparation for a marriage of convenience.[44] Girls reported identifying with the characters in novels, and vicariously living the adventures and emotional traumas described in the plot. Amélie Weiler sighed with 'the virtuous, unhappy and tender Gustave, the young and charming Valérie' of Mme de Krüdener's novel *Valérie*, and with Dumas' *Isabel de Bavière*, although her mother had given her permission to read neither.[45] But it was the novel *Corinne* that brought the conflict with her mother to a head:

> Madame Schneegans, whom we went to visit in the afternoon, talked to me about Madame de Staël's *Corinne* which all my friends read at fifteen, which people discuss frequently, but which Mama finds appropriate to forbid me at nineteen [...] There is no more danger for me [in reading it] than for a recluse in the depths of her convent; my thoughts never penetrate the walls of my prison, and how can a vivid imagination be dangerous when no-one is there to understand? It's not enough that I'm deprived of all the pleasures of my age, they want to throw a blanket of ice over my most innocent emotions as well.[46]

Corinne was controversial at the time, not only because it dealt with 'romance', but also because it dealt with the question of female talent and ambition. The heroine Corinne was a woman who challenged social norms and chose life as an author over marriage. Despite the fact that the heroine did not live 'happily ever after' in this book, its plot raised questions about women's lives which daughters of the bourgeoisie were advised not to ask.

Romances presented complex messages to their readers, and their impact on young women's perceptions of their assigned roles could not be controlled. On the one hand, they proclaimed the model of affectionate and companionate marriage that promised emotional fulfilment. This fulfilment was what girls were offered in the 'separate spheres' model, in compensation for limited choice and a predestined lifestyle. 'Romance' also expressed the acceptable ideal that women should surrender themselves to love, seeking fulfilment only in devotion to a man. But bourgeois marriages were typically arranged unions, not based on a romance between two partners. Choice and 'romance' had therefore to be contained. But girls' access to novels in the home – authorised or not – suggests that their mothers were reading these books. Presumably they judged the emotions aroused by such novels to be acceptable for themselves, even if dangerous for their daughters. Perhaps novels provided them with the emotional release that marriage failed to produce.

Girls were encouraged instead to read literature that reinforced the female virtues of modesty, conformity and self-sacrifice. Such books showed the pitfalls of rejecting the normative female role. In one example a feminist character, who argued that women should be able to become lawyers and have the same political and civic rights as men, was ridiculed as bizarre. These stories taught that men would not love women who strove to be different or who stepped outside their assigned roles,[47] but the need for these messages to be reiterated indicates that questions about marriage and about women's limited roles were not without controversy.

By reading 'good books', girls were taught that the most important consideration for a successful future was to be pleasing to others, especially men. Catholic views on marriage dovetailed neatly with the Civil Code, which required wives to obey their husbands, and 'good literature' for girls reinforced this model. Girls were advised to imitate the fictitious Isabelle, who declared: 'I am happy to be submissive, even more happy because affection makes obedience easy.'[48] This sentiment was reiterated in girls' diaries. Recording a discussion with her friends on whose will should submit to the other in marriage, Caroline Brame wrote: 'I believe that it is woman's, but at the same time I believe that if a wife truly loves her husband,

this will not be a sacrifice for her.'[49] Similarly, Lucile le Verrier
accepted the prerogatives of her fiancé Lucien while commending to
him the 'authority of tenderness': 'My ideal of a true union is when
a wife obeys without her husband commanding.' In return for his
support and protection, she promised him 'plenty of love and
submission, my dearly-beloved lord and master'.[50] This was the
Rousseauian ideal in action, and it reiterated the legal relationship
between spouses under the Civil Code.

Being pleasing to others also implied being physically attractive.
Girls pursued the idealised figure of the wasp-like waist and
delicate features, if necessary by undertaking dramatic and dangerous diets.[51] Lucile le Verrier's young friend Laurence summed
up the importance of beauty for girls of the bourgeoisie, whose sole
destiny was marriage: 'when you are rich you have to be pretty in
order to be chosen for yourself; well I am rich and not pretty. From
another angle, when you are poor you need to be pretty in order to
be chosen at all. So the conclusion is that it is always good to be
pretty.'[52]

Being 'chosen' was critical, because it was regarded as inappropriate
for a young woman to pursue a profession or a career. Some found
this difficult to accept. In 1836, Stéphanie Jullien was criticised by her
father for being melancholy and lethargic. She replied:

If one had envisaged giving me a profession or a means of
supporting myself I would certainly have pursued it with a zeal
and an enthusiasm that seemed useless to expend for nothing [...]
with no useful or productive employment, no calling except
marriage and not able to look myself for someone who might suit
me, I am surrounded by cares and anxieties [...] I would regain
my courage and enthusiasm very quickly if I had some mission to
fulfil or some goal to pursue. That is not the case, I have no calling
and cannot have one: that has been my most ardent wish and it
has been refused to me.[53]

Similarly, Amélie Weiler's father refused to countenance her desire
to become a governess: 'I spoke to my father about it yesterday,
I told him that a young man is free to choose the profession for which
he feels an inclination: why am I not free to choose? [I told him] that
my whole life will be ruined if he doesn't let me leave.'[54] It would
take another 16 years, and a financial crisis in the family, before she
fulfilled this ambition. Examples like these illustrate the constant

need amongst the elites to reaffirm gender norms and contain young women's expectations.

Women as 'wives': marriage among the elite

For most elite women in the nineteenth century, the question was not whether they would marry but whom they would marry, and on what basis. Marriages among the elite were shaped by family considerations. Marriage was a useful way of bringing capital into the business and extending the web of professional contacts.[55] There was a high level of professional and social endogamy among the bourgeoisie. The children of textile manufacturers in north-eastern France tended to marry within those circles. A similar exclusiveness prevailed among the silk magnates of Lyon, the arms manufacturers of Marseille and the ribbon-weaving elite of Saint-Etienne.[56] Family and financial considerations also governed aristocratic marriages, with the additional preference that blood-lines be protected. While wealthy bourgeois would happily marry their children into the nobility, then, the nobility were less enthusiastic about such unions.[57]

Marriages of this kind were described as 'marriages of reason' or 'marriages of convenience', meaning that rational calculations took priority over emotional attachment. Love matches were not unknown although ones like that between 39-year-old Pauline de Meulan, the educationist, and 25-year-old François Guizot, historian and future Prime Minister, were rare.[58] Many people remained sceptical about whether the emotions provided a sound basis on which to build the futures of individuals and families. If one could 'fall in love' today, one might equally fall out of love tomorrow. Only after the 1870s did 'marriages of inclination' become more widespread. Until that time, most families sought to match couples on the basis of similar background, lifestyle, wealth and social standing.

Once children reached their mid-teens, families turned their minds to the quest for a suitable marriage partner. If a girl was considered a 'good catch', like Marie d'Agoult, who had both wealth and noble ancestry, the propositions might begin the day she left school.[59] Discreet enquiries would be made about the background, family, prospects and character of a possible spouse. Their health was important (venereal disease and insanity were greatly feared), as was religious and political compatibility.[60] If the reports were favourable, negotiations between families would begin and the young couple would become involved in the process. In Paris, a stroll in the Bois de Boulogne or a visit to the Louvre might be organised to enable them to catch sight of each other. They might then be brought together for a brief conversation before the official proposal of marriage by the prospective groom. The young woman would be allowed a little time to decide, and unless she was resolutely opposed, the marriage would take place soon afterwards. In many cases, however, the two families would be known to each other, and many young people found their partners within the social groups in which they had been raised.[61] Marriages between cousins were not uncommon, but such marriages only went ahead if they were regarded as suitable matches. Some cousins were prevented from marrying by relatives who feared, for instance, that the extended family's fortune would be co-opted by one branch at the expense of others.[62]

Brides were often much younger than their husbands. This was partly due to the fact that men delayed marriage until their education was finished and their careers established. However, it also reflected a belief that a man should 'complete' the education of his wife, shaping her to his own ideas and preferences. The best-known exponent of this view was Jules Michelet, who advised marrying someone who had 'not yet received a definitive imprint' upon her character. Her husband would then 'exercise a remarkable ascendancy of authority and tenderness' over her.[63] Others doubted whether couples of widely different ages could be happy, and doctors warned of the health problems and weak progeny that they produced.[64]

Since a young woman's entire future rested on the decisions made at this point, it is not surprising that marriage was a major theme of girls' diaries. They discussed the marriages of their friends and acquaintances, noting the age differences between the spouses, rumours about the financial settlements involved and reports of the bride's enthusiasm or otherwise for the union.[65] Girls expressed a desire to be chosen in marriage because they were loved: a priority different from that of their parents and closer to the scenes played out in novels. Caroline Brame hoped for a tender and loving husband like the man her close friend had just married.[66] Amélie Weiler declared that she would never submit to an arranged marriage: 'If I find nobody in the world who loves me for myself and who doesn't worry about whether he is making a good investment by offering me his name and his hand, well! I will remain single',[67] as indeed she did. Lucile le Verrier noted: 'I dream of marrying a young man who chooses me himself and whom I know well',[68] unlike an acquaintance who was to marry a man she had known for only three weeks:

> People are amazed at my firm ideas on marriage, on love in marriage. But I am amazed in turn at the courage of these young girls who give themselves completely and with no turning back to a man who was a stranger to them yesterday and today is indifferent to them.[69]

Lucile's hopes were realised. In April 1873 she met and fell in love with Lucien Magne, and they were married in February 1874.

Since women hoped for marriages based on affection, they sometimes transferred their romantic expectations onto the husband selected for them by others in arranged matches. On the basis of a first glimpse, Caroline Brame decided that Ernest Orville 'could not be more loving'. Having met him twice, she was enraptured: 'Dear God, yes, I will be happy with him, he is so good, so tender. We promised to love each other very much and forever.' His customary gift of a bouquet of flowers to mark acceptance of the proposal was interpreted as a sign of attachment: 'I am being spoilt already!'[70] Amélie Weiler, more sceptical and rebellious, was scathing about such naivety. When a friend 'fell in love' with the partner selected for her, she wrote:

> Oh the carefree, the happy, the stupid girl! she believes that he lives only for her, that he has only ever lived for her! Poor child, distrust these deceitful promises, these false oaths of love [...] Young women are not very fussy and not very careful! Too pleased to find a husband, to be able to play the madam, they attach themselves to a man, in good faith, often without worrying about his past, believing they see the fire of a love that will last for eternity in the most superficial, the most banal homage. It must be an immense sorrow to realise later that they alone loved and that their tenderness has been repaid only by ingratitude and infidelity.[71]

Marriage required the bride's consent, but girls were not well positioned to give 'informed consent' to arranged marriages. They had limited contact with men and hence no basis for assessing the character or compatibility of the prospective husband, particularly when they had little opportunity to get to know him prior to marriage.[72] Young women trusted their family to see to their best interests, and rarely opposed their parents' choice of husband. In fact, Marie d'Agoult became so tired of the selection business that she left the choice to her mother and brother.[73] To refuse a marriage to which one's family was committed was a gamble, particularly when there was no guarantee that the next suitor would be any more appealing. Besides, considerable pressure could be brought to bear on reluctant brides, with the priest sometimes playing a significant role.[74] So long as little value was placed on mutual attraction, and so long as the gendered social model virtually precluded women from choosing not to marry, they remained relatively powerless. Their consent often amounted to a blind act of trust.

Many girls therefore contemplated the step into the unknown with considerable anxiety. Divorce was illegal from 1816 to 1884 and then became possible only with great difficulty, so marriage was for life. Sophie Günther confided her fears in her friend Amélie Weiler at the moment of her betrothal, as Amélie noted in her diary:

> [S]he told me that when it came to pronouncing the solemn yes which determines a woman's entire life, she almost fell ill: frightful struggles, painful hesitations turned her whole being topsy-turvy and disoriented all her thoughts. She felt neither love nor repugnance [...] Now she has made her decision and is adjusting to the idea of being betrothed.[75]

Caroline Brame resorted to prayer when she learned that a marriage was under consideration for her. The critical day came on Sunday 25 February 1866: 'My destiny is hanging by a thread so to speak, and it only remains for me to pronounce the solemn "yes", the consequences of which I do not know.' Having met 'Mr Ernest' at the Luxembourg Museum that afternoon and found him charming, she decided to consent. On Monday she met his parents. On Tuesday he proposed to her in the Bois de Boulogne. They were married on 19 April.[76]

Lucile le Verrier, in love with Lucien Magne, faced a different problem: she knew her own mind but had to persuade her father, because the marriage could not proceed without paternal consent. She spent an anxious hour in prayer as her mother pleaded their case:

> [A]t first my father refused absolutely. Poor Mama was in despair. But then she made such a good case, offsetting against Lucien's

youth his steady qualities and the solid wealth of his family, that [...] my father gave in, while saying that it was absurd. Then I arrived, I hugged him, and he no longer said it was absurd [...] he told us to invite the Magnes to dinner to facilitate his discussions with the father.[77]

Older and more mature women were sometimes less resigned to their fate than those married off in their late teens. Stéphanie Jullien's father was annoyed when she delayed giving her consent because, at 29, she was already well beyond marrying age and could ill afford to be choosy. She tried to explain her position:

> I have repeated over and over to myself all the arguments you put to me; I recognise all the benefits which lie with the one presented and which it will be difficult, perhaps impossible to find elsewhere, and that is what makes me hesitate for so long, that is why I have not said no for three months [...] I am asking for time, and it isn't too much to see and get to know a man for six months, a year even, when it's a matter of spending your life with him. There are no grounds for objection, you say. The most serious, the most important one is this: I do not love him. And lest you think that I am speaking here of a romantic and impossible passion, of an ideal love that I do not hope to experience, I am speaking of a feeling which means that one takes pleasure in being with someone who is loved, that one looks forward to seeing him, that his absence is painful, that his return is awaited, that one is interested in what he does, that one desires his happiness.[78]

Stéphanie asked only for time to decide. Amélie Weiler rejected a suitor when she was 30, against the advice of her family. She had learned the lesson of making rational calculations about her future. To say no almost certainly meant to remain unmarried for life, with the consequent need to ensure her own financial security, but she estimated that she was better off alone:

> To marry wig, spectacles and tobacco pouch, 45 years and a mediocre and uncertain financial position, you would need a thirst for a husband which happily I do not possess [...] If M. Roederer offered me a situation which was if not brilliant, at least comfortable, I would take him [...] as a necessary inconvenience, but to chain my life to a doubtful situation and to a man who inspires no

sympathy in me, is something a wise and prudent woman does not risk.[79]

For the vast majority of elite women, marriage marked the beginning of sexual knowledge and experience. Their sheltered upbringing was designed to protect them from 'premature' sexual awareness, particularly in Catholic circles where innocence was linked to ignorance, and where virginity was prized as a spiritual, not merely physical, condition.[80] Accounts of the drama of the wedding night sometimes served as a 'ritual dramatization' of the norms of feminine modesty.[81] Discourses around sexual behaviour typically offset feminine innocence against masculine knowledge; feminine reluctance and passivity against masculine virility and conquest. But where 'sex education' amounted to learning what was forbidden – exposing the body, touching the body, familiarity with the opposite sex[82] – the overturning of those precepts with no forewarning might be perceived as (and sometimes was) a violent attack. It is impossible to know how widespread negative experiences were. As late as 1906 one woman reported:

> From the first night, he trampled underfoot any sentiment of modesty. He treated me like the last of his prostitutes. With no consideration for youth, or innocence, or pain, he didn't lay down his arms until having satisfied his brutal passions. He frightened me and injured me at the same time. I have never been able to forgive him.[83]

Doctors urged men to treat their wives gently and with consideration. This message reaffirmed the model by which sexual activity had different meanings and chronologies for the two sexes, and the need to create a model of sexuality consistent with the notion of companionate marriage.[84]

Other evidence reveals a growing eroticisation of marriage by the late nineteenth century, with women expecting and finding emotional intimacy and sexual satisfaction. Their mothers sometimes found this astonishing and scandalous. Inès Fortoul's mother-in-law remarked disapprovingly in 1884 that men now treated their wives like their mistresses.[85] From the 1840s, in fact, 'experts' had encouraged a view of marriage as an intimate partnership based on affection and sexual compatibility. Dr Debay's *Hygiene and Physiology of Marriage* emphasised women's capacity for sexual pleasure but included helpful hints to cure 'frigidity', showing a particular fondness for flagellation as an aphrodisiac. The book went through 173 editions between 1848 and 1888.[86] Similarly, Gustave Droz's *Monsieur, Madame et Bébé* went through 121 editions between 1866 and 1884. It also promoted marriages based on intimacy:

> It is nice being an angel, but, believe me, it is either too much or not enough [...] A husband who is stately and a little bald is all right, but a young husband who loves you and who drinks out of your glass without ceremony, is better. If he ruffles your dress a little and places a little kiss on your neck as he passes, let him. If he undresses you after the ball, laughing like a fool, let him. You have fine spiritual qualities, it is true, but your little body is not bad either, and when one loves one loves completely.[87]

As Adeline Daumard points out, too, love was not necessarily absent from marriages that were not originally contracted on the basis of love. Many couples developed a deep affection and respect for each other and some, at least, came to love each other passionately.[88] The shift towards love matches in the last decades of the nineteenth century, therefore, was a shift in degree rather than in kind. Ideas promoted for decades gained wider acceptance. Rituals of courtship changed, with couples allowed more privacy before marriage, getting to know each other more fully, exchanging love letters, and developing greater intimacy.[89] The case of Lucile le Verrier, married for love, illustrated a perception that love matches promised personal happiness and fulfilment, as romantic novels suggested:

> More than three months have passed since my marriage to my dearly-beloved Lucien [...] I have become the happiest and most blessed of women, blessed in the love of my husband which is so pure, in his esteem, in his confidence. It seemed that I would never meet my ideal man; I dreamed of someone simultaneously strong like a man, chaste like a young girl, healthy and honest to the depths of his soul [...] Well! All that has come true. How I love him, how I respect him, how I admire him, my dearly-beloved, the husband of my soul as well as of my body![90]

Love letters to their wives by late nineteenth-century politicians, particularly where the expressions of intimacy surpass the established conventions of address, also suggest deep affection between some couples. For Jules Ferry, Minister for Education in the 1880s, Eugénie Risler was the 'adored one' whose 'infinite tenderness is my refuge and my glory'. Similarly Eugène Chaper, who represented the Isère in the lower house of the National Assembly, wrote to his wife in 1871: 'I will not close this letter without repeating again that I miss you constantly, that living alone, separated from you, is my greatest sorrow.'[91] Inès Fortoul and her husband Joseph invented a secret code in which to write sexually explicit messages when they were separated.[92] Nevertheless, the eroticisation of marriage was still contested by a Catholic lobby which warned against sexual indulgence, and which argued that sex should be preserved for procreation.[93] Besides, while formal separation and (after 1884) divorce were rare amongst the elite, women vastly outnumbered men as applicants. This suggests that marriage, and thus the idealised lifestyle for which women had been prepared from infancy, proved less satisfying than they may have expected.[94]

The destiny of motherhood

Motherhood lay at the heart of the Rousseauian ideal. The maternal-centred family was lauded as the basis of a stable society and the wellspring of civic virtue. The supposed incompatibility between childrearing and public life also provided the justification for 'separate spheres' and for women's necessary dedication to the 'private' domain. The maternal-centred family distinguished the 'bourgeois' model of womanhood from the aristocratic pattern in which mothering had played only a minor role. The creation of a domestic ideal centred on motherhood thus marked a cultural shift, the transformed feminine ideal reflecting the transition in political life produced by the Revolution. In the post-Revolutionary decades, the growing ascendancy of the Rousseauian model of womanhood amongst the elites highlighted and assisted the increasing ascendancy of the bourgeoisie and the decline of aristocratic cultural and political domination of French life.

Many elite women accepted the view that aristocratic women had undermined the Old Regime by pursuing a life of pleasure or meddling in serious affairs of state. They aimed to raise girls for motherhood, now perceived as a new and more valuable social role.[95] Young aristocratic mothers sought to instil a more serious lifestyle – defined as maternal dedication – in their daughters. They openly rejected the lifestyles of their own mothers and were reluctant to allow their mothers to influence their children or even, in some cases, to see them.[96] Texts on education, including those by women like Madame de Rémusat and Madame Guizot (both members of the political elite in the early nineteenth century) sought to impress the maternal model on girls' minds. The 'mother–educator' role – the role which made women the primary educators of their children – would give women a social purpose, and unite women of the diverse post-Revolutionary elite in a shared mission of social stability.[97]

The child-centred family with the mother at its heart was increasingly promoted as the ideal during the nineteenth century, and it was embraced even amongst the aristocracy. Marie d'Agoult remembered a childhood surrounded by love and caresses. 'Never a punishment, never a reproach. Some rules, no doubt, but flexible and not coercive.'[98] Gustave Droz, advocate of erotic marriage, was a key exponent of this model of family intimacy. Fathers were encouraged to surrender some of their paternal dignity, playing with their children and developing close emotional ties with them.[99] The mother's role was pivotal within this family model because her closeness to her children was believed to come more naturally. She should treat each child as an individual, studying its character, encouraging its physical and moral development, and endeavouring to correct its faults. Her aim was to instil self-discipline in the child by means of gentleness and affection. This model of parenting rejected corporal punishment, although it placed the child under emotional and psychological pressure by exploiting its desire for love and security. Gestures of affection would reward good behaviour while maternal withdrawal, refusing the good-night kiss for example, served to punish bad behaviour.[100]

By the 1820s even the royal family needed to project an image of domestic intimacy in order to maintain elite support. The traditionalist Bourbons, who regained the throne in 1815 and ruled until 1830, failed to do so. Their model of personal relationships, like their political model, remained locked in pre-Revolutionary patterns.[101] It was no coincidence that conservative theorists across the nineteenth century also promoted an authoritarian model of family life shaped around the dominant father. They argued that hierarchy and obedience were the essence of both a well-ordered family and a well-ordered society.[102] A leading exponent of this model in the early nineteenth century, Louis de Bonald, saw democracy and the egalitarian family as equivalent social evils, and linked his campaign to restore the monarchy of old to a campaign to restore paternal authority in the family. 'In order to wrest the state from the hands of the people', he wrote, 'the family must be wrested from the hands of women and children'.[103]

By contrast with his Bourbon cousins, King Louis-Philippe (the 'Bourgeois Monarch'), brought to power by the Revolution of 1830, took pride in being a father. Ruling couples in the past had had separate apartments, but Louis-Philippe delighted in showing off to visitors the double bed he shared with Queen Marie-Amélie. She resembled a bourgeois mother and strove to present a model of the sentimental family to the nation. The Queen bore ten children of whom eight survived. Despite her official duties, she devoted each evening between 4 and 5.30 p.m. to them. The older ones gathered around their mother to read, draw and do handwork, eating pastries and discussing politics. The younger ones were incorporated into this family gathering (known as 'the club') as they grew older.[104] Similarly, Empress Eugénie in the 1850s and 1860s took pride in the fact that she raised her child herself like an ordinary mother.[105] Motherhood had become a central metaphor for the suitability to rule, representing the nation as a family bound together by mutual support under the aegis of a paternal monarch and his compassionate queen.

Throughout the nineteenth century, the glorification of maternity in literature, religious teachings and cultural models of femininity fostered the maternal aspiration in girls. They were told that it was both 'natural' and a critical social function. As mothers, they would hold 'within their hands the integrity of the family, the honour and peace of the home, the prosperity of the household'. They would be responsible for 'a great part of the destiny of our beautiful country'.[106] Motherhood, rather than marriage, conferred adult status on women and gave them a purpose in life. It also offered some women the emotional fulfilment that they did not find in marriage.[107] Nevertheless, the glorification of motherhood was not reflected in the legal status of mothers, who remained juveniles with no official right to make decisions concerning their children. The cultural messages girls received about motherhood were therefore ambiguous in that the prestige with which it was surrounded in theory was not evident in practice.

Motherhood was also the goal for which girls were prepared from infancy, and to which they aspired at marriage. Bourgeois families in the Nord expected news of pregnancy soon after marriage, and most wives delivered their first child within 11 months.[108] Given women's powerful emotional investment in motherhood, failure to conceive was a source of considerable anxiety, and a problem for which they assumed responsibility. In 1866, after four months of marriage, Caroline Brame was bitterly disappointed that she was not pregnant, as she had thought. 'Oh! How proud and happy I will be when I can say "My son, my daughter" [...] Dear God I pray you to grant us a little child who will bring our joy to completion.' Sixteen months later, she was still not pregnant: 'I cannot throw off the sadness that weighs on me! Dear God, you know my great sorrow, it is that I don't have a baby, which I would love so much and which would make me accept the sober [sérieuse] life I lead.'[109] It would take 14 years of prayers, pilgrimages, water cures and medical treatment before she finally produced a child.

Pregnancy brought a woman special status. Doctors emphasised that her diet, her comfort, her cravings should all be satisfied. Her husband should avoid doing anything that might upset her, becoming a 'slave to her wishes and even her caprices': a reversal of roles that was probably attractive to women.[110] The sense of fulfilment at the successful delivery of a healthy infant was made more poignant, perhaps, by the fact that childbirth was a dangerous event. Women of the elite were at less risk of death than their poorer and more hard-worked counterparts. However before the widespread practice of antisepsis in the years before the First World War, they were not exempt from the dangers of infection or the deaths of their babies. Lucile le Verrier witnessed the deaths in childbirth of two childhood friends:

> During my first pregnancy I lost Elisabeth, who like me was having her first child; during the second I lost Isabelle, who like me was having her second child. Last January, Mme Roger [Peyre, Isabelle's sister] gave birth with great difficulty to a fine boy, whom she lost a fortnight later. This must be a bitter disappointment. I was devastated for her, putting myself in her place.[111]

Lucile had already lost her sister-in-law, who died following an operation to repair a tear to the peritoneum incurred during childbirth. She had also had a miscarriage, and suffered from peritonitis and other serious problems after her second child was born.[112]

Bourgeois women in the department of the Nord produced large families, averaging five children in the 1840s and seven in the late nineteenth century. This was quite unusual: most women born in 1881, for instance, had no more than two.[113] Moral reformers became increasingly alarmed by couples' failure to produce children. From mid-century, women's 'selfishness' in rejecting their 'natural' role became the subject of public debate. The slow rate of population growth in France was contrasted with that of neighbouring countries, particularly following France's defeat in the war with Prussia in 1870. In the last quarter of the century, many conservatives and natalists argued that 'depopulation' was looming.[114]

Family limitation was practised in elite circles as it was amongst other social groups, because the financial pressures created by equal inheritance laws affected noble and bourgeois families alike. Besides, the cult of motherhood was associated with a desire to invest more time in each individual child, which was more difficult if families remained large. This did not necessarily imply the level of close personal care of children that became typical in the twentieth century. Amongst Parisian social elites in the late nineteenth century, at least, women were regarded as good, attentive mothers if they spent a few hours per day with their children, leaving them with servants for the remainder of the time.[115]

A mother's first duty was to breastfeed her child, as doctors constantly reminded her. According to Dr Debay, it was a 'law of nature' beneficial for the mother's health and that of the infant.[116] But where breastfeeding had been advocated in the eighteenth century as a 'moral' duty – infants supposedly absorbed moral principles with their mothers' milk – it was increasingly portrayed as a national duty in the nineteenth. One of the first signs of the decline of the Roman Empire, Dr Debay insisted, was the abandonment of maternal nursing.[117] Doctors' insistence on the importance of breastfeeding suggests that women were reluctant to take their advice. Rather than sending their infants to the countryside to be nursed, however, bourgeois women usually brought the nurse into the family home, where she was supervised by the mother with the doctor's guidance. There were 3880 such nurses living in Paris in 1860.[118]

The restrictions that doctors imposed on breastfeeding mothers may have contributed to women's reluctance to nurse their own infants. They were instructed to watch their diets, to avoid strong emotions, to avoid balls, soirées, and the theatre, and above all to avoid sex. On this point doctors repeated a longstanding popular belief that sex would spoil the milk. This restriction also gave husbands an interest in limiting the period of maternal nursing. It was the prominent writer Victor Hugo, rather than his wife Adèle, who decided that Léopold should be given a wetnurse in 1823: 'You can imagine how hard it was to persuade our Adèle, who took such great joy in the effort of nursing', he wrote to his parents.[119] Similarly, Lucile le Verrier resorted to a wetnurse after three months partly because of her husband's unhappiness, although nursing her baby had been an 'unspeakable joy'.[120]

Doctors' intervention in the processes of childrearing placed increasing pressure on mothers as the century progressed. Their entry into the bourgeois home, caring for bourgeois women and children, was critical to the professionalisation of medicine.[121] Elite women read the books that doctors wrote, paid for their advice, and suffered the anxieties created by medical criticism of maternal inadequacy. Doctors simultaneously insisted on women's maternal 'destiny' and emphasised their unfitness for the role. As Dr Caron proclaimed in 1858: 'Mothers, like nurses, don't know how to nurse babies': they acted on instinct, whereas the doctor brought 'science' to the task.[122] By the mid-nineteenth century, doctors were advising against demand-feeding and in favour of strict regulation of infant care. They provided advice on clothing, weaning, toilet-training and infant hygiene. The medical reinvention of mothering reached its pinnacle in the 1890s with Dr Pinel's invention of 'puericulture': the science of childrearing. This alone, its proponents asserted, would enable France to overcome the 'depopulation' crisis. 'Puericulture' transformed maternal education into a national, and nationalist, crusade.[123] As it indicated, too, the 'separate' sphere of domestic life where women reigned supreme was neither so separate from political concerns, nor so fully under women's control, as the model implied.

The 'social motherhood' of elite women

The rhetoric that made women responsible for well-regulated homes and well-educated daughters emphasised the all-encompassing nature of these tasks. The role of 'mother–educator' demanded, in theory, total commitment and preparedness to sacrifice one's individuality and interests to its requirements. The pundits predicted personal disaster and social collapse should woman fail in this duty.[124] While motherhood was revered as a role of great significance, it also placed women outside the sphere of public life. They were taught to envisage themselves as the mothers of citizens, rather than as citizens themselves.[125] The 'mother–educator' role restated the Rousseauian ideal in the nineteenth century, therefore, and confirmed the Revolution's exclusion of women from public life. Nevertheless, elite women also assumed important roles in the broader society. The ideal woman of the elite turned her maternal virtues – her compassion, her moral strength and practical accomplishments – to the benefit of the less fortunate. In doing so, she undertook the task of preserving social order by easing suffering, teaching self-improvement and instilling resignation in the poor. Simultaneously, too, she broadened the boundaries of her 'separate sphere' to carve out roles that gave her a 'social sphere' of increasing significance; roles that both accentuated the gender division in social life, and pointed to its artificiality.

Charity work had a long aristocratic pedigree within the social system of the Old Regime. Led by the Royal family and inspired by Christian teachings, aristocrats had distributed aid in times of need in return for deference and submission by their inferiors. The aristocracy continued to play an important philanthropic role in post-Revolutionary society, but as the elite became increasingly diversified, so too did the practitioners of charity. Philanthropic work enabled bourgeois women to demonstrate their status and claim membership of the elite.[126] Charity also 'proved' that the wealthy were necessary to society, and helped to maintain social order by alleviating misery.[127]

Social events for the well-to-do often doubled as fundraisers for charity. Fairs and lotteries were extremely popular. A charity ball in aid of those affected by the flooding of the Rhône River in 1840 attracted 3000 participants, who each paid 20 francs to attend.[128] Church collections for the poor continued as well. Women's charity work increasingly focused on the needs of poor women and children, aiding those who were unable to live the Rousseauian ideal of maternal devotion and family intimacy. There were crèches for the children of working mothers; associations for educating poor children and for assisting them into apprenticeships; organisations for the care of orphans; refuges for homeless and indigent women; societies to aid women in prison and on their release; organisations to assist reformed prostitutes; and a variety of societies for aiding poor mothers in childbirth and after delivery. Many of these organisations had mixed membership or were under the patronage of eminent men, but women did much of the daily work and undertook the fund-raising activities.[129] In the period before social welfare systems existed, the philanthropic work of wealthy women filled an urgent need in alleviating misery.

Women were expected to devote one or two afternoons per week to charity work, and they spent many additional hours producing items for sale at charity bazaars. Girls began to take part in this work from adolescence, generally as part of their religious education.[130] At 14, Lucile le Verrier's activities were confined to making donations, although she dearly wanted to be allowed to visit the poor. At 18, Caroline Brame took up the collection for orphans at Sunday Mass, visited working women in their homes, and visited a shelter for impoverished women and children in Lille, where she distributed 'toys, cakes and useful objects'. Her experiences brought home to her the gap between her own life and the lives of the women she aided:

> They have spent a terrible winter, some have got into debt, others have been ill, others are overburdened by children and exhaustion. Dear God when you see such misery close at hand, you can no longer complain about your own lot! How mild are my little privations compared with the terrible struggles these poor people must endure in order to eat.[131]

Women's particular role in philanthropic work was justified by the belief that it was an extension of their maternal role. Regulations drawn up in 1816 for a 'Society for Maternal Charity', an organisation to assist poor women in childbirth, stated: 'The Society for Maternal Charity has been established by women, because they are the ones whom Providence has summoned particularly to aid children and indigent mothers.'[132] As creatures of sentiment, women were believed to respond instinctively to misery and suffering. Besides, their relationship to the poor was construed in 'maternal' terms as a hierarchical but compassionate one. Since women 'naturally' protected and guided children, and supervised their moral development, they were well placed to perform a comparable role amongst the poor, who were also perceived as 'children' in need of guidance.

Women's charitable activities were therefore understood as a form of 'social motherhood'. They set out to instil a range of good behaviours in those they assisted, reflecting the widely held belief that the poor were largely responsible for their own plight due to ignorance, if not ill will. Religious observance and bible reading were often required of beneficiaries, given that many organisations were inspired by their members' Catholic, Protestant or Jewish faith. Unemployed women in one Parisian charity workshop in 1848, for instance, had to endure two to three hours of morally uplifting reading as they worked, before receiving their soup in the evening.[133] Since the bourgeois family model was assumed to have self-evident virtues, legal marriage and an orderly personal life were often required to qualify for assistance from the maternal charities and the crèches. Many groups also sought to instil the 'virtues' of saving and thrift, along with cleanliness, order and hard work.[134]

While well-to-do women were no doubt genuine in their desire to alleviate human suffering, their charitable activities rested on the premise that moral reform (rather than social reform) was the solution to poverty. Aid was also designed to counter worker militancy and the threat of socialism. This was particularly evident following the workers' uprising of June 1848 in Paris, which produced an upsurge in charitable activity. The Revolution was eventually defeated at the cost of considerable bloodshed, but the outcome was interpreted by some women as evidence of the success of the social system, rather than as an illustration of its failure:

> The anger, the hatred against society have been appeased; the ladies who visit are received everywhere as angels of peace [...] The worker, formerly so dangerous, has finally understood that only Christian charity can equalise the ranks of society without mixing them; and he accepts gratefully the alms which are offered to him with sympathy and love.[135]

This rationale for charity, which emphasised the social bonds created as the rich came to the aid of the poor, also accepted the inevitability of poverty. That idea was challenged throughout the century by socialists who argued that poverty was created by an economic system that benefited capital at the expense of workers. However, serious official measures to eliminate poverty rather than assuage its effects only began once the Republicans came to power in the 1880s. The Republicans recognised public assistance for the needy as a right, not a privilege, and passed laws providing pensions to the aged and infirm, financial assistance to large families, and paid maternity leave for working mothers.[136]

The development of a formal Republican programme of public assistance in the late nineteenth century extended women's 'maternal' role within the community and opened up professional opportunities for women as 'social assistants'.[137] Building on the earlier appointment of a handful of women to inspect nursery schools and women's prisons, the Republicans created new roles for women in the overview of services to children assisted by the State, and as labour inspectors. In the Paris region women were also employed to check on the well-being of children placed with wetnurses, and mothers receiving breastfeeding subsidies. As one prominent Republican stated in 1887 in earmarking funds for such jobs: 'Women are especially qualified to understand the services for children and to devote themselves thereto; to note their gaps, to discern pragmatically the reforms that they require.'[138] In this period, therefore, charity began to be transformed into social work, which would emerge as a female profession after the First World War. This transformation reflected the belief that women had an intuitive sense of the needs of women and children, or a particular capacity to attend to their needs. So the perception of women's special nature, their differences from men and their particular female role, defined the nature of the task and women's suitability for that task. As Linda Clark suggests, the 'inspectresses' of the late nineteenth century were 'state-supplied mothers and sisters' to needy women,[139] just as the women benefactors of earlier decades perceived themselves as maternal figures in the lives of poor women. Republican principles may have legitimated roles for women outside the home, but the definition of women as 'maternal' beings remained paramount.

The lives of elite women in the nineteenth century, therefore, were shaped by the politics of 'difference' and the ideal of 'separate spheres'. The view that their destiny was fundamentally different from that of men and dominated by motherhood was widely held, by men and by women. From infancy, girls were prepared for this role and educated to accept different rights and prerogatives from men. However, girls' frustrations at their socialisation into this role reveal that, far from being 'natural', the maternal ideal was inculcated with considerable difficulty and at considerable personal cost to women.

Many women found great satisfaction in their roles as mothers, but they also managed to extend its boundaries in ways that provided fuller social engagement than domesticity itself afforded. The maternal ideal that designated women's exclusion to a 'separate', 'private' sphere therefore simultaneously justified their participation in and leadership of philanthropic activities in the public domain. Women's 'public' activities were defined as 'maternal', and hence as an extension of their 'private' role, but this rhetorical sleight of hand camouflaged only poorly the fact that the 'gendered' social order was an artificial construct that bore a limited relationship to reality. Not only was the conduct of women's maternal role in the home subjected to public scrutiny and shifting political considerations (as the debate over depopulation demonstrated) but 'motherhood', a notion encompassing compassion, altruism, and care for the needy, had an impact on politics and public policy. Furthermore, generations of feminists were to utilise the prerogatives of 'motherhood' as a powerful argument for extending to women the social and political privileges men had claimed for themselves by constructing 'separate spheres' in the first place.

2 Urban Working Women

The modern gender order based on 'separate spheres' presupposed women's economic dependence on men and their dedication to home and family. But the 'domestic wife' was unknown amongst the urban labouring population, where a 'family economy' based on production in the home generally prevailed. Artisanal and shopkeeping couples shared productive activities, although a sexual division of labour allowed women to combine their productive tasks with their household and childcare duties. From the early nineteenth century, however, changes in the broader economy were placing this household model of production under pressure. The family workshop was being undermined by factory production, and by competitive pressures that drove down earnings and forced both men and women into wage labour outside their homes. The family wage economy, based on the wage labour outside the home of all family members, began to replace the older pattern. These changes also disrupted women's ability to combine income-earning and family responsibilities.

The processes of urbanisation and industrial development created enormous anxiety and provoked considerable public debate. Discussions of women workers were at the heart of these debates because their conversion into wage-earners, especially where this work was removed from a family context, highlighted the transformation in economic structures and social mores which was occurring. The ways in which the urban working woman was perceived reflected attitudes to the emergent economic order of competition and mechanisation. Commentators sought to reconcile economic change with an idealised model of the family in which women still played a family-centred role. Rather than admit that this family model was incompatible with a low-wage economy, commentators condemned the failure of women workers to conform to the idealised image. The woman wage-earner challenged their theories about the benefits of economic change to workers, and about independent individuals making rational economic decisions in the marketplace. Caught between 'dependence' as mothers and 'independence' as wage-earners, women struggled with the double burden of 'productive' and 'reproductive' labour in a capitalist wage economy.

Urban development and working families

Less than 10 per cent of the French population lived in cities at the beginning of the nineteenth century, but while the population increased by 38 per cent over the century, the urban population grew by more than 300 per cent. Three-quarters of the population were still defined as 'rural' in 1846 and this fell to only half by 1911, indicating that French urbanisation was less frenetic than that of its main European neighbours. But Paris was already a vast metropolis in 1801. Its population reached one million before mid-century and two million by the end of the century.[1] Extraordinary growth also characterised the new industrial towns that sprang up around textile mills. In the north-east of France, the population of Roubaix swelled from 8000 to 34,000 and that of Mulhouse from 6600 to 29,600 in the first half of the nineteenth century.[2] Mulhouse's population more than doubled between 1831 and 1846.[3] Similarly, spinning mills gave birth to thriving industrial towns in the early nineteenth century around Saint-Etienne and Saint-Chamond in central France, and in the southern regions of the Vaucluse and Languedoc.[4]

Urban growth was due largely to the movement of under-employed villagers into the towns. In the second half of the century permanent immigration to urban centres began to replace temporary relocation.[5] This urban drift was stimulated by the upheaval in rural manufacturing that undermined hand-spinning as a form of domestic employment for women. The long agricultural depression from the 1870s to the 1890s also saw an exodus of agricultural wage-earners, including many women.[6] Migrants were drawn to the city by the prospect of better-paid and easier work than the village offered. The city promised the opportunity to earn regular wages, which might be sent back to the family or saved as a dowry.[7] It also presented dangers perceived to be worse for young women than for men.

School readers for rural girls warned against the attractions of the city, while boys were encouraged to see it as a place of opportunity.[8]

Urban development was a subject of considerable debate amongst social commentators in the nineteenth century. It is no coincidence that the towns most discussed were the industrial centres, where the contrast between the wonders of the new industry and the brutalisation of the working population was most pronounced. Reports of urban problems were not simple descriptions of reality. Rather, they expressed complex and varied responses to the city and to the new forms of industry. For some, the city was associated with progress and human perfectability. For others it was a place of perdition, symbolising the loss of the 'traditional' society based on rural values. For still others, it highlighted the exploitation of the poor by the rich and the destructive social impact of new patterns of economic organisation. All social commentators had an opinion on the city, and all focused their attention to some degree on urban women to argue their case.

Observers of all political persuasions identified the same worrying features in discussing modern towns. Reports emphasised the consequences of rapid growth: severe overcrowding, substandard housing, the virtual absence of sanitation, and the public display of destitution on a large scale. Workers lived in appalling conditions, despite spending a large proportion of family income on rent. Even at the turn of the twentieth century, between 25,000 and 30,000 Parisian working families each lived in a single room, as did poor families in Lille and Roubaix.[9] Jerry-built housing sprang up to meet the expanding market, but often constituted just a higher-quality slum.

The absence of sanitation facilities meant that sewage and household garbage contaminated the streets. In the late nineteenth century, a single tap and a few courtyard toilets served each apartment block housing thousands in Lille.[10] In Paris, apartment blocks might have only one toilet on each landing. Nightsoil carts emptied their contents into the Seine creating a health hazard. Apartments often had no running water above the first floor where wealthier tenants lived. Fetching water – a 'woman's task' – was onerous, as was disposing of wastewater. Since there were no bathing facilities, personal hygiene was poor.[11]

Poor hygiene had its inevitable consequences for workers' health and life expectancy. Periodic outbreaks of cholera, caused when drinking water was infected with sewage, produced significantly higher death rates in worker suburbs than in wealthier suburbs. The epidemics of 1832 and 1849 were testimony to this. Overcrowded, damp homes assisted the spread of infectious ailments like influenza, typhus and tuberculosis, which were major killers of adults in the nineteenth century.[12] The poor diets of workers made them prey to deficiency diseases like rickets, which in turn gave rise to bone deformities in adulthood and, for women, to problems in childbirth. Little meat was eaten, and it was generally reserved for the men as primary breadwinners.[13] Infant mortality remained high. Overworked and undernourished mothers produced sickly babies and often returned to work immediately, but there was no safe form of artificial feeding until the late nineteenth century. Outbreaks of diphtheria, whooping cough and measles decimated the ranks of children. Women workers often witnessed the deaths of their children, while many children lost one or both parents before reaching adulthood.[14]

These problems seemed worse because they were occurring on a larger scale than previously. They also took on new meaning as strikes and revolution increased fear of social and political disorder in the cities. By the 1830s the labouring classes were increasingly identified by the well-to-do with 'the dangerous classes': urban riff-raff given to a life of vice and criminality.[15] It was no coincidence, then, that the Revolution of 1848 gave rise not only to measures to control workers' political activities, but also to slum clearance programmes designed to eliminate the breeding grounds of criminality and rebellion.

Commentators attributed urban poverty to workers' improvidence. Workers, they said, lacked restraint, married young and produced too many children. They spent their earnings on alcohol, tobacco and prostitution. Working women abandoned their infants to public welfare. Critics proposed various solutions to these problems. Political economists defended the free market. The 'iron law of wages' punished the improvident by reducing them to destitution, they argued, but workers' conditions would improve as competition and mechanisation made industry more efficient. Paternalistic conservatives supported constraints on the market, but also insisted that the problem was primarily a moral one. They argued for measures to reform workers, to teach them to budget, and to instil the moral principles that were the basis of family life and ultimately of material comfort. Workers, they argued, had to learn to be self-sufficient and not to rely on charity.

Socialists confronting the same problems saw a populace brutalised by the 'iron laws' of capitalism, which treated human beings as disposable instruments of production. Socialists argued that structural changes in the economy and unjust government policies disadvantaged workers to the benefit of employers. They saw emerging a 'class' society marked by inherent inequality. Socialists condemned the lack of regard for the human and social consequences of unimpeded economic development, a view shared by many Catholics committed to social reform. Discussions of the place of women in the city, and their roles in labouring families, reflected these disparate assessments of the social and economic changes that France was undergoing.[16]

From the family economy to the family wage economy: manufacturing and female employment

Economic change transformed employment patterns for both men and women in the early nineteenth century. Within the 'family economy' the labour of the entire family was pooled for the production of goods and thus for a collective income. This family-based mode of production could take several forms. In the textile trades, for instance, a typical household comprised a male weaver, his wife who spun thread, kept the accounts and handled business arrangements, and children who assisted their parents in the home workshop. Younger children ran errands, while older children learned to spin or weave, and collected and delivered materials. Where the business was large enough, apprentices might also be employed, living with the family.[17]

Gender identities within these households were defined by both economic roles and family responsibilities. Male artisans prided themselves on their 'skill', which was regarded as a 'masculine' prerogative, and by their position as heads of household production units. Male authority within the family was regarded as natural. It was fostered by the camaraderie of mutual aid societies and trade associations, from which women were generally excluded. The patriarchal assumptions widespread in workers' circles were illustrated by support for the ideas of Pierre-Joseph Proudhon (1809–1865). He advocated a small-property-owning society based on peasant and artisan households. In these households, women's domestic and income-generating tasks could be performed alongside each other. Infants could be fed and small children cared for in the course of a day's work.[18] The status of women in such households rested on their ability to manage their domestic and productive responsibilities competently. A good wife was a capable worker as well as a mother and domestic manager.

The so-called 'industrial revolution' did not overturn this system entirely and it certainly did not do so overnight. It did, however, gradually transform the family economy into the family wage economy, in which family members worked for wages outside the home. Until the mid-nineteenth century, only spinning was mechanised in France, so small-scale manufacture long remained the norm.[19] The mechanisation of spinning had major significance for women's employment, however, because spinning had traditionally been 'women's work'. It was a female task in urban textile-manufacturing households, and rural families also relied on domestic spinning to supplement the income from agricultural labour. The increasing use of 'spinning jennies' driven by water power forced many women into spinning mills located in towns.[20] It became much more difficult to combine spinning with childcare.

The industrial revolution sometimes reinforced home-based production alongside factory-based production. If the spinning jenny took female workers into large-scale manufacture then the invention of the *tricoteuse*, a small knitting machine, meant that hosiery developed as a largely home-based industry, with 70 per cent of its 56,000 workers employed at home in 1900. A number of factors favoured the resurgence of outwork in the late nineteenth century: the economic crisis of the 1880s, the existence of a pool of labourers willing to work cheaply at home, restrictions on the hours of work of certain categories of employees in factories, developments in transport.[21] The census of 1906 revealed that 60 per cent of France's blue-collar workers worked at home or in firms with fewer than 10 employees.[22]

The lives of workers were nevertheless transformed by industrial change during the nineteenth century, though the effects were different for men and women. Artisans fought a running battle with entrepreneurs to preserve craft skills, as well as to maintain control of the location of work and the manufacturing process.[23] They had varying levels of success in this endeavour. Metal workers were well placed, because new machines meant an expansion of their trade and increased demand for their services.[24] In the garment trades, on the other hand, women (along with unemployed tailors) were employed doing piecework at home for derisory wages, to the detriment of male workers endeavouring to preserve their artisanal status.[25]

Changes in manufacturing therefore had very different implications for workers in different sectors of the economy, and for men and women workers. Many men saw their skill lose its value in a new economy. They lost status and felt dishonoured and disempowered (even within their families) as their economic position declined. Women workers frequently struggled to combine work with their domestic responsibilities. Both family relations and gender identities were thrown into turmoil by such economic changes.

As the industrial wage labourer came into being in the early nineteenth century, the gendered identity of that labourer was constructed and the inherent inequalities between men and women workers thereby justified. Women came to be defined as 'cheap labour'.[26] Much ink was spilt to explain why women should not be paid the same rates as men. The key argument employed in the early nineteenth century proved enduring: a man's wage (regardless of whether he had a dependent family or not) must be calculated to support a family, whereas a female wage (regardless of whether she had a dependent family or not) must be calculated as a supplement to a male wage. Political economists reasoned that women's labour was less productive than men's. J.-B. Say argued in 1841, for instance, that men were responsible for the costs of reproducing labour power, that is, for ensuring that a new generation of workers was produced to enter the workforce. But he did so by defining women as 'dependent' regardless of the actual tasks they fulfilled, and defining their home-based work as 'consumption'. This circular argument justified the claim that men's labour was more 'productive' than women's, and that they should receive higher wages.[27]

Significantly, too, working men's investment in the notion of male superiority in the workplace meant that they often reacted to women's low wages, not by calling for equal pay for equal work, but by attempting to reverse the changes forcing women to become wage labourers in a factory environment. The printing trades became renowned for hostility to women, and their longstanding attachment to a Proudhonian model of the working-class family. In the so-called 'Couriau Affair' of 1913, their union went so far as to expel Louis Couriau for 'allowing' his wife Emma to work in a printing shop and to join the union. This event marked a turning point in the acceptance of factory work for women amongst skilled workers, and a final defeat for the 'family workshop' model of production. It was finally recognised as a thing of the past.[28]

Single women in the urban labour force

According to the 'bourgeois' model of womanhood, the proper place for women was within the family or within a familial environment.

Paid labour was not necessarily incompatible with this vision, but work performed outside the home was. Debates around women's roles in the urban economy hinged upon this principle, as commentators and critics endeavoured to latch a model of female domesticity onto a model of a wage economy. This principle was applied even to young single women without families of their own. Assumptions about their idealised future role as housewives marked perceptions of the work they did, and prescriptions of the work they should do.

Emerging roles for women in large-scale manufacture raised the greatest alarm, despite the fact that only a small percentage of women were employed in such work. As textile manufacture became mechanised and factory-based, it became predominantly work for single women. In Saint-Chamond, for instance, both the silk-processing workshops and the braid mills relied heavily on a labour force of young women from surrounding rural areas. They were housed in dormitories during the week, returning to visit their families on Sundays. An enterprising silk mill owner at Cavaillon, in the Vaucluse, had a special multi-tiered bus constructed to take his workers home on Saturday evenings and collect them on Sundays.[29] Female employment was also significant in the textile regions of north-eastern France. Nearly half of the workforce in the woollen mills in Roubaix in the 1870s was female and those women were mostly unmarried. One of the main attractions for migrants to this town was precisely the availability of work for young people: an adult male could not support a family and the wages of the entire family were essential.[30]

The employment of young women in factories, outside the family, was highly contentious. Approval for employers who housed young women on site and used female overseers, or for workshops run by nuns, stemmed from the perception that women should work in a 'family' environment, or at least in a protected situation. While essential in the emerging wage economy, and desirable to employers because it was cheap, female waged labour removed women from their 'natural' sphere, the home. This posed a dilemma for observers committed to both the capitalist wage economy and a family-based social model in which women remained dependent on men.[31]

Despite the fact that young factory workers had no children, their employment nevertheless conflicted with women's idealised roles as mothers of children and as the moral guardians of the family. Conservative critics feared that women factory workers were exposed to tasks that were dangerous to their health (by which they usually meant their reproductive health). Their potential as mothers was therefore undermined. More importantly, they were exposed to moral danger. Well-to-do critics were alarmed about mixed work-places, and even about men and women mingling as they arrived at and left work, seeing factories as places of debauchery. This was a key element in Villermé's condemnation of the factories of Lille in 1840:

> What! You mix the sexes in your workshops when [...] you could so easily separate them? Are you then ignorant of the licentious discourses which this mixture provokes, of the lessons of bad morals which result [...]? Even among children, doesn't the mixture of the sexes lead to a licence in relations, and, even in the most vulgar acts of life, a scorn for decency, which must later bear its fruits? [...] You will never be able to escape the reproach of having allowed girls to be lost whose morals you could have saved by wise and honest precautions.[32]

Such critics seemed to believe that, outside the workshops, male and female workers lived (or should live) segregated lives. They expressed a desire to contain workers' animal natures. There were certainly sexual problems in some workplaces: male overseers sometimes preyed on women employees, distributing tasks and overtime according to sexual compliance.[33] But these problems were rarely the focus of the critics' attention, which focused on disciplining women workers more closely.

As Joan Scott has argued, concern amongst the social elites about the vulnerability of women workers and about sexual disorder in the workplace often expressed broader anxieties about social change. To emphasise the dangers of mixing the sexes, and thus of allowing distinctions between male and female spaces and tasks to break down, was to condemn the social disorder and disruption which the reorganisation of work seemed to entail.[34] In actual fact, spaces and tasks within the factory were often clearly defined along sexual lines, and family groups were often employed there. Besides, as the feminist Julie Daubié pointed out in 1866, women workers were not victims of an abstract system but of the policies and practices of men. The well-being of women factory workers could best be protected, she suggested, by paying them adequately for their labour, thus removing the prime cause of their sexual vulnerability.[35]

While the factory was a major focus of debates about women workers, the domestic garment trades provided a more common form of employment for young women as seamstresses, or in specialities like lacemaking, lingerie, hatmaking and artificial flower making. These trades were quite diverse in the skills required and in rates of pay. Artificial flower making required a three-year apprenticeship and years of practice. Wages in this trade were 40 per cent higher than in other female occupations.[36] The lingerie trade required only limited skills, so this trade was poorly paid. Many home workers in the garment trades were dependent on sub-contractors for their employment: a system known as 'sweating' which drove down wages. They also suffered months of unemployment in the dead season.

Home work in the needlework trades appeared to be suitable work for women, but the impoverishment of women in these trades was also apparent. Their low wages were the subject of public debate across the nineteenth century. Personal accounts of women workers attest to the hardships they faced. When Suzanne Voilquin was forced to become a worker in the 1820s, following the bankruptcy of her father's hatmaking business, she took employment in a dressmaking shop. Wages were low, but real poverty set in when she was laid off and forced to resort to piecework at home, earning one franc for an 18-hour day.[37] Sixty years later, Jeanne Bouvier was considered 'rich' as a regular worker in a dressmaking shop, but she worked at home after hours in order to increase her earnings. Nevertheless, she was better off than others in her apartment building, who were driven by poverty and hunger to commit suicide or to work the streets.[38] Seamstresses and garment workers provided a significant percentage of single mothers giving birth at the public maternity hospital in Paris. Their infants were sometimes the fruit of consensual unions (which provided another solution to starvation wages), and sometimes a product of the 'fifth quarter' of the day – selling sex in return for bread.[39]

Images of the impoverished seamstress, working long hours alone in her attic for a pittance, driven to prostitution in order to survive, or alternatively preserving her virtue against all odds, were staples in the discussion of women's work across the nineteenth century. The virtuous Rigolette was a key character in Eugène Sue's popular serial novel of the 1840s, *The Mysteries of Paris*.[40] Such images had compelling cultural resonance in the nineteenth century. From one perspective home-based needlework was ideal work for women. However, home workers were frequently isolated, living and working alone rather than in the idealised family workshop. Rather than being under the control and guidance of a male head of household, earning a supplementary wage, the home worker was isolated. For exponents of the domestic ideal, the image of the impoverished seamstress validated views about women's natural dependence on men, and the unnaturalness of economic arrangements that subverted that dependence. For socialists and feminists, on the other hand, the image highlighted capitalism's destruction of love, innocence and family life.[41]

Because women's work was defined as unskilled or low-skilled, low-paid female handwork supported a vast expansion of production in the garment trades without major capital investment. The invention of the domestic sewing machine meant that workers themselves carried the costs of mechanisation in the trade when it did occur. Although many home workers were married and were often the primary wage-earners for their families, the evocative image of the vulnerable young seamstress was central to debates over women's work and social roles. For some observers, it highlighted the need for further economic development; for others, the need to preserve valued social norms; for still others, the need to reform society in ways that would alleviate working-class misery and disadvantage. Few, however, argued for a living wage for women workers to enable them to support themselves independently with dignity.

Domestic service best approximated the 'ideal' form of wage labour for young women in the nineteenth century, because it seemed most compatible with the ideal of domesticity. It was carried out in the home, occupied young women at domestic tasks that prepared them for their future roles as wives and mothers, and subjected them to the 'maternal' influence of their elite employers. Service in the household of another had long been common for young people. In the nineteenth century it became increasingly an urban occupation. After 1850, it became increasingly feminised. Where 69 per cent of servants were female in 1851, more than 80 per cent were female by the turn of the twentieth century. About half a million urban households had at least one servant at that time, but demand was rising as families of the petty bourgeoisie aspired to the status achieved by employing domestic help.[42] The 'maid of all work' was frequently a young rural woman for whom going into service was a means of escape from the village, or from the hardships of service on the farm.[43]

Despite its location, domestic service had significant drawbacks for women. Wages were extremely low. Rather than being protected from vice in a 'moral' environment, servants remained vulnerable to sexual coercion and exploitation.[44] Domestic servants were over-represented in the statistics on premarital pregnancy in nineteenth-century Paris. They comprised one-fifth of unwed mothers giving birth at the main public maternity hospital in the 1830s, and two-thirds in 1900: an increase greater than their increase in the city's population.[45]

The tale of the young servant seduced by the master of the family or his son, and abandoned to raise her illegitimate child alone, presents an extreme example of the perils of the job. Such cases were not unknown, as servants' trials for infanticide in the late nineteenth century attest.[46] More commonly, however, servants became pregnant to men of their own class. Servants frequently shared rooms in the garrets of apartment buildings. They were isolated from both their families and their employers, and worked alone all day except for the critical oversight of the mistress. Loneliness may have made them vulnerable to sexual advances, especially if accompanied by the promise of marriage. Besides, the tale of the young servant girl, seduced and dismissed, was sometimes told as a moral tale rather than as a depiction of reality. It reiterated the vulnerability of women working outside their own homes, as well as presenting a critique of relations between the classes.

In some respects, servants might be seen as 'victims' of their circumstances. They worked 15 hours per day, and their employers had considerable power over them. They were excluded from the provisions of the 1906 law, which gave workers a right to a day off per week, on the grounds that they were not 'employees' but 'extensions of the family'! The 1898 laws on workplace accidents were not applied to domestics until 1923, and even then they only applied if the servant could prove that the fault lay with the employer, which was virtually impossible.[47]

Anne Martin-Fugier argues that conditions for maids in petty bourgeois households were particularly severe. Wages were low and jobs poorly defined, while inexperienced employers relied on manuals for guidance. Having a servant was also critical to the employer's status and sense of identity, making her keen to assert her authority.[48] The Weiler household at Strasbourg provides some support for this argument. The marginal bourgeois status of the family is evident in the amount of domestic labour that the women undertook, for instance in assisting the laundresses on washdays. Twenty-year-old Amélie became mistress of the household on the death of her mother in 1842, and her relationship with a series of domestic servants is a key theme in her diary. Having given one maid notice in May 1844, after 'tolerating her faults for five years', she found the next employee a very raw recruit: 'sixteen years old, with the best will in the world, but [she] knows neither how to wash a glass, nor to wield the broom, nor to dry a plate'. The following year Amélie was seeking a new maid, questioning applicants on their liking for dances, on whether they had boyfriends, whether they could cook fish and dress poultry (even though her family rarely ate either):

> I tell each one that I am extremely particular about cleanliness. I consider whether their clothes demonstrate that innate taste which each one says she has and that one rarely finds in any of them. I examine whether their hands are as well manicured as is possible for a woman condemned to hard work, whether their fingers appear nimble.

In 1846 she was again at her wits' end, threatening to send an incompetent maid back to her village, a threat also made in 1847 to one who was labelled 'as useless and ugly as a beast unhitched from the plough'. In mid-1847, Amélie was dealing with her fourth servant in three months. In June 1851 she dismissed yet another maid, partly because she could not cook, but also because she was not sufficiently 'attached' to the family. The unrealistic expectations evident in Amélie's diary for what was undoubtedly a poorly paid position perhaps reflect her youth and inexperience, but they also explain why servants tended to stay only briefly in the Weiler household and others like it.[49] However, if employers were quick to dismiss servants, frequent job-changing was servants' most potent weapon, given the anxiety caused for employers by the constant search for 'good help'.

New employment opportunities for young single women opened up in the tertiary or service sector in the late nineteenth century. Developments in finance, telecommunications, government services and bureaucracy led to the rapid expansion of clerical jobs in banks, insurance companies, the post office, telephone and telegraph work. Developments in the retail sector opened up positions for sales clerks in department stores. If the expanding metallurgical and chemical sectors provided high-paying jobs mainly to men, young women, now almost universally literate, were willing and available to take up employment in the expanding tertiary sector. In 1890s Paris a vacancy at one department store drew 100 applications, while 1000 women competed for 25 jobs at the Bank of France, and 5000 women competed for 200 post office jobs.[50]

Despite its location away from the home, 'white-collar' work was defined as suitable work for young women in this period. Sales clerks' positions were unskilled, a period of in-house training (often remunerated only with room and board) providing the necessary preparation. This had the added advantage of inducting malleable young women into the required culture and behaviour. The provision of lodgings for female employees was a legacy of the paternalism of the past. It provided the 'familial' context in which the work of single women was ideally located. It thus reassured families of their daughters' well-being, but it also enabled employers to control workers' lives outside working hours.[51] Clerical positions also required limited skills because office functions were broken down into separate tasks: typists did not do the filing. This created a hierarchy of skills and remuneration amongst employees.[52] Employers welcomed the opportunity to enlist women on wages lower than would have been required for men. Women did not need to be offered a career structure, either, because they could expect to leave the job on marriage. Many young women were attracted to this work because it was less strenuous and better paid than factory work or domestic service. They came to see white-collar work as an ideal form of employment, though they generally regarded it as a prelude to marriage.

Marriage, childbearing and the maternal ideal

The feminine ideal for women of the labouring classes focused on marriage and motherhood. But industrial development based on cheap wage labour put increasing pressure on marriage and family life, and made childcare particularly difficult for women to integrate with paid work. Contemporaries frequently lamented the breakdown of urban family life. Women were subjected to particular criticism, given their central role in bearing and rearing children. Their failure to approximate the maternal ideal of the bourgeois imagination focused attention on the 'condition' of the workers, however, and helped shape new government policies on the family by the later nineteenth century.

The urban craft tradition linked marriage with the establishment of a new economic unit. Marriage occurred after a period of training and saving, when the couple had the resources to establish their own workshop. The silk weavers of Lyon illustrate this pattern. Endogamy was strong: weavers' daughters frequently married weavers, and their complementary skills enabled the couple to work as a team. In the early nineteenth-century silk workers married young, but by the

1840s the age at marriage was rising. Economic change was forcing young people to save for a longer period before they could afford to set up their own businesses. However, unmarried couples often lived together and legitimised their children when they married.[53] Similar marriage patterns characterised other artisanal groups, while the need to save a dowry delayed marriage for some non-artisanal groups such as domestic servants.

Other forms of employment encouraged earlier marriage. This was particularly true of industries where large numbers of unskilled workers, notably children, could be employed in the production process. The 'proto-industrial' production of goods, where merchant capitalists provided raw materials to families and paid them at piece rates, was highly conducive to this arrangement, as was factory-based textiles manufacture. Young people had no incentive to delay marriage, having no expectation of becoming independent or inheriting property. Children increased the family's earnings – crucial to the family wage economy – because they could be employed in these enterprises from a young age.[54]

For the bourgeoisie, large families were proof of workers' lack of self-discipline. Manufacturing centres certainly appeared to be overflowing with children, as did the workers' quarters of most towns. However, the populations of manufacturing towns were comprised largely of young migrant workers: the age profile of these towns, rather than the reproductive behaviour of the inhabitants, explains their high birth rates. Overcrowded urban slums also gave the impression of large families, when in reality several families were living together in the same dwelling. High infant mortality was due to the same poor conditions, and meant that while working women might bear more children, not all those children would survive to adulthood.[55]

The impression that impoverished workers were having large families was no doubt reinforced by the fact that many observers visited the industrial towns of the north-east, where large families were indeed common. Families in Lille and Roubaix averaged four to six children in the 1880s, although some were as large as eleven or more. These families pooled their wages to survive, especially where adult wages were low: a pattern that encouraged large families. High infant mortality, and the inability of working mothers to breastfeed their children, also facilitated a high birth rate because breastfeeding helped to prevent conception. Flemish culture, moreover, was strongly marked by Catholicism, which may have made couples reluctant to employ family limitation, and it was also renowned for a love of children: bourgeois families in this region were also uncharacteristic-ally large, often consisting of 12 or more children.[56]

The Nord was atypical, however. Elsewhere economic incentives encouraged workers to limit the size of their families. Lyon's silk-workers had on average only 3.2 children in the early nineteenth century, even though wives tended to be in their early twenties at the time of their marriage. Such small families would be most unlikely without contraceptive measures, particularly since these women nor-mally sent their children to wetnurses in order to maintain the rhythm of their work in the family business.[57] Families were larger in nearby Saint-Chamond. Nevertheless, the pattern of births was not 'natural': women were having fewer children in the early nineteenth century than in the eighteenth century.

Differences between the reproductive histories of ribbonweavers' wives and nailmakers' wives in Saint-Chamond illustrate the impact of different family economies on reproductive behaviour. Ribbon-weaving, like silk manufacture, depended on the co-operative labour of husband and wife. Women in these families tended to have several children rapidly after marriage. They put children out to wetnurses to minimise disruption to their work. This quick succession of preg-nancies had the advantage of enabling the couple to get through the period of infant dependency as quickly as possible. Once they had got through this stage, they produced very few children and at quite long intervals. This suggests that they used contraceptive techniques once the desired family size was achieved.

Nailmaking in Saint-Chamond, by contrast, was men's work. Nailmakers' wives worked in other branches of domestic industry, particularly silk production. This employment was more flexible than the work of ribbonweavers' wives, and more easily rearranged around childcare. Breastfeeding was common among nailmakers' wives and provided the main brake on pregnancy. Although these women were generally poorer than ribbonweavers' wives, therefore, they continued having children over a longer period. The example of Saint-Chamond suggests that the need to co-ordinate the employment of husband and wife in a family enterprise was a stronger incentive than poverty to restrict the number of children.[58]

In the textile towns of north-eastern France couples were slower to limit family size. The birth rate in Roubaix was still 42.8 per thousand in 1861, but fell rapidly to 36.4 in 1891 and 29.9 in 1901. This was clearly due to deliberate measures of family limitation. A gradual rise in adult wages over the period reduced the need for children's earnings. Legislative controls on child employment and compulsory schooling reduced the economic value of children by the 1880s. Where wage-earning children in these towns had paid the costs of their own subsistence in the early nineteenth century they now became a 'cost' to parents, having to be housed, clothed and fed for long periods before being able to contribute to the family's income. Under these circumstances, workers – mostly unskilled and with limited earning power – simply could not afford to have large families. The need to limit births became more urgent amongst this sector of the population too.[59]

Social commentators, concerned that workers had too many children, were even more scandalised by the irregular domestic arrangements of many workers and the illegitimate children who resulted. They complained that workers saw no harm in 'giving rein to their passions', producing 'illicit relations without consecration or responsibility – young men without moderation, young women without modesty, children without families – in a word, all the inconveniences of hastily arranged marriages minus the moral bond and sanctity of legitimate unions'.[60] 'Concubinage', as contemporaries described it, was common in some urban communities. The work of the Society of Saint-François Régis, established in the early nineteenth century to facilitate legal marriage amongst workers and to legitimise their children, claimed credit for the celebration of nearly 42,000 marriages between 1826 and 1850.[61]

Historians have paid particular attention to women's motives for entering consensual unions. Edward Shorter argued that this development reflected a 'sexual revolution' led by working women. As they became individual wage-earners in the towns, escaping the controls and taboos of village life, they added to their newfound economic independence a desire for personal freedom and fulfilment.[62] However, as other historians have pointed out, such women gained a very dubious 'freedom' in the towns. Michel Frey's study of Paris showed that it was women with the lowest earnings who were most likely to enter consensual unions. Where Shorter saw women's 'economic liberation', Frey argued that increasing economic dependence forced women into relationships with men in order to survive. Furthermore, the Napoleonic Code had abolished women's right to seek support from the fathers of children born outside marriage. All in all, women had little power to require men to accept the responsibilities flowing from sexual relationships, and 'concubinage' was frequently the result.[63]

There is evidence that some women believed consensual unions allowed them more freedom than marriage, and Frey cites court cases where they challenged men's attempts to keep them within such relationships.[64] However, there is little evidence to suggest that workers rejected marriage as an institution. As Lynch points out, socialist theories of 'free unions' gained little support among workers.[65] 'Concubinage' was commonly a preliminary to marriage, as among Lyon's silk weavers saving to establish their own workshops. Similarly, the high percentage of children born within nine months of their parents' marriage in Saint-Chamond in the 1860s suggests that workers formed relationships akin to marriage, rather than that they behaved promiscuously. Pregnancy brought forward marriages that had been delayed, often for economic reasons.[66] Contemporary observers also noted that the irregular liaisons in towns like Mulhouse and Reims were nevertheless stable family units. The high rates at which infants born out of wedlock were legally recognised by their fathers in many communities support this view: for instance, almost all infants were recognised by their fathers in mid-century Lodève.[67]

Working women outnumbered men in seeking to have their relationships regularised. This may reflect women's higher levels of religious practice,[68] but they also had other reasons for desiring marriage. Labouring communities often accepted consensual unions and did not distinguish between 'legitimate' and 'illegitimate' children, but it was extremely difficult for women to support children unaided. Women with children were unlikely to see consensual unions as a source of 'freedom', then, and may have seen marriage as a promise of economic security. Women were also under greater pressure than men to conform to prevailing codes of conduct. They were deemed responsible for keeping men on the straight and narrow, and their sexual misbehaviour was more heavily criticised. From this perspective, women may have found in marriage the respectability that men found through such criteria as skill and earning power.

Finally, there were practical advantages for women in legitimising their unions. Marrying their partner might not bring direct financial gain, but it did open up new avenues of assistance for needy families. Women were the ones who balanced the family budget and who, when wages ran out, faced the humiliation of seeking assistance at the public welfare bureau or from private charitable organisations. But these institutions usually had strict moral criteria and refused to aid women living in consensual unions.[69] Religious observance was often required as well.[70] Since the public welfare bureaux were usually administered by the same local elites that ran the private charities, the needy had few options but to conform to their expectations. The periodic need for charity, therefore, exposed women to religious influence and moral pressure. Even if women did not see marriage as morally preferable, as the elites hoped, they had good economic reasons for seeing it as desirable.

Combining work and family: the challenge for urban mothers

The paid employment of married women was particularly contentious in the nineteenth century because it frequently conflicted with the cultural model of the family-centred and maternal woman. A larger proportion of married women continued to work in France than in England, however, because the small-scale system of production remained more common, and because the lower rate of population growth limited the supply of available labour. Low wages continued to favour a family wage economy rather than a male-breadwinner model. Around the mid-nineteenth century, 40 per cent of married Frenchwomen and 25 per cent of married English women were in paid work.[71] Despite the myth that women's wages were supplementary to those of a man, many women were supporting themselves or their families. Their earnings were needed for rent or to buy food: the two main reasons cited by women during a government enquiry. Some working men were unwilling to support their families, seeing that as their wives' responsibility. In law, however, husbands controlled married women's incomes until 1907.[72]

Despite the criticism they received for neglecting their maternal duties, women with families sought work that could be interwoven with family responsibilities. Women with children tended to occupy particular niches in the urban economy and to do different jobs from women without families. Combining the idealised role of mother and helpmeet with the economic imperative of 'making ends meet' – also a female responsibility – presented major problems.

The economic contributions of mothers within the family wage economy varied with the life-cycle of the family and the employment structure of the town. The most difficult years were those when a couple had young children because this was when extra income was most needed but when it was also most difficult for the mother to earn unless she worked at home. In most communities, women with family responsibilities did not work outside the home unless absolutely necessary. The higher a family's standard of living, the less likely the mother was to work.[73] Where there were jobs for children, they often became wage-earners in preference to their mothers.[74] When their income was essential mothers sought jobs that enabled them to control their own hours and to care for their children. In north-eastern France they performed piecework, became laundresses or cleaners, or sold produce on the streets or in their homes. Working in the factory was a last resort and a mark of poverty in these communities.[75]

Piecework at home in the garment trades provided one of the major forms of employment for married women into the twentieth century. The Labour Office Enquiry into the lingerie trade, conducted in 1908–1910, discovered that the great majority of home workers were married or widowed, while the majority of shopworkers were single. Women's motives for taking on homework, despite its low wages, were complex. Cultural norms which valued the domestic wife were one factor. Women also made practical calculations that greater earnings would flow from working at home, where the legislation limiting the hours that women could work did not apply. It was cheaper than travelling to the shop, and more readily combined with caring for children. Homework was an economic choice for some women with domestic responsibilities, while for others it more closely approximated the ideal of domesticity.[76]

In factory towns, however, women with families who needed employment were often forced to take work in factories since little else was available. In Roubaix, demand for workers was high and male wages were low, so mothers of even young children were forced into factory work.[77] Only 17 per cent of married women had paid employment there in 1872, but more than half of the married women who worked were employed in the textile factories. In Lille and Roubaix, many women textile workers did not leave their jobs on marriage or even when their children were born. They entered the mills between 10 and 12 years of age, and remained there for the rest of their short lives (life expectancy for such women was less than 40).[78] In 1896, adult women comprised more than a third of the textiles workforce in the Nord.[79] In Saint-Chamond, mothers were also a significant percentage of the workforce in the braid factories, and their representation increased rather than decreased during the century.

Restrictions on child labour from the mid-nineteenth century, and the law of 1874 that prohibited women under 21 from working night shift, encouraged employers to rely on older women. In 1890, more than 60 per cent of employees were women over 21, and most women over 21 were married.[80] Employers argued that working night shift suited the needs of women with families: 'Married women take the night shift so that they can do housework at home in the morning, take care of children, prepare food at noon for the family, and then [...] earn a salary.'[81] Had employers really supported the domestic ideal of womanhood for their workers, they might have concluded that shift-work was impossible for women with young children. Women's maternal role, so significant for the well-being of their families and the moral education of their children, might have suggested the need for women with children to be supported in the fulfilment of that social function, perhaps by paying men higher wages. But such a view would have cut across employers' vested interest in preserving this low-paid female workforce by defending the work of married women. Their solution was to present an image of working-class superwomen, who put their domestic responsibilities first but still performed paid work, and had no need for sleep.

Public opinion was often hostile to married women's employment in factory work precisely because it was seen as incompatible with the performance of their 'duties' as mothers. Many women seem to have shared this view, which is hardly surprising given that their 'duties' as mothers had to be performed on top of a long day at the factory. Debates about the paid employment of married women outside their homes focused on family breakdown, which was regarded as its inevitable consequence. If the mother was unable to devote her time to the family, the result was a dirty and neglected home, and dirty and neglected children. This argument was reiterated across the nineteenth century. The economist Adolphe Blanqui noted in 1848:

> Family life is becoming increasingly rare amongst manufacturing workers, especially in the towns, where their confined or unhealthy dwellings are only regarded by them as fleeting nocturnal shelters. The family dissolves very quickly on contact with the foul air of the cellars of Lille and the attics of Rouen.[82]

Men fled these bleak homes for the tavern, he declared, and thus fell into alcoholism. In the 1860s similar points were made by another prominent social critic, Jules Simon.[83] Like Blanqui, he contrasted the destitute and demoralised families of urban workers with an ideal working family in a rural environment. Simon praised the silk-processing families in the countryside around Lyon, where 'intemperance is more rare, family life more common, the influence of woman almost always predominant'.[84] These were the impoverished families whose meagre earnings were helping to reduce artisanal families to poverty within Lyon itself.[85]

In contemporary observers' eyes, the central problem with the employment of married women was that it conflicted with their role as mother. Observers described women 'torn' from their families, unable to feed and rear their infants, unable to create proper homes. Rather than emphasising the exploitation of women's labour through starvation wages, critics recounted the destructive effects on the maternal body of excessive or incompatible employment, which made women incapable of bearing healthy children or of nursing and nurturing them.[86]

Concerns about the harmful effects of female employment had some basis. But problems were not confined to the new industrial occupations. Flora Tristan had expressed similar fears about the reproductive health of the laundresses of Nîmes in 1844. They worked in a very traditional branch of women's industry but were now working in water contaminated with dyes and chemicals.[87] Condemning the effects of employment on women's reproductive capacity highlighted a change in the experience of work under new economic conditions. Woman's maternal function, and hence maternal values more generally, appeared to be threatened by the processes of economic change.

The expression of anxiety about the employment of women and its attendant effects, which first emerged in the early nineteenth century, therefore articulated deeper concerns about change. Woman's role within the family became vital in this context. She was held responsible by social commentators for maintaining the home and preserving the family. She was also charged with keeping her husband from the attractions of the tavern, and raising her children as good citizens and workers. The maternal ideal attributed enormous power to women. It also exposed them to criticism for failing to achieve the desired results.

By the late nineteenth century, concerns about working mothers had acquired new dimensions. Anxieties about a falling birth rate accelerated after France's defeat in the Franco–Prussian war of 1870. Women's inability or refusal to bear children became a key focus of these 'depopulation' debates.[88] Politicians were increasingly prepared to take legislative measures to facilitate childbearing, to provide financial assistance to poor mothers and to parents with large families, to control wetnursing and subsidise sterile milk for needy mothers, and to ensure the survival of even 'illegitimate' children. If the leaders of the Second Empire (1851–1870) played an active role in supporting charitable organisations, the Republicans who then came to power espoused a philosophy of social solidarity. This led to the idea of a minimum standard of living for everyone in the community, and hence the needy person's right to 'public assistance': no longer should people be forced to rely on charity. The beginnings of the French Welfare State emerged in the pre-First World War period.[89]

Women workers were key targets of the legislative reforms of the 1880–1914 period. The employment law of 1892 restricted them to an 11-hour day, as well as banning children's employment and limiting the hours of adolescent workers. These measures were strengthened in the Millerand–Collier Law of 1900. It also decreed that, where men and women worked together, the restrictions should apply to both, although family workshops were exempted. In 1893, poor women became eligible for free antenatal care. In 1909 the maternity protection law entitled women to up to eight weeks' leave before and after childbirth, with their jobs guaranteed. The Strauss Law of 1913 introduced four weeks' compulsory leave after childbirth, and paid mothers a small daily allowance during this period with an additional stipend for breastfeeding.[90]

Working mothers benefited as greater recognition was given to the economic pressures under which they suffered. However, this two-pronged attack on the problems of working mothers served to emphasise the primary function of motherhood in women's lives, and in some respects disadvantaged them as workers. Mary Lynn Stewart argues that the law of 1892 locked women into low-paid jobs, since employers had good reason to prefer male employees.[91] It also led employers to devise innovative counter-measures such as split shifts, which made women's working days longer.[92] By reinforcing the secondary nature of women's paid employment, it strengthened the impact of the 'double burden'.

The focus of reformers' attention, however, was not so much the burdens endured by women, but the effects of women's employment on their children. Even 'illegitimate' children and their mothers were beneficiaries.[93] Many overburdened women probably shared the image of themselves as mothers first and foremost. This model was idealised not only by conservatives, but also by feminists and socialists in the nineteenth century.[94]

By 1914, a broad community consensus had developed about the maternal destiny of women, even working-class women. This consensus was broken only by occasional radical calls for a broader understanding of women's potential and rights. Women nevertheless remained an important supply of cheap labour for industry, and carried considerable economic responsibility for their families.[95] Low wages supplemented by social welfare payments became the solution to economic change, allowing wage labour for women to coexist with their ongoing responsibility for their families. At the beginning of the twentieth century the double burden remained for urban women of the labouring classes.

3   Peasant Women

Peasants comprised the majority of the French population throughout most of the nineteenth century. The French Revolution had enshrined peasant ownership of the land, and family-based farming underpinned the economy throughout the century. Economic change eroded this model of agriculture, however, just as it undermined the urban family workshop. Small farms became less viable as market agriculture replaced subsistence farming. The development of market agriculture in the north of France was supported by the agricultural labour of landless peasants, just as cheap labour by workers supported economic development in the towns. Women were an important part of the agricultural labour force, both as peasant farmers and as agricultural labourers. As men departed for work in the towns in the nineteenth century, women's role in agriculture increased. They comprised 30 per cent of the agricultural labour force in 1854, but nearly 40 per cent in 1911.[1]

Women's lifestyles in rural France reflected a variety of socio-economic situations and regional cultures. An increasingly powerful urban culture began to challenge local beliefs and practices in the nineteenth century, leaving its impact on gender roles. But peasant women, like urban workers, hardly resembled the domestic woman idealised by the social elites. The economic imperatives of rural life, and peasant cultural expectations, prevented peasant women from devoting themselves predominantly to home and children. Like urban working women, peasant women combined 'productive' labour on the farm with responsibility for 'domestic' tasks. The two were difficult to distinguish on the farm. Gender norms in peasant society created an imbalance of power between the sexes, although their dynamics differed from the bourgeois model. The impact of the dominant culture in the late nineteenth century, however, was to strengthen the inequalities in conformity with the urban model.

The dynamics of marriage in peasant communities

Peasant society was strongly marked by gender divisions. In James Lehning's words, gender was 'firmly rooted in every aspect of daily life, from the physical spaces people walked, to the tasks they performed, to the secrets they possessed, whether these were about working a field or having (or not having) a child'.[2] But the norms of femininity and masculinity differed from those in the bourgeois world. Marriage and family patterns were dominated by the need to keep a fragile economic bark afloat. The distinctiveness of female and male tasks, and the qualities valued in men and women, reflected economic imperatives. Bourgeois observers often lamented the absence of romantic love and affection between peasant couples. They interpreted peasant life through their own urban lens, often misinterpreting it in the process. Nevertheless, pragmatic decisions did prevail in peasant society because survival was the paramount consideration.

Marriage was a family-undertaking in village society, as it was in the bourgeois world. It brought two families into close economic and social relations with each other, hence the need to ensure a suitable match. The degree of family interest in a potential union depended upon a variety of factors. A distinction is often drawn between the northern regions, where peasant women had higher status and more authority and hence more say in choosing their husbands, and the patriarchal society of the south.[3] Marriage patterns in the Briançonnais region, in the Southern Alps, support this picture of male-dominated southern society. Women generally had no control over marriage arrangements there in the nineteenth century. To take one example, Catherine Vallier and Joseph Allais were married in the late nineteenth century because their families viewed the partnership as economically advantageous. The bride's desire to marry someone else was irrelevant.[4]

But this case also illustrates that marriage arrangements were shaped by economic structures and imperatives, not simply by 'tradition' or male power. The Briançonnais was a poor mountainous region. Family survival was more important than individual choice in such areas. Marriage between suitable partners provided a means for ensuring that marginal farms were as productive as possible. Furthermore, property was owned individually in this region, so the marriage of the heir was a matter of great family importance. French law dictated that all children inherit equal shares of family wealth, but the eldest son received the farm in the Briançonnais. The prospective wife had to be an accomplished worker of sound character to help that farm prosper, and she had to come from a family of equivalent status so as not to disrupt village hierarchies.

Marriage had less serious economic implications for younger sons and daughters, and in areas where land was owned communally. Children had greater freedom of choice, although those who did not inherit land might not marry at all because the economic prerequisites for family life were lacking.[5] While Catherine Vallier was not permitted to marry the man of her choice, her daughter Catherine (whose marriage did not affect the inheritance) married the local cheesemaker in a lovematch without upsetting village relations or economic imperatives.[6] Village dynamics were also critical in areas where political events (especially the conflicts of the French Revolution) had created sharp divides between socialists and conservatives. Such divisions limited the choice of acceptable marriage partners in the Var (in south-eastern France).[7]

The age at marriage in peasant communities was declining in the nineteenth century. In the early decades brides were on average nearly 26 when they married and their husbands 28, but by the turn of the twentieth century brides were normally about 23 and their husbands 26.[8] However, national averages camouflage a wide variety of local patterns based on demographic, socio-economic and cultural factors. Developments in the Department of the Loire (near Lyon) illustrate the factors shaping marriage patterns in the countryside. Women's age at marriage declined here between 1851 and 1891, but more women remained unmarried. A clear difference emerged between the lowland and the mountain regions, demonstrating the impact of economic considerations on marriage patterns. In the lowland regions, farms were larger, land was more fertile, and production became more market-oriented. Few people left the village for the town, and a pattern of earlier and more universal marriage emerged. In the more isolated upland regions, however, farms were smaller and less adapted to market production. Many young people (especially young men) left the village because they could not find work. Economic insecurity and a shortage of potential husbands ensured that the pattern of late marriage continued in these areas.[9]

Economic considerations were so fundamental to peasant marriage that for much of the century courting required family approval. Marriage often proceeded quickly once approval was obtained. Parents were unwilling to sanction a daughter's marriage into a family that was indebted. In protecting the bride's assets, they protected the family's assets and social standing. Martin Nadaud recounts of his youth in the Creuse (in central France) in the 1830s that he was denied the right to court one girl because of his family's debts. However, the family of the woman who became his wife placed more emphasis on his sound character and his reputation as a hard worker.[10] This account suited Nadaud's image as a self-made man whose hard work resulted in financial success. Emile Guillaumin made a similar claim for Etienne Bertin, the landless labourer whose life he recounts in a fictional autobiography, *The Life of a Simple Man*. When Bertin sought Victoire Giraud in marriage, her family ignored the poverty of his background and consented because of his reputation for hard work.[11] Even a landless man who was not drunken or dissolute and did not shirk work could be a suitable husband, because he could maintain a family by his labour if not by his patrimony. He could still be the head of a family enterprise, though one based on wage labour rather than the desired family farm.

Marriage brought status to peasant women, and was widely sought by them. It did not give women the independence that men acquired in becoming heads of households. Passed from father to husband, peasant women remained less autonomous than men. The unmarried woman, however, had no autonomy. She lived her life as a dependent, usually a servant in the home of one of her siblings, and she was reliant on their goodwill for her livelihood. By becoming mistress of a household, a woman could earn respect for her management skills, and fulfil the most prized role by bearing children. It is hardly surprising that peasant women strongly desired marriage.[12]

Each region had its traditional practices for girls fearful of not finding a husband. These ranged from wearing lucky stones to bathing in sacred springs and making pilgrimages to holy places. In the mountains of the south-east, girls seeking husbands made a pilgrimage to the shrine of Saint Nicholas in June. In Normandy they laid coins on the stone dedicated to Saint Nicholas de la Chesnaie, a custom still observed in 1933.[13] Near Bordeaux, and in farming communities around Paris, the customary prayer invoked a multitude of saints:

> Kyrie, I should like
> Christe, to be married
> Kyrie, I pray to all the saints
> Christe, that it should be tomorrow [...]
> Saint Frederick, may I have a good husband.
> Saint Bartholomew, may he be handsome.[14]

Marriage partners generally came from the same village or a neighbouring village: the range of social interaction for most peasants until the late nineteenth century. Marrying locally was most common in isolated mountain communities and in Brittany, where available partners were limited and where the demands of daily labour made it desirable that plots of land brought together by a marriage should not be too far apart.[15] Even where peasant men travelled outside the area to work, they customarily married a woman from the local area. This was one means of controlling property relations in the village. In the Vaucluse, endogamy began to decline about 1900 as young women began to seek town dwellers rather than agricultural workers as partners.[16] This change also suggests that male control over marriage was not universal in the 'patriarchal' south, or was in retreat by this time.

Patterns of courtship varied with region and economic status, but attraction, affection and family suitability were intimately entwined throughout the nineteenth century.[17] Village dances, the communal winter work-sessions known as *veillées*, and even Sunday Mass provided opportunities for the young to interact. The degree of intimacy allowed courting couples reflected economic and social patterns in each region. In Savoy and Upper Brittany – where property was controlled communally – it was not unknown for courting couples to sleep together, as happened in the Basque country.[18] Marriage simply followed more quickly if the woman fell pregnant. But where marriages were based on economic alliances and a pattern of individual inheritance, courtship was strictly supervised because premarital sexual liaisons had to be prevented.[19] In the Briançonnais, where individual inheritances were strictly controlled, a premarital liaison could provoke a murderous reaction in a young woman's father.[20] Lack of experience in mixing with the opposite sex could then prove an obstacle to the courting process once a suitable spouse was selected. Martin Nadaud had difficulty making conversation with his fiancée, whose mother acted as both chaperone and prompt.[21] By contrast, Guillaumin describes young people in the Allier region pairing off to walk home following the winter *veillée*, providing the opportunity for a degree of sexual experimentation. Village youths also exchanged tales about women prepared to advance sexual favours outside marriage.[22]

Urban-style dances became popular in the village in the late nineteenth century, to the consternation of priests who feared that sexual licence would be unleashed by close bodily contact. Despite the fears of the priests, it did not take the arrival of the waltz in the village to provide the opportunity for 'immorality'. At 18, for instance, Etienne Bertin's relationship with his young neighbour was portrayed as passionate but careful: 'I took her in my arms, pressed her to me in a passionate embrace, and gave her a long lover's kiss [...] But our relationship never went beyond innocent hugs and long, long kisses [...] Young and shy as we were, timidity, modesty, fear of consequences – all these things hindered us from the consummation of our love.'[23]

Guillaumin composed his fictionalised memoir in the 1880s, describing practices purporting to date from the mid-century.[24] However, the language of 'falling in love', if not the feeling, dates from the late nineteenth-century urban world. Couples were likely to express their sentiments in different ways prior to that time, especially in peasant society.[25] Guillaumin's desire to present a positive image of peasant life to an urban reading public who often despised peasants may well explain this romantic tone.[26]

Urban observers noted the 'brutal' ways in which courting couples expressed their intimacy in rural France. Rather than embracing in a display of tenderness they slapped or thumped each other, threw pebbles at each other, squeezed or twisted each other's hands to the point of pain or dislocation.[27] These practices reflect a world in which physical endurance was a prized quality. If feminine 'weakness' was inculcated in bourgeois girls, 'delicacy' was not valued where hard labour was the norm for both sexes. In regions where daughters-in-law joined their husbands' families, they became part of its labour force, hence the importance placed on fitness, skills and competence rather than beauty or delicacy in the choice of marriage partners. The qualities desired in a wife were the same as those essential in a good husband: health, strength and endurance. Communal events such as the threshing of a local farmer's grain could provide an occasion for the public display of strength and stamina for girls as well as boys, and thus the demonstration of one's worth as a prospective marriage partner. '[Girls] knew that even if they were beautiful enough to get some heir to lose his head, lurking in the background were a mother and a father who would not believe everything they were told.'[28]

Physical attractiveness was not irrelevant, however, and peasant girls prayed for handsome husbands.[29] But notions of beauty reflect cultural norms. At the turn of the twentieth century a suitor in the Vendée, in western France, praised his fiancée by saying: 'I think you are so lovely, my great big darling [...] I can't do better than to compare you to a field of young cabbages before the caterpillars have been through it.'[30] Peasant couples had other ways of expressing intimacy too. They exchanged traditional gifts like handkerchiefs or carved spoons but often did so silently.[31] Gestures were the currency of affection in the village. As Etienne Bertin declared, 'We love each other just as much, but we are never so liberal with tender words.'[32]

From the 1880s, the impact of compulsory education promoted widespread literacy in rural France. This brought the newspaper, with its serialised novels and fashion pages, to a mass audience. The mail-order catalogue put new consumer items within reach of rural-dwellers. These developments transformed many aspects of rural life, not least notions of fashion and sex appeal, and the practices of intimacy. The peasantry began to be brought under the sway of urban cultural norms. Young peasant women began to desire the dresses and crinolines, as well as the ribbons and finery, they saw in urban magazines.[33] They began to wear brassières that exhibited their figures rather than tight bands camouflaging them.[34] Individual happiness assumed greater priority in the choice of marriage partners, while the love letter began to provide a new way of expressing personal feelings and articulating expectations of personal happiness and fulfilment.[35] Peasant couples gradually acquired ideals of beauty and means of expressing their feelings which were more in line with the practices of urban society. Nevertheless, these processes were slow and uneven.

If marriage created a new economic partnership, it did not necessarily create a new domestic unit immediately. The new couple frequently took up residence with parents or other family, sharing sleeping and living spaces (which were often the same single room) and having little of the privacy expected today for a married couple. Middle-class observers wavered between horror at the potential for promiscuity in peasant living arrangements, and confidence that communal sleeping arrangements allowed the *pater familias* to prevent such promiscuity.[36] However peasant expectations may have been different from those of urban, middle-class couples. Martine Segalen suggests that the multiple-member household, with its separate sex groups, remained a more important social unit than the couple. Pairing off superimposed a new relationship on the peer group relationship, but work and leisure were often conducted in same-sex groups, both before and after marriage. In bourgeois homes, the bedroom became demarcated as a particularly private space during the nineteenth century. But, given the customary living arrangements, peasant couples may not have associated the bedroom with sexual intimacy.[37] Where a newly wed couple slept alongside their parents, for instance, mowing the hay in the alpine fields offered the privacy unobtainable in the home.[38]

Determining peasant attitudes to sex is extremely difficult. Sexual behaviour is not usually the subject of written records except when things go wrong, especially in peasant communities where an oral culture rather than a written culture prevailed. The hardship of daily life, the fact that many marriages rested on economic consider-ations rather than sexual attraction and, in religious areas, the Church's insistence that sex should be used for procreation rather than pleasure, may all have diminished the erotic aspect of peasant relationships.[39] And while children may have deduced something about the facts of life from observing the life of the farmyard, sexual ignorance may also have inhibited eroticism.[40] Peasant memoirs suggest enormous individual variation in patterns of tenderness and sexual compatibility: a variety found in all social groups then as now. Emilie Carles contrasts the blissful happiness of her sister and brother-in-law, who married in 1914, with the sexual brutality of some village men towards their wives, and with other relationships marred by the ignorance of the bride at marriage.[41] Marie-Catherine Santerre, married in 1909 at the age of 18 to an agricultural labourer like herself, reflected many years later on a very happy marriage:

His eyes, my God! They were so beautiful, so blue, so good. Ah, Auguste, my kind, my tender Auguste, it was that day, before you left several weeks later for the country, it was then that I fell in love with you, like that, blindly, in one instant! [... H]e knew neither how to read nor write – but so tender, so attentive to his 'Marie-Cat'. How I miss him now.[42]

Such twentieth-century accounts reflect the widespread adoption of a romantic sensibility that has been defined as 'modern'. They illustrate the spread of literacy in rural areas and the integration of peasants into a national affective culture. What they do not tell us clearly is how peasant relationships changed as a result. The historical silence of their predecessors preserves the secrecy surrounding peasants' intimate relationships.

Peasant women and motherhood

Motherhood was the archetypal role for women in the bourgeois model of 'separate spheres'. In this model, women's bodies defined their social purpose, and the female capacity for reproduction designated women's 'difference' from men. Reproduction made women dependent on men for support and protection, according to the theorists, and defined the nurture of children within the home as their destiny. This vision of womanhood was incompatible with peasant lives. Motherhood was highly valued, but it was nevertheless only one of the roles a woman had to fulfil. It could not, and did not, have the priority it assumed in elite circles.

The newly married couple expected to produce children, which began to arrive soon after marriage. For this reason, marriage was often delayed (as we have seen) until it had a sound economic basis. Fertility brought honour to a married woman, and only a married woman had the right to exercise her reproductive capacity in peasant society. The status attributed to motherhood derived from the production of heirs and labour power for the farm, rather than from sentimental notions about the bond between mother and infant.

Since marriage and reproduction were linked in the peasant worldview, rural wedding celebrations incorporated rituals involving such customary fertility symbols as grain, hens and cabbages. Ancient rites overlaid with a Christian veneer, such as dancing around local 'bride stones' surmounted by a Cross or a statue of the Virgin, also remained part of the wedding ceremonies in some regions in the nineteenth century. Given that the physiology of reproduction remained a mystery even to doctors, women's reproductive capacity was understood within a broad naturalistic concept of the cycle of life and death. Like the field made fertile by largely incomprehensible processes, the woman was made fertile by the forces of nature. She provided the fertile ground in which her husband fixed the seed and gave the infant its uniqueness. Divination and cosmology could therefore play a role in assisting fertility. Customary practices were also invoked if a woman failed to conceive. Local fertility sites, particularly wells and springs, and herbs such as wormwood and mandragora, might be called upon to restore the honour of the childless woman and her family.[43]

The image of the hardy peasant woman, impervious to pain, giving birth rapidly in the fields before returning to her duties, became a metaphor in the nineteenth century for the superiority of the 'natural' over decadent urban practices. It was cited by Dr Debay to highlight the inadequacies of bourgeois mothers.[44] But it reflects a dehumanised view of the peasant woman, whose 'animal' qualities are thereby highlighted. As Jacques Gélis points out, to give birth under such circumstances was a sign of extreme poverty and deprivation in rural society, as it was in urban society.[45] Peasant women, like urban working women, did continue to perform their normal duties until the onset of labour, but childbirth was an important social event and its rituals were observed with care.

Childbirth normally took place before the kitchen fireplace or in the stable: sites that were warm and easy to clean. It also took place within an entirely female setting, and the new mother remained in the company of women until the religious ceremony of purification some days after the birth.[46] Women in labour continued to wear 'birthing stones' or 'birthing bags' to ease pain and ensure a successful delivery until well into the nineteenth century. They provide another example of the 'christianisation' of more ancient rituals. A birthing bag from Aurillac in 1924, for instance, contained a variety of magical items and recipes, along with medallions, rosary beads and other religious objects.[47] Following the birth, other rituals surrounded the cutting of the umbilical cord and the burial of the placenta: a practice that continued in some regions into the twentieth century.[48] The increasing presence of doctors at childbirth around the First World War began to break down the sexual divide. It also saw women begin to give birth lying down rather than in traditional birthing positions.

The safe delivery of a healthy child was celebrated. But poor nutrition and the heavy work of rural women meant that complications were common. Miscarriage levels tended to rise in summer, when the demands of farm labour were at their highest, and in times of economic hardship. Women expecting their second baby, who were weakened by breastfeeding and the additional work of caring for a child, were more at risk than first-time mothers, as were older women expecting their sixth or seventh child.[49] Inadequate nutrition in infancy also had long-term effects, creating pelvic deformities that made normal delivery difficult. At its worst, this could lead to the deaths of both mother and child. Infection was also a significant threat due to the insanitary conditions of rural life. Doctors frequently blamed complications on poorly educated rural midwives, who were the last to benefit from improved medical education. However, if doctors trained in the use of instruments could be beneficial in some difficult deliveries, they could also infect mothers since asepsis was not practised until late in the nineteenth century.[50]

While fertility was highly valued, having too many children threatened the survival of poor families and the viability of the family farm. A delicate balance had to be achieved between the potential labour of children and the burden they imposed on the family's resources. Landowning families feared the subdivision of property that made farms unsustainable, so local customs favouring a single heir sometimes prevailed despite the law of equal inheritance.[51] Late marriage and the maintenance of high levels of celibacy had traditionally functioned to control family size, highlighting once again the link between economic well-being and family formation. In the nineteenth century, however, pressures on landownership and the desire to obtain or ensure the viability of farms led to the adoption of additional contraceptive measures, most likely the withdrawal method. Historians regard this as the most satisfactory explanation for the fall in rural birth rates in a number of regions between 1820 and 1850.[52]

Desperate situations sometimes called for more desperate measures. It has been estimated that one act of infanticide occurred for every 583 births in the first half of the nineteenth century. However the figures were much higher in some extremely impoverished regions. Rates of child abandonment were also extremely high in impoverished areas – up to 1 in every 24 babies born. Prosecutions for infanticide increased until the 1860s, when they averaged about 200 per year, and then began to decline.[53] The number of offences, however, was undoubtedly much higher than this.[54] Marie-Françoise Chailan, aged 23, a day labourer of no fixed abode, seen concealing a dead baby near Auriol in 1832, typifies the woman most likely to be investigated for this crime. She was a young, unmarried woman from the lower echelons of rural society, economically vulnerable, and with little likelihood of obtaining an abortion compared with her urban counterparts. Typically, too, her story made it difficult to determine whether the baby died of natural causes as she gave birth alone, or whether she deliberately allowed it to slip from her apron onto the floor of the pigsty where she had taken refuge.[55] Most of the cases of infanticide that came to the attention of the authorities concerned unwed mothers, revealing the marginality of women outside family networks in rural society.[56] They also highlight the incompatibility of sentimental models of motherhood with the extreme poverty that some populations endured.

Rates of illegitimacy were generally low in rural France. Sexual contact between unmarried couples was severely constrained in areas where inheritance governed marriage arrangements, as we have seen, while in more egalitarian areas local customs placed pressure on men to marry pregnant women.[57] Unmarried mothers were therefore relatively rare and the butt of discrimination.[58] The rate of premarital pregnancy began to rise in some areas in the nineteenth century. Roger Price suggests that this reflected the impact of industrialisation, which broke down traditional social structures and patterns of authority. He cites industrialising Sainghin-en-Mélantois in the north-east, where the rate rose from 15.2 per cent of women marrying in the mid-eighteenth century, to rates varying between 40 and 58 per cent in the first half of the nineteenth century. This compares with the more remote Bilagrés d'Ossau (in the southern Pyrenees), where the rate fell from 7.76 per cent in the mid-eighteenth century to 2.8 per cent in the first half of the nineteenth century.[59] Information on premarital pregnancy is limited, and different regional patterns are probably due to a variety of factors. Nevertheless, rising numbers of premarital pregnancies and unmarried mothers have been linked to economic change in both rural and urban communities.[60]

Urban critics insisted that peasant women were poor mothers, and their failure to replicate bourgeois norms and expectations was roundly condemned. Contemporary observers' descriptions of harsh and negligent peasant mothers have contributed to trickle-down theories of the 'invention' of mothering and the 'discovery' of childhood amongst modern historians. If the wealthy classes 'discovered' childhood and family intimacy in the seventeenth century, it is suggested, peasant families still failed the test of affectionate child-rearing in the nineteenth.[61]

Peasant childrearing practices were governed by custom and the harsh realities of peasant life. Peasant mothers were not indifferent to the fate of their infants, but had different understandings of how their infants' well-being might best be protected. Newborn infants were swaddled tightly for the first few months, in the belief that their bones were soft and prone to deformity. Binding them tightly ensured that limbs maintained their proper shape while the bones hardened. In some communities, 'giving the child its feet' was a ceremonial occasion and the ritual release of the swaddling bands took place in the church, accompanied by prayers and rejoicing.[62] Hooked onto a nail, the swaddled infant was also safe from dogs and chickens that wandered in and out of peasant homes. Besides, swaddling kept babies warm in poorly heated houses. For this reason the practice survived in Brittany until the early twentieth century, and in mountain regions until 1945.[63]

Peasant mothers keen to assist their children's development employed a number of methods scorned by urban authorities. Some of these practices were magical, although protective rosaries, scapulars and medals gradually replaced pagan talismans.[64] Other practices reflected customary beliefs and the frequently harsh conditions of rural life. The fear of washing babies was consistent with longstanding notions that dirt was protective, that urine was good for the skin, and that the scab on a baby's scalp protected the fontanelle. Infrequent washing of babies was hardly surprising when adults rarely washed beyond their hands and faces (a pattern prevalent in both rural and urban areas for much of the nineteenth century). Besides, in draughty and unheated homes peasant mothers may have been wise to resist the baths advocated by doctors. The lack of running water made all washing a chore, and the lack of means for drying infants' clothes in winter was a further disincentive to practising the standards of hygiene advocated by the late nineteenth century.[65] Poor living conditions were hardly conducive to the ideal of spotlessness promoted by urban elites.

Peasant childrearing practices could be harmful to their children, even if well intentioned. Infrequently washed but immobile infants were prey to vermin and skin diseases. The belief that crying was good for babies and a sign of vigour contributed to the prevalence of hernias, while in the Vaucluse the belief that green diarrhoea was a sign of health rather than of dehydration could be fatal. But in case of illness, peasant women had few options. They turned to traditional remedies, and consulted village 'wise women'. The high levels of infant mortality in rural France in the nineteenth century suggest that these methods were ineffective.[66] Rural communities experienced a lower death rate than their urban counterparts, thanks to their less-crowded conditions and the wider prevalence of maternal nursing. But gastro-enteritis, diarrhoea, respiratory infections and contagious diseases decimated the ranks of both rural and urban infants. In the early nineteenth century 180 infants per thousand died in the first year of life, and this had declined only to 170 per thousand in the 1890s.[67] In the rural Vaucluse, one in every two children died before reaching the age of five, a pattern that was not unique.[68]

Breastfeeding was the focus of medical campaigns throughout the nineteenth century and became one of the hallmarks of the maternal ideal. The fact that peasant mothers breastfed their infants, unlike their urban counterparts, was their chief virtue in the eyes of many critics, although maternal nursing was not given the same emotional weight as some doctors would have liked. Breastmilk had many advantages, being cheap, sterile, nutritious and readily available to most mothers. The link between breastfeeding and the reduced likelihood of conception was also understood in peasant communities by the late nineteenth century.[69] Mothers' milk was often supplemented with other foods, however, according to local custom. *Bouillie*, cow's milk thickened with wheaten flour, was believed to help infants grow more quickly. They might also be fed bread boiled in water, either as a substitute for milk in very poor families, or as a supplement. Herbal teas and soups were offered to infants in an effort to prepare them for adult diets, while substances like coffee, spirits, and cider were sometimes believed to have fortifying properties.[70] Most of these supplements had little nutritional value, but their main danger lay in exposing infants to infection from unsterile bottles and cups.

Peasant women's work roles often prevented the close attention that the maternal ideal demanded. Peasant babies were left alone during the day, except for intermittent visits by neighbours or siblings, until they were old enough to be taken into the fields. Pierre-Jakez Hélias relates the story of his own infancy in early twentieth-century Brittany, as told to him by his mother:

[A]ll day long, for hours at a time, I was there by myself, despite hasty visits from two neighbourhood children who had been asked to look in and see how I was doing. My mother was out in the fields, my grandfather on the road crushing stones, and my father felling trees or working as a pit sawyer [...] In the morning my mother would leave for the Méot field with her cow, after having gorged me with her milk. When the Angelus rang at noon, she'd return for a quick meal, change my diaper, nurse me again, and go off to plough up the ground until four or five o'clock.[71]

Maternal 'neglect' was condemned by doctors, but was the result of necessity. Mothers assumed the overwhelming responsibility for childcare, particularly for the first two years. Strict taboos excluded men from washing and changing infants, and from feeding and caring for unweaned babies.[72] But a mother had other essential tasks to perform. The infant was part of a family unit whose overall survival was a constant struggle. The mother's work on the farm could not be neglected lest the whole family, including the infant, suffer.

Mothering was less intensive in the nineteenth century, too, because the childbearing years of peasant women were more extended. They bore larger numbers of infants than urban women, yet could devote only a portion of their time to childcare. Their limited maternal investment in each infant was compensated for to some extent by the role of siblings in caring for infants, and birth order could produce very different childhood experiences for children within the same family.[73]

Peasants and the affectionate family

The maternal-centred family idealised by urban elites was also an affectionate family. Parents were encouraged to base their relationships with children on kindness and encouragement rather than harsh discipline. Many peasant memoirs written in the late nineteenth century discuss attitudes to parenting because peasant practices seemed at odds with this model. The harsh peasant mother, in particular, confounded bourgeois images of maternal affection and true womanhood.

Peasant authors attempted to explain peasant norms and practices to an uncomprehending urban public. Etienne Bertin, in Guillaumin's fictional autobiography of a sharecropping family, described harsh discipline and physical punishment, particularly when a child failed to fulfil the duties on which the good of the family depended. But he also noted moments of intimacy and affection from his parents. Commenting on his own role as a father, he attributed the absence of cuddling and petting to 'the laborious life' his family led as share-croppers,[74] and noted how things had improved since the years of his own childhood: 'When I compare my childhood with that of the little ones today, who are petted and cared for tenderly, and are not obliged to do any manual labour before they are twelve or thirteen years old, I feel they are really lucky.'[75] This suggests that the author, now an urban-dweller himself, had come to share the sentiments of his urban counterparts.

It is particularly difficult to disentangle autobiography from fiction in this case because Guillaumin, who was born in 1873, wrote his memoir in 1901 but set it in the early nineteenth century. His fictional self, Bertin, supposedly born in 1823, shows considerable affection for his sickly daughter, but whether this reflects peasant attitudes in the 1850s, or Guillaumin's views in 1901 as a critic of the earlier less-expressive world, is impossible to say.[76]

The memoir of Emilie Carles is more straightforward because she claimed to provide an autobiographical account of peasant life rather than a fictionalised one. Nevertheless, like Guillaumin, she set out to explain and account for peasant behaviour that was often misunderstood by its critics. She reported that, when she fell two stories onto the threshing floor at the age of six, her father refused to call a doctor. He headed off to collect a bull, as arranged, instructing his older children to contact the carpenter for a coffin if she should die. This might seem the height of parental indifference. However, as Carles explains, 'in those days [1906] our mountain peasants led such harsh, wretched lives that death could hardly move them [. . .] It was not indifference it was something else. Harsh language may have been a defense against pain.'[77] Her lasting memory was her father's gentle kindness as he tried to compensate his six children for the premature death of their mother.

Overt displays of affection were also unusual in Hélias' Breton community, where kissing did not become customary until after the First World War. However, Hélias also describes a childhood shaped by close family ties. His mother was unable to devote her time exclusively to him, as the idealised model of motherhood dictated. But the care with which she prepared his sugar soup each morning before she left to work in the fields indicated her affection, and the constant companionship of his grandfather revealed strong emotional bonds within the family.

In the more prosperous Mistral family, who owned a successful farm in southern France in the early nineteenth century, young Frédéric was indulged as an only child. His worst infant escapade, in repeatedly going down to the stream, aged four or five, attracted by the irises growing there, initially brought punishment and confinement to bed. But his fearful parents soon devised an alternative strategy: 'The patriarch, the Master, my honored father himself had gone to pick the flowers that made me happy. And the Mistress, my beautiful mother, had put them on my bed.'[78]

Then as now, parental indulgence owed something to financial security, since children from comfortable rural families were not required to labour, and their mothers were more likely to have time to devote to their children. However, poverty does not automatically produce indifference: a point on which Marie-Catherine Santerre, born in 1891, insists in her memoir of childhood in northern France. Her family were amongst the poorest of the rural poor: the landless labourers who combined winter weaving with summer agricultural work on commercial farms. She paints a picture of a happy but poverty-stricken family life. Her father never beat his children, although she notes that some did. Santerre describes devoted parents who found simple and inexpensive ways to 'spoil' their children, even if kisses were an annual birthday present and formal modes of address, rather than affectionate ones, were the norm. As she notes: '[My parents] didn't know how to read or write, they had no contact with the outside world. The radio was unknown, of course; newspapers were expensive, and you had to be able to read to understand them. Nevertheless, they were both intelligent, sensible, and kind. Their kindness towards us children was endless.'[79] Peasant memoirs of parental affection and love cannot necessarily be seen as representative of broader patterns, particularly since they often set out to dispel myths of peasant peculiarities and savagery. But neither can it be assumed that they were falsified or atypical.

Gender roles in peasant families

Gender demarcation was the norm in peasant families, although it did not replicate the divide in elite families. Its motivations were primarily economic. The demands of a viable family farm required the productive labour of all rather than a model of 'separate spheres'. Notions of masculinity and femininity revealed a pattern of gender complementarity in peasant households, therefore, but not a model of female domesticity. Both work roles and patterns of authority were delineated by the sex-segregated structures of peasant society, rather than by the gender opposition of the bourgeois family model.

Daughters had lower status in peasant families than sons. When a woman gave birth to a daughter in Alsace, the commemorative tree was planted in the communal fields rather than near the house: the site reserved for the son who would inherit the family property. In Lamarche, in the north-east, the mother was fed bread dipped in salted milk rather than in sweetened wine, because a daughter was less welcome than a son.[80] A preference for male children was reflected in attempts to ensure that the expected child would be a boy. Long before Dr Debay published his 'scientific' instructions on how to produce a son,[81] peasant families applied to human reproduction the principles they used in sowing their crops and breeding their animals. An early nineteenth-century observer wrote: 'It is commonly believed that the woman who conceives under the new moon bears a boy, and that she has only a girl if she receives her husband's attentions in the moon's last quarter.'[82]

This preference for boys reflected the emphasis on the family line-age. Even if there was no land to pass on, the preservation of the family name was critical. It could only be passed on through the male line, despite the fact that in regions such as Brittany women retained their own family names at marriage.[83] Peasant men also preferred sons. They would become part of their fathers' world in this sexually demarcated society and share the heavy agricultural tasks allocated to men. In a world that relied on physical strength rather than mechanical power, masculinity was primarily defined by physical capacity and it carried superior value.

Women's status and self-esteem derived from producing sons. Nevertheless, a peasant woman might welcome a daughter to share the household tasks and act as her assistant.[84] A peasant farm could not operate without the contribution of women and girls, whose tasks were generally distinct from those of men. Besides, if a dowry was a financial burden and a disincentive to welcoming female children, a marriageable daughter could also be a means to enter an alliance through which landholdings could be extended and family status enhanced.

Gender demarcation began at about the age of five, when boys were dressed in trousers as the first sign of their entry to the male world. But in some respects girls' lives still differed little from those of boys at that age. As children began to contribute to the household economy, which could afford few unproductive members, their tasks were designated by age rather than by sex. Minding the sheep, collecting eggs, gathering berries or fruits were tasks that required little strength or skill, and were done by the youngest children. However, the apprenticeship in adult tasks was also underway.

Millet's mid-century paintings show girls learning to knit and sew from a very young age, while shepherdesses wielded their spindles from childhood. These romanticised images of peasant life tended to replicate a bourgeois model of femininity too closely. Nevertheless, the production of textiles and clothing would be peasant women's constant occupations throughout their lives.

At age 12, children in Catholic France made their First Communion. This marked the transition to adolescence, when the lives of girls and boys began to differ more markedly. In Emile Guillaumin's account, Catherine assumed the domestic chores on their farm when she turned 12, replacing the hired servant girl. Tiennon, aged seven, was then charged with the care of the sheep, which were formerly Catherine's responsibility.[85] Catherine's new role did not indicate that she was destined henceforth for a life in the home: her mother was working in the fields, which was why domestic help was needed.

Urban (and essentially bourgeois) models of the sexual division of labour are particularly inadequate for describing peasant households that required the productive labour of all their able-bodied members. Catherine's mother was responsible for overseeing the smooth functioning of the household, while her husband was responsible for decisions affecting the crops and the livestock. This division was a conventional one in peasant households, but it did not amount to a division between domestic chores and farm labour. Instead, responsibility for running the household involved many tasks that were performed outdoors rather than indoors, such as fetching water, feeding the domestic animals (pigs, chickens, rabbits), milking the cow and tending the kitchen garden. In poorer regions, where a farming family also did paid labour for others, the wife might essentially do all the farm labour while her husband worked elsewhere. The father of Pierre-Jakez Hélias worked as a pit-sawyer, leaving his mother to plough the field.[86]

Women's labour, like men's, was essential to the productivity and success of the family farm. Women had their tasks in the fields as did men, but a sexual division of labour normally prevailed. This was true even for tasks that were carried out communally, such as sowing, harvesting and threshing. Frédéric Mistral's account of the harvest on his family's farm near Arles in 1848 describes separate male and female tasks: men, working in teams, wielded their sickles rhythmically to the instructions of the foreman, while women followed binding the sheaves.[87] Similarly, Hélias' early twentieth-century account of threshing in his native Brittany describes men wielding their flails while women turned the husks and swept up the grain.[88]

Space was gendered in the peasant world. Women's space was domestic and localised, generally encompassing areas close to and inside the farmhouse. Men occupied broader expanses both physically and culturally.[89] The division of roles was also based on physical capacity and strength. But rather than confining peasant women to the home, this division utilised the strength of young women in farming work, leaving domestic chores and childcare to young girls and older women. The roles of peasant men and women were complementary, since their co-operation in carrying out the tasks of the farm was the fundamental requirement for family survival and for the success of the enterprise.[90]

The division between 'productive' and 'domestic' tasks on peasant farms was often difficult to determine. Women sold surplus produce from the farmyard at the market, just as men sold grain and livestock. All these commodities were produced by the shared labour of the peasant family economy. An even clearer example of the overlapping of domestic and market activities concerns wetnursing. Until the First World War peasant women in the poorest regions contributed to the family economy by taking in urban nurslings. Their breastmilk became an economic commodity, supplied at very cheap rates to urban working women. Only the increasing range of employment opportunities for rural women in the late nineteenth century, and the decline in demand as safe forms of bottle-feeding became available, saw the decline of this rural industry.[91] Wetnursing reveals, moreover, that both rural and urban women were slow to embrace the Rousseauian model of maternal nursing. Here, too, economic considerations conflicted with sentiment.

The contribution of peasant women to agricultural production was also evident amongst landless rural families, where women's lives were governed by wage-earning rather than domestic duties. Women and girls provided a substantial portion of the hired agricultural labour force. In the Carpentras region (near Avignon) young rural women worked as strawberry pickers in the early twentieth century. They laboured in silence from dawn to dusk breaking only for midday soup.[92] The family labour unit prevailed on the large commercial farms of northern France in the nineteenth and early twentieth centuries. Ten-year-old Marie-Catherine Santerre joined the village migration from Avesnes-les-Aubert, near the Belgian border, to Normandy as a seasonal worker in 1910. She did so as part of a family labouring team of five, including three daughters. From May to November they worked at thinning, weeding and harvesting the sugar beets, clearing stones from the wheat-fields, spreading nightsoil as fertiliser, and gathering the harvested wheat into sheaves. No distinction was made between male and female workers, or between adults and children, in the performance of these tasks. These landless rural workers provided the cheap labour that contributed to the late adoption of mechanisation even on large commercial estates. While their wages improved gradually across the nineteenth century, they remained amongst the poorest workers, had few possessions, rarely ate meat, and led very hard lives.[93]

Despite the interdependence of husband and wife, the subordination of peasant women to men has frequently been seen as the norm. Nineteenth-century observers often described male contempt for women, the use of physical violence against women, and women's deference or even submission to men. They noted, too, the preferential treatment accorded to farm animals over women, so that the veterinarian would be summoned more readily than the doctor. Relationships between men and women were, however, sometimes misinterpreted by outsiders. For instance, the practice of women serving men at table before having their own meal was regarded as a mark of women's inferiority. But, as Hélias explains, in his Breton community it indicated women's domestic authority as they presided over the meal. His mother took pride in serving the food she had prepared, accepting the acknowledgements of her competence, and fulfilling one of the responsibilities that marked her out as mistress of the household.[94]

Peasant proverbs have often been cited to illustrate negative attitudes towards women in peasant society: 'Women are not people' (Provence); 'Women are like chops, the more you beat them the tenderer they are' (Languedoc); 'Good God on high, take my wife but leave my horses' (Upper Brittany); 'The death of a wife is not a disaster, but the death of a cow is' (Alsace).[95] But as Martine Segalen points out, the interpretation of such expressions is not straightforward. In some instances, they reflect the harsh reality of peasant life. Given the desirability of marriage for women, for instance, a widower would generally be able to find a new wife to help manage the farm, whereas the cost of replacing farm animals made their loss an economic disaster. In other cases, proverbs served to express the norms of communal life; the desirable patterns to which all were encouraged to conform. Statements describing the boundaries between the male and female realms of activity, or assigning men authority over women, would fit into this category. Segalen notes that such statements outlined the norm rather than defining the practice,[96] which varied between communities and between families. The need to reiterate such boundaries suggests the difficulty of maintaining them in practice. Proverbs authorising the use of physical force against women also indicate that it needed justification rather than being taken for granted. Customs like *charivari* – the ritualised mockery of those transgressing community norms – restrained and ridiculed men who beat their wives as well as men who were under their wives' thumbs.[97]

Power relations between men and women in rural society reflected a public/private divide, as they did in urban culture. The separation of male and female roles meant that male domination was limited, and forms of female authority acknowledged. Ultimately, however, the formal authority of men over women prevailed in the village as elsewhere, since French law enshrined patriarchal power. In the late nineteenth century that authority was reinforced by official efforts to integrate rural men into the national community through military service and citizenship rights. Peasant society began to resemble urban society more closely, but the forms in which male power was expressed there remained different from those prevailing in the bourgeois world.

Part II
Sex and Citizenship, 1814–1914

4 Women, Politics and Citizenship, 1814–1852

The early years of the nineteenth century were marked by a search for political stability after a decade of Revolutionary upheaval. The restoration of the monarchy had little public support, and a variety of political groupings – monarchists, Bonapartists and republicans – struggled for power. The period saw two further revolutions (in 1830 and 1848) and a coup d'état in 1851 that brought the nephew of Napoleon I to power. France became an Empire again in 1852.

Women supported a variety of political causes in this period. Political divisions in the community ran deep, and women's political views were shaped by their social origins, just as those of men were. Their self-identification as monarchists, republicans or supporters of the Empire usually echoed family traditions, amongst both the elite and the population at large.

The property-based suffrage system of the early nineteenth century gave the vote only to selected men. But their eligibility for the suffrage was based on the taxes paid by all family members, and they received the vote in their capacity as family head. The division between enfranchised and unenfranchised was between families and not between the sexes.[1] Within this model it was possible to think of women as political participants, although participants whose activities were indirect. The roles of elite women were consistent with this understanding of politics, although some women from the propertied classes were vocal in support of greater equality for women. Among the unenfranchised masses, the shared interest of women and men in extending the franchise was often subordinate to their shared interest in redressing their economic difficulties.

The extension of the suffrage to all men in 1848 was a definitive political moment for women. It created a distinction in political rights based solely on sex and thus made the question of women's rights in French society more prominent. The Revolution of 1848 was thus to see a revival of the debates about citizenship that had first surfaced during the French Revolution. It was also to see the renewed exclusion of women from the political community.

Women and 'Ultraroyalism': the Restoration period (1814–1830)

When the European powers defeated Napoleon in 1814, they placed Louis XVIII (brother of the executed Louis XVI) on the throne. The Bourbon restoration was highly unpopular. Louis XVIII was forced to accept a Charter limiting Royal power, and a two-chamber assembly. The Chamber of Deputies was to be elected on a narrow property franchise, while members of the Chamber of Peers were appointed by the king. Political representation was confined to the wealthiest section of society. Louis was prepared to accept some limits on his powers but his brother, who succeeded him as King Charles X in 1824, espoused a strict definition of monarchical power. He remained personally committed to undoing many of the Revolution's reforms. A powerful clique of intransigeant nobles supported this 'Ultraroyalism', which dominated the politics of the Restoration period and particularly the years after 1824.[2]

The 'Ultraroyalist' vision of society was highly conservative. Its adherents aspired to create an idealised imaginary France: peasants would labour for loved and respected noble landlords, who in turn would aid and protect 'their' peasants. Democracy was alien to their philosophy, as were notions of equality. Instead of equality, the Ultras emphasised paternalism and the legitimate rule of traditional elites. They also emphasised the 'natural' hierarchy between male and female.[3] Ironically, these nineteenth-century monarchists accepted Rousseau's bourgeois model of relations between men and women rather than the aristocratic patterns of the Old Regime.

The two key theorists of Ultraroyalism, Louis de Bonald and Joseph de Maistre, linked the establishment of a stable society in post-Revolutionary France to male control of women. This reflected arguments that women's escape from such control was responsible for the Revolutionary upheaval in the first place.[4] In 1816 Bonald proclaimed that the political task of the Restoration was 'the destruction of Revolutionary doctrines, the re-establishment of religion, the security of the throne, the happiness of the nation, good order within families'.[5] His renowned formulation of the 'familial' theory of political life made 'good order within families' the basis for political order, and the patriarchal family the foundation of good government.

Bonald was the driving force behind the repeal of the divorce laws in 1816. Divorce was a political issue, because it threatened good government and social stability by disrupting the 'natural' hierarchy of the family. 'Divorce was in harmony with democracy', he wrote. 'It meant disorder in the family and disorder in the State.'[6] Hence, '[i]n order to wrest the state from the hands of the people, the family must be wrested from the hands of women and children'.[7]

Bonald's well-ordered society was one in which the gender divide was clear-cut. Women were destined for motherhood. Education must prepare girls for 'domestic usefulness' and boys for 'public usefulness'. The possibility that women might aspire to 'involve themselves willingly in the government of the State' was as preposterous to Bonald as that men might aspire to a domestic life. De Maistre agreed, although stressing the importance of women's role as the shapers of citizens.[8]

Both theorists called on 'nature' to demonstrate the subordinate status and domestic destiny of women. By citing 'nature', for instance, Bonald avoided the need to justify female 'destiny' on rational grounds. He asserted: 'Women understand better than men how to run domestic affairs, which proves better than lengthy arguments that nature does not summon them to control public affairs.'[9] De Maistre argued that women had never excelled in intellectual or creative endeavours, attributing this to nature's design rather than to their historical exclusion from such undertakings. He presented reproduction as a form of creativity comparable to men's intellectual creativity. While he argued that women's role in shaping the next generation was greater than that of invention or artistic creation, he also believed that motherhood destined women to remain under the guardianship of men.[10] The ideas of these two theorists were to be widely publicised in the early nineteenth century.

With the Restoration of the monarchy the old aristocracy attempted to reassert its dominance of society as well as its control of politics. Women featured prominently in the symbolism that under-pinned the reassertion of royal authority and aristocratic social supremacy. This can be seen in the court rituals reinstated with the returning Bourbons in 1814. Evenings at Court were a formal re-enactment of the rules of social hierarchy, as Marie d'Agoult recalled:

> Seated at the top of a circle which stretched out in the shape of an almond from each side of her armchair, Mme la Dauphine[11] worked on a piece of tapestry. In this circle, where each one was seated according to rank, it was not appropriate to converse with one's neighbour [...] From time to time, with apparent spontaneity but really according to etiquette, [the Dauphine] addressed a brusque question to one or other of those ladies seated around her. The reply, in the midst of general silence, was [...] as brief and banal as possible.[12]

In resuming their places at court in 1814, noble women demonstrated their acceptance of the dominant values of the Restoration: hierarchy, rank and deference. By busying themselves with needlework, however, they revealed the impact of Revolutionary critiques of aristocratic behaviour. They illustrated the impossibility of a return to Old Regime norms even as they asserted a continuity between present and past that symbolically elided the Revolutionary interval.[13] The official role of the Duchess of Berry, wife of Charles X's younger son, was also designed to emphasise the durability of royal bloodlines and the longevity of the regime. As the mother of the infant prince, the only hope of succession for the inbred Bourbon dynasty, she played an important symbolic role in the Bourbons' effort to reclaim their right to rule and the loyalty of their subjects.[14]

Many noble women embraced Ultraroyalism passionately. They promoted its tenets and insisted on marrying only *émigrés* who had proved their Royalist credentials by leaving France during the Revolution. Defence of the Ultra vision depended on the aristocracy's fulfilling its traditional roles, and hence on aristocratic women's exercising the social and cultural patronage assigned to them. Their salons were critical, not only for asserting the nobility's cultural leadership, but also for defending the Ultra world view, since politics was a common subject of discussion there. Similarly, women's commitment to philanthropy was essential to the Ultras' defence of a social model based on paternalism.[15]

Noble women's political activities reflected a 'sexual division of labour' consistent with the notion of a 'familial' model of political life. As mothers, they played significant roles in passing on the sense of exclusivity and the grievances about the Revolution which formed the basis for noble politics in the post-Revolutionary era. Mothers instilled in their children the genealogical data establishing the impeccability and longevity of their bloodlines: Louis de Carné's mother gave him a treat each time he recognised the name of an ancestor in his history of Brittany. Oral histories (real or fabricated) of struggle, persecution and martyrdom reinforced in the young a sense of heroism and virtue, and a sense of their elite status.[16]

The wives of 'Ultra' politicians also played crucial supportive roles, illustrating that the model of female domesticity was interpreted flexibly even in these conservative circles. Céleste de Montjustin provides one outstanding example. She was married to Louis de Vaulchier, Marquis du Deschaux, a Minister in the Ultraconservative Villèle government in the 1820s. As a leading salon hostess, she performed the social duties that underpinned patron–client relations and ensured her husband's electoral success in Besançon. In addition, she filled a range of important political functions. She provided a sounding board for Vaulchier's political decisions as he negotiated the factionalised Ultra world. She also passed on confidential information to selected contacts in his electorate, sometimes selecting those contacts herself. She explained her husband's voting decisions to his electors, and kept him abreast of sentiments in the electorate while he was in Paris. She alerted him (for instance) when his votes in the Chamber seemed insufficiently 'Ultra' for his reactionary electorate. Céleste de Montjustin also channelled requests for patronage to her husband, making recommendations as she passed them on.[17] She acted as his campaign manager or electorate secretary as well as his wife.

Ultraroyalist politics eventually proved unsustainable. Few people in France saw benefits in a return to the old hierarchical regime, and many were afraid of losing the gains they had made since 1789. The return of the Catholic Church as partner of the monarchy aroused considerable hostility. The Church's 'rechristianisation' campaign, preaching repentance for the sins of the Revolutionary interlude and condemning all who had supported it, sparked widespread agitation. Despite his Ultra convictions, Charles X had to restrain the Church's missionary zeal in face of popular protest.[18] Otherwise, however, Charles' overt support for monarchical supremacy and his heavy-handed tactics won him few friends. His repeated restriction of the franchise in an attempt to secure co-operative Chambers created hostility amongst the educated and propertied classes, who were determined to resist a return to 'despotism'. Many peasants feared the restoration of feudal dues, and the reclaiming of their land. In the towns, the excesses of Ultraroyalism were held responsible for the economic depression and unemployment of the 1820s. By 1830 Charles X had alienated most of his subjects.[19] The Revolution of 1830 ended his reign, and with it the rule of the Bourbon dynasty over its historic kingdom.

Elite women and the 'Bourgeois Monarchy', 1830–1848

The Revolution of 1830, in Paris and the provinces, was carried out mainly by aggrieved workers. The first victim of government fire was reputedly a woman. Her corpse became a symbol of the contest between oppressive government and 'liberty': a king who allowed innocent women to be shot could hardly claim to be a loving father to his people. Although some women took part in the fighting, the majority participated in ways regarded as more appropriate for their sex. They built barricades, threw stones and strewed broken glass on the streets to impede the horses of government troops. They carried their husbands' provisions, reloaded their muskets and nursed the wounded.[20]

The political opposition amongst the well-to-do was led by lawyers and journalists. A loose coalition of like-minded men rather than a formal political party, they shared a commitment to a constitutional monarchy that would ensure the 'rights of man', protect against royal 'tyranny', and guarantee representative and accountable government. They would have preferred a peaceful transition in regimes, like the Glorious Revolution of 1688 in England that featured prominently in the opposition press prior to the Revolution. But when the popular insurrection forced Charles X to abdicate, these oppositional groups quickly seized control. They invited Louis-Philippe to assume the throne as a constitutional monarch, heading off popular support for a Napoleonic or Republican leader.[21]

The new regime was known as the Orleanist regime, because Louis-Philippe represented the House of Orléans (they were cousins of the Bourbons). It also became known as the 'Bourgeois Monarchy', because it saw the rise to political dominance of an elite characterised by wealth and education rather than by birth. Under this regime, those landed nobles who rejected its principles withdrew from political life and busied themselves with their country estates. The catch-cry of the Revolution of 1830 was 'Liberty', in contrast to the 'tyranny' of Charles X. 'Liberty' had been represented since the 1790s as a female figure, carrying a sceptre to indicate personal autonomy and wearing the Phrygian cap of the freed slave. That same female image featured prominently in the 1830 Revolution, immortalised in Delacroix's renowned painting of 'Liberty leading the people'.[22] It supposedly represented a real woman, although this cannot be clearly established.[23] But the Orleanists who assumed power in 1830 did not regard 'liberty' as applicable to women. Their regime marked a high point of women's exclusion.

The Orleanist case for the political exclusion of women had a foundation different from that of their predecessors. Despite being divided on a number of issues, the Orleanists shared a commitment to a limited form of representative government based on individual 'capacity': the entitlement to political rights required proof of the capacity to exercise them rationally. François Guizot, leading theorist of a faction known as the 'doctrinaires' and Prime Minister in the 1840s, noted that 'numerous classes of individuals, women, minors, domestic servants, the great majority of men are denied political rights everywhere' because they could not demonstrate 'the capacity necessary to exercise them in the interests of society'.[24] 'Capacity' was demonstrated by successful management of one's own affairs, which in practice meant the acquisition of wealth. On this basis, then, the property suffrage was extended only as far as the '200-franc taxpayers'. It did not include 'the people', whose lack of property meant they did not pay the property tax and had not proven their own 'capacity'. Nor did it include any women, whether they were taxpayers or not: even very wealthy women were not legally responsible for their financial affairs and remained under male control in the family. Besides, the ideas and actions of 'the people' (like those of women) were supposedly motivated by passion and not by reason.[25] This further demonstrated their unsuitability for political rights.

The political factions that dominated the Bourgeois Monarchy therefore shared with the Ultras a belief in the natural superiority of some over others, although they attributed that superiority to 'capacity' or merit rather than to birth. Women and 'the people' were destined for a subordinate position in both cases. Arguments for excluding all but the wealthiest men from the franchise were couched in terms of their unpreparedness for that role: they needed to be educated for it; trained in the self-control and rational judgement which would enable them to fulfil its duties. More urgently, as social unrest continued in the early 1830s, they needed to be educated to accept the hierarchy of merit, and to submit to the authority of those qualified to rule. This explains the regime's emphasis on boys' education. When the Guizot law of 1833 required communities to provide elementary schooling, the law was mandatory only for boys: schooling was envisaged specifically as preparation for citizenship.[26]

Women's lives and roles were seen as different from those of men within this hierarchical worldview. Women were not envisaged as citizens, even in the future. Guizot (like the Ultra theorists, Bonald and de Maistre) regarded paternal authority within the family as an example of the 'natural authority' of some over others and, revealingly, as an example of true 'democracy' at work. 'Power stems from superiority', he declared.[27] The logic by which all women were placed in an inferior position to all men appears suspiciously like a remnant of birth privilege, but it was attributed instead to men's superior reason and powers of judgement. The family was seen as a 'natural' unit, marked by sexual difference and bound together by affection. It was not a homogeneous unit of similar individuals bound together by contractual relations, which defined the State.[28] The father's role of authority and guidance in the family became a model for the rule of a social elite, capable of rising above the passions of the rest and of making decisions in the public interest.[29] The political agenda of the ruling coalitions during the Bourgeois Monarchy was to maintain the dominance of 'reason', that is, of the 'reasonable class'. If the masses – uneducated and prone to strong emotion – were excluded by their criteria, so too were women.

Under the Bourgeois Monarchy, women of the liberal aristocracy and upper bourgeoisie continued to dominate social life, but the elite was more open and welcomed new members on the basis of their 'merit'. The court of King Louis-Philippe practised a less formal etiquette than the Bourbons and was open to newcomers, including politicians and men of finance. Its atmosphere was more 'bourgeois', which gave it credence in bourgeois circles and amongst the liberal aristocracy, although it was scorned by the 'Ultra' royalists.[30]

The support base for the Orléans family lay in a part of Paris known as the Palais-Royal, while that of the Bourbons centred on the Faubourg Saint-Germain, heartland of the pre-Revolutionary aristocracy. The Faubourg Saint-Germain was exclusive and snobbish. The society of the Palais-Royal, by contrast, included distinguished bourgeois figures. Marie d'Agoult recalled, 'I met there that upper bourgeoisie which journalism, the bar, the tribune and the arts singled out and accepted already as the elite of the nation.'[31] These people began to distinguish themselves under the Orleanist regime, which undermined the social pretensions of the Faubourg Saint-Germain:

> [With the Bourbons gone] we felt liberated from a surveillance which had not allowed us until then to open our salons to new people, to men of modest station, bourgeois, ennobled men, writers, artists, whose renown had begun to awaken our curiosity. The Duchess de Ranzau was the first, I believe, to shake off prejudice [...] She attracted to her soirées Messieurs Sainte-Beuve, Eugène Sue, Liszt etc.[32]

As d'Agoult's reminiscence indicates, the salons of elite women were vital to the cultural life of the early nineteenth century, but cultural events were also occasions for political networking. Women's patronage was vital to young men seeking to establish themselves in administrative and political careers. While 'merit' was gaining influence as a criterion for advancement, an overcrowded job market ensured that personal contacts still counted heavily in the quest for public office.[33] Elite women groomed promising candidates by educating them in the rituals and manners of polite society, introducing them to the right people, and even organising suitable marriages. The debates chaired by women in the leading salons educated aspiring politicians in the conventions of political discourse.[34] Women also intervened to secure ambassadorships and prefectures for their favourites. Women's support could still be vital, then, to the prospects of a young man of modest origins or modest means. Equally, women could hinder the prospects of a man who did not win their support.[35]

Women in Orleanist circles also demonstrated the interest in and flair for politics that enabled Céleste de Montjustin to be such an asset to her husband, but they did so in support of a different political cause. Women's enthusiastic attendance at sessions of the Chamber of Deputies was widely remarked upon in the 1830s.[36] For some, like the Duchesse de Broglie or Madame Guizot, it was part of their role as wives of leading politicians, but they often contributed to such politics in their own right. The correspondence of the Duchesse de Broglie was intended as a vehicle for political discussion. It explored a range of political ideas and offered advice to Guizot and other leaders of the 'Doctrinaire' faction.[37] Her salon (and that of Pauline Guizot) provided a forum for the Doctrinaires to discuss ideas and strategy, just as Céleste de Vaulchier's salon had done for the Ultras.

François Guizot's two wives played major roles in his political career. Pauline de Meulan was 34 and Guizot 20 when they met, and she already had an established reputation as a writer. They married in 1812. Their collaboration began with Guizot writing articles under his wife's name. She later contributed articles to his newspapers and carried out research for him, while they jointly founded and directed an educational review.[38] Pauline Guizot also wrote most of the editorials for the newspaper, Le Courier, which the Doctrinaires established in 1819. Her premature death in 1827 was a profound loss to her husband, professionally as well as personally. However his second wife, Elisa Dillon, filled a similar role in his life.[39] A telling example is provided by Guizot's maiden speech in the Chamber of Deputies, shortly before the Revolution of 1830, when she advised him to take a more clear-cut stand in response to the political crisis:

> I found, and told him when he talked with me about the plan of his speech, that since he was already sufficiently known as a man of government, it was as an opponent that he ought to show himself, and that a little more ado about liberty would suit his situation better [...] The speech was striking for its eloquence, for its views, and for its spirit, but did not have the success as an act of opposition that we ought, I believe, to have sought.[40]

Elisa Guizot's identification with her husband's political objectives was explicit here, as was Pauline Guizot's before her.

Although Guizot relied on his wives' intellectual competence and political judgement, he nevertheless insisted on women's exclusion from politics. This was consistent with his idea of marriage. The marital partnership was a 'fusion of two beings',[41] but they were opposite beings whose roles were complementary. Guizot's colleague, Alexis de Tocqueville, shared that view.[42] Guizot was unable to imagine that women's capacities were equivalent to men's, but he saw no contradiction in relying on the competence of wives whose political 'incapacity' was preordained. Insofar as their views on women and politics were concerned, Guizot and his peers, and indeed their wives, revealed themselves as products of their times.[43]

Such women as Pauline and Elisa Guizot, like Céleste de Montjustin before them, might be described as 'helpmeets' of their politician-husbands. While their roles were 'hidden' behind those of their husbands, however, and while their husbands benefited from the career-support provided by female scribes and assistants,[44] women's activities reveal the extent to which such marriages were political partnerships. Within their own circles, women were respected as political, not merely personal, allies. However there was a sexual division of political labour, enshrined in law, by which only the male could play a formal political role, and both women and men in these elite circles accepted that division.

Women and radical movements in the 1830s and 1840s

Republicanism was a radical political ideology in the nineteenth century. During the French Revolution it had become associated with the 'tyranny of the majority' and with popular violence, and it remained a feared and often proscribed movement. Suspicion of popular extremism meant that democracy and its proponents were regarded as a threat by monarchs and the propertied classes for much of the century. To avoid the threat of prosecution, Republicans adopted the label 'radical' from England.[45]

Republicans in the early nineteenth century sought to foster 'equality' in public life, in the tradition of the French Revolution they deeply admired. Their leaders were lawyers and journalists drawn from the wealthy educated bourgeoisie, but they rejected hierarchies of birth or capacity and rejected monarchical rule.[46] Even though they saw themselves as 'democrats', however, they were unable to conceptualise the inclusion of women as political participants. Like their forebears in the French Revolution, they subscribed to a gendered social model in which women's world was separate from the world of politics. Political society was an 'imaginary society of brothers'.[47] In recruiting working men to the cause in the 1830s, therefore, Republicans reiterated a view of 'the sovereign people' that was entirely masculine, and saw citizenship as a male prerogative.

They were 'radical' in regarding working men as fit to be citizens, but not in their views on women.[48]

Women acted as messengers and publicists for republican groups, made cartridges, hid arms and propaganda in their homes, sheltered political fugitives, hosted prohibited meetings, and on occasion took part in armed insurrection.[49] The wives of leading Republican politicians assisted their husbands' political careers just as more conservative women did. Marianne de Lamartine conducted research for her husband's publications, copied and corrected his drafts, handled his correspondence, and kept press clippings of importance. When Lamartine became head of the Provisional Government after the February Revolution of 1848 she organised a range of charitable measures, in conjunction with other politicians' wives, in an effort to calm the popular discontent that threatened her husband's government.[50]

The separation between the private world of women and the world of public action nevertheless remained a feature of Republican thinking in this period. Republicans shared Guizot's commitment to public education, but like him saw it as valuable only to boys. Alphonse de Lamartine, an Orleanist in the 1830s but a Republican leader by 1848, stated: 'Public education is only appropriate for those who are destined like us for an active public life.'[51] Women were not 'like' men and therefore were not destined for such a life.[52] Republican women writers explored ideas for more democratic family models that were compatible with greater autonomy for women.[53] But, for men, women's dependent status within a hierarchical family unit was taken for granted.

Only among the ranks of socialist men, on the margins of political respectability, did a vision of politics emerge that had the potential to undermine women's political exclusion. 'Socialism' was born in the early nineteenth century to contest the 'individualism' espoused by liberals.[54] Socialists advocated a radical restructuring of society to end the inequalities and inefficiencies they saw around them, and which they linked to the unbridled pursuit of individual interests. This individualist ethos led directly, they argued, to the exploitation of 'the largest and poorest class', as well as to the subordination of women: joint 'losers' in the struggle for domination. The socialists identified both material and moral flaws in society, and they offered both material and moral solutions. To use Charles Fourier's terms, they sought to construct simultaneously 'a new industrial world' and 'a new world of love', revolutionising methods of production, and revolutionising the moral values governing society. Peaceful class collaboration, based on a just distribution of wealth and social benefits, was their goal.

Like other theorists of their era, the early socialists regarded sex as a significant marker of talent and potential, but they valued feminine qualities and assigned great significance to the 'liberty' of women. The Saint-Simonians were the most prominent socialist group in the 1830s.[55] Belief in the complementarity of the sexes was a key plank of their philosophy: '*Man and woman*, that is the being whom God created; *man and woman*, that is the social individual.'[56] From this dualism arose the idea that all social functions should be performed by a couple, thus combining male reason with female emotion and maximising human potential. On this basis, and because social roles were to be defined by talent rather than by birth, the Saint-Simonians envisaged a broad range of social roles for women. In their theory, the presence of women in government would symbolise a new mode of social authority based on love and persuasion:

> Today no-one can command by the use of violence, men no longer accept imposed authority; before obeying, they want to love and understand. So, who knows better than woman how to make herself obeyed by gentleness and persuasion? What word inspires tender respect and conviction more than hers does? Who possesses more than she that fine and delicate tact, which so clearly detects what is acceptable and what is repugnant? Therefore, woman can govern; because, in the future, to govern is to make oneself loved and understood.[57]

Saint-Simonian theory was radical in some respects, but it also shared some of the assumptions of more conservative theories. The concept of sexual difference, if not the uses to which it was put, was commonplace for the period. On this question the radicalism of the Saint-Simonians' main competitor, Charles Fourier, was remarkable. He too linked masculinity with activity, rationality and strength, and femininity with passivity, sensuality and weakness. But he alone differentiated between sex and gender: masculine and feminine talents differed, but were not automatically equated with male and female persons. In fact, he predicted that, once children were no longer subject to the current processes of socialisation, up to a third of each sex would display the talents and capacities more typically found in the opposite sex. In the ideal world of the future, which he called Harmony, women would play all roles just as men would, according to their inclinations.[58]

The legacy of these socialist theorists was mixed as far as women's participation in political life was concerned. The 'separate natures' model could provide a justification for their political participation, but only if women's specific talents were defined as essential to public life. This was rarely so, as the longevity of the 'familial' model of political representation demonstrated. Emphasising women's 'difference' served to provide a basis for their exclusion from public life by some socialists, as well as by more conservative theorists. Pierre-Joseph Proudhon's definition of women as either 'housewives or harlots' is the best-known example.[59] Similarly, Etienne Cabet, founder of the 'Icarian' communist movement, assigned women a dependent role in the community and gave them no voting rights.[60]

Furthermore, the emphasis on the sexuality of women in some socialist theories alarmed public opinion and tarnished all ideas of 'feminism'. Charles Fourier and Prosper Enfantin (the Saint-Simonian leader) believed that female sexuality, once released from the shackles of male control and monogamous marriage, would have transformative power. But the world was not ready for this message in the 1830s. The socialists' attack on the injustices and 'tyranny' of the family system, their calls for women to be freed from its clutches and to play broader social roles, were linked in the public mind with theories of 'free love'. The association between 'women in public' and 'public women' (or prostitutes) was strengthened as a result, making even modest challenges to male control of the public world more difficult.

Feminist politics in the early nineteenth century

If women's political engagement was often shaped within a family context, the early nineteenth century also saw the emergence of a feminist movement through which women made demands on their own behalf and in their own interests. Although the term 'feminist' was not coined in this period, it serves to capture a diverse set of ideas which challenged the subordinate position of women in French society: a subordination enshrined in the Civil Code of 1804.[61] Demands for reform of the Civil Code dominated the concerns of feminists throughout this period. This issue was debated at length in the emerging women's press, and headed the demands of bourgeois women's magazines in the 1830s. The *Gazette des Femmes* waged a campaign calling for civil disobedience by women until their rights were recognised. It sought an end to the legal requirement that women obey their husbands, which gave husbands wide-ranging powers over their wives. It also campaigned for the right to divorce; for an end to discriminatory legal penalties against women for crimes like adultery; for mothers to have the same rights as fathers in relation to their children; and for women to have the right to sit on juries.[62] The *Journal des Femmes* likewise attacked the marriage system, which it likened to a traffic in women. Its editor, Fanny Richomme, wrote: 'I call on you to revolt, ladies, let us all devote ourselves to finding our own ways of waging a war to the death against money marriages [...] let each of us use all her resources, all her credit, all her intelligence, all her initiative to abolish the matrimonial industry.'[63]

Petitioning was the only avenue available to women to effect such changes, and it was used mainly by women of the educated bourgeoisie. They petitioned the Chamber of Deputies for marriage law reform, as well as demanding that elementary schooling be required for girls, not only for boys.[64] Furthermore, women called for a 'serious' education for older girls, rather than a focus on the accomplishments, because this was essential for women's autonomy and for their understanding of matters of public interest. Women's enthusiastic attendance at public lectures, and their enrolment in Eugénie Niboyet's *Athénée des Femmes* – an unofficial university in Lyon where women heard lectures on social science, political economy, education, history, literature and morals – revealed the demand for such education.[65]

The female press generally espoused a conservative version of 'feminism' in the early nineteenth century, challenging the application of the laws as they affected women, but rarely challenging the position assigned to women in society. The *Journal des Femmes*, for instance, helped to construct, rather than to deconstruct, the model of the domestic wife.[66] But some women sought a more radical social transformation in order to advance women's 'liberty'. Feminists in the early nineteenth century were often socialists because, in seeking to shape a better world, socialism frequently envisaged significant changes in the roles of the sexes and was sympathetic towards women's grievances. Involvement in organisations like the Saint-Simonian movement gave women the opportunity and the confidence to express their own ideas about women's lives, even in opposition to those of socialist men. The Saint-Simonian women's movement, for instance, gradually developed an independent stance, challenging its male leader's views on women and their social roles.

The magazine produced in 1832–1833 by working women associated with the Saint-Simonian organisation, variously entitled *La Femme Libre* (The Free Woman), *La Femme Nouvelle* (The New Woman) and *La Tribune des Femmes* (The Women's Tribune), was the first magazine of its kind in France. Its concerns included those raised by the bourgeois women's journals, but it also called for professional training and well-paid work for women to enable them to be economically independent. It called for an end to the 'slavery' of the home and sought to reform the household as well as production. It publicised problems of rape and sexual harassment, and suggested co-operative workshops for single women where they could live and work in safety.[67]

Saint-Simonian women also grappled with the controversial pronouncements of their male leaders on sexual freedom. Some women welcomed the call to utilise their sexuality in positive ways, occasionally even offering themselves to men in a gesture of healing. As Pauline Roland wrote in entering a relationship with a troubled young man, 'My desire as a woman is to give myself mainly for the good that I can do for the man to whom I give myself.'[68] Even more radical was the view of Claire Démar, who argued for women's right to experience sexual pleasure and to live a sexual life freed from the constraints of law and public opinion. She advocated 'unlimited liberty' and believed that a woman 'might simultaneously give satisfaction to the love of several men'. She also argued against the emphasis on motherhood and childraising as women's destiny.[69] The majority of those whose views were recorded, however, were hesitant to abandon accepted moral conventions, at least in the immediate term. Marie-Reine argued:

> Surely we must recognise that all freedoms must advance simultaneously; and, in order to be *morally* free, we must be *materially* free; for wouldn't our moral liberty be a sham if we were still forced to rely on men for our material needs?[70]

Few women publicly demanded political rights for women in the early nineteenth century. As Michèle Riot-Sarcey points out, it was difficult for women to conceptualise themselves as political actors when the entire culture constructed such figures as male.[71] Only occasions of extreme crisis, when heroism was required of all, enabled the sexual taboo to be lifted. Hence the female role models identified by women activists were their 'foremothers' of the French Revolution, or the heroines of the Polish Revolution of 1830.[72] Outside such situations, it was difficult for politically active women to claim legitimacy.[73] This helps to explain why even women who did take part in 'political' activity did not always construe their actions in this light.

Nevertheless, some women were persuaded that only male 'tyranny' explained men's monopoly on political power. The Revolutions of 1789 and 1830 had produced 'liberties' for men, but Revolutionary men had refused to allow those 'liberties' to be passed on to women. Charges of 'usurpation' and 'despotism' were therefore made by women, who employed the same political language used earlier by men to justify their challenges to tyrants. Marie G. declared: 'men have stripped us of our natural rights to liberty and to any voice in political affairs by their abuse of force'.[74] The self-styled 'woman of the barricades', Claire Démar, concurred: 'if your laws are illusory for men, in how many ways are they not for women, for women whom you keep in servitude, for women whom you exclude from all political leadership'.[75] She continued: 'the time has come; woman must finally claim her rights of ownership, her right to be an elector, her right to free and spontaneous consent, not only in the government of the family, but in the government of the city and the kingdom'.[76]

Women's roles and women's rights in the Revolution of 1848

The Orleanist Monarchy was overturned by revolution in 1848. It had been a compromise between the threat of Ultraroyalism on the one hand and Republicanism or Bonapartism on the other, and it became progressively unpopular. Legitimists (supporters of the Bourbons) continued to attack it, and those in the lower ranks of the bourgeoisie were alienated by its close ties to elite bankers and financiers. Workers blamed it for the structural changes in the economy that created hardship. Protests accelerated, especially once widespread depression affected Europe in the 'Hungry Forties'. Despite the regime's initial self-promotion as liberal and constitutional, too, it became progressively more despotic. Laws on censorship and assembly were tightened in response to criticism and protest.[77]

As workers or the wives of workers, women suffered from the unemployment and hardship that fostered working-class militancy during the 1830s and 1840s. In times of hardship, women attacked grain carts, looted bakeries and ransacked food stores. They conducted rent strikes, and hanged landlords in effigy. They invaded town halls to protest to mayors about the exorbitant price of food, and conducted 'popular taxation' at warehouses, selling off grain at 'just' prices.[78]

When popular hostility to the Orleanist régime erupted into revolution in February 1848, women helped men defend their communities, though rarely as combatants. Women built barricades and nursed the wounded, and they also assumed their symbolic function, this time as the personification of the Republic.[79] Women joined political clubs (although in many they were not permitted to speak) and produced newspapers. They joined men in urging the government to remain faithful to the vision of a 'democratic and social' republic that would defend workers' rights. Suffering from unemployment like men were, they campaigned for 'national workshops' to provide jobs for women too.[80]

When the government demonstrated its unwillingness to meet these demands, many Parisian women joined with men in a desperate second revolution, the June uprising. This uprising was widely condemned as a treacherous attack on the fledgling Republic by criminal elements, and the women associated with it were vilified as symbols of the depravity of the government's opponents. As politically active women, who thereby challenged both the social and the gender order, they were seen as proof that the uprising was an attack on the civilised values of French society.[81] Women revolutionaries, like men, were shot in cold blood as the uprising was suppressed. They were prosecuted, imprisoned and exiled by courts martial, although some were pardoned more quickly than men, particularly if they had dependent children. When the short-lived Second Republic was overthrown in a coup d'état in 1851, women also joined the bands of rural insurgents in Southern France who sought to defend La Belle (the 'beautiful republic') against the troops of Louis–Napoléon Bonaparte. The tiny village of Saint-Etienne-les-Orgues provided 33 rebels, including two women who marched with their husbands and, like them, were sent to prison in Algeria as punishment.[82]

The year 1848 was a definitive one for women because the new Republic extended suffrage to all men. A distinction in political rights based solely on sex was created. Anne Verjus interprets this development, not as the denial of political rights to women, but as the continuation of a family-based model of citizenship. All men were potentially, if not actually, heads of families, so all men were enfranchised.[83] But the fact that family headship, and hence suffrage, was impossible for women reflected a sex-based distinction that was contentious in 1848 and afterwards. Besides, many of the arguments about suffrage focused on individual autonomy, and the possibility of individual autonomy for women was rejected. Arguments about the family rested on underlying ideas about sexual difference, therefore, that made the 1848 decision a sex-based one.

Some women, at least, expected to share in the advent of 'democracy' in 1848. Eugénie Niboyet reported that she had heard 'a cry of astonishment from so many women' when they discovered that they were excluded from the new suffrage provisions. As a result she made her newspaper, La Voix des Femmes ('Women's Voice'), a forum for women's demand for a truly 'universal' suffrage.[84] Throughout March and April of 1848, in the lead-up to the first elections under manhood suffrage, women lobbied Republican men, especially the Provisional Government, to acknowledge women's political rights. Many of these women had been active in socialist or republican organisations in the 1830s, and now enjoyed – like men – renewed freedom of action and renewed confidence in the prospect of change.

The former Saint-Simonians Pauline Roland, Désirée Gay, Eugénie Niboyet and Jeanne Deroin all made calls for women's proper share in the 'sovereignty of the people' and for their 'rights of citizenship'.[85] Roland even attempted to cast a vote in the municipal elections at Boussac, and laid an official complaint when she was prohibited from doing so.[86] But belief in the justice of this cause was not confined to a handful of practised activists. Delegates from a 'committee for women's rights' lobbied the Provisional government.[87] Manifestos by working women, whose main priorities lay elsewhere given the dire hardship of mid-1848, also declared suffrage to be 'the cornerstone of women's rights',[88] and an integral part of women's emancipation under the Republic.[89]

The grounds on which feminists demanded the rights of citizenship in 1848 called into question the 'familial' model of citizenship espoused by others, including most Republican men. Women presented a variety of arguments, attempting to find one that might prove persuasive. They defined women as individuals who were thereby entitled to represent themselves as citizens. But they also defended a view of family relations that challenged men's right to represent those families. Women claimed the right to participate in society alongside men both because they were individuals, and because they were mothers of families. Drawing on the divided feminist tradition which dated to the French Revolution, they argued sometimes that women possessed rights because they were identical to men, and at other times that they possessed rights because they were different from men. The 'paradox' of women's relationship to a normative male citizen was fully evident as women attempted to make the case for suffrage in 1848.[90]

'Jeanne-Marie' exclaimed in April of that year: 'Women, don't lose heart, what you are asking for is justice, it is not licence but liberty.'[91] From women's perspective, simple justice required that they gain the rights newly acquired by men. Pauline Roland put the philosophical case that women were inherently free beings like men, with a right to autonomy.[92] Others preferred more pragmatic arguments. Women were obliged to pay taxes and obey laws like men, they noted, so justice required that they have a say in the shaping of those laws.[93] Deroin quoted Olympe de Gouges' famous words from 1789: 'Woman has the right to mount the scaffold, equally she must have the right to mount the speaker's rostrum.'[94] Besides, women noted that they were not actually excluded from voting under the terms of the suffrage declaration, which eliminated only those convicted of serious offences and those who were mentally ill: 'since women's eligibility does not fall under either of these categories, so far as we are aware, electoral rights belong to her'.[95] These arguments implicitly rejected the notion that men could represent the interests of women, though they did not contest it openly.

More importantly and at greater length, however, feminists contested the 'blind spot' in men's definitions of Republicanism that allowed them to ignore or deny women's rights. From women's point of view the situation was simple: the February Revolution had overturned 'privilege' and established 'liberty, equality and fraternity' as the bases of the Republic. Rights could not be denied to women if the Republic was to be consistent with its own principles. Women appealed repeatedly to the Republican motto to make their case. A 'simple proletarian woman' exhorted her brothers in the Club Lyonnais: 'Citizens, you have done a lot in proclaiming the Republic, but it isn't enough. The Republic has taken for its motto these words: *Liberty, Equality, Fraternity*; these must not be for you alone, but also for women.'[96] The Society for the Emancipation of Women claimed that everything stemmed from this 'holy trinity': 'Women demand their emancipation. They seek the inauguration of the genuine reign of true liberty, true fraternity [...] They are seeking what is their due.'[97] The newspaper *L'Opinion des Femmes* also appealed to 'the three great principles which underpin the future of our society', noting 'We will constantly demand, in the name of Equality, the complete abolition of all privileges of *sex*, of race, of birth, of caste and of wealth.'[98] But women felt it necessary to explain the link between Republicanism and women's rights simply, for those who could not grasp it:

> The Republic means the regeneration of society. Society consists of men and women. The most profound principle of social regeneration proclaimed by the Republic is Equality. *Social* equality. The Equality of all members of Society. Therefore irrefutably, Equality of men and women: – therefore the same rights, the same duties for men and women [...] To say to women: you are not electors, you are not eligible for election, and you will not be, and we do not wish you to be, – is to refuse to establish the Republic whilst proclaiming it, – it is to dishonour a victory achieved for the good of all – it is to monopolise in an unworthy fashion the public and shared results of the triumph, – it is to be Republicans no longer; – let us put it plainly, it is to be *Aristocrats!*[99]

In arguing for 'liberty, equality and fraternity' to be applied to women, feminists claimed the essential similarity between the sexes: there was no fundamental reason which justified women being treated differently from men as far as 'rights' were concerned. They also explicitly contested men's right and ability to represent women. Men could no longer claim to be the sole embodiments of 'humanity', they declared. Besides, if men voted as heads of families, thereby representing their wives and daughters, why did the head of the family not represent his sons, who also had the franchise? Rather than accepting the argument that male suffrage was justified because all males were potentially heads of families, women insisted that male suffrage was a form of sex privilege.[100]

If women asserted their own individuality and their right as individuals to represent themselves in public life, they also formulated arguments for female suffrage that emphasised their unique contribution as women to society. Motherhood represented their uniqueness. As Jeanne Deroin asserted, in principle 'the mother of future generations, she from whom the glorious citizens of a regenerated world will be born, must not be a slave'.[101] Besides, mothers raised citizens, and slaves could not teach their children to cherish liberty. Désirée Gay declared: 'the future of our children and peace in society depends on the exercise of our rights, because woman influences the character of new generations through the education she provides'.[102] Women's qualities as mothers were therefore beneficial to society more broadly. A mother was typified by her love, devotion and self-sacrifice for others. Women would bring these qualities into public life, as befitted a Republic imagined as a caring 'mother'.[103] Men may have dominated society under the 'reign of force', but the new politics was a politics of healing and rebuilding: tasks for which women were eminently suited.

The most articulate exponent of this view was Jeanne Deroin. As well as cataloguing the horrors of a world run by men – unjust laws, the unequal distribution of wealth, slavery, the servitude of wage labourers, corruption, ignorance and misery[104] – she declared: 'We must be at your side and share your glorious struggle when it's a matter of fighting egoism, of regenerating humanity, of delivering it from moral and material suffering.'[105] Women's influence would transform the politics of violence into the politics of peace:

> Only woman, who is innately opposed to war, because the principles of love and peace are inherent in her nature, can make everyone understand that the temple of brotherhood cannot be constructed on foundations of bloodshed[...] And she must take her place in the city in order to abolish war and transform this improvident, oppressive and unfair politics, which is the source of wars of aggression, of civil strife and of all the sufferings which damage humanity. It is up to her to inaugurate the reign of universal peace and the politics of work and conciliation.[106]

This argument relied on an essentialist view of female nature, but it also showed the essentialist dimension in arguments for male suffrage. If all men were citizens because they were potentially fathers, all women should be citizens because they were potentially mothers.

Feminists were aware that their calls for equal rights in society were deeply disturbing to some men. They therefore insisted that women's roles as citizens would be complementary to their roles as wives and mothers. As Deroin put it, they would be 'citizenesses' but they would remain attached to 'the sacred duties of the family'.[107] Michèle Riot-Sarcey notes the tension between women's desire for 'liberty' in 1848, and their desire to conform to the ideal of woman-hood that was prized in their society. Only a family that was compatible with women's 'liberty' promised to allow the resolution of that tension, hence women's attention to transforming the family, as well as the State, in 1848.[108] Women's many proposals to establish co-operative workshops, crèches, communal laundries, restaurants and kitchens illustrate their attempt to manage their overburdened lives as working women and make space for their roles as 'citizenesses'.

These proposals also represented an opening up of the family to society. They envisaged a transformation of the 'private' sphere into a communal space, because defining the domestic sphere as 'private' had naturalised women's dependent status and political exclusion. The rejection of the idealised 'private' family was also reflected in feminist arguments that women's various roles existed on a continuum as men's did. Deroin argued:

> The life of every intelligent being is a holy trinity, *one [and] indivisible*; individual life, family life, social life, that is a complete life. So let us live the life in society [*vie sociale*] which gives a new impetus to the noblest faculties of the soul; to repress them in us would be an odious tyranny, a social crime.[109]

But the problem was not only one of transforming 'roles' but of transforming relationships. The manifesto of the 'society for the emancipation of women' spelled out the issue: 'First of all we must work out how the principle of liberty can be introduced into the family without its harmony and hierarchy being disturbed. How can the liberty of the wife be made compatible with that of the husband?'[110] We might ask instead: was the 'liberty' of the wife compatible with ongoing hierarchy in the family at all? Political rights for women represented both the flowering of their liberty, and the overthrow of the domestic 'Old Regime'. Women realised pessimistically that this made it a threatening and unrealistic expectation:

> So, poor women who welcomed the dawn of this new era with such enthusiasm; who thought for a moment that since the sun of liberty was shining on everybody, some of its rays would reach as far as you, restrain your joy, that isn't how the masters of the world envisage things! In the Republic of 1848, which has as its mission to abolish all privileges, there will still be pariahs, and those pariahs will be you![111]

Women did not vote in 1848, but their demands for suffrage continued. Jeanne Deroin became the first woman political candidate when she stood for the National Assembly elections of 1849. Her candidature was declared illegal (although 15 democratic socialists voted at the electoral committee meeting for her right to be included on the list of candidates).[112] In prison and in exile after the overthrow of the Second Republic in 1851, Deroin continued to defend women's political rights, as did her fellow prisoner Pauline Roland. Roland declared: 'woman is a citizen by right, if not in fact, and, as such, she must involve herself in public life, in social life'.[113] Deroin insisted: 'we will not stop demanding women's political rights [...] And because, in current society, political rights are the highest expression of man's rights as a member of this society, it must be the same for woman who is also a member of this society'.[114]

As Anne Verjus points out, feminist demands for political rights in 1848 were out of step with the dominant view that men should represent their families in civic life. In extending the right of family representation to all males, she points out, the suffrage of 1848 was 'universalised' in comparison with the limited suffrage that preceded it. As she also notes, however, the exclusion of women needed to be justified explicitly, not least because feminists challenged its underlying assumptions.[115] They challenged the definition of the 'political individual', as well as the notion of a private family represented in public by a male head. Feminists also outlined the positive benefits of a specifically female contribution to public life, adopting a 'particularist' rather than gender-neutral perspective.

Joan Scott notes that it was paradoxical for women to call for a share in the rights of an undifferentiated gender-neutral citizenry on the basis of their feminine particularity. But appeals to women's special nature were historically produced, in a situation in which male definitions of 'universalism' were masculine rather than gender-free.[116] To see the feminist case as regressive for focusing on the particularity of women, as Verjus suggests, ignores the fact that women also argued the individualist case more strongly and more logically than Republican men. Women were not immune from pervasive cultural assumptions of sexual difference. But men's refusal to acknowledge that women and men shared a common humanity made alternative arguments for female suffrage essential.

5 Women and the Creation of Republican France, 1852–1914

The Second Republic was born in hope in February 1848, mortally wounded in the June uprising, and killed off by Louis-Napoléon Bonaparte's coup d'état of December 1851. Twelve months later Louis-Napoléon established the Second Empire and became Emperor Napoleon III. Martial law was imposed in December 1851, and strict limits on rights of assembly prevented any public discussion of political ideas. Republican organisations and publications were banned, and activists imprisoned or driven into exile. Women who had been prominent in the campaign for women's rights were amongst those prosecuted, especially committed socialists like Jeanne Deroin and Pauline Roland. Deroin fled to England, while Roland was imprisoned in Algeria. The undemocratic Second Empire was not receptive to arguments for female political rights.

Republicanism developed after 1848 as an embattled movement whose victory remained far from assured. According to Judith Stone, this produced a politics of nostalgia.[1] The halcyon days of the First Republic served as a reference point for an abstract Republican ideal, and for a masculine Republican self-image. In drawing on the history of the First Republic to define the citizen, Republicans of the mid-nineteenth century also adopted its theory of sexual difference: citizenship for women was rejected, as it had been in the 1790s. Despite the roles played by women in the movement, and the Republican credentials of feminists, most Republican men proved unable to accept an inclusive notion of democracy.

Women and politics during the Second Empire

Under the Empire, women's ability to exert political influence and wield authority stemmed from their family position, as it had under earlier dynastic regimes. Empress Eugénie led the way, taking an interest in matters affecting women, especially their education. In 1862 she intervened personally to allow the first woman (Julie Daubié) to take the *baccalauréat* examination required for entry to university-level study. She also authorised women to enter the faculties and take degrees. Very few women were able to benefit from such measures, however. The Falloux Law of 1850 required communities to establish elementary schools for girls, but these remained firmly in the hands of the Church. Nuns were exempt from provisions requiring teachers to be qualified. The standard of girls' education remained abysmal and many women remained illiterate.[2]

Empress Eugénie also supported philanthropic measures for women. Like queens before her, for instance, she became patron of the Society for Maternal Charity that provided assistance for poor women in childbirth across France. Eugénie responded positively to direct appeals from regional Societies for special assistance or increased funding. The wives of Empire officials also played leading roles in this organisation. In Avignon, for example, the wife of the Prefect normally headed the Society for Maternal Charity.[3] This was consistent with the Empire's personalised style of politics and the hierarchical model of society that it espoused.

The Second Empire restored the universal male suffrage instituted in 1848, although it diluted the impact of democracy by means of inducements, manipulation and the promotion of 'official candidates' who had the Emperor's favour. The political gulf between the sexes implicit in a regime of male suffrage was not absolute in practice, however, and the family-based electoral procedures of the July Monarchy endured. The government's attempt to predetermine election results even brought women directly into the election process. Restrictions on opposition campaigning forced candidates to rely largely on family members, particularly their wives, for assistance. The wives of official government candidates also played a role, urging women to ensure that their husbands voted 'wisely'. On occasion women cast the ballots on their husbands' behalf and they were even involved in vote-counting, which sometimes occurred in the mayor's kitchen. Furthermore, since public positions were awarded according to political criteria, women who held such posts were required to provide active support to the government despite having no official political standing. For instance, the postmistress at Crèvecour (Oise) was sacked in 1863 for having displayed hostility to the government candidate. Voting was not so clearly 'men's business' in this period as it was to become during the Third Republic.[4]

In the 1860s a less repressive Empire allowed more open political activity. Those exiled in 1851 were allowed to return to France in 1860, and relaxation of censorship and assembly laws in 1868 made public meetings possible. A new generation of feminist activists emerged, most famously Maria Desraismes, André Léo and Paule Mink. A series of public lectures in Paris addressed a range of issues affecting women, including the unequal marriage laws and the plight of working women. Newspapers and societies for 'women's rights' were established.[5]

While these developments occurred in the final years of the Empire, they were the work of Republicans. Despite steady growth in support for the Republican cause, however, only the Emperor's ill-judged war with Prussia and his capture on the battlefield at Sedan allowed the Third Republic to be proclaimed in 1870. It was to be another decade before committed Republicans won effective control of government, and only then did they manage to put a Republican stamp on policy and politics.[6] The question of women's place in the Republic remained on the political agenda throughout this period.

Women and the establishment of the Third Republic

From the 1850s, women played vital roles in shaping the culture of Republicanism and making it a genuine alternative to monarchy and empire. With many Republicans in exile, women devoted themselves to keeping the Republican faith alive amongst the scattered community through their correspondence. Their letters were read in salons of the Republican elite in Paris. These private gatherings were occasions for political discussion while public meetings remained illegal.[7]

In exile or at home in France, women assumed responsibility for creating a domestic environment permeated with Republicanism and raising children with Republican values. They also sought to strengthen the Republican network through their choice of marriage partners for themselves or their children.[8] The marriage in 1869 of Charles Floquet, future Republican prime minister, and Hortense

Kestner, daughter of a wealthy Alsatian industrialist and Republican leader, illustrated the blend of personal and political attraction that underpinned many elite Republican marriages in this period. Her sister explained to a friend:

> My sister wants me to tell you that in becoming the wife of Floquet, she wishes to become not only the adored wife of a man she loves, but also the companion of a good soldier of our future struggles. It is certain that our new brother carries in his heart the political tradition of our family and our friends and that the only thing he will love with as much passion as his wife will be the Republic.[9]

As the focal point of passion in Republican men's lives, their wives occupied a central position within the emotional economy that galvanised men's political zeal.

Nevertheless, the circumstances in which the Third Republic was founded gave active political participation by women a negative image. War with Prussia in 1870 was followed by civil war between the newly proclaimed Republican government and the population of Paris. Elections based on male suffrage in February 1871 produced a monarchist majority, shocking Parisians already aggrieved by government 'defeatism'. They rose up against the national government and elected a local administration, the 'Paris Commune', with a broadly left-wing membership.

In the two months of its existence (March–May 1871), the Paris Commune implemented a number of radical social measures. It decreed free, compulsory and secular education for boys and girls, and equal pay for male and female teachers. It paid pensions to widows and children of national guardsmen, whether the couple had been legitimately married or not. A minimum daily wage for soldiers' wives surviving on the manufacture of uniforms was decreed. Women played active roles in the Commune's political debates and decision-making, provided nursing and other support to the soldiers, and even took up arms to defend the Commune against the Versailles government. Militant women took the title *Citoyenne* (Citizeness), and campaigned for their rights in the new society that the Paris Commune aspired to inaugurate.[10]

The Versailles-based Republican government violently crushed the Commune, slaughtering between 15,000 and 25,000 Parisians in one week and imprisoning many more. This episode heightened the Republican government's fear of working-class militancy. It also associated feminism with social disorder. The *pétroleuses* – the mythical women supposedly responsible for setting fire to Paris during the Commune's last days – became symbols of the danger posed by women who abandoned their natural sphere. Conversely, a return to normality seemed to require women's being 'in their place'. In practical terms, the Commune and its aftermath removed militant women from the scene, since they were imprisoned or fled into self-imposed exile. Bourgeois women were wary of being associated with social disorder. Moderation and respectability were to characterise women's participation in the Republican movement, even its feminist organisations.[11]

Monarchists remained the dominant political force in the first decade of the Third Republic. Only divisions among conservatives – Legitimists, Orleanists and Bonapartists supported different candidates and different agendas – prevented a restoration. As Adolphe Thiers (formerly an Orleanist, and first President of the Third Republic) observed in 1872, the Republic was 'the regime that divides us least'. The rise of Republicanism as a political force in the 1870s rested on a broadening of its clientele: as Léon Gambetta said, the Republic meant the advent of the 'new social strata', by which he meant the prosperous new middle class of teachers, doctors, lawyers, retailers and the like.[12] This brought increasing electoral successes, and Republicans finally gained control of all levels of government in 1879.

Republicans were not a unified group in the early Third Republic. 'Opportunists', so-called because of their largely pragmatic approach to policy-making, dominated Republican politics in the 1880s. The factions led by Léon Gambetta and Jules Ferry differed on a number of issues but both were at odds with the 'Radical' Republicans led by Georges Clemenceau, who held sway by 1900.

Republican parliamentary leaders were drawn especially from professional groups; many had modest provincial backgrounds. Léon Gambetta, the son of an Italian grocer, was a lawyer, as was Jules Ferry. Georges Clemenceau was a doctor. Other politicians were journalists, schoolteachers, or emerged from the middle and lower ranks of industry and trade.[13] They lacked the personal fortunes and social graces for mixing with and winning over the elite. To their modest social origins many of these aspiring politicians added personal lives that did not conform to expectations. Many were single or, like Gambetta and Camille Pelletan, lived in 'irregular' relationships. Jules Ferry had a series of mistresses before his late marriage to Eugénie Risler; Georges Clemenceau reversed the pattern, having a series of liaisons after divorcing his American wife. One of the Republicans' greatest political handicaps, then, was that they lacked respectability: they were, in Theodore Zeldin's words, 'parvenus who had not quite made good'.[14]

Social elites sympathetic to Republicanism therefore sought to strengthen links between Republican politicians and Parisian high society in order to enhance their electoral prospects. Women played important roles in this process, continuing a pattern evident in the political participation of elite women, of all political persuasions, since the Restoration. Women like Juliette Adam, Céline Scheurer-Kestner, Madame Arnaud de l'Ariège and the Marquise Arconati-Visconti (daughter of the Republican Félix Peyrat) hosted Republican salons in the 1860s and 1870s. These allowed Republican men from modest backgrounds to hone their social skills and mix with powerful opinion-makers. The writer Juliette Adam, wife of Republican senator Edmond Adam, hosted the most influential salon. It served as a forum where policies were debated and Ministries decided, and Léon Gambetta was a regular participant.[15] Wealthy women also offered financial support to Republican leaders – a significant gesture when salaries were estimated at half of parliamentarians' real living expenses. As well as making her private hotel available to Gambetta, for instance, Madame Arnaud de l'Ariège paid him a pension so that he could live in suitable style.[16]

Women were sometimes more ardent in their commitment to Republicanism than men. It was Eugénie Risler who insisted on a civil marriage in 1875, for instance, when her fiancé Jules Ferry, future anticlerical Minister of Public Education, had been prepared to follow the more expedient course of being married by a priest.[17] Nevertheless, women remained 'companions' of Republican 'soldiers' rather than front-line troops. The military metaphor highlights the gendered nature of the struggle in which Republicans perceived themselves engaged: since politics was a battlefield, it was unsuitable terrain for women.

Sexual difference and the 'masculine' Republic

Republican men remained committed to a social model based on sexual difference and a radical separation of sex roles. In the nineteenth century, they relied increasingly on scientific justifications for sexual polarity. The new nineteenth-century sciences of anthropology and anthropometry (the measurement of the body) confirmed prevailing assumptions about sexual dimorphism. Anthropologists 'discovered' that sexual difference increased as species evolved. Logically, therefore, increasing human perfection meant increasing distinction between males and females. The Darwinians added that the struggle for survival confirmed the inevitability of male superiority. Anthropometrists compared female skulls and skeletons to a male norm, and likewise found evidence of male superiority. Medical scientists 'proved' that female passivity was natural, by comparing the 'passive' female ovum with the 'active' male gametes in the sperm: an observation shaped by prior beliefs about masculine and feminine traits. The female ovaries, which replaced the uterus as the organ deemed responsible for femininity in the nineteenth century, and the discovery of hormones, were also believed to confirm a gender order embedded in 'nature'.[18]

The obsession with sexual dimorphism was not unique to Republicans in this period. But the impact of new scientific and medical insights was heightened by the prominence of doctors and academics amongst Republican activists. The number of doctors elected to the National Assembly in this period was far greater than their proportion in the population overall, for instance. Between 1880 and 1910, one-third to two-thirds of these men identified as Radical Republicans.[19]

Republicans also shared the cultural anxiety underlying this emphasis on difference. Dr Henri Thulié, a militant anticlerical Republican, voiced a broadly held view when he argued that sexual difference was the basis for sexual attraction and hence for the survival of the nation. The alternative – a society in which women were masculinised and men effeminate – would lead to impotence, sterility and race suicide. A clear dichotomy between masculine and feminine in all aspects of life was not merely socially desirable, then, but politically imperative.[20] In the words of another leading Republican who shared those views: 'What was decided among the prehistoric protozoa cannot be annulled by Act of Parliament.'[21] A political decision could not overturn the 'natural' relationship between the sexes.

These developments support the arguments of Katherine Auspitz and Robert Nye that psychological imperatives shaped the emergent Republican ethic in the second half of the nineteenth century. The contest between Republicans and conservatives was not simply about political power but about manhood itself. Like their forefathers in the 1790s, Republicans of this period aspired to create a new Republican man who would demonstrate his fitness to rule by exhibiting 'manliness' – rationality, self-control and civic-mindedness. He would be a citizen and a worker, but also a *père de famille*: the head of a family. In this role his manliness and virility came to fruition.[22]

Since the family was the site where principles were instilled and identities shaped, Republicans were convinced that their political success depended upon the creation of truly Republican families.[23] The two most influential Republican theorists of the mid-century – Jules Michelet and Victor Hugo – emphasised the importance of this task. Michelet attributed the failure of the Second Republic partly to the utopian socialists' attack on the family. Hugo likewise saw the reformed family as the solution to social divisions.[24] As a union of unlike individuals, diverse in age, sex and capacity but united by the bonds of sympathy and affection, the ideal family aptly symbolised a society in which harmony would reign despite class and sex differences, provided that its members shared a united vision. Nevertheless, a tension between equality and hierarchy continued to pervade the Republicans' visions of both family and society.[25]

The centrality of the family to Republican thinking had significant implications for women. In imagining reformed families, Republican men imagined more loving and intimate relations between spouses. Marriage would become a partnership of shared interests.[26] This vision seems to have been lived by many Republican couples including Hortense Kestner and Charles Floquet, Eugénie Risler and Jules Ferry, Juliette and Edmond Adam, and even Léonie Léon and Léon Gambetta. Eugène Pelletan wrote of this ideal relationship: 'I would call it a constitutional government. The husband minister of foreign affairs, the wife minister of the interior, and all household questions decided by the council of ministers.'[27] But what if this council of two disagreed? Intimacy did not mean equality. The ideal Republican family remained a hierarchical unit. Besides, as Ferry declared, 'In the heart of the best of us, there is a sultan.'[28] The Republican man would reign, but reign lovingly, over a Republican woman shaped to man's desires and expectations as Michelet recommended.[29]

Given the Republicans' emphasis on sexual difference, the Republican woman was inevitably cast as complement to the Republican man, counterbalancing the qualities and roles he claimed for himself. Where he was citizen-worker-*père de famille*, therefore, she was imagined as a dependent being, represented by her husband, inhabiting the domestic world as bearer and rearer of his children. Where he was defined as rational, she was defined as emotional, needing male guidance and control. As 'Republicans', then, women shared a theoretically equal civic status with men, but as mothers they were assigned to the private world, outside the civic domain where the bonds of equality prevailed.[30] This contradiction was never resolved by Republican theorists.

The fraternal solidarity of Republican theory was reinforced by the male camaraderie of late nineteenth-century Republican society. The decline of the salon and the conventions of bourgeois life meant that men moved from the male worlds of secondary school and university to the equally exclusive 'Circles', Masonic lodges, fencing clubs and parliamentary debating chamber.[31] The separateness of men's and women's callings was thus reinforced and the female citizen remained a largely inconceivable figure.

Challenging the 'masculine' Republic in the 1860s and 1870s

The glaring gulf between the theory of democracy and the reality of women's exclusion persuaded some women to challenge the male formulation of Republicanism in this period, as women had done earlier. As men elaborated their view of Republicanism from the 1860s, women did likewise. Women proposed egalitarian models of the Republican family and promoted a view of women as independent individuals, challenging notions of women's 'difference' as they did so.

Republican women shared men's emphasis on the importance of the family. Maria Deraismes, pioneering feminist and leading Republican in her hometown of Pontoise, stressed the social benefits of marriage rather than the 'free unions' favoured by some socialists. So did Jenny d'Héricourt and Léodile Champseix (who used the male pseudonym André Léo). But like their predecessors in 1848 and earlier, women insisted that the seedbed of a democratic Republic must itself be democratic. George Sand, Hortense Allart and Marie d'Agoult wrote fiction about families where women were not confined or subordinate, and where permeable boundaries between the private and public worlds allowed women to combine their responsibilities in both.[32]

Other women did not rely on fiction, but challenged Republican men's attachment to female dependence in the family directly. Jenny d'Héricourt and André Léo targeted the contradiction between democratic political models and hierarchical family models, particularly those developed by Jules Michelet and Pierre-Joseph Proudhon. André Léo wrote of the authoritarian Republicans:

> These self-proclaimed lovers of liberty, if they cannot all take part in ruling the State, at least need a little kingdom for their private use, each one for himself. When divine right was reduced to dust, it was so that each male (in the Proudhonian sense) could have a little bit. Order in the family seems to them to be impossible without hierarchy. Well then, what about in the State?[33]

If marriage were to be a true union, d'Héricourt noted, it should be a partnership involving joint names, joint property and joint custody of children. It could not result in one partner being absorbed by the other.[34] Women also argued that there was no justification for limiting woman's existence to her reproductive function. 'Woman is born for life, as much as man is, as her diverse aptitudes show.'[35]

Women took issue with male pronouncements on 'female nature'. Exposing the absurdity of many of Michelet's claims, d'Héricourt argued that 'female' nature was 'normal' for women. It was not an inferior variant of male nature.[36] Léo made similar points. Both women also dismissed as absurd the idea that knowledge and intellect had distinct 'masculine' and 'feminine' forms. 'Can you prove to me, a woman, that I desire to possess knowledge differently from you?', asked d'Héricourt.[37] Léo pointed out that 'it's difficult to imagine two ways of teaching and understanding the properties of a ray of sunshine or the murder of Henri IV'. She challenged men to 'demonstrate the two faces of justice, the two sexes of the mind!'[38]

The issue of women's 'difference' from men was at the heart of the debate between the 'masculinist' theorists and their feminist opponents, because arguments about 'difference' justified the male view of women's circumscribed rights and social roles. Women's exclusion from Republican citizenship hinged upon their supposed non-conformity to the required model of the rational, independent and self-directed individual. As Joan Scott has argued, the question of 'difference' posed a major tactical and theoretical problem for women. Since Republican men's image of 'the citizen' was based on a male model, the extension of 'rights' to women required either denying that women were 'different' from men, or convincing men that women's 'difference' was inconsequential. Both these approaches were fraught with difficulty.[39]

Some women, like Juliette Adam and Maria Deraismes, promoted 'equivalence' between the sexes. This term combined the notion of 'difference' with that of comparable worth. For them, 'difference' was not a justification for subordination but was perfectly compatible with full civil and civic rights for women.[40] Others argued, however, that 'difference' was a slippery notion that was particularly appealing to opponents of women's rights. Jenny d'Héricourt and André Léo asked how any 'natural' differences between the sexes could be identified before women had the same education and opportunities as men: a notion accepted by some Republican men.[41] They suggested that 'difference', if it did exist, was socially constructed and therefore mutable.[42]

Women attacked masculinist formulations of womanhood from two standpoints. First, they claimed the 'rationality' that men sought to deny them. They claimed to present the 'undeniable facts' about women, in place of the distorted notions of men, and argued that their view of women was based on impeccable methodology, logical argument and rigorous analysis.[43] They also undertook detailed refutations of male supremacist arguments, in which they constantly questioned the evidence men presented and the conclusions they drew from it. In this process, they claimed the territory of reason and science for women.[44]

At the same time, female theorists asserted that men's arguments about women rested on emotion. The 'woman' presented by many theorists was a figment of the male imagination, they contended, not a real person. Michelet indulged in 'poetical metaphysics', d'Héricourt charged. His ideas about women were 'opposed to reason, to science and to truth'. She challenged men: 'Stop creating an imaginary type of woman to serve as the standard for judging real women.'[45] André Léo went further, describing such theorists as 'monuments of illogicality'; their views on women were simply 'fiction'.[46] But 'when it comes to woman', she suggested, 'man doesn't want to be logical and doesn't seem to be able to be logical'.[47]

From women's perspective, therefore, men did not demonstrate their much-heralded 'reason' in discussing women. They relied on emotion, and especially on fear. Pondering men's resistance to full and free education for women, for instance, Léo asked: 'Why this senseless, illogical fear of knowledge, of reflection, of the free development of the person? Because from knowledge flows will, just as uncertainty flows from ignorance. A person who thinks and knows wills; all despots feel (*sentent*) that.'[48] The issue was a political one, the definition of women's 'nature' ultimately designed to deny them independent existence and self-determination. As Jenny d'Héricourt asserted: 'terrified by the emancipating movement [men] call to their aid false science to prove that woman is beyond the pale of right'.[49]

Significantly, then, in an era when notions of sexual difference (and hence of different 'rights') pivoted on the distinction between male reason and female emotion, Republican women exposed men's deep emotional investment in female dependence, and the illogicality of their arguments on the subject. By reversing the gender order that labelled reason as men's domain and emotion as that of women, feminists challenged one of the theoretical lynchpins of Republicanism. To define men as 'irrational' was a serious charge, given Republican men's commitment to reason as a mark of their progressive politics. However, since 'a logical woman was an illogical combination' (to quote Joan Scott), women's criticisms could be ignored or attributed to the 'emotion' presumed to dominate them.[50] Republican feminists faced the impossible task of trying to persuade men of the logic and hence validity of their arguments. But the alternative was equally difficult: accepting that woman, as a 'different' being, was destined by 'nature' for a dependent and subordinate position within the Republic.

Woman as 'Muse' in the 'masculinist' Republic

Despite women's formal exclusion from politics, the relationships of Republican politicians with their wives and female friends illustrate that women participated actively in political debate and endeavoured to shape Republican policy. Consistent with the discourse of 'difference', women's role was often represented through the discourse of the Muse – woman was the 'inspiration' of man. This language of abstraction concealed a pragmatic role for women in advising, challenging and supporting men, just as women in leading political families had done under earlier regimes. Republican women regarded politics very much as their business, then, but some women accepted a private and confidential political role, and hence a 'different' place for women within the Republic.

Women were deeply interested in the struggle for control of the Republic in the 1870s, and keen to be kept informed of developments.

This was reflected in the correspondence of Léon Gambetta, who was emerging as a Republican leader in this period. Gambetta responded to queries from a number of women, outlining the tactical battles in the Chamber of Deputies, reporting on the outcome of votes taken and on the prospect of Republican victories on forthcoming ones. He also sent out tickets to the public gallery when an interesting debate was looming.[51] Gambetta readily acknowledged the commitment to Republicanism that inspired women. As he wrote to Céline Scheurer-Kestner, wife of a Republican colleague, in 1874: 'I know too well, from experience, how passionate you are about all that concerns the destiny of the Fatherland, not to consider it a duty to keep you informed about whatever may threaten or improve it.'[52]

Gambetta's political relationship with Juliette Adam was particularly significant.[53] Her salon provided Gambetta with a forum for his ideas and the two debated political matters, particularly foreign affairs.[54] Assessing the results of the elections of 1874 in the southern Department of the *Alpes-Maritimes*, for instance, Gambetta wrote to Adam:

I wish to express my thanks for the various replies you gave to my questions. It's truly a report of a plenipotentiary minister, I have reflected on it at length and I am fully disposed to believe that our French friends acted imprudently in failing to attract the annexed Italian segment of the population[55] [. . .] After having ceded to you completely on this point, I nevertheless persist in believing that the hand of Mr. Bismarck has meddled in our affairs [. . .] How can you believe that he could remain inactive in such serious and important matters?[56]

Gambetta nicknamed Adam his 'beautiful Egeria', a reference to the water nymph consulted by King Numa in Roman legend.[57] This gave her the status of muse or oracle, and defined her perspective as particularly 'feminine'. She understood the politics of Bismarck better than 'many diplomats of the strong sex', he asserted, but she did so by 'feeling' or intuition: 'I place the greatest weight on your intuition (*sentiment*) as a Frenchwoman', he wrote, 'and I am ready to believe it much more infallible than all the arguments of the diplomats'.[58]

If Adam's perspective rested solely on intuition, it was superfluous to debate the relative merits of different policies with her. But Gambetta's belief in intellectual complementarity reflected the Republican view that sexual differentiation characterised all aspects of human life and even cosmic existence, just as it characterised every organ of the body. As Jules Michelet argued, there were 'two sexes of the mind', not just two sexes of the body. Women arrived at truth through feeling or emotion, while men arrived at truth through reason. Together they achieved the fullness of knowledge.[59]

Gambetta's belief in intellectual complementarity was also evident in his relationship with Léonie Léon, which lasted from 1872 until his sudden death in 1882.[60] It produced a correspondence in which passionate love was inseparable from a passion for politics, and in which the political partnership was framed as a sexual division of labour between male action and female inspiration. Gambetta assigned to Léonie Léon a key role in his political decision-making: by 'our foreign affairs', he noted, he meant 'ours, not those of the government'.[61] He reported to her on political events, sought her opinion constantly, and attributed many of his successes to her influence or inspiration. She was his 'inspiration', his 'guiding star' the 'inspiring genius' of his patriotism. Her 'infallible instinct' for politics was invaluable.[62]

Classical allusions provided the reference points for Gambetta's description of his 'special genius'. Léonie Léon resembled Andromaque, faithful and trustworthy companion, rather than Cassandra, whose insights went unheeded.[63] But the image of Minerva, goddess of war and symbol of knowledge and wisdom, was most frequently invoked to describe Léonie's role in Gambetta's political life. He wrote to her: 'You are for me the advisor who is always clear-sighted and steady [...] you are always the inspiration of my best deeds, the surest guide of my actions, and I love you as the enlightened Greeks used to love their own special genius, their own personal Minerva.'[64]

If Léonie Léon was frequently invoked as Muse, she nevertheless played a very real role in influencing Gambetta's political decisions. Her advice was critical, for instance, in 1878, when Gambetta briefly resolved to pay a visit to Bismarck in order to improve Franco–Prussian relations in the wake of the war of 1870. Gambetta wrote to Léonie:

> The most daring, and probably the most fruitful venture of my career, is born of your inspiration and of the clarity of your intelligence. Everything that happens and unfolds in this regard illustrates that you have read things correctly and that I would have searched elsewhere in vain for the means to raise up and restore our unfortunate and noble country.[65]

The precise nature of Léonie Léon's advice is unclear, although she certainly encouraged him to attend the Congress of Berlin which Bismarck was chairing. She may even have suggested he seek a personal interview with Bismarck.[66] But whatever her recommendation, her 'harangue' on the matter 'electrified' and initially persuaded Gambetta:

> I cede arms to wise Minerva; your final words have triumphed over my last hesitations, and if people are to gather in Berlin under the presidency of the Monster, one must be there, especially if the invitation comes from him. I spent the evening with the Minister and when I got home I found this wonderful and decisive letter; I made up my mind and am about to prepare the memo to defend the course of action (*sentiment d'action*) that you have so vigorously outlined. The terrible words, cowardice or aggression, sum up everything and I am going to prove how correct you are.[67]

'I am the disciple; you are the master', he noted.[68]

This episode is interesting because Gambetta's two 'muses' disagreed on this particular question. Léonie Léon's views conflicted with Juliette Adam's entrenched anti-Prussian stance, as well as with Gambetta's more pragmatic foreign policy. Despite being convinced by Léonie Léon at this point, Gambetta was eventually persuaded by Adam (and by his colleague, Eugène Spuller) not to undertake the venture.[69] Women's political views, rather than having special 'intuitive' qualities that made them 'infallible', were shaped by a variety of political perspectives just as men's were.

While Gambetta welcomed women as political confidantes, however, he did not support a public role for women in politics. He even insisted that women (apart from the hostess) be excluded from Republican salons.[70] Similarly, Jules Ferry made his wife Eugénie his political confidante, but he believed that her political acumen was unusual and consulted her only in private. He wrote to her in 1876: 'my darling, advise, give your opinion, your thoughts are sound, which can't be said of all women, not even the best'.[71]

From today's perspective, there appears to be a contradiction in the Republican leaders' stance. They opposed an overt political role for women while relying privately on women's political advice and affirmation. Gambetta and Ferry, at least, were fully cognisant of women's political interest, zeal and shrewdness. However, within the worldview that dominated nineteenth-century French Republicanism there was no such contradiction. 'Difference' was compatible with political insight, but it was not compatible with women filling the same political role as men. Many Republican women seem to have accepted the 'difference' model and to have valued their roles as political confidantes of their politician husbands.

Sexual difference and women's rights within the Republic

The Republicans' commitment to sexual difference helped shape the policies they implemented once they gained control of French political life in the late 1870s. They sought to enhance the position of women within society in ways dictated by their gendered vision. Their goal was to create mothers committed to the Republic and to their Republican husbands, who would devote themselves to the welfare and education of their children. A range of reforms directed at women was enacted between 1880 and the First World War.

Republican feminists contributed significantly to the impetus for change. Many feminist leaders in this period were the daughters, granddaughters or wives of Republican politicians.[72] They were committed to the Republic in principle, and believed that a philosophy dedicated to the rights of the individual should be receptive to women's claims for rights. Nevertheless, their close link to Republican politicians inhibited their tactics and agenda. They were reluctant to pursue policies that might destabilise the Republic, or bring comfort to anti-Republican forces. As a result they focused on civil rights and sought a gradual improvement in women's position. Their approach (which reflected the fact that the great majority of feminists were middle class) alienated working women, who organised instead within the socialist movement.[73]

By the turn of the twentieth century, a broad array of organisations participated in the campaign for women's rights. The majority pursued the gradualist approach pioneered by Maria Deraismes and her collaborator Léon Richer in the late 1870s. They described their approach as *la politique des brèches*. This meant chipping away at weak points in the structure where a 'breach' seemed possible, rather than making an all-out assault on the edifice of male superiority.[74] Such gradualist tactics were influential in expanding women's civil rights once the Republicans were in control. Feminists counted a number of laws as successes for this approach: secondary education for girls

(1880); the reintroduction of divorce (1884); laws allowing married women to control their own earnings (1907); laws increasing women's rights over their children (1906–1908); and the legalisation of paternity suits (1912).

As they contemplated and enacted such legislation, however, Republican men continually exhibited the tension between their philosophy of egalitarianism and their belief that women's 'difference' was incompatible with full equality. First, the Republicans' 'maternal' image of women shaped the legal reforms affecting working women in the pre-war period, as we saw in Chapter 2. Laws limiting women's working hours and protecting them in the workplace were designed predominantly to ensure the welfare of their children and to safeguard their childbearing potential. However, small family workshops in which most women were still employed were excluded from the provisions of this legislation.[75] The Republicans' defence of the rights of the *père de famille* within his own home clashed with their interest in overseeing women's childbearing function. Laws protecting women and children from exploitation, and setting up an emergent welfare system for those whose husbands and fathers were unable or unwilling to provide for them, also exposed the cracks in the idealised picture of the Republican family.

Reforms to girls' education also reflected the Republicans' commitment to a supportive and dependent role for women, rather than a desire to enhance their independence. Many Republicans believed that women were under the sway of the Catholic Church, that girls were inculcated with monarchist ideas and with an anti-rational and anti-progressive worldview in religious schools. Some also resented the pressure priests exerted on women in the confessional to obey Church teachings on sexual behaviour. Jules Michelet, writing in the 1860s, had described the priest as 'the secret enemy' of the husband.[76] Jules Ferry, the architect of the Republican education reforms, later argued: 'The bishops understand clearly: whoever controls the wife controls the husband [. . .] That is why the Church wants to hold onto women, and it's also why democracy must choose, under pain of death [. . . W]oman must belong either to Science or to the Church.'[77]

Republican policies on girls' education were therefore closely bound up with their anticlericalism, that is, with their battle to diminish the influence of the Catholic Church in French society. The Republicans put their faith in the secular school to transform women into suitable partners for 'men of progress' like themselves. In devising the Republican schooling system, Jules Ferry aimed to create 'Republican companions for Republican men'.[78] 'Republican companions' would be partners of men but under their authority, and the dignity and sexual prerogatives of the *père de famille* would be safeguarded.

Nevertheless, the establishment of the Republican schooling system greatly improved educational opportunities for girls. The laws of 1879–1882 made elementary education free and compulsory, and established a network of secular schools. Girls benefited, in particular, from the establishment of training institutions for female teachers, and the requirement that religious teachers hold a teaching certificate: in 1880, only 15 per cent of women teachers (who were mostly nuns) had a certificate of competence.[79]

The Republicans' establishment of a network of secular secondary schools for girls, enacted in 1880, was also a significant step for bourgeois girls (few workers of either sex received a secondary education in this period). Girls were not offered Latin and Greek and hence could not matriculate, but the new schools offered a broad curriculum in the sciences, languages, history and geography that expanded their horizons. In 1913, 19,700 girls were enrolled in high schools and colleges, and another 37,800 were attending upper primary schools.[80] Camille Sée, architect of the law, saw his task as preparing girls to be 'mothers of men'.[81] Nevertheless, the reforms undermined the assumption that they were destined irrevocably for domestic life.[82] The problem would be to contain girls' ambitions and expectations within the limits set by 'difference'.

The Republicans remained ambivalent about the implications of educating women. Jules Ferry rejected the belief that women were intellectually inferior to men, though he did not go so far as denying the significance of 'difference'. He advised women to read John Stuart Mill's *The Subjection of Women*, observing:

> [Y]ou accept this subjection of woman, based on her intellectual inferiority, and people have repeated it to you so often that you have ended up believing it. But you are wrong, ladies, believe me [... Mill] will teach you that you have the same faculties as men [...] it is impossible to say, given the current state of their education, that [women] won't be something else, when they are raised differently. Therefore, given our ignorance of the true aptitudes of woman, we don't have the right to mutilate her.[83]

Nevertheless, Ferry did not wish to 'create learned women, unbelieving women'. He merely sought to ensure that 'the habit of reasoning, the scientific method, should penetrate women's education a little more than it has until now'.[84]

Political pragmatism may explain Ferry's caution in envisaging a radical change in girls' education because he needed to ensure a broad coalition to push through his reforms. However, a sense of 'the eternal feminine' remained influential in his thinking. Girls now had access to a career in school teaching. By 1906, about 78,000 authorised women teachers were working in state schools, and a further 5000 in religious schools.[85] But women's potential as teachers rested not on their intellectual ability, in Ferry's view, but on their innate maternal sentiment. He declared:

> Gentlemen, I myself am profoundly convinced of the superiority of woman as far as teaching is concerned. It is a general law that maternal sentiment is the most fundamental resource of education, that the woman teacher who remains unmarried finds in teaching other people's children the fulfilment of this maternal sentiment, of this great instinct of sacrifice which every woman bears within her, that nature has engraved on your hearts, ladies, and which constitutes the nobility, the dignity and the power of your social action.[86]

A career in teaching was envisaged as an alternative expression of motherhood for the single woman. Women's fitness for it was determined not by their intellect but by sentiment.

Other professions were harder to envisage in maternal terms, and were opened to women in a piecemeal manner during the early Third Republic. Women who sought careers in law and medicine had to study privately, since girls' schools did not prepare them for the *baccalauréat* until 1924.[87] They then had to confront protests and riots by male students opposed to their presence at university. In 1895, 842 women were enrolled in degree courses. The first woman lawyer graduated in 1892, but women were not admitted to the bar until 1900. The first woman doctor graduated in 1875, and in 1914 there were 400 women in medical school. But a long struggle was required before women gained access to the residency and internship periods essential for becoming fully qualified. Male interns campaigned against women's admission on the grounds that they lacked the necessary 'masculine' qualities of strength, courage,

independence and judgement.[88] The incompatibility between medicine and motherhood was emphasised in Camille Pert's 'Practical
Guide' for women in 1901:

> Familial and maternal tasks are hardly compatible with the
> professional duties of the doctor, and even less with the obliga-
> tions of the woman student. Medical studies will occupy the
> years designated for motherhood in women. Those who devote
> themselves to medicine regarding it as the moral purpose of their
> existence, and the material basis of their life, will therefore almost
> always have to renounce motherhood, which could only hinder
> their career without being exercised in the favourable conditions
> it demands.[89]

By conforming to the 'maternal' image, however, women were able
to carve out a niche for themselves in the profession. The ninety-five
women practising medicine in France in 1903 worked mainly in
maternal and child health.[90]

Women's entry into journalism posed a specific challenge to the
ideal of the domestic and dependent woman. The first feminist daily
newspaper, *La Fronde*, launched in 1897, was staffed and produced
entirely by women. This meant that women journalists covered all
subjects, including politics, crime, finance, sport and international
affairs. Its director, Marguerite Durand, had to get permission for
women to enter previously exclusive male worlds like the Stock
Exchange, the Senate and Chamber of Deputies, and municipal and
departmental councils. *La Fronde* played an important role in creating
an image of women as interested in and knowledgeable about a
range of public affairs.[91] By 1914, the consequences of opening up
secondary education and the professions to women were beginning
to be noticeable, but the implications of this change for a social model
based on 'difference' remained to be addressed.

The suffrage question, 1880–1914

In the nineteenth century, the majority of French feminists did not
give suffrage the priority it assumed elsewhere. Their gradualist tactics
led them to defer the claim for the vote: a response to the political
situation in early Third Republic France. At the Paris Exhibition of
1878 that marked the rebirth of an organised feminist movement

after years of repression, Marie Deraismes and Léon Richer confined discussion to civil rights in the hope of government tolerance.[92] This decision was opposed by Hubertine Auclert, whose name became synonymous with suffragism in the 1880s. Auclert insisted on the need to pursue female suffrage first and foremost:

> Political rights are the keystone that will [...] guarantee all other rights. As long as woman does not possess this weapon – the vote – she will be forced to submit to the system of patriarchy. All her efforts to conquer her civil and economic freedom will be in vain.[93]

Once women voted, Auclert argued, they would set their own agenda and their interests would carry greater weight with male politicians. For many years her argument had little impact. By the early twentieth century, however, even moderate feminist organisations had come to support suffragism, despite remaining cautious about the tactics to achieve it. The fact that some Catholic women had begun campaigning for female suffrage stung them into action in order to demonstrate their 'progressive' politics.[94]

Suffragists in the pre-war years rested their case on natural justice and consistency with Republican principles. The French Union for Women's Suffrage (UFSF), founded in 1909, quoted the Declaration of the Rights of Man and Citizen, making the egalitarian foundations of Republicanism the basis for their claim. But they also mustered pragmatic arguments in their cause. Like Hubertine Auclert before them, they pointed to the injustice of classing women as citizens for purposes of levying taxation or punishing their crimes, but not for purposes of enacting laws or consenting to taxation.[95] Besides, French suffragists listed the measures supported by women voters in other countries, arguing that the social effects of female suffrage would be beneficial for France too. The USFS branch in Besançon argued in 1913:

> All women will *want* to:
> *Fight against alcoholism*, from which they suffer much more than men;
> Establish laws of hygiene and public assistance;
> Obtain the regulation of women's and children's labour;
> Defend young girls against prostitution;
> Finally prevent wars and submit disagreements among peoples to arbitration courts.[96]

In making this case, suffragists emphasised the benefits to be derived from women's 'difference' and from their unique perspective as moralising agents in society.

The question of women's 'difference' from men also underpinned the arguments of opponents of female suffrage. 'Woman's nature', meaning particularly her destiny for motherhood and family life, was seen as disqualifying women from political participation. A feminist pamphlet summed up this argument in order to challenge it:

> Because of her natural aptitudes, which are completely different from those of man, and entirely oriented toward life in the home, woman does not understand and will never understand politics. She is unsuited to the functions of governing and administering the country and the city.[97]

Opponents of female suffrage argued that it threatened women's 'essential functions' and hence 'the race'.[98] It challenged a 'natural' hierarchy between the sexes, they claimed, dividing families and introducing political conflict into the home.[99]

Suffragists had simple replies to these objections. Women's reproductive role would hardly suffer from 'duties' exercised once every two years, they noted. Voting would not inhibit women's role as mothers, therefore, any more than it hampered men in their roles as doctors or lawyers. Feminists insisted that 'family harmony cannot be bought at the price of women's silence and subjection'. They argued that it was in the interests of the family and the race that woman, 'the mother and educator of tomorrow's men', should exercise all her faculties and all her talents.[100] And if women did not pay the 'blood tax' of military service, suffragists noted, they paid an even higher 'blood tax' in bearing sons to defend the country.[101]

But the key question was whether women's 'difference' had political significance at all. Ferdinand Buisson, Radical Republican Deputy for the Seine, and one of a minority of Radicals who supported female suffrage, argued that it did not. Buisson headed the Commission on Universal Suffrage and in 1911 produced a lengthy review of the operation of female suffrage elsewhere in the world. He quoted approvingly the claim that 'woman is different and even opposite [to man] in nature, but of equivalent value', adding: 'Equality does not imply identity [...] And it is not necessary that woman be the same as man to be his equal.'[102] Where he defined 'difference' as irrelevant, however, the UFSF used it to justify their claim that men could not represent them: 'In fact, *since woman has her aptitudes, her tendencies, her particular ways of thinking and feeling, by what right does man claim to speak in her name*, since he can only express his own ideas, his desires, his own feelings?'[103]

The most popular argument against women's suffrage, especially in the ranks of the Radical Republicans, stemmed not from philosophical conviction but from political expediency. Ferdinand Buisson summarised that argument:

> Giving women the vote at the local or State level, would throw onto the electoral scales an enormous weight that would lean to the side of reaction. This is not to claim that woman is inherently conservative and set in her ways. But until now, in France, she has remained under the influence, or even under the domination of the clergy.[104]

Georges Clemenceau, leader of the Radical Party and Prime Minister from 1906 to 1910, stated bluntly: 'The number of women who escape from the domination of the clergy is ridiculously low. If the right to vote were given to women tomorrow, France would all of a sudden jump backwards into the Middle Ages.'[105] Clerical domination of women was seen as a factor distinguishing France from states that had already given women the vote, which were overwhelmingly Protestant.

If women's 'clericalism' was the real issue worrying Republican men, we might expect that clerics themselves would have been denied the vote as enemies of the Republic. But this was not the case. Maria Deraismes had made the point in 1879: 'One would be led to believe that clericalism was the invention of women. But who really introduced the priest into politics? Who made him an elector, a deputy, a senator, if it is not the Constitution that was drafted by men?'[106] Priests had inalienable rights as citizens that permitted them to oppose the Republic legally, while the fear that women might do so was used to deny them the vote. We might also expect that the Republicans' faith in their secular schools would have produced a politics of gradualism on the question of female suffrage. But this was not the case either.

The increasing influence of the 'Radical Republicans', who dominated the Chamber of Deputies and governing Cabinets by the turn of the twentieth century, was a major factor in delaying bills on women's suffrage or rejecting the possibility outright.[107] Their militant anticlericalism, and the hostile views of their provincial lower middle-class constituency, produced a strong resistance to the idea of votes for women. There were exceptions like Ferdinand Buisson, but the fervently anti-suffrage views of Georges Clemenceau were more widely shared. Feminists noted the self-interest that lay behind the Radicals' position:

> The deeper cause hidden behind this objection is the opposition that all parties in power, in every country, always present to demands for the extension of the suffrage, for fear of losing their majority. And without denying the value of the ideas which they serve, let us nevertheless note that this excuse of political interest has nothing in common (as several of their members admit themselves) with right and justice, with the democratic principles they proclaim.[108]

The fear that women would vote as the priests instructed was no doubt genuine for many Republicans, highlighting a deep-seated male anxiety over control of women. More fundamentally, however, Republican men continued to regard suffrage as a masculine prerogative for which no amount of 're-education' could prepare women. The image of the citizen remained the self-governing, free-thinking and rational male – a self-image to which even the most lowly and impoverished Republican man could aspire, and which gained force by its contrast to the image of the dependent woman under his authority.

Part III
Women in the Era of the Great Wars, 1890–1944

6 'New Women' in the Era of the Great War, 1890s–1920s

The Great War of 1914–1918 brought to an end the 'Belle Epoque', the quarter-century before the war when life for Europe's bourgeoisie reached its finest flowering. The war dramatically affected European and world history. It undermined assumptions about Europe's 'civilised' values.[1] In France, where much of the conflict took place, the war left an impact that can still be distinguished today.[2]

For French men, the First World War marked a rupture with normal life. More than eight million men aged between 18 and 46 were mobilised, and 43 per cent of the male population fought in the trenches. Of that number 17 per cent (1.4 million) never returned, and those that did were scarred and traumatised psychologically, if not physically. Overall, 63 per cent of Frenchmen of mobilisation age were killed or mutilated.[3] The impact of this fact on France in the 1920s cannot be underestimated.

Women were not isolated from the war or immune to its effects. They lived without men for four years, and many suffered the loss of fathers, sons, husbands and brothers. But, as feminist historians note, the periodisation of women's history has often differed markedly from that of men.[4] To understand the patterns in women's lives at the turn of the twentieth century, we need to focus not just on the war years themselves, though these were particularly significant, but on the period from 1890 to the late 1920s. In cultural terms, these years formed a more coherent whole for women than for men, and the war had the effect of accentuating developments already in train in 1914.

The 'modern' woman – educated, employed in white-collar or professional work, wearing 'sensible dress', and more independent than the 'traditional' woman – made her appearance amongst urban elites before the war. Her appearance contributed to, and symbolised, the collapse of the cultural certainties that had shaped the world of the Belle Epoque. Like the new generation of writers, composers and artists who overturned creative conventions in this period, the 'modern woman' was culturally threatening, if not as immediately dangerous as the strikers and anarchist bombers who challenged the power structures of the Third Republic. She rattled the cage of 'traditional' womanhood, and hence the gender structure on which bourgeois society was built.

War strengthened the movement for change in women's social position, at least by default. Rich or poor, urban or rural, women took on new roles and assumed new responsibilities. Some did so eagerly, others because there was no alternative. As France faced the new conditions of the post-war world, therefore, the question of women's place in that world was central. The aspirations of 'new women' were opposed by those who desired a society with distinct male and female roles. This pattern of sexual relations seemed to promise normalcy and security in a world shattered by conflict. The 1920s were therefore marked, not by the triumph of 'new women', though they refused to go away, but by ongoing tension over women's appropriate roles.

The changing lives of women in the Belle Epoque

In 1883, Emile Zola's new novel *Au Bonheur des Dames* addressed a popular theme. This novel ('Ladies' Delight' or 'Ladies' Paradise' in English) was the story of a department store closely modelled on the Paris icon, the Bon Marché. Zola's novel vividly portrayed the irrational and impulsive behaviour, the temptation to indulge to excess, the narcissism and self-gratification, which the department store supposedly fostered. Its main characters were women. By the Belle Epoque, shopping had become a pastime for well-to-do women, and the 'consumer' or 'shopper' was one image that defined the 'modern' woman. If the modern man was portrayed as a *flâneur*, who strolled the urban streets as spectator and observer, the female shopper was perceived as a *flâneuse*, who explored the commodities on display in the department store as shopper and consumer.[5]

Bourgeois women had long been consumers of luxuries. Their roles in purchasing commodities and decorating their homes were seen to have cultural value, creating work for others and establishing their family's place within bourgeois society.[6] Mass production made available a wide array of goods at cheaper prices, and created a broader social range of consumers: a trend disturbing to those who feared the blurring of class boundaries.[7] Anxieties about the new consumer-driven world were expressed in negative representations of women as consumers. Like Zola, psychologists and doctors warned of real dangers in unrestrained consumption by women. The upsurge in kleptomania in this period was attributed to women's inability to resist the temptations posed by the new shopping experience. Kleptomania was a 'modern' disease, and it was also coded 'female'.[8] Anxiety followed, therefore, as women carved out new roles in the public domain, or as a new society evolved in which women played central roles.

The suggestion that a 'new woman' might be replacing the familiar one by the late nineteenth century brought even greater consternation. Some women had begun to envisage themselves in this guise. For instance, when some anonymous male correspondents of the feminist paper *La Fronde* asked its readers in 1899 what they thought of men, one woman replied: 'Are you addressing the Woman of the Past (*la Femme Ancienne*), gentlemen, or the New Woman?'[9] 'New Women' were identified by their appearance which, along with their freer lifestyles, indicated a new set of aspirations and expectations. The fact that those aspirations were exhibited on the body – in their hairstyles and dress – made them highly visible and controversial. The physical appearance of the 'new woman' was a statement of her autonomy and her desire to live a new kind of life. That desire threatened the balance of relations between the sexes. While 'new women' were confined to a small elite in the pre-war years, their presence brought a strong reaction from all who feared the demise of the dependent and domestic woman.

Changes in fashion were the first sign of the emergence of the 'new woman'. The dress reform movement had accelerated from the 1880s in response to the exaggerated ornamentation of bourgeois women's dress, with its voluminous skirts and its assortment of decorative bows, bustles and trains. Besides, white-collar and professional women, who were becoming more numerous in this period, required a practical form of dress. Tailored suits became fashionable for daytime wear, although high collars ensured that women's bodies remained covered, and until about 1910 stays ensured that they conformed to the requisite hour-glass shape.

Changes in clothing were accompanied by changes in hairstyles. Belle Epoque hairstyles were elaborate to complement the extravagance of bourgeois dress, with false hairpieces to increase volume, and extensive use of combs, feathers, fruits and flowers as ornamentation. The shift towards simpler dress was accompanied, then, by a 'modernist' challenge to 'classicist' hairstyling. Hair tinting became more common, especially after the invention of L'Oréal's safe and durable colour in 1909. The avant-garde began to make their mark with blue and green tresses. Whereas washing the hair was considered a health risk in the nineteenth century, regular shampooing at the salon became fashionable. The permanent wave was all the rage, suiting the desire of increasing numbers of fashionable women for simple and convenient hairstyles.[10] Emile Long, a leading Paris hairdresser, noted in 1911: 'Ladies [...] prefer their coiffures to look simple; they reject any complications, because this would no longer be in keeping with the outline of their garments, and especially with the modern bearing and gait.'[11]

Short hair for women also began to make its appearance in the early years of the twentieth century. This was particularly shocking because short hair was culturally associated with masculinity. Noting this trend, Emile Long associated it with a change in relations between the sexes: 'Whilst gentlemen are permitting their hair to grow in order that they may curl and dress it after the style of the 1830s, ladies will cut theirs, so that they may curl it, too, and so contribute to the equalization of the sexes, which is their dream and ambition.'[12]

In identifying something described as a 'modern bearing and gait', Long also identified a shift in the aesthetics of the feminine ideal. This, too, marked a change in the power relations between the sexes. As Hollander has argued, between 1910 and 1915 the ideal shape of women's bodies was transformed. The hour-glass image, achieved by means of a rigid undergarments, gave way to the disappearing bustline and waist that would denote elegance in the 1920s. The volume of female clothing was reduced, dresses became shorter, undergarments less restrictive, fabrics thinner and more transparent. The physical distance between the sexes, maintained and expressed by the rigidity and cumbersomeness of clothing, was diminished. A 'modern' female image marked by the visibility of feet and legs – by a sense of movement – began to appear.[13]

The new cultural image of mobile and agile women was high-lighted by their participation in a diverse array of leisure pursuits in the Belle Epoque. Bourgeois girls had long been restricted by adult fears for their 'delicacy', and a concern to instil modesty and physical restraint. The range of acceptable activities was still limited in the Belle Epoque, but well-to-do women nevertheless took up a number of new pursuits. They flew airplanes, rode bicycles, played golf, sailed yachts, and drove automobiles. Some even took up weightlifting.[14] The Duchess d'Uzès was the first woman to gain her driver's licence in 1893, and Mme Camille du Gast competed in the 1903 Paris-Madrid Rally.[15]

La Fronde proclaimed in 1897:

Sport and Women! Two words that clashed when they were put together just a decade ago and which, today, evoke only very pleasant and very gracious images. Illustrations and sculpture have popularised the harmonious and slender lines of our women cyclists and yachtswomen. Tennis, horseriding, hunting, even the motor car, have thousands and thousands of practitioners in feminine circles.[16]

La Fronde ran a regular Thursday supplement on 'Games and Sports'.[17] It recommended appropriate forms of dress for a range of fashionable activities, thereby linking changes in women's lifestyles with the consumer revolution that was also gaining momentum at the turn of the twentieth century.[18]

The bicycle was the most significant invention for women in this period because it brought them the opportunity for physical mobility and independence. It was not just a mode of transport, but a source of liberation.[19] Advertising posters for bicycles frequently used female models. The intention may not have been to foster female independence, but the images of abandon and escape they presented were appealing to women. By 1902, France had one bicycle for every 32 inhabitants.[20] Sales statistics do not distinguish by sex, but women were recognised as a potential market to be tapped and Touring Clubs had many women members in the 1890s.[21]

The woman cyclist also made her appearance in the literature of the day. One of Proust's heroines in his multi-volume novel, *A la Recherche du Temps Perdu*, was the young Albertine, introduced to the reader as she wheeled her bicycle along with her 'gang' of friends. Albertine was described as:

> a girl with brilliant, laughing eyes and plump, matt cheeks, a black polo-cap crammed on her head, who was pushing a bicycle with such an uninhibited swing of the hips, and using slang terms so typical of the gutter and shouting so loudly when I passed her (although among her expressions I caught that tiresome phrase 'living one's own life') that [...] I concluded [...] that all these girls belonged to the population which frequents the velodromes, and must be the very juvenile mistresses of racing cyclists.[22]

These were not the modest, sedate and sheltered young women of 'times past'. Rather, Proust linked the bicycle with female immorality, and a claim for independence that was already 'tiresome'.

Journalists and cartoonists of the 1880s and 1890s satirised the woman cyclist just as those of the 1830s and 1840s had satirised the 'liberated' women of that period.[23] A survey of publications for the year 1889 listed riding a bicycle as one of the three faults that identified the 'new woman'.[24] The controversy surrounding the woman cyclist illustrated anxiety about the breakdown of 'natural' sex differences and appropriate sex roles. Much comment focused on women's health, and attempted to reassert the norm of female weakness and physical incompetence which the female cyclist was undermining. Commentators suggested that women cyclists should always be 'protected' by a male companion. Even doctors who favoured cycling as a means to improve women's health set limits for them: no cycling during pregnancy or when menstruating; no trips of more than 40 or 50 kilometres; and a gynaecological examination before taking up the sport! Above all, they prohibited competitive racing, although it took some years for this prohibition to come into effect. Until that time (1912), women performed creditably in both road and track events, with times close to those of male competitors.[25] *La Fronde*, for one, reported on women racers like Louise Roger and 'little Lisette'.[26]

The debate about female cycling, or about women and sport in general, focused on normative patterns of femininity. Public acceptance depended upon the compatibility of particular activities with a poorly defined but compelling distinction between 'feminine' and 'masculine' pursuits. Competitive sport, in particular, was a hallmark of masculinity, requiring proof of strength, aggression and courage.

In the late nineteenth century, it was linked to the project of rebuilding male self-confidence and military strength following the defeat of 1870, and to the colonial conquest. The sporting arena doubled as a training ground for the battlefield, where women had no place.[27] The revival of the Olympic Games in 1896 was intended to promote male physical and moral fibre, therefore, and women were excluded.[28]

If the quintessential male role was to be victorious in battle, the quintessential female role in an era obsessed with fears of 'depopulation' was to marry and have children. Arguments supporting sporting activities for women were often couched, therefore, in terms of their contribution to female reproductive health. Doctors favourable to female cycling declared that it would make women better child bearers. One advertisement, mindful of this debate, portrayed a woman cycling whilst breastfeeding a baby, so easy was this particular bicycle to control![29] In advocating sport for girls, too, *La Fronde* rejected 'masculine' activities like boxing and football in favour of 'cycling, gymnastics, tennis, fencing and skating'. These would 'regenerate' women, producing 'impeccable mothers and good wives', yet allowing young women 'a little of that liberty which we have begun to allow boys'.[30]

Female sport added to the debate over clothing, and accentuated the association between clothing and power. Culottes or bloomers for cycling were controversial, as was the 'harem skirt' created in 1911 for dancing the tango.[31] The possibility that women might begin wearing culottes as a matter of course horrified even some women, and the authorities issued a directive in 1892 permitting such garments only for cycling.[32] Culottes, and the visibility of women's calves, aroused fears of a loss of feminine modesty and reserve.They suggested a more sexual and independent woman, associating this image with supposedly 'respectable' bourgeois women rather than with women of 'ill-repute', as in the past.

Cycling presented new opportunities for women to escape surveillance, accentuating concerns about female sexual behaviour. The woman on a bicycle evaded the constraints that had surrounded women in the age of chaperones and limited female access to public space. Advertisements emphasised the 'intense pleasure' of riding a bicycle, employing the same term used to refer to sexual pleasure. Doctors debated whether the movement of pedalling produced pleasurable sensations in women, raising fears about nymphomania and leading some priests to declare that women cyclists would burn in hell for their sins.[33]

Not only was the female cyclist free of male supervision, then, she was free to experience sexual pleasure that did not depend on men. This nightmare scenario was reflected in advertisements and post-cards portraying female cyclists in compromising situations, not only with their male suitors, but with other women. The linkage between cycling and lesbianism was explored in Proust's novel cited above: women who ignored the accepted conventions of behaviour were portrayed as keen on either or both these activities, and Proust's protagonist Albertine was constantly forced to deny that she favoured 'that sort of thing'.[34] The moral panic generated by the female cyclist betrayed a deep anxiety about female freedom, about sexual freedom in particular, and about men's loss of control over women.

The link between clothing, sexuality and female independence associated with the bicycle was widely perceived and brought diverse reactions. Madame Gaches-Sarraute, a medical doctor, observed:

> If, as I believe, woman has above all seen an element of liberation in the bicycle, it was quite natural that she should demand the right to wear the outfit of her companion when practising this sport, because man alone has been free until now, and he has made his clothing a symbol of his freedom.[35]

More hostile commentators predicted that women cyclists would become 'virile' or even become 'a third sex' who switched sexes as they switched from skirts to riding outfits: an image illustrating the strong association between the wearing of trousers and masculin-ity.[36] Sarah Bernhardt, a leading actress and hardly a model of maternal domesticity, also saw the trend as fraught with danger:

> I believe that the bicycle is transforming our morals more pro-foundly than people generally seem to realise. All these young women, all these young girls who go off roaming the wide-open spaces largely renounce life in the home, family life [...] Moral considerations must prevail and I believe that this life in the open air, for which the bicycle multiplies the opportunities, may have dangerous and serious consequences.[37]

Translated literally, Bernhardt referred to women 'devouring space', an expression which conjures up images of women hungry to explore the world and enjoy the thrill of speed. It was precisely this

aspect that other women welcomed. For J. Hudry-Menos the speedy
cyclist defined the 'modern woman':

> Here she is in the saddle, a turn of the pedal and her bicycle
> carries her off so quickly that she is already out of sight.

> Skating first procured for us a foretaste of this mad flight across
> space, an immaterial flight which gives the whole organism a
> sense of intense life.[38]

The sense that the bicycle 'freed' woman 'from the prejudices
which made her an unfortunate recluse destined only to care for
children and do the cooking'[39] thus aroused the concerns of traditionalists and the admiration of feminists. Both reactions illustrate
the perception that women's lifestyles were beginning to change
even before the First World War. By 1900, *La Fronde* was declaring:
'The *Parisienne* of today goes everywhere, does everything, is interested
in everything. Her life has changed completely.'[40]

Women's roles in the war years

Germany declared war on France on 3 August 1914. The following
day the German army swept rapidly through Belgium and into
France. The French victory at the first Battle of the Marne in
September halted the German advance towards Paris, but the battle
front was nevertheless only 90 kilometres from the capital. The
initial reaction to this situation for many people was shock and fear.
The general mobilisation of French forces on 1 August had suggested
that war was threatening, but the German advance was nevertheless
unexpected. Catherine and Auguste Santerre, agricultural labourers
in Normandy, were working in the fields when the alarm rang on
3 August. 'What war?', they asked as they joined the crowd fleeing
back to the farm.[41] And it was not only rural illiterates who were
taken by surprise about developments in far-off Sarajevo. As Françoise
Thébaud remarks, Parisians were busy planning their summer
holidays. They were distracted from international affairs by the trial
of Henriette Caillaux, wife of a cabinet minister, for the murder of
the editor of *Figaro*. War was the last thing on the minds of most.[42]

Despite reluctant separations, the mobilisation proceeded
smoothly. The war was presented to the French public as an act of

German aggression, making defence of the nation a patriotic duty. There was no need for the government to implement the emergency measures it had devised in case of public resistance. As young men assembled at the recruiting stations they reiterated the widespread optimism that the war would be won quickly and they would be home by Christmas.[43] Unfortunately, however, military tactics had not kept pace with advances in weaponry. The horrors of trench warfare, broken only by suicidal assaults, comprised the experience of male combatants for the next four years.

The war affected women on the 'home front' in diverse ways, but invariably required them to adopt new roles and act more independently than in the past. Thousands of women and children became refugees in northern France as they tried to escape hostilities or were ordered out of the combat zone by the military. The battle of Verdun in 1916 saw 600,000 uprooted; the second Battle of the Marne in 1918 another 700,000. Some towns remained in the firing line for years. Reims, for instance, was bombarded almost constantly. About 20,000 civilians lived underground in the champagne cellars, maintaining schools, shops and church services as best they could, until they were evacuated in 1917.[44]

More than two million French people in 10 Departments, mostly women, lived under occupation. Normal economic life was shut down, and hunger was soon the dominant concern. Food and valuables were requisitioned. People ate whatever they could find or steal, even the hay fed to the officers' horses. Some young women were deported from their homes to work in other parts of the occupied zone: a practice which only ceased following a massive international outcry. Other women were required to do forced labour in their own villages, working up to 13 hours a day in the fields to feed the German army. The movement of the population was closely controlled, and infractions of the occupiers' rules brought fines, imprisonment or beatings. Few families were able to communicate with their loved ones elsewhere, especially with men at the front.[45]

In some areas women were raped, even gang-raped, during the invasion. Rape was recognised as a way of demonstrating German prowess over French men, who were unable to protect French women. It was widely reported in the press, along with other atrocities, to demonstrate the 'barbarism' of the enemy. The rape of women also became a metaphor for the 'rape' of Belgium and France, and helped justify France's claim to be the victim of German aggression. The fate of real women was sometimes lost sight of in this discourse. But an anguished public debate over 'the children of the enemy' resulted in policies enabling women pregnant from such attacks to give birth, where possible, in secrecy and surrender the infants to orphanages.[46]

Conditions were less severe outside the occupied zone, though the demands on women's labour were enormous everywhere. War broke out at harvest time, the busiest time of year in rural France. On 7 August, Prime Minister Viviani summoned women and children to become warriors on the home front: 'Rise up, women and children of France, daughters and sons of the nation. Take the place in the field of labor of those who are now on the field of battle.'[47] But they had already done so. Across the country observers reported:

'Women in large numbers brought in the harvest'; 'Women, old people and children were anxious to finish the harvest and get on with the sowing'[. . .] 'Women, children, old people all set to work [. . .] to take the place of the men on the farms and in the fields'.[48]

Farming was not a reserved occupation so few farmers were exempt from military service. For the next four years, responsibility for feeding the country lay primarily with 3.2 million women, aided by men too young or too old for military service.

Women added men's jobs to their already extensive responsibilities on the farm. Many of their new tasks were designated 'male' because they demanded considerable strength. They were even more difficult given that horses were requisitioned for the war.[49] Women and teenagers kept farms going against the odds because idle farms could be requisitioned. With her brother and brother-in-law at the front, for instance, Emilie Carles worked the farm with her elderly father and young sister: 'I had seventy-five sheep, eight cows, I made the butter in a hand churn, I took care of the hay and the harvests, I was sixteen years old.'[50] Nevertheless, the efforts of women and youths could not ultimately be sustained. Harvests gradually declined in quality and quantity over the next four years. Women's health was also affected, with miscarriages and stillbirths common.[51]

Urban women faced different problems in the absence of fathers and husbands. Unlike rural women they could not provide their own food, so earning an income to feed their families was the first priority. Women comprised about a third of the industrial workforce before the war. But many of their jobs, especially in the luxury goods sector, disappeared as the industrial economy was reshaped for war production. The first impact on urban working women, then, was unemployment. Gradually they were re-employed in sectors that were previously male preserves. Female workers at the Renault motor plant rose from 4 to 32 per cent of its workforce. Women became dockworkers for the first time, and moved into the chemicals, soap and drugs industries in more significant numbers. In August 1914 they were authorised to become conductors and drivers of trains and trams. Their visibility in these roles helped create the impression that women were newly becoming workers. The number of women employed on the railways rose from 8 to 14 per cent of its workforce during the war years.[52]

The most controversial form of employment for women was in the munitions and war industries. Employers hired women as a last resort, and only after all other possibilities had been exhausted.[53] By 1918, 119,966 women were employed in the metals industry compared with 17,731 before the war, an increase of 650 per cent. Of these, 362,000 worked in war factories (684,000 women were employed in this sector at some stage of the war). Women comprised one-third of armaments workers in the Paris region, the heartland of war production. Their contribution enabled massive increases in production of armaments and ammunition. As General Joffre acknowledged, if women had left the war factories, France would have lost the war.[54]

Women were attracted to war work, at least initially, by the high rates of pay compared with traditional female industries. Most had never worked in industry before and had no experience of operating industrial machinery. They therefore performed the least-skilled jobs. The work was difficult and conditions of employment were terrible. Pre-war regulations governing the workplace were suspended, allowing nightshifts of up to 14 hours. Women often finished such shifts in time to undertake domestic tasks, queuing for lengthy periods to buy rations and returning to work without proper rest. The number of workplace accidents – 69,606 in 1917 – may have reflected this fact.[55] Marcelle Capy, a trade unionist and pacifist who worked incognito in a factory for a period, wrote: 'Never say that women factory workers are privileged. Never make light of their sufferings. Never judge their work lightly. Say what I say at this moment: one must be hungry to do this job.'[56] Trade unions accused women of accepting conditions that male workers would not have tolerated. Women did protest to their employers and petition the authorities, but often preferred to seek work elsewhere. From 1916, they began to participate in strikes over their poor conditions.[57]

Employers took the opportunity presented by the war to economise on labour costs. As well as paying women less than men doing the same tasks, they reduced staffing levels. On the Paris Métro, for instance, women were one franc per day cheaper than men, and 11,000 men were replaced by 7000 women. In the postal and telegraph service, 11,000 women replaced 18,000 men. Employers also appreciated the 'docility' of women workers. Moreover, in retaining the differentials between male and female rates (despite government directives requiring the same rates), and in confining women to unskilled and repetitive tasks, employers ensured that sex-based distinctions in the labour force would be preserved in the post-war period.[58]

Professional and white-collar workers faced less onerous tasks than industrial workers, but they too saw their lives transformed by war. Women teachers began to teach boys, and to assume positions of responsibility. The woman teacher often became the voice of officialdom in her village, acting as go-between with Paris, signing official documents and completing official reports. Staff shortages sped up the entry of women into higher-level jobs in commerce and administration. However, women in such posts were referred to as 'substitutes' to indicate their temporary tenure of such posts.[59]

The lives of those on the 'home front' were often difficult, despite literature claiming that women were 'living it up' in their husbands' absence. Wives of servicemen received an allowance of 1.25 francs per day, plus 50 centimes per day for each child under 16. This payment was often more than rural labourers had earned before the war, but they had been able to live outside the cash economy to a considerable extent. For urban families, however, allowances were often substantially lower than the earnings of a skilled male worker in 1914.[60] Those in de facto relationships received nothing, and nor did dependent mothers or sisters.[61] A decline in income for urban families coincided with steeply rising prices for necessities, making their lives precarious.

Despite the moratorium on rents, purchasing power in Paris dropped by 10.5 per cent between 1914 and the end of 1916.[62] Like their foremothers in subsistence crises of earlier centuries, women mobilised against profiteering and marched on town halls to demand relief. The sharp price increases in the spring of 1917 were the last straw for many. By May 1917 coal was three times its pre-war price, and butter, eggs and cheese had doubled in price. Necessities like meat and sugar were in very short supply and milk was rationed.[63] One housewife and mother of three petitioned her local representative in July:

> We are tired of our life of hardship and deprivation. The situation is becoming serious and is no longer tenable when we are forced to deprive our children of the most basic necessities. *Monsieur le Député*, would you yourself be able to live on 1.25 francs a day and feed your children on the modest sum of 75 centimes. They must not only be fed, but clothed and provided with shoes etc [...] No money, no credit, we will soon be forced to resort to pillage to live, if someone doesn't help us [...] We ask for 2 francs for the mothers and an increase of one franc for the children.[64]

Civilian exasperation, spurred by news of the failure of yet another 'final' offensive, erupted in a series of major strikes in 1917. Women shouted 'give us coal or give us back our husbands'. A significant wage increase in a number of industries followed, although prices continued to rise.[65]

Middle-class and aristocratic women also threw themselves into war work in significant numbers, but as volunteers rather than through economic necessity. They organised charitable organisations to support soldiers and their families, held sewing and knitting bees, and organised a pen-friend system, the *marraines* or 'godmothers', who wrote to soldiers regularly. Volunteer nursing also attracted large numbers of women. By 1918 the Service for Military Health controlled 120,000 women, of whom 30,000 were salaried employees and 70,000 volunteers. Most nurses worked outside war zones where the wounded were evacuated, but with the creation of mobile field hospitals in 1915, nurses also worked under fire and some were killed.[66]

Gender relations during the war

Women's roles in and experiences of the war were diverse, but the emotional impact of the war on the community overrode its varied socio-economic impacts. For four years, the adult male population was largely removed from French society, which became a world of women. Men had only a transient presence, and in many cases their absence became final. This situation had a major impact on gender relations.

Women were forced to assume economic responsibility for their families to a greater extent than previously. As well as having to earn an income, which was new for some women, they assumed full responsibility for family finances, and often took over management of the family farm or the family business. Women became responsible for decision-making in their families, taking charge of matters previously barred to them at law. From 1915, married women were allowed to exercise 'paternal authority' in urgent matters when the husband could not be contacted – a grudging official recognition that there was no alternative.[67]

The long separation of husbands and wives affected relationships in a variety of ways. Some couples had no contact for the duration of the war – for instance, where the wife lived in the occupied territory. More commonly, women had intermittent contact with absent men through correspondence and brief periods of leave. Lack of contact, along with strict government censorship of information, helps to explain the misunderstandings of soldiers about life back home. It also hindered civilians' ability to appreciate the horrors of trench warfare. Only ignorance could explain the suggestion that life in the trenches turned indolent youths into men, returning them 'pink-cheeked and chubby, full of health, transformed by a year of war'.[68] It also helps to explain the pervasive anxiety in soldiers' wartime literature that women were getting on very well without them. This view was expressed forcefully in Henri Burbusse's bestselling novel of 1916, *Le Feu* ('Under Fire'). The gulf in experiences and understanding was sometimes difficult to fill after the war.

Catering for soldiers' sexual needs was deemed essential for morale, so the war saw a return to State-licensed brothels and military bordellos. Prostitutes were still condemned as immoral, and the army feared they would spread venereal disease among the troops. But two-thirds of cases among women were caused by husbands returning on leave.[69] The conditions of sex workers in the mobile brothels near the front lines were onerous: '50 to 60 men of every colour to do per day, under the constant threat of the planes, the bombardments [...] eighteen hours hard work a day [...] but you earned 400 to 500 francs a day and that was almost a fortune'.[70]

Many women on the 'home front' suffered from the lack of male company and marriageable partners. They saw the future they had anticipated disappearing as their male friends died. But the extraordinary conditions of wartime were not seen as a justification for female sexual misdemeanours. As Joan Landes has argued of the

Revolutionary period, love of the nation was fostered metaphorically by the nation's representation as a woman (La France, or Marianne).[71] The notion that they were defending hearth and home mobilised men, but the myth of nationhood was endangered if women did not play the role of devoted wife. The sexual misdemeanours of women were therefore perceived to undermine the project of national defence and threatened to make the war meaningless. Female adultery was regarded as a betrayal of the country and the war effort, not just of the individual. It brought imprisonment if the husband was at the front; a fine otherwise. Soldiers who believed themselves betrayed were acquitted of 'crimes of passion', sometimes to public applause.[72]

Some married women did have affairs. The illegitimacy rate rose from 8.4 per cent of births in 1914 to 14.2 per cent in 1917, although the number of illegitimate children remained below the pre-war level. Soldiers' literature took as one of its themes the unfaithful wife, but she was probably more a fear than a reality. Even so, this did not mean that relationships escaped the war unscathed. Divorce rates rose sharply in its aftermath: having almost halved to 7952 in 1915, they rocketed to 16,500 for mainland France immediately following the war, and to more than 30,000 for the two subsequent years. Clearly, couples could not always resume pre-war lives easily, given that both partners had undergone new and different experiences during the war.[73]

Attitudes towards women appear to have hardened during the war, perhaps reflecting an increasing resentment of the war itself. Initially women were fêted as heroes for their contribution to the war effort. One writer praised:

> the prodigies of virile heroism and of smiling energy, of invincible tenacity and sublime abnegation, of physical or nervous strength placed in the service of the most vigilant and most ingenious solicitude, indeed of the thousand prodigies that French women, whatever faith and social class they belong to, have accomplished with a fullness of heart, a fullness of soul which equals the exploits of our combatants.[74]

Women's united efforts symbolised the unity of the nation, which set aside internal differences in face of foreign attack. Updated accounts of the exploits of Joan of Arc or Geneviève de Paris, legendary saviours of France, appeared in the press and on the Paris stage.

These historical references were familiar to the populace from school readers.[75]

But the threat to normative gender roles implicit within this model may have disturbed some readers. 'Virility', 'energy' and 'physical strength' suggested a 'masculinised' woman. These qualities were offset, then, by more conventional appeals to women's 'natural' qualities. Devotion, abnegation and solicitude for others were the traits more commonly praised in women as they committed themselves to the war effort. The characteristics of the nurse outlined by Dr Camille Fromaget, for instance, were those found in the ideal *bourgeoise*. She should be 'devoted, obedient [...], discreet, calm, methodical, cool-headed and needless to say, morally irreproachable'. The nurse, in other words, was the incarnation of the eternal feminine: 'woman is predestined for these very delicate tasks of tending the sick [...] she is a born nurse, a nurse without knowing it'.[76] The same could not be said of the woman doctor. The army was reluctant to employ women doctors, and many found work as nurses instead.

By 1916, the heroic Joan of Arc figure was giving way on the Paris stage to unflattering stories of working women who were authoritarian and immoral. The female heroines of these plays did not fight to save their husband or the nation, but were obedient and passive, accepting their fate. Representations of female submission became even more pronounced as the war drew to an end. The *poilu* was portrayed as victorious, both on the battlefield and in the bedroom, and motherhood was presented as the surest path to happiness for women.[77]

Françoise Thébaud links the shift in attitudes towards women with the realisation that the war would be a long, drawn-out struggle by the entire community, rather than a short and heroic contest by its soldiers.[78] People no longer envisaged a brief suspension of the norms of behaviour but realised that women needed to play new roles indefinitely. The longer the war went on, the more entrenched the new pattern of gender relations seemed to be. Women, it appeared, had not only moved into men's jobs but taken over their world; a world from which men felt they had been exiled. Women had replaced them as 'heads of families', primary or sole wage-earners. They had become financially independent, autonomous, accustomed to living alone and making decisions for themselves and their children. Men seemed to be redundant. With the end of the war, the power relations between the sexes became the focus of a new contest.

The 1920s: sending women home

When the Armistice was officially declared on 11 November 1918, nearly 1.4 million Frenchmen were dead. Almost 900 French soldiers had been killed per day for the duration of the war, including one officer in three and one private in four amongst the infantry.[79] The general rejoicing that greeted peace was tempered by the presence of black-clad women everywhere. Those who were children at the time remembered this fact vividly, along with the wounded and disfigured soldiers. Little Josette Foleo thought that the word 'l'armistice' had something to do with tears since the two words are similar in French.[80] The 'Prayer for a Dead Child' written by Jane Catulle-Mendès no doubt expressed the grief felt by many parents:

> I gave him life, nothing can enable me to give him back a breath of life [...] The most sublime of causes could not make me accept that my child no longer exists. No-one loves France more than I do. But one loves nothing more than one's child.[81]

Grandparents felt the injustice of outliving the young. The grand-mother of Maurice Gallé created a shrine of his bedroom, and prayed there every day until she died in 1927.[82] The grief of the bereaved was perhaps worse for being so commonplace and unexceptional, and it remained ultimately inconsolable. Nevertheless, some 700,000 widows needed to make new lives, and the State assumed responsi-bility for a million war orphans.[83]

In many respects, the end of the war appeared to close the oppor-tunities that had opened for women in the absence of men. The dominant interpretation of the 1920s emphasises the conservative impact of the war on French society. The shifts in women's roles while men were at war, it suggests, proved temporary and were soon retrenched. The post-war years were marked by a determined reac-tion against the cultural changes signalled by the freer lives of urban women from the 1890s, which had accelerated during the war. In this interpretation, the post-war period largely restored the bour-geois model of female domesticity, and emphasised women's duty of reproduction and men's right to command in both the public and private domains.[84]

Despite efforts to return to an idealised past, however, this was not fully possible. To begin with, the desired 'past' was an imaginary one; a time of unchanging security and certainty evoked by the image of the maternal woman. Besides, the domestic life presented as the norm was impossible for many women, who were forced to become breadwinners due to the death or incapacity of their husbands. Furthermore, the economic and structural impacts of the war need to be distinguished from its impact on the encounters between men and women in their daily routines. It was possible to remove women from 'male' sectors of the workforce and to use economic measures to encourage female domesticity. It was possible to pass laws to prevent contraception and abortion and to try to force women to bear children. It was possible to resist laws allowing female autonomy and citizenship. But it was not possible to undo experiences and perceptions. Insofar as women had had new experiences and come to see their lives in new ways, they could not simply revert to a former sense of identity.

Women welcomed the return of men, therefore, and many no doubt regarded their release from paid labour with relief, but this did not mean they welcomed a reassertion of male dominance. Restoring men's power and authority in civilian life potentially conflicted with women's heightened sense of their own abilities, due to the roles they had assumed during men's absence. Gender conflict in the post-war years reflected the changed basis of the encounter between men and women, whose lives had diverged dramatically during the war and who now had to rebuild relationships on new foundations.

The attempt to wind back the clock was particularly visible in the workplace. A 'return to normal' required getting men back into paid employment, and this required removing many women from their positions. There was an important difference between rural and urban France. The high death rate amongst the peasantry, which was over-represented amongst the infantry, meant that women continued to comprise a high proportion of the rural workforce after the war.[85] Having recruited urban women into the industrial workforce a few years previously, however, the government now offered financial incentives for them to leave. It urged them to 'return to the home' as though they had not been employed before the war.[86]

The war accelerated trends in female employment already underway before 1914. First, the percentage of women in paid employment declined across the twentieth century and the pattern only reversed after 1968. It reflected the pressure on women to undertake reproductive rather than 'productive' roles, and suggests women's desire to be relieved from the double burden of paid and unpaid labour. Nevertheless, statistics probably under-represent female activity levels, because much female employment either was not counted for statistical purposes, or was not reported. Nor were married women registered as unemployed even if they were seeking work. Traditionally, mothers of families had utilised a variety of strategies to make ends meet without necessarily entering the formal labour force. Christine Bard estimates at one million, rather than the census figure of 250,000, the number of women who did paid work in their own homes in 1936.[87]

Secondly, the wartime transfer of women into 'male' sectors of the industrial workforce could not simply be reversed, because the structure of industry was changing. A number of formerly 'female' occupations – particularly in textiles manufacture and domestic service – had declined permanently.[88] Although many women were removed from 'men's jobs' as soldiers were demobilised in 1918 – the Metalworkers' Federation estimated that the number of women in their industry alone had declined by 500,000 in April 1919 – women remained more highly represented in the expanding sectors of metallurgy, engineering, electrical and chemical industries in the 1930s than before the war.[89]

The employment of women in the tertiary sector also continued to rise, strengthening a third pre-war trend. The numbers of women in white-collar work grew from 7.9 per cent of the female labour force in 1906 to 23.5 per cent in 1936, when more than one million women held such jobs.[90] This trend was accentuated by the increased number of single women after the war. The Postal Service led the way, with women comprising 52 per cent of its employees in 1921. Although such jobs were better paid than industrial work and highly sought after, discriminatory practices kept women on inferior pay and conditions compared to male employees. Besides, the sexual division of labour was deeply entrenched, producing a 'hierarchical complementarity of the sexes' even in this increasingly feminised sector.[91]

The 'feminine professions' also expanded in the post-war years: a development linked with the increasing tendency for the daughters of the bourgeoisie to earn a living. The fact that girls could study for the baccalauréat at State schools from 1924 widened access to tertiary education.[92] Besides, the war had undermined the French economy and ruined many of the bourgeoisie who could no longer afford dowries for their daughters (Simone de Beauvoir is a case in point). Economic necessity thus coincided with young women's desire for education and independence to produce increasing numbers of professional women in the post-war period.

Many bourgeois parents still regarded the employment of their daughters as a sign of their failure to maintain social standing. Jules Isaac tried to change their minds in 1922: 'How many of our daughters will not marry? How many years will they wait before finding a favourable opportunity, a husband worthy of them, a man capable of supporting them and their children?' He recommended that young women take up a career and contribute to the family's income rather than remaining idle. A young woman should be allowed to 'work for herself, for her dowry, for the costs of setting up her own household'.[93] However, as Christine Bard argues, the strong cultural investment in notions of femininity tended to confine women to a limited number of professional areas. The 'caring professions', especially teaching and nursing, were conceptualised as a form of 'symbolic motherhood', bridging the gap between the accepted understanding of women's 'nature' and changing female lifestyles.[94]

The 'new woman' after the war

During the 1920s, debates about women's changing lives reached a new intensity. While alarm about the 'new woman' does not necessarily reveal a great deal about the numbers of women assuming that guise, there is considerable evidence that women were adopting the 'modern' look in larger numbers. It was no longer confined to the fashionable sectors of society as in the Belle Epoque, but became a common sight amongst women of all social strata in the cities. There is also evidence that many of the constraints on bourgeois women's lives had broken down during the war, as they began to acquire more independence of action. Public debates about 'new women' reflected a range of anxieties about post-war society, then, which were voiced through a focus on women's changing appearance and behaviour. They also show that the war did not put an end to the cultural changes that had produced the woman cyclist in her sensible dress, but reinforced those changes.[95]

In the post-war years, the trend towards short hair and short skirts for women clearly accelerated. Bobbed hair was all the rage at the victory balls in 1919, and its popularity was increasing.[96] Emile Long reported:

The fashion of short hair for ladies has become so general in Paris, that all the French papers, even the most serious, are dealing with the question at the present time [. . .] It must not be supposed that only the young and frivolous have taken to this fashion; today coiffures of short hair [...] may be seen in every circle, even among the upper ten [per cent], and amongst certain elderly ladies with light grey hair.[97]

The hairdresser René Rambaud estimated that 90 per cent of women visited a salon regularly by the end of the 1920s, whereas only 10 per cent had done so before the war. Few working women could afford the 900 francs per year that Rambaud suggested was spent by the 'average' woman. But the development of cheaper dyes, and new forms of permanent waving using curlers, did allow them to adopt the fashion for waved and tinted hair. Cheaper salons in workers' districts opened late in the evenings to cater for workers. The war and the new hairstyles requiring more frequent visits to the salon also opened up hairdressing as an occupation for women. By 1926 nearly 20 per cent of hairdressers, and nearly 35 per cent of those in Paris, were women.[98]

The war accentuated new trends in fashion, and new patterns of consumer spending. Simplicity in dress had become the norm during the war, partly because of the limited availability of fabrics, but also because even wealthy women wanted to show their sympathy for the war effort by rejecting extravagance. But the trend did not reverse after the war. Skirts rose to knee-height by 1925, and the 'flapper' style – a low-waisted, straight shift – came to the fore in the late 1920s.[99] Bare arms and sheer stockings led to the development of new beauty routines. Emile Long reported in July 1919: 'corsets have, so to speak, disappeared; and the habit of applying a depilatory beneath the arms has been acquired [...] Safety razors now have a place in almost every lady's toilette cabinet, being used after bathing to embellish the legs'.[100] Such investments in personal beautification were probably confined to the leisured women who comprised Long's clientele.

The 1920s saw a fascination with youthfulness, symbolised by the boyish female image known as the 'garçonne'. Youth was idealised and romanticised. 'Mature' women began to cover grey hair and aspire to slimness in order to maintain a youthful appearance. The ideal was encapsulated by Suzanne Lenglen, the Wimbledon tennis champion in the early 1920s, whose dress and hairstyles conveyed the athleticism and activity of the 'modern' woman.[101]

The leading fashion designer of the 1920s, Gabrielle 'Coco' Chanel, also epitomised the new trends. She was the embodiment of the 'liberated' professional woman, who had risen to prominence through her own talents rather than through marriage. Her fashions reflected the relaxed and more casual style of the era. Chanel herself was a fashion icon, whose designs illustrated the emerging notion of fashion as an art form. Nevertheless, Chanel linked fashion and the everyday by employing a range of ordinary fabrics and by allowing her designs to be copied for mass production. Few women could own a Chanel original, but many could wear a style like hers.[102]

The strengthening of consumerism in the early twentieth century helps to explain the development of a 'mass' demand (in the cities, at least) for the new styles of dress and haircut. A range of new beauty products appeared in the 1920s, and advertising made them increasingly desirable to consumers. The fact that women embraced the new fashions in larger numbers shows that they also embraced the ideal of beauty that they represented. As Mary-Louise Roberts suggests, women aspired to the 'fantasy of an ideal self, liberated, free in her movements in a social space devoid of constraints', that the fashions of the 1920s proclaimed. This may have been an illusion, but it was an appealing illusion to many women, especially the young.[103]

The association between the new fashions and an ideal of female independence, however imperfectly realised, was also evident to contemporary critics. Emile Long explicitly linked 'Revolutionary' hairstyles with 'Revolutionary' politics. Likening the recent war to the 'cataclysm' of the French Revolution, he declared: 'All the great political revolutions have brought an upheaval in fashions and notably as regards ladies' hair. Read history.' He was particularly alert to the sexual politics of changing fashions:

> There is also another reason: feminism is rising, carrying with it principles which evoke equality between the sexes. Is not women's long hair a sign of servitude? Short hair typifies a programme of franchise, as we are given to understand, when a wise woman orders her hair to be cut and dressed à l'indépendance.[104]

The sense of a 'revolution' underway in women's identity provoked extreme reactions in some. Priests, who had seen the devil lurking in the female cyclist of the 1890s, now detected a Masonic plot to destroy Christian womanhood in the new fashions, and tried to pronounce on morally acceptable hairstyles. Doctors gravely predicted either baldness or facial hair for women who challenged 'nature' by cutting their locks. Fathers and husbands assaulted or sued hairdressers who cut the hair of 'their' women without permission.[105] These critics grasped that physical appearance conveyed serious messages about gender and gender relations. As Anne Hollander has argued: 'At any moment, women's clothes express attitudes about women held by themselves and by men, and especially about the bargain struck between the sexes concerning visual expression of their relations.'[106] The shift in female appearance denoted a shift in gender relations that many found threatening and unacceptable, and determined to resist.

The renewal of conservative ideals

The conservative ideal of femininity continued to emphasise mother-hood as the ultimate achievement of a woman's life. For some, indeed, it remained the only achievement to which a woman could legitimately aspire. For this reason, the sex imbalance exacerbated by the war created great concern. The 1921 census recorded 6.2 million women in the 20–39 age group compared to only 5.1 million men. This meant a large number of women who were unlikely to marry.

In the post-war context, the single woman became another indica-tor of changing gender relations, and hence for many a 'problem' to be solved. The label 'surplus woman' indicates that a woman without a man was deemed a cultural, if not a biological, anomaly. It was inconceivable or terrifying to some that she might live happily with-out a husband. Feminists, on the other hand, suggested that women no longer saw marriage as their only option. As Madeleine Pelletier wrote, 'Prince Charming has lost his prestige.'[107] Rather than being a victim, the single woman was represented as an independent woman: an image particularly disturbing to traditionalists, and one which made her a key symbol of change.

In some respects, the figure of the single woman overlapped with that of the 'new woman'. Both were perceived to represent a new model of femininity distinct from the dependent and reproductive woman. The defence of single motherhood for 'surplus' women thus served a similar function to popular novels in which the 'new' woman had a child and was transformed. Both exorcised, at least in an imaginary way, the threat of an alien woman.

Claude Vautel's 1924 novel, *Madame ne veut pas d'enfant* ('Madame does not want a child'), explored this issue by portraying a clash of gender models. Its cover portrayed a 'modern' woman, with short hair and flat chest, wearing pyjamas and smoking a cigarette in the arms of her lover. The central character, Elyane Parisot, preferred pleasure and sexual indulgence to the demands of motherhood. She and her husband – dressed identically to her and with a similar hairstyle – adopted a monkey, rather than surrender those pleasures. By contrast, the Duvergers – a working-class couple with six children – represented 'traditional' family values, now fading away in a world of gender confusion. The contrast of gender models is made even more explicit in the novel by two professors at a public lecture: one proclaims the 'suppression of the sexes' and sees love as the coming together of 'two identical bodies'; the other objects: 'I am in favour of a clear demarcation between the masculine and the feminine sexes.' Similarly, the working-class Louise contrasts herself with bourgeois Elyane: 'she has that figure that is à la mode: nothing in front and not much behind! ... *I'm* a woman with long hair, breasts and hips, a *real* woman who doesn't cheat or play around with her sex.' The novel concludes, as do other similar works, with Elyane discovering the joys of motherhood. She no longer betrays her sex as a 'modern woman' but becomes a 'real' woman and lives happily ever after with her husband and son.[108]

Vautel's novel, as well as engaging with themes of sexual identity, tendered explicit support to the natalist campaign which flourished in the post-war years. Concerns that the French population was declining, or not increasing fast enough, had a long history, but the slaughter of 1914–1918 gave added impetus to such fears. The threat of depopulation was linked, however, not with the deaths of Frenchmen, or with longstanding legal and economic incentives to limit the number of heirs, but with the failure of Frenchwomen to do their reproductive duty. For this reason it was often discussed alongside the question of women's 'natural' roles.

In the post-war context, the Catholic Church was won over from suspicion of fecundity (which indicated excessive sexual activity) to support for the natalist campaign.[109] The view of the French bishops that the faithful should 'fill the void created by death, if they wish to keep France French and ensure that she is able to defend herself and to prosper',[110] thus coincided with the view of Republican war time Prime Minister Georges Clemenceau: 'If France stops producing large families, you can put the grandest clauses in the treaty [of Versailles], confiscate all Germany's cannon, do anything you please and it will be to no purpose: France will be lost, because there will be no more Frenchmen.'[111]

In 1920, the French parliament outlawed 'inciting' to abortion, as well as selling or even providing information about contraception methods. This law was supported by 521 votes to 55, only the French Socialist Party (SFIO) voting against. Another law of 1923 ensured that even passing on the name of an abortion practitioner was an offence, and shifted abortion cases to magistrates' courts because juries acquitted 80 per cent of those charged.[112] These punitive measures were supplemented by a range of administrative measures intended to encourage large families. The new Council on Natality oversaw the introduction of payments for families with three or more children, and the 'medal of the French family' for mothers with five or more legitimate children. It also introduced 'mothers' day' in 1926. Other legislative measures and incentive payments encouraged women to breastfeed their babies, while some proponents of large families also suggested (unsuccessfully) that fathers of such families receive two votes as a mark of their contribution to national welfare.[113]

The effects of such measures were mixed. The threat of prosecution inhibited the campaigns of birth control activists, and a number suffered imprisonment for defending the right to information, or (worse still) assisting women seeking abortions.[114] But more women were active in the often-conservative family organisations than in the reproductive rights movement. Even most feminists supported the promotion of motherhood, and devoted their efforts to improving the economic and legal situations of mothers.[115]

There is little evidence, nonetheless, that the combination of 'carrot and stick' measures was actually effective in preventing family limitation, although it may have made it more difficult. Birth rates remained low and the urban 'middling' classes had fewer children than before the First World War or after the Second World War. As Siân Reynolds points out, the inaccuracy of birth control measures in this period was a greater obstacle to successfully preventing conception than legal statutes.[116]

While active promotion of birth control was limited, public opinion seemed quietly to support the right to limit pregnancy. Jurors' unwillingness to convict, and Catholics' desire to find morally acceptable ways of preventing conception, provide two sources of evidence for this view. Catholics regularly wrote to the Abbé Viollet asking about the acceptability of various sexual practices intended to prevent conception.[117] Abortion, the resort when contraception failed, remained common. Recent estimates put the figure at 120,000 abortions per year in the interwar period, about double the pre-war level.[118] Women who were prosecuted explained their actions by saying that they had too many children, too many pregnancies close together, or were unable to support another child. This coincides with the anxieties expressed to the Abbé Viollet about why Catholic couples sought to prevent pregnancies.[119] As feminists and others tried to argue, couples would only consider larger families when their economic security was addressed. The authorities appeared less willing to address these issues, or to develop a national policy on child welfare.[120]

The futile struggle for women's suffrage

With the coming of war, feminists had patriotically set aside their demands for the duration. Cécile Brunschwicg, leader of the UFSF, wrote in 1916: 'The vote? We demand it more than ever [but] it would not be suitable or beneficial for our cause to undertake an ardent suffragist campaign [...] at the moment when our fatherland is battling against a barbarous enemy.'[121]

After the war, the question of female suffrage was rarely off the political agenda for two decades. Most famously, the Chamber of Deputies (the lower house) voted 344 to 97 in favour of female suffrage in 1919, but the Senate delayed debate on the proposal until November 1922. By that time, post-war elections had produced a more conservative outcome and the Senate rejected the bill. During the next 14 years, proposals for female suffrage were regularly considered and often approved, but died in the Senate.[122]

The strongest support for suffrage in this period came from the French Communist Party (PCF). It had an extensive women's programme and even stood female candidates in elections. Nevertheless, the PCF was not yet a significant political force, and its crackdown on unorthodox views in the 1920s alienated many women members. Many members of the SFIO (the socialists) also supported female suffrage. But the Left generally believed that the needs of women were shaped more by their class than by their sex. Some regarded female suffrage as a diversion from the true interests of the mass of women and denounced feminism as 'bourgeois'. Class struggle took priority. The movement for female suffrage was weakened as a result of such divisions.[123]

Both Communists and Socialists were Republicans, but the main Republican party in the 1920s, the Radical Party, remained anti-suffragist. The Radicals' pre-war anticlericalism and Masonic links had not weakened, and the fact that organisations of Catholic women were increasingly active in the post-war period was grist to their mill. The largest of these organisations, the Patriotic League of Frenchwomen (LPF) had 800,000 members in 1927 and 1.5 million by 1932. It was funded by the Catholic newspaper, *La Croix*, and led by women from noble and upper-bourgeois backgrounds. Women's religious militancy supported the Radical view that female suffrage would hand France over to the religious parties, and that view became more compelling once Pope Benedict XV pronounced in favour of female suffrage in 1919.[124]

The Radicals' stance was consistent with the Republican tradition which, as we have seen previously, enshrined a masculine concept of citizenship and saw the political domain as a male sphere. Some analysts argue that this was not an 'antifeminist' or 'sexist' position, but reflected a particular concept of 'universality' which was incompatible with differentiation of any kind.[125] A concept of 'universality' which is unable to incorporate women seems remarkably non-universal! Besides, many Republicans including prominent leaders and theorists of the movement supported female suffrage: obviously they did not consider it incompatible with Republican principles.[126] Other factors must therefore have been at work.

The dynamics of political power made female suffrage undesirable to many Republicans. Despite the growth of pro-suffrage organisations, suffragist numbers remained small in national terms. By contrast, the political weight of rural France made the electorate socially conservative. The Radicals' support for the ideal of the small independent producer drew a peasant constituency to Republicanism, but not one attuned to ideas like female suffrage.[127] Although elections in 1924 and 1932 produced Chambers less dominated by the centre-left, not until 1936 was the Chamber of Deputies strongly in favour of social reform.[128]

Furthermore, political resistance to female suffrage reflected men's resistance to losing their monopoly on political power. Siân Reynolds has pointed out that the French electorate in the 1920s was the most unrepresentative of the entire Third Republic. Since the war had decimated the ranks of Frenchmen in their twenties and thirties, and since women and resident foreigners were excluded from suffrage, the Republican electorate 'excluded the majority of adults resident on French soil'.[129] Rather than creating a determination to introduce 'universal suffrage', however, it reinforced resistance to the idea. It fed the view that women's 'equality' would really mean women's 'domination'.

Siân Reynolds has analysed the many female suffrage bills passed by the Chamber and rejected by the Senate. She concludes that there was widespread support for female suffrage but strong opposition from a group of very powerful men, in an upper house where the conservative tendency was exacerbated by an electoral system favouring rural areas.[130] This is an effective explanation in political terms, and it is supported by Christine Bard's suggestion that opposition to female suffrage is best explained not by 'rational' motives but by the irrational fears of men faced with increasingly independent women.[131]

This is a recurrent theme of the relations of the sexes in the 1890–1920 period. It percolates through responses to education for women, to female sport, and to dress reform in the 1890s. During the war, soldiers perceived themselves as displaced and marginalised by women who had grown in authority and confidence. They feared returning to women who had 'become authoritarian, imperious, playing the boss and the drum-major'.[132]

A significant gap in understanding between the sexes is therefore apparent as they considered the meaning of the changes in women's lives in this period. One woman assessed the situation in 1921, in a letter to a male journalist enquiring into marriage:

> Five years of war taught women that they could live without the support of the men who made them into eternal slaves. And our desire to create a home and children for our future happiness is no longer enough to make us lose our fear of male egoism, which has been all too well proven. Until now we have been merely passive victims, but there is an end to everything. Now we just want to live our own lives [*vivre notre vie*] without worrying about the fate of future generations.[133]

For the male recipient, the critical point of this letter was its 'egoism': the desire of women to 'live their own lives' and thus reject the sacrificial demands of love and marriage. But the woman writer complained about the unacceptability of male power in marriage, not about marriage itself. It was not the desirability of 'home and children' that she questioned, but the fact that they came at such a high price. The views of this one woman were not necessarily representative of the majority, but a growing desire for individuality and independence – which were not necessarily incompatible with marriage and family – placed many women increasingly out of step with men's desire to feel secure in and through their power over women. At the end of the 1920s, the issue of power relations between the sexes remained unresolved.

7 Taking Sides: Women in the 1930s

The dominant historical interpretation presents the 1930s as the 'triumph of familialism' rather than of the 'new woman'.[1] In this scenario, the period from the 1890s to the 1920s was merely a 'phoney war' of the sexes: change threatened but did not really eventuate. The longer skirts and hair of the 1930s symbolised, in this analysis, the recovery of conventional femininity and the return to domesticity.[2] French films of the 1930s illustrate this pattern, presenting a panoply of female characters who, having dabbled in independence, find their fulfilment in marriage and devotion to a husband.[3]

Debates about women's lifestyles and dress that had preoccupied many in the 1920s certainly receded in the 1930s. This was partly because the political divide and the economic crisis claimed attention, but also because short hair and simple clothing gained wide acceptance. Clothing may have been 'conservative' in the 1930s, but it did not revert to pre-war styles. Bobbed hair and cloche hats were commonplace in the years before the Second World War, and had become respectable.[4]

While pressures on women to subscribe to a maternal self-image were intense in the 1930s, and while motherhood was venerated across the political spectrum, the link between women's family role and their exclusion from public affairs weakened significantly. As the economic and political crises of the decade unfolded, women claimed a role in shaping the world rather than remaining spectators to a world of men. Some pursued a vision of 'traditional' femininity; others a programme of radical transformation. They were active as trade unionists, pacifists and communists, as well as in Catholic political organisations and in the fascist leagues. While women's unequal status

185

with men was reaffirmed in the 1930s, the very crises of the period nevertheless created a new momentum towards their participation in public life as citizens in fact, if not yet as citizens in law.

The depression and its impact on women

The Wall Street crash on 25 October 1929 marked the onset of the 'great depression'. All countries were affected by the collapse of the world's largest capitalist economy, although depression arrived more slowly in France than elsewhere. France was more reliant on agriculture and its less 'modern' manufacturing was more self-sufficient, meaning that its enterprises were less exposed to market fluctuations. Nevertheless, by 1931, France began to see bankruptcies and unemployment on a significant scale. Moreover, it was slow to recover from depression, largely because successive governments pursued anti-inflationary policies rather than trying to stimulate spending. The French economy still remained stagnant in 1938 when recovery was well underway elsewhere.[5]

The effects of the depression on women's employment were diverse, given women's complex relation to the labour market. Siân Reynolds has demonstrated that census categories conceal as much as they reveal about the employment status of women in this period because their work patterns did not conform to the male-derived norm.[6] As in earlier decades, women often side-stepped the 'official' workforce, surviving on a range of casual and part-time jobs. In most cases they were not eligible for the unemployment benefit. Married women were deemed 'dependent' on their husbands. Besides, it was necessary to have worked in the same job for a year in order to register, and women changed jobs more frequently than men. The official unemployment figure, which peaked at 503,000 (4.3 per cent) in February 1935, therefore significantly underestimates the true figure. It largely omits women who were seeking work, as well as excluding the migrant workers welcomed during and after the First World War but now encouraged to return home.[7]

Despite the fact that seven million women were in paid employment in 1931 (48.4 per cent of women aged 15–64 years),[8] work continued to be regarded as less central to women's lives and identities than was the case for men. The 'right to work' was not perceived to have the same meaning for them. One response to the crisis of the 1930s, then, was to argue that women should return to their 'proper place' in the home. This view was popular in the press, and politicians from various parties regularly proposed such measures.[9] Some conservative women's organisations argued for measures that would force women out of the workforce and reward families with non-employed wives, although the Catholic trade union movement opposed this solution.[10] Striking men sometimes demanded the sacking of married women, despite the trade union movement's official resolution in 1933 that women had the right to work.[11]

These arguments were premised on the assumption that women took men's jobs, so that fewer working women would mean fewer unemployed men. However, the sexual division of the workforce had become more pronounced in the twentieth century; men and women rarely did the same jobs even if they worked in the same industries or workplaces. For this reason, returning women to the home did not provide the solution to male unemployment that some imagined. For instance, many more women than men lost their jobs in the Post Office. But these women were primarily employed as switchboard operators and postal clerks in what had become an increasingly feminised sector, so their dismissal was not necessarily to men's advantage.[12] Nor would sacking the typing pools of government ministries have created jobs for men, because few men were willing or able to take on this archetypically feminine work. The idea also ignored the needs of the many families dependent on female wages. These arguments were repeated incessantly by feminist groups in the 1930s, particularly when neighbouring countries began to exclude married women from paid employment. Feminists emphasised the necessity of work for most women, rather than its 'liberating' character. But this argument played into the hands of those who sought to use 'protective' measures to return women to the home.[13]

Given the sexual division of the workforce, women's employment history during the depression was largely independent of that of men. It was shaped by the diverse needs and priorities of employers. Women were laid off in significant numbers in some sectors, but suffered little or no unemployment in others. The depression also accelerated the restructuring of industry, and this affected many women caught in declining sectors. For instance, the textiles and clothing sectors in the Department of the Seine (the region including Paris and its suburbs), which were both more than 70 per cent female, shrank by half between 1926 and 1936.[14] In this region, too, unemployment in 1936 reached 17–18 per cent: the same level reached in other countries during the depression but four times the

French average for that period. Women and men were affected in equal proportions, but female unemployment rose quickly and fell away, while male unemployment rose slowly and gradually overtook that of women.[15]

Age and skill levels affected the employment histories of women during the depression years, but marital status was critical. An unmarried or widowed woman was more readily acknowledged to have a place in the workforce than a married woman.[16] The crisis of the depression increased social pressure on women to give up their jobs, particularly if they had young children. In any case, poor health and exhaustion encouraged women to leave work temporarily when their children were young. Working 50 or even 60 hours per week from their youth without paid holidays (until the Popular Front government legislated two weeks' paid annual leave in 1936), they began motherhood in poor physical condition.[17] Besides, the burden of housework for women in those pre-appliance days made resigning an attractive choice. One woman recalled: 'There was the washing and ironing, which were much more demanding than now; there was mending to do; there were no refrigerators, you had to shop every day, cook every day, etc. The woman did a lot more work than nowadays.'[18]

In many families, however, the mother's 'retirement' became an unaffordable luxury during the depression. The policies adopted by successive governments ignored the economic role of women workers in poor families, not to mention the social function of work in women's lives.[19] Families were only eligible for a full unemployment benefit if the male 'head of household' was unemployed. If he was placed on short hours, or if he was a small proprietor sliding towards bankruptcy, he was not eligible for a benefit and the family struggled to survive. Many rural families also faced dire poverty in these years of plummeting agricultural prices.[20] Even when husbands were eligible for relief, their wives were entitled only to the same assistance as their children: less than half the male rate. This was not sufficient to support an adult, which explains why married women needed to seek work. Rather than driving women into their 'proper' roles as housewives, then, the depression produced a rise in the rate of married women's employment.[21] This was despite the rhetoric of maternalism which pervaded political discussion concerning women in the 1930s.

The threat of unemployment meant that worker militancy was muted during the depression years. But conditions were onerous for many workers in this period, not least for women. At best, women earned two-thirds of men's pay for the same work, while 'female' jobs were by definition poorly paid. Women were expected to perform tasks which came 'naturally' to them – like cleaning their machines and the factory toilets – without pay after hours. They also suffered sexual abuse in some workplaces. One factory inspector reported on the prevalence of this problem: 'male workers impose themselves on the young female apprentices in the bins by touching them inappropriately. Elsewhere young women are hung upside down by the feet until they let themselves be kissed.'[22] Since girls began work at 12 or 13 years of age, they were ill-equipped to deal with such harassment.

Women's shift from declining sectors like textiles into expanding sectors like metalwork and chemicals did not necessarily mean better pay and conditions. Instead, conditions in the newer workplaces with their production lines and scientific management practices were extremely demanding. Young women were regarded as ideal employees where speed and dexterity were required, and were pressured to achieve maximum productivity. Simone Weil, a political activist working in a metal workshop in 1936, reported the constant pressure by the foreman to produce more castings per hour: ' "Four hundred an hour? You must do eight hundred. I won't keep you unless you do." [...] How many of them have I done at the end of an hour? Six hundred. Faster. How many at the end of this last hour? Six hundred and fifty.'[23] Another woman reported of her workplace: 'It was slavery. You had to work, work...The bosses were very tough. If you didn't complete your quota you didn't get paid... Talking was forbidden.'[24]

Women employed in department stores, despite a cleaner physical environment, were also subject to strict workplace discipline. They worked very long hours for low wages. Shop assistants at the *Galeries Lafayette* in Paris, for instance, reported earning only 400 francs per month in 1936.[25] Union membership was prohibited, while socialist and even some republican newspapers were banned.

Despite such oppressive conditions, women were poorly represented in the syndicalist (trade union) movement and rarely took industrial action. This was one factor which made them attractive to employers. Congregated in low-skilled jobs, they were easily replaceable. Besides, trade union culture was strongly masculine. Little attempt was made to integrate women into mixed unions, and unions often resisted women's attempts to organise separately.[26] Jeanne Bouvier, a dedicated syndicalist and leader of the federation of clothing industry workers, found men's attitudes a constant challenge. She recorded in her memoirs:

> I thought that men, returning to civilian life [after World War I], would have been able to appreciate what women had done in their absence. I also hoped that the years spent in the trenches would have ended the sectarianism of those who had fought a pitched battle, between 1910 and 1912, against the women's unions affiliated with the Labour Bureau in Paris. At that time, they had conducted a violent campaign to force them to combine with the male unions. Woe to those [women] who wanted to preserve their independence! [...] The unionists who returned from the war were just as sectarian as their predecessors.[27]

The barrier presented by masculinism to women's industrial organisation is highlighted by the fact that women joined the CFTC, the Catholic trade union movement, in much greater numbers than the more militant trade unions. In fact, women comprised a third of its membership in 1919, when 75 per cent of unionised women belonged to this organisation. The CFTC actively sought to enrol women into single-sex unions, and regarded them as a brake on Left-leaning male militancy in the broader union movement. Women workers appeared to find the CFTC's approach congenial, and many also welcomed its links to Catholicism. This may indicate that its conservative agenda was particularly appealing to women in the tertiary sector, where it was strongest. Like the CGT, the long-term objective of the CFTC was to return women to their 'proper' place in the home. In the interim, however, it defended women's interests as workers, and did so in a manner they found sympathetic and familiar.[28] Ironically, then, the CFTC organised women in the workplace around the vision of female domesticity. It is impossible to determine whether its members were more attracted by its long-term vision of them as mothers, or its short-term support for them as workers.

Communism, Fascism and the Popular Front

The deepening economic crisis of the 1930s intensified the political polarisation in France and in Europe that had ideological roots. The Russian Revolution of 1917 had successfully established a new society based (theoretically) on popular sovereignty. This vision of an egalitarian society attracted many admirers, male and female. French workers, who had streamed into the Socialist Party and trade union movement after the war expecting significant change, were soon disillusioned, and many subsequently placed their hopes in Lenin's approach. When the Communist International was established in 1920 the socialist rank-and-file, including most of the younger and more energetic members, voted overwhelmingly to affiliate. They transformed the Socialist Party (SFIO) into the Communist Party (PCF). Only a minority (mostly older militants and former leaders) resisted and formed a new SFIO.[29] Socialists and Communists were bitterly divided in subsequent years. But the fascist threat encouraged them to set aside their differences and make the defence of the Republic their first priority.

The extent of that threat was revealed in February 1934, when organised rioting by fascist leagues outside the Chamber of Deputies almost brought down the government of the Third Republic. The response of the Left was the formation of a 'Popular Front' against Fascism in 1935 that brought together Radicals, Socialists and Communists. The 1936 elections were a contest between the Popular Front, pledged to defend democracy and give 'bread to the workers, work to the young, and a great human peace to the world',[30] and conservatives mobilised by the Fascist leagues that held the Republic responsible for France's plight. Where the image of 'Marianne' embodied all the positive virtues of the Republic for her supporters, the fascists' hatred of the Republic was succinctly captured in the nickname they gave her – *La Gueuse*, the slut.[31]

The election campaign of 1936 was bitter and violent. Léon Blum, leader of the Socialists, was vilified in the anti-Semitic press, and then attacked and injured by a mob of right-wing youths while women shouted 'death to the Jew'. The victory of the Popular Front marked a political watershed in France. The Popular Front parties gained only a 2.4 per cent swing overall, but the Communist vote doubled and the Radicals lost 15 per cent support. The Socialists won the most seats, and formed a government in coalition with the Radical Republicans, supported by the Communists. Blum became the first socialist – and the first Jewish – Prime Minister. His opponents were hard-pressed to decide which was more reprehensible, his politics or his ethnicity. And while the Communists remained the smallest of the three parties and refused to enter a formal coalition, the threat of communism loomed large in the minds of conservatives.[32]

Gender and the ideological divide in the 1930s

Despite women's exclusion from electoral politics, they shared the widespread sense of crisis in the1930s. They were extremely active in political organisations and debates. Women pursued divergent visions of an ideal and prosperous France and, like men, saw women's roles as critical to the realisation of the ideal. Moreover, in lending allegiance to these political causes, they embraced divergent visions of the appropriate roles of women in society. Even those who joined organisations that promoted female domesticity revealed an active political consciousness by doing so. Women's involvement in the fraught politics of the 1930s demonstrated – in practice, if not always in theory – that the ideal of sexual complementarity was compatible with a broad definition of women's 'sphere' that gave them an important public presence.

On the Left, women were active in both the Socialist and the Communist movements. Given the political priorities of the 1930s, neither party gave women's recruitment high priority despite their commitment to women's rights. Women had comprised an energetic but tiny minority of the SFIO before the war. Most members of the Socialist Women's Group (GDFS) remained with the Socialists when the Communist Party formed in 1920. But the GDFS continued to follow its pre-war strategies under its pre-war leader, Louise Saumoneau. She reiterated that women should avoid feminist demands and place their faith in socialism. Efforts by younger women to develop new strategies for the recruitment of women met with entrenched opposition from Saumoneau and her allies, and evoked little male interest. Despite the generally liberal views of the party leader, Léon Blum (who had published a controversial book on marriage reform in 1911), women remained marginal to the Party's concerns. Women's membership hovered around three per cent of the total throughout the 1930s.[33]

Other committed Socialist women moved into the Communist Party in 1920. At that time the PCF was explicit about its dedication to the liberation of women and adopted a number of policies consistent with this goal. It actively opposed the 1920 law prohibiting abortion and banning the distribution of information about contraception. It was the only Party to support female suffrage, introducing bills to that effect in 1924, 1927 and 1928. It even stood women as official candidates in municipal elections, 10 of them being successfully elected (but later disqualified) in 1925.[34] The PCF developed recruiting strategies aimed at working women, 'to help exploited women understand that only socialism will liberate them by realizing their economic enfranchisement; in order to group them, organise them, and politically educate them'.[35] During the 1920s the Party also welcomed girls into the Young Communist (JC) movement, which subscribed to a gender-neutral model of political activism and Revolutionary agency.[36]

This 'feminist' approach was soon modified, however, as the PCF adjusted its ideas and practices to a number of considerations. First of all, the Comintern's insistence on the primacy of class war made feminism suspect. This, and the 'Bolshevisation' of the 1920s, which enforced Party authority and discipline, saw the departure of a number of women sympathetic to feminist ideas. The Party's confrontational 'style' in the 1920s may well have been unattractive to women, too, just as the tactics and campaigns of the JC hampered the recruitment of young women. The JC's violent confrontations with Fascists in the streets made female involvement dangerous, and conflicted with the social norms of working-class families. Parents, even Communists, generally did not allow girls to mix freely with men or go out alone in the evening, let alone expect their daughters to be beaten up or arrested.[37] Finally, the vision for women modelled on the 'new Soviet woman' – freed to work alongside Soviet man but no longer under his domination – gained little traction in France. The French workers' movement had a long history of resisting female equality, and women themselves were not enthusiastic about the PCF message if membership is any indication. The number of female party members declined from 2600 (3–4 per cent) in 1924 to only 200 (0.6 per cent) in 1929. This was considerably fewer than the Socialists attracted, despite the fact that they largely ignored women.[38]

By the mid-1930s the French Communist Party had adopted a range of policies which conformed more closely to those of mainstream parties, and which were premised on a gendered model of political participation. The defence of reproductive rights weakened and then disappeared, as the PCF began to support population increase and advocate wage supplements for the fathers of large families. More rigid attitudes to sexuality (including denunciation of homosexuality) emerged. With the creation of the Popular Front in 1936 the most radical PCF policies were sacrificed to unity. This was the fate of their stance on abortion and female suffrage, although the principle of women's right to work may have been included in the agreement as compensation.[39] 'Family values' became the order of the day.

This change in outlook led to the establishment in 1936 of the Union of the Young Girls of France (UJFF) as a female alternative to JC membership. The UJFF emphasised sexual difference. It organised an array of recreational activities for girls and published a magazine that combined politics with advice on fashion, makeup and sexuality. As a single-sex organisation, the UJFF also catered to the views of parents who had refused to allow their daughters to join the 'co-ed' youth group.[40] The expansion of UJFF membership – from 5000 in mid-1936 to 19,411 at the end of 1937 – suggests the appeal of this separatist political model.[41]

The UJFF sought to construct an image of the Communist woman that respected social expectations, rather than one modelled on Revolutionary doctrine. UJFF members would therefore be involved in politics but 'retain their charm', in the words of UJFF leader and PCF activist, Danièle Casanova.[42] An idealised image of the Communist mother became the role to which girls should aspire, and which Communist women should emulate. In 1936 the Communist paper L'Humanité transformed its 'Woman's' page into a 'Woman and Child' page, and lauded women who prepared a happy home for returning husbands and sons.[43] Its poster for the 1936 legislative elections showed a family group with the woman nursing a young child, and bore the slogan 'Vote Communist so that the family may be happy.'[44] The political roles of Communist women were envisaged, therefore, within a gendered model of activism that emphasised female nurturance. This reflected broader social concerns about depopulation that the PCF had come to share, as well as workers' desire for family security in face of economic hardship.[45]

The atmosphere of the mid-1930s was not favourable to the vision of female emancipation from traditional gender norms: even in Soviet Russia this radical vision had faded. But this did not mean that women on the Left were envisaged – or envisaged themselves – as apolitical beings. The sex-segregated UJFF had removed girls from the essentially masculinist atmosphere of the JC, but its aim was to politicise them. As Danièle Casanova declared:

> Since the founding of our organisation, we have discovered new and courageous militants. Our work is of interest to them [...] young girls are participating in large numbers in the political life of the Federation of Communist Youth in France. Tomorrow

they will be capable militants, having been well-educated in our best sources of Marxist-Leninist doctrine.[46]

The growth of the UJFF did not necessarily imply that young women embracing the message of Communist motherhood rejected the option of political participation. It may suggest, however, that girls (or their parents) preferred single-sex groups and favoured modes of activism that were compatible with their concept of feminine roles.

The appeal of the UJFF to young women, as Susan Whitney suggests, may have derived from the opportunities for socialising, travel and leadership it offered. Many of the 200 provincial delegates to the first national conference in December 1936, for instance, had never visited Paris before. This single-sex organisation provided forms of personal development generally unavailable to working-class girls once they left school at 12 or 13.[47]

Furthermore, the female leaders of the UJFF were themselves political activists playing public roles, not simply Communist mothers. If their formal message praised motherhood as ideal, therefore, their activities demonstrated that this was compatible with broader social activism by women. They provided models of Communist womanhood that were not confined to family obligations. A number of PCF women maintained their public roles throughout the 1930s, if necessary without Party backing. Women volunteered to fight or nurse in Spain when the Civil War broke out in 1936, for instance, despite the Party's lack of support for their active participation.[48]

The rise of Communism on the Left had its counterpart in the emergence of Fascism on the Right. The 1930s saw a resurgence of extremist organisations which had played an active role in French politics in the 1880s and 1890s, like *Action française* (French Action) and the *Croix de feu* (Iron Cross). Both received funds from François Coty, the perfume magnate. An array of new organisations also emerged in the 1920s and 1930s, including Georges Valois' *Le Faisceau* (the Fasces) and Jacques Doriot's *Parti Populaire Français* (French Popular Party). In 1933 Coty established his own paramilitary league, *Solidarité française* (French Solidarity). These organisations had about 280,000 members in 1933–1934.[49]

Despite their diversity, the Fascist leagues shared a belief that strong leadership, authority and discipline were the cure for social ills. They applauded 'natural' hierarchies in lieu of equality, condemned sexual and class conflict, and rejected democracy as a failure. They regarded the political scandals that rocked the Third Republic as proof of the failure of the Republican system. The immediate aim of the Leagues was therefore the overthrow of the Third Republic: an aim almost realised in February1934.[50]

Some Fascist groups sought to recruit and organise women for the cause. *Action française* had a women's group whose leader, Marthe Borély, was as hostile to 'modern' ideas like women's rights as her male counterparts were. She also shared their antisemitism and racism, calling for a 'France for Frenchwomen' and labelling feminism a 'Jewish invention'.[51] *Solidarité française* (SF) regarded women as political actors and future voters despite espousing the ideal of the domestic wife. Lucienne Blondel, a leading SF activist, proclaimed: 'And women, what do you say? [...] Men vote, therefore we must vote! [...] A simple concern of justice is typically the only reason women give for voting. We propose to offer them some others, for the next epoch when voting will actually mean something.'[52] She urged women to promote the fascist agenda in the meantime.

The largest organisations of women in the interwar period were associated with the Catholic Church. The *Ligue des Femmes Françaises* (League of French Women, LFF) and the *Ligue Patriotique des Françaises* (Patriotic League of French Women, LPF) both grew spectacularly in the interwar period. Membership of the LPF swelled from 500,000 in 1917 to 1.5 million in 1932.[53] These organisations were inspired by the tenets of the papal encyclical *Rerum Novarum* (1891), which emphasised social involvement by Catholics but also defended the 'traditional' family with a male head and a domestic wife.[54] A second encyclical, *Quadragesimo anno* (1931), reaffirmed such sentiments, proclaiming: 'The place of mothers with families lies above all in the home, or in matters linked to the home, and in domestic occupations.'[55] Despite this exhortation, Rome supported the establishment in 1933 of an umbrella women's organisation, the *Ligue féminine d'action catholique française* (Feminine League of French Catholic Action), which had two million members by 1939.[56] 'Catholic action' by women was not incompatible, then, with their confinement to the family.

Supposedly apolitical, these organisations were strongly anti-Republican. They believed women were destined primarily to be mothers, but maintained that women had a duty to influence men in the interests of the nation. The main threat to the nation, from their perspective, was the secularism of the Republic and its immoral policies such as divorce. They therefore supported the electoral success of Catholic political parties in the interests of religion, and

received support in turn from the Catholic clergy. Political parties on
the Right believed that these women's organisations were very effective.
Once papal objection to female suffrage was removed they also
pursued this goal zealously, forming the largest suffrage organisation
in the interwar period.[57]

These organisations were nevertheless antifeminist, seeing feminism
as a product of a misguided perception of womanhood. The encyclical
on Christian marriage, *Casti Conubii* ('Chaste Spouses', 1930), had
put the Catholic view: the sexes were complementary, not identical,
and in the family 'the husband is the head, the woman is the heart'.[58]
Feminism was not merely misguided but unnatural:

> [Feminists] want women to be freed at their own volition (*à leur
> gré*) from the conjugal and maternal duties of the wife [...] They
> want a woman, even without her husband's knowledge, and
> against his will, to be free to have her own business interests, to
> run them, administer them, without concerning herself otherwise
> with her children, her husband, with her whole family.

This 'false liberty and this equality with her husband' were 'not
natural', it declared, and dethroned woman from the 'truly royal
position to which she had been raised by the Gospel within the walls
of the home'.[59] In accord with this view, the Catholic *Union Féminine
civique et sociale* (Feminine civic and social union, UFCS) supported
female suffrage, 'always providing that family hierarchy, on the one
hand, and on the other, the mission of wife and mother which is
a source of honour for women, are safeguarded'.[60]

The ideal of the domestic wife was promoted amongst working
women as Catholics, too, endeavoured to recruit the young. While
Socialists and initially Communists had neglected women, Catholics
quickly became aware of their importance. The Young Christian
Workers' organisation (JOC) had been established in 1926, but in
1928 a special organisation for young working women – the JOCF –
was set up, and became the largest organisation of its kind in the
1930s.[61]

The JOCF sought to imbue young women with the ideals of Christian
womanhood, emphasising moral purity, the centrality of motherhood and the significance of the mother's role in the working-class
family. It aimed ultimately to create a new working class – Christian,
morally rejuvenated and non-Revolutionary – through the influence
of mothers. In line with this objective, JOCF meetings included

discussions on the qualities of a good husband and a good mother, and taught skills like mending and cooking. But the JOCF did much more. It involved its members in a series of investigations into workers' lives and in campaigns for improved conditions for working women (separate toilets and change rooms, washing and eating facilities, workplace safety, freedom from sexual harassment). It also taught them a range of skills which they would never have acquired otherwise, extending their education just as the Communist UJFF did for its members. Girls learned to prepare reports, write pamphlets, and speak in public. Like the UJFF, too, the JOCF offered recreational opportunities that girls of their background would not otherwise have received. It promoted camping, cycling and other outdoor activities, and it fostered travel for JOC girls, most notably a pilgrimage to Italy in 1934.[62]

Despite its principle of returning women to the home, therefore, the JOCF created young militants who envisaged their role as a social one. Like the Communist youth movement, its message to girls was ambiguous. Both groups instilled in girls a sense of independence, competence and dignity which were not necessarily compatible with a destiny of selfless motherhood and submission to a husband. The JOCF produced many women who were active in Catholic organisations and, ironically, it sometimes produced militant Communist women who attributed their preparation for such roles to the Catholic youth movement.[63]

As Susan Whitney has noted, the similarities between Catholics and Communists in their approach to young women were more remarkable than their differences. Despite their diametrically opposed political goals, their visions of women's social roles were similar, as was the maternal rhetoric in which those visions were expressed. Yet the terms in which they envisaged women's specificity enabled women to create significant public space for themselves, and even to assume public roles.

The strikes of 1936

In 1936, the largest strike wave in French history to that time erupted. The strikes were sparked, first of all, by the deteriorating working conditions of the depression years. At the Renault plant, which employed 30,000 men and women on the outskirts of Paris, for instance, 8000 workers had been laid off between 1930 and 1933, and wages cut by 10 per cent.[64] But political factors were also significant. The election of a Popular Front government in 1936 gave workers confidence that the government was now sympathetic to their interests, breaking the perceived alliance between previous governments and employers. Simone Weil wrote of the strikes in June 1936:

> The decisive factor, it must be said, is the government of the Popular Front. In the first place, people could at last – at last! – go on strike without police and without mobile guards [...] Every worker, on seeing the socialist party gain power, had the feeling that, confronted with the boss, he was no longer the weaker.[65]

The strikes were particularly significant in manufacturing and large-scale commerce, including the major department stores. Twelve thousand sites were affected, nine thousand workplaces were occupied, and two million workers downed tools.[66]

The industries most affected were those which were least unionised, and all employed significant numbers of women. This reflected the fact that these strikes often arose spontaneously from the 'grass roots': the labour movement struggled to control them.[67] While it is sometimes difficult to identify women's precise roles in the strikes, their attitudes to the strikes were diverse. On occasion, women found themselves coerced into striking when they were reluctant to do so. In other instances, they were willing industrial militants for the first time in their working lives. These different responses reflected the unevenness of women's integration into the political culture of the workplace, as well as the fact that loyalty to good employers was sometimes strong.[68]

Strike action was often gendered, particularly in the wave of factory occupations that characterised the 1936 movement. Women usually returned (or were sent) home in the evenings while men slept at the factory. At the Renault plant at Billancourt, the strike committee (two women and four men) imposed this rule to prevent 'anarchy' and to show that the strikers were serious in their claims. The only exceptions were 'a few old grandmothers' who fried chips for the strikers.[69] They did not present the threat of sexual disorder that had long been raised by critics of women's presence in mixed-sex workplaces. Like these 'grandmothers', women often took charge of provisioning the strikers and preparing meals. They frequently occupied themselves with knitting, rather than making the strike a time of inactivity and leisure as men often did. As striking workers, women still felt responsible for 'female' tasks like feeding men and clothing their families.

But women also downed tools, joined delegations to air their grievances, rejected settlement provisions, and demonstrated in their thousands. A female delegate at negotiations with the grocery chain employers surprised them by putting the case for a wage increase herself.[70] Alexander Werth, Paris correspondent for the *Manchester Guardian* and an observer of the 1936 strikes, noted that 'women were the most vociferous of all' when the striking Renault workers marched from their workshops down to the Seine. Non-working wives visited the plant with their children, inspecting it 'with a landlordly air', thus participating vicariously in the workers' campaign for greater control over the workplace.[71]

The strikes in the department stores were particularly notable as a mark of female participation, given that they employed a predominantly female workforce. Alexander Werth reported on 5 June:

> The most spectacular new development was the extension of the strikes to the Grands Magasins [department stores], most of which, including the Galeries Lafayette, the Louvre, the Samaritaine and the Trois Quartiers were declared to be occupied that morning. At the Galeries Lafayette a notice was displayed in the windows with a large title: 'Prostitution or Hospital for Consumptives?' It spoke of the sweated female labour in the big shops, and appealed for the moral support of the general public.

The shop assistants' demands included a wage increase of 50–75 per cent, no overtime, and the right to join a union. As Werth noted, the 'young girls' may have been enjoying the strike but they were grimly serious about their demands.[72] Women were also present in large numbers at the great 'victory demonstration' organised by the Communists on 14 June, when most of the strikes had been settled.[73] Nevertheless, they were settled without according equal pay to women despite the fact that the CGT had previously subscribed to that policy. Women workers rarely protested about this inequity, content to have made gains and fearful that pay hikes would make them unattractive to employers.[74] The strikes of 1936 confirmed, in several respects, that women workers were perceived as 'women' more readily than as 'workers'.

Women's rights and the maternal ideal

In theory, the election of the Popular Front government in 1936 looked promising for women's rights. Prior to this election the Socialists and Communists had both been more sympathetic to women's issues than the Radical Party, the dominant Republican political group. The Radicals' resistance to political rights for women had not shifted since they first came to prominence in the 1890s: this despite the fact that most feminists were republicans. Women were only admitted as members of the Radical Party in 1924 whereas the Socialists and Communists had always had women's groups. A trickle of women joined the Radicals, including a number of feminist leaders. Some even became part of the Radical Party bureaucracy. Yet this did nothing to weaken the Radicals' resistance to female suffrage and civil rights. Radical Senators still led the campaign to stymie a change to the law, just as they had before the First World War.[75]

Following the Popular Front victory in 1936, Léon Blum informed the Radical leader, Edouard Daladier, that he proposed to include two Socialist women in his government. Despite the Radicals' history of hostility to women in politics, Daladier insisted that a Radical woman be included as well. Cécile Brunschvicg, feminist leader and Radical, thus joined Irène Joliot-Curie, sympathetic to the Communists, and Suzanne Lacore, a long-time SFIO activist, as the first women to hold ministerial appointments in France. Women were thus in the strange position of being in cabinet before they were eligible to vote or to stand for election. Moreover, both Brunschvicg and Joliot-Curie were legally minors because they were married.[76]

There were precedents at lower levels for these appointments. Women had been co-opted onto a number of boards and committees, and in the 1920s local councils began to appoint women as adjuncts on matters like infant welfare and hygiene. These were perceived as 'women's issues' and not surprisingly the women 'ministers' were allocated to these areas as well. Joliot-Curie, the Nobel prize winner, was made Under-Secretary for Scientific Research, Lacore was appointed Under-Secretary for Child Welfare, and Brunschvicg became Under-Secretary for Education. In making these appointments, Blum was fulfilling a promise made six years previously to the feminists that he would move to advance women's rights despite parliamentary delays.[77]

The appointment of the women 'ministers' was a gesture, however, rather than a political breakthrough. Indeed, as Siân Reynolds argues, it was a gesture towards 'trustworthy' individual women whose political behaviour inspired confidence, rather than towards the masses whom the feminist movement sought to enfranchise. A female electorate was still mistrusted by the Popular Front parties. This was particularly true of the Radicals, but many Socialists were also uneasy about the potential impact of female suffrage on the Left. Joliot-Curie had not been associated with feminism, and Lacore, a member of the GDFS, had shared its view that feminism was a 'bourgeois' concern.[78] Brunschvicg was only included once she resigned from leadership of the UFSF, the French women's suffrage association, and undertook not to advocate for female suffrage during her term.

Feminist expectations that this marked a new era of trust for women were therefore misguided and disappointed. The appointments were short-lived, since the Blum government survived only until June 1937, and Joliot-Curie effectively resigned after two months in office. She, too, regarded the appointment as a gesture and was keen to return to science.[79] The women also struggled to insert themselves into the bureaucracy, and to be taken seriously in their portfolios. This was not surprising, given that none had the preparation for public office that men normally received. Bureaucrats posed problems for many new ministers until they were able to assert their authority: something difficult for women as political outsiders to do. But perhaps the frustrations of Cécile Brunschvicg, who found it difficult to obtain the resources and authority that she needed to do the job, indicate that she expected *not* to be a figurehead, unlike her fellow women ministers.[80] The oft-quoted words of Léon Blum to Suzanne Lacore, the provincial teacher baulking at accepting a post as Under-Secretary in the national government, are suggestive of his intentions in 1936: 'You will not have to command, but to inspire (*animer*). Above all, you will just have *to be there*, since your presence alone will mean a great deal.'[81]

Blum was no doubt sincere in wishing to make a gesture towards women. The gesture was significant in that it did demonstrate that women – even unprepared by progression through the normal channels of political initiation – could hold high office without the sky falling. The tactful approach taken by the women may also have reassured those who feared an opening of the feminist floodgates.

But if Blum might be criticised for not being prepared to go out on a limb by pushing for female suffrage, his difficult position must be recognised. The Popular Front coalition was shaky despite their victory in the polls, particularly because the PCF refused to do more than offer measured support. The Communists provided no ministers, and remained free to launch criticisms from the sidelines. A powerful array of interests confronted the Blum government, too, as employers joined forces to resist concessions to workers. The strikes, which were a measure of workers' faith in the government, played into the hands of those who believed, or who had an interest in persuading others, that France was on the verge of revolution. Blum's Jewishness aroused anti-Semitic interests and added to the Right's hatred. As Julian Jackson says, 'the celebrated phrase "rather Hitler than Blum", may never have been uttered but it did encapsulate an attitude'.[82] Besides, many in the SFIO itself would have revolted at female suffrage.

It is not surprising, then, that Blum adopted a cautious strategy to show his measured support for women. He reiterated that support in 1937, shortly before his government fell: 'By taking two women into the government, the Socialist party has virtually made the equality of the sexes a reality. But the paradox whereby women can be ministers without being *députés* cannot and will not last.'[83] If Blum's initiative had really meant the 'equality of the sexes', however, it is likely that he would have evoked much more criticism than he did by these appointments. As we have seen, equal pay was not considered a viable proposal by those involved in the strikes: 'equality' of that kind threatened not only to upset employers but also to provoke male voters. Blum's government preferred to settle the strikes without considering such a step, and no pressure was exerted on the Senate to accept yet another vote for female suffrage in July 1936. As historians have noted, then, the virtue of the women ministers was that their presence did not disturb established power structures.[84]

Yet, as Siân Reynolds has argued, their appointment was one more step in the ongoing infiltration of women into public life in the interwar years. Through their roles in an array of organisations and even political parties, women had emerged from the shadow of men to put their own views in the public sphere.[85] They also made some significant gains in the interwar period, even if these were intended to reinforce women's maternal role. With the advent of a more conservative, Radical-led coalition in 1937, the Civil Code was finally revised. But this reform had come only slowly and grudgingly, prodded by decades of feminist activism. The Radicals had previously conducted a three-year enquiry (1925–1928) into the issue: a typical delaying tactic. The report had advocated reforms, but they were only enacted in 1938 and then largely, perhaps, to head off the onslaught of female suffrage bills. The law of 1938 ended the legal status of women as minors, with no rights over their own persons or property, but it left men's 'headship' of the family in place. Husbands therefore retained the right to choose the couple's place of residence, to prevent their wives from working, and to exercise authority over the children (women's equal parental rights were only recognised in 1970). Feminists remained dissatisfied with the result, but the Radicals' undaunted determination to resist any major assault on male privilege was clear. Besides, as the feminist newspaper *La Française* noted, when it came to debates on women's rights 'Right and left disappear, and a touching sacred union forms to resist the peril of women's emancipation. All the parties are antifeminist in their own way.'[86]

In November 1938 the Radical-led government also introduced nation-wide family allowances which increased with the number of children in a family. In early 1939 a Family Code provided for an extra 10 per cent of wages to go to workers whose wives stayed at home to raise children.[87] There was no guarantee that these sums were channelled to the wives and children who needed them, unless employers paid them directly to mothers. Only a 'birth bonus' was paid directly to mothers: a concession only forced through at the last minute and perhaps because it did not threaten the status of the male 'head of the family'.[88] Feminists were critical of these policies, particularly of the way they were delivered, believing that they were surreptitiously designed to limit female employment. Cécile Brunschvicg argued that the allowances were too small to enable women to retire and mainly benefited those who had not previously been working.[89] The Family Code was therefore consistent with the view that 'returning women to the home' was a panacea for social ills. It also supported the aim of increasing the birth rate by increasing the penalties for abortion.[90]

'Maternity' was the catch-cry of all in the 1930s, including the Radicals and many feminists. Nevertheless, as we saw in the previous chapter, the birth rate remained low. French couples had on average 2.05 children in 1935, despite the pronatalism of all political parties and of the Catholic Church; despite financial inducements and repressive laws against birth control and abortion.[91] As scholars have commented, 'French men and women were convinced Malthusians.

But in the collective imagination, the more or less mythical figure of the mother-housewife had pride of place.'[92]

The discourse of 'motherhood' touched powerful emotional chords and elicited passionate responses. In the 1930s, that discourse expressed the clash of political values: the Communists' mother-activist vied with the Fascists' ideal woman to convey the image of a remade world. Nevertheless, the models presented by Left and Right were remarkable for their similarities. As Susan Whitney has suggested, the Communist Party's adoption of a maternalist view of women was a sign that they had rejected their previous emphasis on violent revolution and subscribed to French cultural values, in which the woman as mother held pride of place.[93] To emphasise a maternal role for women was to blunt the weapons of the Right, who had attacked them as anti-family in a period when concerns about 'depopulation' were strongly felt. Jeanette Vermeersch, wife of party leader Maurice Thorez, was the 'Communist mother' incarnate: she appeared constantly with her four strapping sons, but was also a leading Party activist and head of the PCF's women's organisation. Within the Socialist Party, Thérèse Léon-Blum's adoption of her husband's full name was perhaps an attempt to emphasise her family status in the absence of children.

Preserving women as 'mothers' of families meant simultaneously preserving family 'headship' for men.[94] This, too, was a discourse that enabled men to imagine themselves in familiar roles and to imagine relations between the sexes continuing along familiar, hierarchical lines. The emphasis on women as mothers, then, reasserted the importance and preservation of sexual difference and gender hierarchy in a changing world. But the pattern of gender relations was susceptible to modification, at least for some.

The Radicals proved least able to grapple with the challenge posed by the prospect – indeed, the reality – of independent and autonomous women. Parties on both their left and right, however, found ways to reconcile the concept of sexual difference with political roles of various kinds for women. On the Left, an ideological commitment to equality and women's rights prevailed despite failures to put it fully into practice. On the Right, a pragmatic assessment of the likely benefits of female suffrage carried the day despite an ideological rejection of equality for women. The Radicals remained tied to a static view of women's rights, playing King Canute before the tide. Radical women remained the driving force of suffragism. But without any real support from their party they, too, were left with nowhere to go. Both suffragism and the Radicals were overtaken by the tide of events as the international situation deteriorated in the late 1930s.

Women and the peace movement

Women of all political affiliations gravitated to peace activism in the 1930s as another major conflagration loomed. This was not a new concern for women, but a continuation of their anti-war activities during the First World War. An International Women's Conference held in The Hague in May 1915 had attracted 1200 delegates from 12 countries, but the French feminist organisations refused to attend until women of the 'enemy countries' disassociated themselves from the 'crimes of their governments and their armies'.[95] Dissident members of the National Council of French Women, unable to get travel visas, nevertheless sent a message of support to the conference:

> Women must speak, in the place of men, who believe that they must stay silent [...] Women know that their sufferings are the same everywhere, that the million dead, that the three million wounded and made prisoner calculated at the beginning of March, are mourned with the same tears by women of all countries [...] Women must defend the ideas from which an equitable peace will be born.[96]

A small group of women in Paris organised a branch of the International Committee of Women for Permanent Peace (later the Women's International League for Peace and Freedom, WILPF) established at this conference, but struggled to make an impact. Socialist women were also active in promoting peace, while teachers (often those active in trade union or political organisations) formed a small but widely dispersed anti-war pressure group. They were kept under surveillance and in 1917 several were prosecuted for promoting 'defeatism'. Some were jailed while others received suspended sentences.[97]

Rather than bringing an end to peace activism, the post-war years witnessed increased efforts to ensure that such a slaughter never happened again. By the 1930s, peace was no longer the preserve of intellectuals and militants but had increasing popular support, particularly amongst women and returned servicemen. The League of Mothers and Female Educators for Peace (LIMEP), established in 1928, reached out to the mass of French women in the countryside.[98] It claimed 70,000 members across four countries in 1932, mostly in France.[99]

The interwar peace movement was divided between those who favoured 'integral' peace, rejecting violence under any circumstances, and those who accepted that self-defence might be necessary on occasion. Women were found on both sides of the divide. Gabrielle Duchêne, active in the French branch of the WILPF, called herself a 'realist pacifist': she was prepared to fight for peace if need be.[100] The LIMEP adopted a legalistic approach, advocating treaties, arbitration and resort to the League of Nations to solve international disputes.[101] Others condemned war outright. Madeleine Vernet called for the abolition of standing armies, and rejected as doublespeak measures to 'civilise' warfare, such as the Geneva Conventions.[102] Similarly, Nelly Roussel wrote to her 'sisters':

> Faced with the Monster [war], only one response is acceptable from us: contempt, inaction, STRIKE [...] The time has come for bold, forceful and precise resolutions. We want no more false 'pacifism' of the drawing-room or the electoral treatise. We demand WAR ON WAR.[103]

Given the message, the violence of the language is startling. But women were often critical of the ways they themselves had supported the war effort in 1914–1918, and now urged a 'strike': no more nursing, no more war work.[104] These attitudes, as Christine Bard points out, were shaped by memory of the slaughter of the First World War, not by an 'antifascist' mentality. Many were slow to realise that the threat they faced in the late 1930s was of a different order, and some would modify their views as the Fascist 'monster' revealed itself.[105]

Women's involvement in peace activism was widely seen to reflect their 'natural' aversion to violence and their commitment as mothers to life. Their arguments and activities during the First World War had drawn a comparison between women's inherent pacifism and men's inherent proclivity for violence. Hélène Brion declared at her trial for 'defeatist' activity in 1918: 'I am opposed to war because I am a feminist. War is the triumph of brute force; feminism can only triumph by moral force and intellectual weight; there is absolute opposition between the two.'[106] Romain Rolland's 1915 'appeal to women' was equally certain that women were (or should have been) the peacemakers at that time. He urged them: 'Be living peace in the midst of war, the eternal Antigone, who refuses to hate and who cannot distinguish enemies amongst her brothers when they are suffering.'[107]

Similar views of women's inherent pacifism marked the peace movement of the 1920s–1930s. Madeleine Vernet argued that men were 'blinded' by politics. 'They tear one another apart in party conflicts. Instead of all uniting to present the combined force of their brains and their arms to the growing evil, they divide into many factions, enemies of each other.' She therefore turned to 'Women! – mothers! – wives! lovers! Sisters!' 'It is up to us, as women, to be the redeemers', she wrote. 'Because we are Mothers, creators of life; and the millions of soldiers killed six years ago were brought into the world by us.'[108]

As Mona Siegel suggests, whether or not women believed in their natural affinity for peace, the language of sexual difference provided the only language in which women could hope to be heard in the cultural context of interwar France. The idea that women had a mission to educate men for peace provided a valuable justification for women seeking to validate their intervention in public affairs. Vernet's newspaper, 'The Mother-Educator', urged women to raise children with pacifist principles, and campaigned against militaristic toys for children. But her paper also called for women to influence public affairs, thus implicitly condemning the exclusion of women from that role. Like the pacifist teachers who read her newspaper, she was seeking to create a political culture responsive to women's concerns and shaped by their input.[109]

Arguments that women were inherently pacifist could be utilised to support the case for broader rights for women in society. Historians have distinguished between this 'feminist' pacifism, which linked pacifism to female suffrage and female participation in public life, and 'feminine' pacifism, which argued for women's influence largely in the domestic sphere.[110] The LIMEP was in the latter camp, noting: 'It is not for us to speak in assemblies in favour of peace. Our field of action is the family and our small circle of acquaintances.' Even so, it published brochures and organised campaigns for disarmament and arbitration which brought it onto the broader public stage.[111] Women cited their 'instinct for peace' to reassure their audience as they engaged in public debate. Even referring indirectly to women's inherent qualities established a woman's credentials to speak on issues like international relations. Some feminists hoped that, if women became involved in peace activism – a topic on which many women felt they had a right to speak – they would develop self-confidence and come to believe in their right to act politically. In this context, Mona Siegel notes, 'the rhetoric of maternalism and pacifism could disguise a more radical agenda of legitimizing the politicization of women throughout the country'.[112]

The prevalence of appeals to maternalism in the 1930s supports the claim that this period saw the 'triumph of familialism' rather than a transformation in the ideal of womanhood. Nevertheless, this interpretation can also be misleading because 'familialism' could mean a variety of things. Both the Right and the Left espoused maternalist views of womanhood. But the similarity of their ideals suggests that the discourse of motherhood was largely strategic, aimed at enlisting women in defence of a political cause. The 'mothers' of the 1930s were not advised to rock their cradles and pay no heed to politics, as had happened in the past. Rather, they were urged to commit themselves wholeheartedly to the political contest. Fascist women, even while seeking to 'return' women to their maternal destiny, called for equality before the law and female suffrage, and tried to mobilise women against the flawed Republic.[113] The Communists sought to foster motherhood, but also to mobilise women in defence of democracy. Women – mothers or not – answered the call. Political groups had long argued that the influence of mothers was paramount, but had construed that influence in domestic terms. But in the 1930s women were organising publicly in political and quasi-political organisations for the defence of 'motherhood', that is for the defence of an ideal vision of France: a significant difference.

8 Vichy France: Reviving the 'Natural Woman', 1940–1944

When Germany invaded Poland on 1 September 1939, Britain and France declared war. The Communists were excluded from the Assembly almost immediately because Russia was allied with Germany. Their exclusion meant the final collapse of the 'Popular Front' coalition that had become increasingly divided over relations with Hitler's Germany. The defeat of France within six weeks in May–June 1940 led to the resignation of Prime Minister Reynaud. He was replaced by 84-year-old Marshall Pétain, hero of the First World War. On 10 July 1940 the Third Republic was formally dissolved when the Deputies voted to extend 'full powers' to Pétain and establish a new constitution.[1] Pétain declared himself 'leader (*chef*) of the French State', rather than President of the French Republic, signifying the change of regime. 'Liberty, Equality, Fraternity' was replaced by 'Work, Family, Fatherland.' This government made its headquarters in the town of Vichy, in the centre of France, and became known as the Vichy government.

The Vichy government decided on a course of official collaboration with the Nazi regime. In addition, however, it set out to conduct a 'national revolution' within France to restore the country to its true path. This 'revolution' was conceptualised in gendered terms: restoring natural sex roles and relationships was defined as fundamental to re-establishing the moral foundations of the country. This agenda reflected a highly traditional view of women's roles, and a reaction against their 'abandonment' of those roles in previous decades. Nevertheless, Vichy needed to politicise women in order to

210

pursue its desired 'revolution'. It also needed to utilise their labour to meet the demands of economic collaboration. These contradictions made the programme untenable. Many women were absorbed by the sheer task of survival during the war years. But their mobilisation for political purposes in the 1930s also bore fruit as women aligned themselves with the conflicting political forces of the era. Despite the rhetoric of maternalism and the attempt to return women to the home, therefore, women remained deeply involved in the economic and political life of Vichy France.

Women, War and Occupation

The declaration of war was accompanied by a general mobilisation of Frenchmen aged between 20 and 40. For many families this began a separation that would last for six years. But the following seven months were a 'phoney war'. Hitler did not attack France, and the French High Command undertook a defensive strategy. Their confidence in the impregnability of the line of fortresses across northern France (the Maginot line) was quickly shattered, however, when the Germans unleashed their *Blitzkrieg* (lightning war) on 10 May 1940. The speed of the Germans' motorised invasion had not been foreseen and soon overwhelmed dispersed French units. Within days French forces were in full retreat.[2]

Civilians in the north, terrified by stories of the German invasion of 1914–1918, were desperate to escape the war zone. Their 'exodus', as it became known, made roads impassable. Fleeing civilians became caught up amongst troops trying to regroup, while German planes strafed the chaotic columns. When the government decided to leave Paris on 10 June panic increased. Simone de Beauvoir, who also left that day, recalled:

> I had my first glimpse of one of those tumbril-like wagonloads of refugees that I was to see so often afterwards. About a dozen big carts came by, each one harnessed to four or five horses and loaded high with hay, [...] the bicycles, the trunks stuck out at each end and in the middle the people huddled together.[3]

About two million Parisians were on the road south when the Germans entered Paris on 14 June, and by mid-July about ten million people, including many refugees from elsewhere in Europe, were trying to reach the unoccupied zone in southern France.[4]

The well-planned attack and the inept defence strategy resulted in the capture of almost two million French soldiers between September 1939 and 25 June 1940, when the armistice came into effect. This was part of the German strategy to provide a labour force for its war effort.[5] It meant, however, that the war was very different from the First World War for combatants and non-combatants alike. The number of men killed was low but many would spend the war as prisoners and forced labourers. Many French women would spend the war in an occupied country as the wives of Prisoners of War (POWs), struggling to survive as best they could.

The Armistice that Pétain accepted imposed punitive conditions on France. The northern half of France and the Atlantic seaboard were occupied and controlled by German forces. The Vichy government retained control over the remainder until November 1942, when the Germans occupied the entire country. France was to pay 'occupation costs' of 400 million francs per day.[6] It was also to supply Germany with vast quantities of foodstuffs, machinery, coal, transport and equipment, wool and cotton, and human labour (in addition to POWs).[7] From 1943, the German demand for labour would necessitate a 'compulsory labour service' (STO), which would see many French citizens shipped to the Reich. While the STO was initially confined to men, 44,000 French women were working in German factories in 1944.[8]

In 1940 some 790,000 women were wives of POWS, including 616,000 who became 'heads' of their families as a result of their husbands' capture.[9] Sarah Fishman's study of prisoners' wives suggests that this was not perceived as a liberating experience. They suffered economic hardship, and any autonomy they may have gained was undermined by State surveillance of their activities, public scrutiny of their behaviour, and severe laws about their sexual conduct.[10] They received a small allowance from the government but many had to find work to supplement this allowance. One woman summed up the situation: 'It's simple, my husband left for the front and I was left with two children including a baby of 3 months, I had to do something. I had never worked in my life but I wrote to Dewoitine to ask for a position.'[11] Rural women faced a different problem. The mobilisation of the men meant that many women had no-one to help run the family farm. Besides, their animals, trucks and cars were requisitioned while fertiliser, tools and seed were hard to obtain.[12]

Many women did not know for some months whether their husbands and sons were dead or alive. Knowledge that those men were prisoners, while a relief, meant eking out rations to send them food parcels. Prisoners' mail was limited and strictly censored, so it provided little scope for intimate exchange. Some women, reflecting on this period of separation from their spouses, regretted the loss of their youth together, particularly if this meant that they never had children. Those with children struggled to raise them alone, and to deal with their children's grief, confusion and fear.[13]

Civilian life for the duration of the war was dominated by the struggle for survival. Constant fear of bombings, of manhunts and roundups, of seeing France once again become a battlefield, made these years traumatic, particularly for those living in border zones or near obvious military targets. Le Havre and Brest suffered heavily from bombing raids, for instance, and the bombing of the Renault factories at Billancourt in 1942 caused 623 deaths in the heart of Paris. Overall, about 60,000 people died in bombing raids.[14]

Civilians also faced a daily struggle to feed themselves as requisitions cut deep. The French had access to only a third of their pre-war coal supply and a tenth of their oil, so obtaining fuel for heating and cooking was a major problem. New clothing was a luxury. Shoes were particularly difficult to obtain and required special authorisation.[15] Finding adequate food was the most pressing problem. Urban women queued for hours to obtain rations, creating the new occupation of 'queuer', who took another's place for a fee.[16] Food shortages were severe in the cities and the south, and a black market soon developed. Peasants found surreptitious ways of evading requisitioning, and city-dwellers with contacts in the countryside were able to supplement their rations as well. Suzanne Lehmann Lefranc was one of the fortunate ones. A friend of her cook (who had been with the family for 28 years) sent butter from Brittany, and an aunt there sent eggs. A cousin in the Loire sent potatoes, and a friendly butcher provided her with meat.[17]

But urban families spent up to 80 per cent of their resources on food alone. Even so, people consumed on average only half to three-quarters of the necessary daily calories, and malnutrition became an increasing problem.[18] One observer reported in 1942: 'There are whole families who have nothing but their daily bread ration each day. There is great unrest. You can see mothers of families weeping in the streets.'[19] Families with adolescent children and non-working wives were particularly hard-pressed to make ends meet. As a result, adolescents from working-class backgrounds or from the families of minor civil servants suffered high mortality, and those that survived had growth deficiencies of up to 20 per cent.[20] The focus on survival was also to blunt the Vichy government's attempt to impose new values on the populace, not least on women.

Vichy and women: 'queens of the home'

Major historiographical debates surround the Vichy regime, its ideology, and the extent of its collaboration with Nazism.[21] Vichy was not a monolith. It brought together 'traditionalists' inspired by an idealised image of the French past, many of whom had been active in the Fascist leagues of the 1930s, and 'technocrats' who admired German efficiency and technological achievements. There were also some committed Nazi sympathisers who welcomed a Nazi victory and wanted France to play its part in the 'new world order'. These groups coexisted uneasily, but the 'traditionalists' were generally in the ascendancy.[22] Pétain was in this camp, and played a key role in both defining the regime's goals and arbitrating between the antagonistic factions.

The Vichy government and its allies, rather than merely meeting the demands of the victors, wanted to reconstruct French society on new foundations. Their 'national revolution', as they called it, aimed to restore an imagined 'true France', which had supposedly been destroyed by democracy and Republicanism. France had abandoned its cultural roots in the family, its foundation in the land and in a sturdy peasantry, its faith in Catholicism, and its political traditions as a hierarchical society under strong leadership. Its defeat, the traditionalists maintained, was a divine punishment and its sufferings an atonement. Regeneration required a return to the values of the past.

One illustration of the desired 'national revolution' showed two houses, the first collapsing in ruins, the second firm and stable with a fire in the hearth. The foundations of the former house were labelled 'laziness, demagoguery, internationalism'. Its crumbling pillars included 'democracy, communism, radicalism, capitalism, antimilitarism, freemasonry and Jewry', as well as greed and alcohol. The foundations of the second house were labelled 'work, family, fatherland'. Its pillars – 'discipline, order, thrift, courage' – supported 'the school, the artisans, the peasantry, the Legion'. A woman was flinging open the shutters of this house over which hovered the Marshall's insignia, while a red flag surmounted by a Star of David hung over the ruins of the other.[23]

This illustration incorporated many of the themes of the Fascist leagues of the 1930s, particularly their attacks on democracy, their anti-Semitism and anti-Communism, and their claim that the Third Republic was morally decadent. It also incorporated their belief that salvation lay in a return to France's 'traditions' of social hierarchy. The image of the woman inside the Vichy house was particularly significant. It demonstrated that the 'woman at home' was central to Vichy's social vision, just as her absence from the Republican house – her failure to fulfil her 'proper' role – signified the decadence and unnaturalness of the Republic. In this respect, too, the illustration reflected the views of pre-war extremists who had excoriated the working woman and the woman who 'refused' to have children; who had condemned the breakdown of patriarchal authority and railed against the evils of feminism. As one official from Vichy's Propaganda Ministry later asserted, the 'national revolution' was 'a virile and human reaction to a feminized Republic, a Republic of women and inverts'.[24]

Vichy's representation of gender – the ways it constructed masculinity and femininity through its rhetoric and policies – was a central way of expressing its 'Revolutionary' vision and the ideals it espoused, as the illustration of the two houses demonstrates. The traditionalists who dominated Vichy were determined to resist what they regarded as the perils of change and 'modernity'. Change was perceived as decline, and the blurring of 'natural' sexual boundaries (evident in feminised men, masculine women, and sexual 'inverts' or homosexuals) was a clear indicator of that decline. Sexual 'confusion', in Vichy parlance, demonstrated the abandonment of the laws of nature and the loss of the moral certainties on which national well-being depended. Redefining relations between the sexes was critical to the Vichy project, therefore, and the 'national revolution' set out to reconstruct both men and women. The defeat of 1940 was attributed not just to the failings of women but also to the failings of men: failings represented in 'feminine' terms. Men had become soft and decadent, seduced by pleasure and comfort. They had become weak and unmanly and had lost their cultural roots. Vichy devoted great attention to restoring 'masculinity' (particularly through reasserting male power and authority), as well as to reshaping women.

In Vichy ideology, women were envisaged, above all, as mothers. In the words of one Vichy writer, women should be 'rooted in nature without horizon beyond their hearth and without any aspiration beyond the joys of motherhood'.[25] The regime's iconography abounded in images of 'the mother', babe in arms and surrounded by children.[26] Mothers' Day was promoted as an important Vichy celebration, and a *Little Guide to Mothers' Day* was published to assist (and regulate) its observance. People were urged to reflect at home on what they owed their mothers. State officials, clerical and secular, led public celebrations.[27] Pétain's address to French mothers in 1941 captured the reverence surrounding motherhood under Vichy: 'Mothers of our dead, mothers of our prisoners, mothers of our cities who would give your lives to save your children from hunger, mothers of our countryside, who, alone on the farm, bring in the harvest, glorious mothers, suffering mothers, today I express to you the gratitude of the entire nation.'[28]

Mothers were characterised by self-sacrifice and devotion to others. An education manual for young peasant women reiterated that theme constantly. Devotion was described as woman's 'vocation'; she must be 'ready for every sacrifice' without complaint. '[Women] must think of others! If we don't, who will?'[29] The language of motherhood thus expressed the overarching Vichy ethic of devotion to the nation, to the 'larger' family. It also reflected the idea that people were not valuable in themselves but in the roles they played and in the social institutions of which they were part. It articulated the anti-individualist message behind Vichy's corporatist social model. Women were not individuals with different talents and aspirations, but 'mothers' biologically destined to reproduce the French 'race', just as men were workers or farmers producing the necessities of life. Motherhood was defined as 'woman's National Service', but unlike men's military service 'it lasts for all her life in the home and it is through motherhood that she pays her "blood tax"'.[30] The feminist argument – that the risks of childbirth equalled those of military service and thus entitled women to the vote – was here turned against women. Duties, not rights, and certainly not desires, were what mattered.[31]

Motherhood best represented the 'natural' differences between the sexes by which the Vichy regime justified its political programme. Constructing women as 'mothers' rather than as individuals or citizens enabled a three-pronged strategy to address the major concerns of the Vichy traditionalists: depopulation, male unemployment and the decline of the family.

Vichy was a victory for the pre-war anti-contraceptive and pro-family lobbies, which constantly pressured officials to introduce

stronger measures promoting reproduction.[32] Women were coaxed
to have children and penalised for not doing so. Peasant women, in
particular, were urged to accept this duty in order to facilitate Pétain's
promise to revitalise France through a return to the land: 'In the
city, children can be a burden: in the country they are *a bounty*
[*richesse*].'[33] An official anti-contraception leaflet insisted: 'Motherhood
alone gives woman the fullness of her potential.' Women 'needed at
least four pregnancies to attain normal health', it asserted.[34] Ancient
myths about the physiological benefits for women of absorbing male
semen were revived, thereby implying that the female organism was
incomplete in itself.[35]

But this promised to be a dangerous argument, for only procreative
sex was sanctioned. Vichy embraced the maternal woman, sober and
responsible. The vamp, the seductive woman, was a social danger.
Sexual desire was associated with dissoluteness, with 'individualism
[...] adultery, seduction, cohabitation, divorce'; with 'selfishness';
with 'sex which does not accommodate its natural result: the birth of a
child'. Its ultimate result was the 'scourge' of abortion.[36] Nevertheless,
men's 'desires' were regarded as inescapable. State-controlled brothels
were maintained to deal with men's 'needs' in an orderly way, while
the women who satisfied those 'needs' were condemned.[37]

The Vichy discourse of femininity harmonised with its authoritar-
ianism to produce policies designed to force women into marriage
and childbearing. These measures also reflected Vichy's strong
natalist ethic. Divorce became difficult to obtain under a law of April
1941, and required a reflective period of seven years. Abortion
became, first, an assault on 'national Unity, on the State and the
French People' (September 1941) and then 'a crime against State
security' that brought the death penalty (February 1942). The efforts
of a specially constituted police force saw the number of convictions
for abortion rise from 1225 in 1940 to 4055 in 1943. Attempts to
promote natalism also underlay measures against infanticide, and a
1941 law allowing the legitimation of children born outside marriage. This law shocked some Vichy traditionalists, however, because
it conflicted with the emphasis on 'family values'.[38] Laws against
homosexuality also reflected Vichy's focus on reproductive sex as
well as being consistent with the family ethic. Men were targeted
more than women for performing 'unnatural acts', however, because
gay men transgressed against the norms of 'masculinity' as well as
those of natalism, and their presence was more visible than that of
lesbians.[39]

Despite the adulation of motherhood, the situation of real mothers was extremely difficult under Vichy. The hardships of the occupation meant women were exhausted, struggling to care for the children they already had. Conditions were not auspicious, either physiologically or economically, for women to bear more children. Besides, many of the fathers of those proposed children were absent. Estimates put the number of abortions performed in the Vichy years at between 400,000 and 1 million per year, and married women who already had children were prominent among those seeking abortions.[40] This also suggests the link between economic hardship and resistance to childbearing.

Attempts to construct the new 'maternal' Eden by removing women from the workforce enjoyed limited success as well. Like attempts to promote reproduction, approaches to the 'problem' of working women demonstrated the gap between theory and practice, as well as the tension between the 'traditionalist' and 'efficiency' strands within Vichy. Vichy propaganda declared that 'the woman who distances herself from the home to work outside therefore betrays her vocation', but many mothers were forced to work in order to survive.[41]

The history of women workers under Vichy was complex. The outbreak of war saw a major wave of dismissals as employers braced themselves for the conflict. The Vichy regime then attempted to enforce preferential treatment for men through laws regulating employment. A series of proclamations in October 1940 called for the dismissal of married women from public sector employment to reduce unemployment: the implementation of a pre-war policy of the Right. Women with fewer than three children and a male breadwinner were dismissed. Priority was given to fathers with more than three children, demobilised soldiers and widows with more than two children.[42] However, the government was forced to exempt 'war widows, wives of soldiers not yet demobilized, women family breadwinners, unmarried women without means and women employed in industries whose labor force is traditionally feminine'.[43] Male unemployment fell as a result of these measures, but female unemployment rose from 26 to 60 per cent of the total.[44] Women continued to seek employment during the war because husbands, even when they were not absent as POWs, were often unable to support their families. It has been estimated that the income of the 'ideal' Vichy family, with three children and only a male breadwinner, would have been about half what was necessary for survival in 1941.[45]

Nevertheless, as Catherine Omnès has demonstrated for the Paris region, female unemployment owed more to the savage cuts in the metallurgical sector following the armistice than to government decrees. Many women did remain unemployed for the duration of the war, but this was due to the strangulation of industry and a sluggish labour market rather than to Vichy ideology. Sex-segregation in the workforce had strengthened during the depression, and there was little demand during this war for women to diversify into tradition-ally 'male' sectors of the economy as had happened in 1914–1918. This meant that many 'feminine' industries retained their demand for women's labour during the war. Fashion houses remained at work for an international market, and skilled seamstresses kept their jobs. Furthermore, the shortage of clothing and fabrics created strong demand for altered and remade garments for the domestic market, keeping small workshops and independent workers busy.[46]

Sacking women also conflicted with the requirements of collabor-ation: if women were to be dependents there had to be men in France to support them. But the Nazi war machine needed endless supplies of workers to do forced labour for its war effort. Married women were therefore summoned back into the workforce in 1942, when the provisions of the 1940 law were reversed. In that year, too, the demands of war saw single women pronounced eligible for compul-sory labour service in Germany. In 1944 the Vichy vision of the domestic and maternal woman unravelled completely, when all women aged 18–45 were subject to the compulsory labour provisions.[47] Vichy was simply unable, given the political situation, to implement its familial ideal.

If the rhetoric of motherhood was empty, so too was the rhetoric of the family with which it was associated. The family was at the heart of the Vichy vision, as its motto indicated. Again, this expressed a criticism of France's recent history when the family had (supposedly) been torn apart by the forces of individualism. Family policy, too, reflected the influence of powerful natalist and Catholic lobbies attached to Vichy. The family was defined as a 'natural' unit, but that 'natural' unit was a patriarchal family in which members had distinct roles and responsibilities. Article 54 of the draft constitution stated: 'The husband is the head of the household, the father is the head of the family.' Justifying this formulation, one commentator wrote: 'Some people are arguing about this, but the majority of minds accept that it must be so in the order of nature.'[48]

The subordination of women within the Vichy family model was evident in the 'Family Charter' of December 1942. This established a 'Federation of French Families', the first step in establishing the family-based State advocated by the Right before the war. This Federation grouped families in each Commune (area of local government). Each family was represented by its 'head', and heads jointly elected the committee by 'family suffrage'. This meant that the head's vote was supplemented by additional votes according to the number of children in the family. As Christine Bard notes, this was a major assault on the principle of individual rights that had underpinned progress towards democracy in France to that point. Men no longer had the vote as individuals, but as representatives of their families. And while women could be family 'heads' under certain circumstances, the model assumed their effacement behind their husbands.[49]

The husband's responsibility was to make 'the important decisions concerning the family', while the wife's responsibility was 'to give all the good examples'. A guide to marital duties (which Pétain wanted widely distributed) instructed the 'queens of the home' that their role was to give 'thoughtful counsel' but no more. A manual for peasant girls spelled out what was true for all women under Vichy's prescription of marriage: that men's 'headship' could be a licence for male self-indulgence and self-assertion. Women were reminded to accept a husband's bad temper, his raised voice, his neglect of his wife's feelings, with a smile.[50] Morale would be boosted for everyone if women sang.[51]

The hierarchical family also served broader political purposes, as Marshall Pétain indicated by linking it to the new authoritarian social order. Dismissing democracy as 'a relatively short interlude in the history of our country', he added: 'A people is a hierarchy of families, of professions, of administrative responsibilities, of spiritual families [in which] a small number advise, a few direct and *at the summit there is a leader who commands*.'[52] The accentuation of the role of the male 'head' within the family was paralleled by the replacement of Marianne with statues of the Marshall in all the town halls of France. Authority triumphed over Liberty in the Vichy State, as it did in the Vichy family.[53]

Attacking the 'new woman'

Vichy's 'national revolution' was shaped by a range of preoccupations, the desire to revert to a 'traditional' model of womanhood being one of the most important. The breakdown of a clear gender divide in the Third Republic, according to Vichy, had illustrated the social confusion of democracy where 'equal rights' overrode different competencies and natural divisions. The issues of gender and class, and also of racial differences and hierarchies, were closely related in this worldview.[54] Depopulation and family breakdown were cited as evidence that, in trespassing on men's territory, women had abandoned their own. Women, rather than incompetent military leaders, were largely responsible for the plight that had befallen France.

The construction of femininity under Vichy was partly, therefore, a reaction against the 'new woman', against whom conservatives had been railing for several decades. This was evident in the attack on female independence. A Catholic-inspired publication on *Woman in the New France* (1940) condemned the ' "exaggerated emancipation of woman", her "competition with man", the fact that she wanted to "live her life, follow her whims, win her freedom to lead an existence without control" '.[55] Independence in women was regarded as selfish, and as the abandonment of woman's natural destiny within the family. Female intellectual ambitions were also undermined. The education of girls was re-designed to instil submission and docility. Home economics was made compulsory in 1942 and their academic curriculum was downgraded to 'de-masculinise' it, but this proved impossible to implement because there were too few teachers available.[56] Nevertheless, the newspapers now felt free to ridicule women who earned the *baccalauréat* rather than doing their knitting.[57]

Since the 'new woman' had expressed her liberty through her physical appearance, the return to 'tradition' also required women to abandon the external trappings of the 'modern woman'. Women were instructed to adapt their clothing to the 'revolution', and wearing trousers was forcefully condemned. A maternal image was recommended in the Vichy press: 'Women's bodies now reflect their rediscovered maternal role. Breasts and hips are more prominent; their form has matured.'[58] This era also saw the introduction of maternity clothes for expectant mothers. The newspaper of the official *Légion française de Combattants* urged its members: 'Let us no longer give our favor, our applause to music-hall starlets, sterile women, divorced movie stars, or to all the painted and plucked figures that go about with short hair in men's attire [...] we must honor the dignity of women who are mothers.'[59]

A new female aesthetic which would replace the 'painted and plucked' woman with the 'natural' woman was therefore encouraged in Vichy literature. Hairdressers, couturiers and beauticians were summoned to the task, and the magazine *Votre Beauté* ('Your Beauty') re-designed the familiar 'before and after' portrait: 'This woman used too much makeup; we returned her to her true nature.'[60] Bodily conformity to a prescribed 'natural' femininity was to begin in childhood. An elementary school teacher warned parents:

> Under the influence of fashion and the movies in particular, parents see their little daughter only as a budding star. The havoc caused by Shirley Temple's polished smile is incalculable. Accustomed to overly elegant clothing [...] the little girl becomes a demanding and frivolous doll. Ten years later, she is a coquette and an egotist.[61]

This attack on the signs of modernity, like film and advertising, and its anti-American focus recalled pre-war diatribes about foreign influences that resurfaced in 1940 to explain the defeat.[62] It also reflected the regime's hostility to 'permissiveness' and moral decadence, especially among the young. The young people who 'pedaled towards the countryside' or joined the 'exodus back to the beaches' needed to be educated about duty, responsibility and the virtues of labour.[63] Peasant girls were warned against the 'ridiculous but alluring stories' portrayed at the cinema as well as in books, which made them discontented with a simple life. They were also warned against placing too much importance on modern luxuries like electricity and running water.[64]

But women's 're-education' took a special form shaped to specifically reproductive purposes, and was therefore particularly restrictive. The 'natural' woman was to be physically restrained and controlled, her physical space limited, her intellectual space reduced, her freedom of action contained. This would begin in childhood with the disciplining and shaping of her body. Not surprisingly, therefore, Vichy envisaged a reformed physical education programme. The Commissariat General for Sports regretted that women were 'too much masculinised' under the previous regime. Rugby, soccer, cycling and combative sports for women were prohibited in favour of exercises like gymnastics and swimming that encouraged flexibility and balance. The goal was to prepare their bodies for reproduction as their minds were trained to accept renunciation and selflessness.[65] The ideology and policies of the Vichy regime raised the maternal ideal to new heights, therefore, and linked it to severe restraints on women's rights and freedoms. But the realities of war created a significant gap between ideology and daily life for women.

Collaborators and resisters

Women's responses to the Vichy regime were diverse. Initially, in the trauma of invasion and defeat, the assumption of control by Pétain was reassuring. He had made his reputation as 'the hero of Verdun', and his grandfatherly appearance and paternalistic style were comforting. The letters written to him by women reveal confidence in his leadership of the country.[66] Conservative women affiliated with the pronatalist and familial movements were also enamoured of the 'national revolution', while the overt support of the Catholic Church for the Vichy regime (particularly at first) persuaded many that it deserved support.[67] In later years, some women still recalled the period of Pétain favourably: ' "Work, Family, Fatherland", it was an ideal, and later all that was dragged through the mud, I really don't understand. A pure France, a happy France where everyone would be happy [sic], but then it was a bit chauvinistic, they wanted France to dominate, a bit.'[68] As John Sweets has argued, too, the line between self-preservation, obligatory co-operation and active collaboration could sometimes be difficult to negotiate.[69] Certainly many French people supported the Vichy regime initially either from commitment to its ideals, or because desperate situations called for desperate remedies.

Little work has been done on active collaboration by women: their active support for the beliefs and policies of the occupiers. As Paula Schwartz suggests, the idea that women might denounce others, or undertake 'anti-French' activities, seems to 'threaten ideas deeply rooted in the collective mentality' and destroy the comforting image of the peace-loving female figure.[70] Estimates nevertheless suggest that women comprised 15 per cent of the *Milice*, the paramilitary police who became a French version of the SS. Most of those women were wives or daughters of male collaborators, although the significance of that fact is not clear. Women also represented 25 per cent of members of collaborationist parties.[71] Christine Bard points out that this was not inconsistent with their pre-war mobilisation by conservative groups and Fascist leagues, and nor was it incompatible with the pre-war sympathy of many women for the natalist and family lobbies.[72]

The politicisation of French women, and their active contribution to the political causes they supported, was evident in their attachment to both collaborationist and resistance organisations during the Vichy period. Some women collaborated wilfully, avowing their commitment to the ideals of Vichy or the Nazis. Some women denounced others, though whether they were more likely to do so than men remains unclear.[73] Some women worked for the Gestapo, betraying resistance networks, and did so with full intent to serve the Nazi regime. One woman who was later executed as a Gestapo agent declared at her trial: 'I proved my zeal and I am very proud of it.'[74] In other cases, women's collaboration was less clearly based on political commitment. Denunciations were sometimes sparked by personal rather than political motives, for instance, though again there is insufficient evidence to indicate whether this differed from the male pattern. Margaret Weitz cites the example of someone who denounced a Jewish woman who was having an affair with her husband.[75] Other women collaborated at least indirectly, and possibly wilfully. They were members of families that acquired confiscated Jewish assets at bargain prices, or grew wealthy on German military contracts.

Sexual relations between French women and the German occupiers were to attract savage criticism after the war. About half a million children were born of such liaisons.[76] Elite women socialised with German officers, Coco Chanel (for one) demonstrating her right-wing political ideas, but such women mostly escaped punishment. The 'madams' of brothels patronised by German soldiers made good money from the trade, particularly in the capital.[77] Paris had 32 brothels for German soldiers in 1941. The German authorities estimated that some 80,000–100,000 women worked as unregistered prostitutes as well, though many of them probably did so from need rather than as supporters of the Nazi agenda.

The summer of 1942 marks the point at which public support for Vichy began to erode, and some evidence suggests that women were disillusioned more readily than men. One element was certainly the inability of the Vichy government, not merely to fulfil its agenda, but to feed its population. According to one historian, Vichy lost the French – and especially French women – in the shops and marketplaces.[78]

But a second element was the government's implementation of highly visible anti-Semitic measures in mid-1942, breaking the cone of silence which had surrounded Vichy's anti-Semitism to that point.[79] The regime passed its first measures against French Jews only one week after Pétain's induction and further punitive decrees followed rapidly. This attack reflected longstanding cultural anti-Semitism, a desire to please the Germans, and a desire to exploit Jewish wealth before the Germans did. Vichy's bureaucratic zeal on this front meant that, when the Germans decided on the 'Final Solution', Jews in France were easily identified. Vichy leaders co-operated fully in Eichmann's plan, providing French police to carry it out. The first major round-ups on 16 and 17 July 1942 netted 3000 men, as well as nearly 6000 women and 4000 children. The inclusion of Jewish children in the deportations was the initiative of Vichy Prime Minister Pierre Laval. According to Rita Thalmann, 'the brutal spectacle of the round-ups of Jewish old folk, women and children' was a key factor in producing public resistance to the Vichy regime.[80] Catholic Bishops began to speak out publicly against anti-Semitic measures, and Catholic and Protestant organisations emerged to shelter Jewish children. Nevertheless, more than 75,000 Jews perished through Vichy's efforts, including about 24,000 French citizens.[81]

Other groups also suffered under Vichy's illiberal and collabora-tionist policies, particularly the Communists. Camps originally established to contain Republican refugees from Spain were soon filled with political prisoners, plus prostitutes and common crim-inals. Two camps were designated women's camps and held nearly 10,000 women.[82] More than 100,000 people were deported from France for political 'crimes', and about 25,000 died.[83] Resistance in France increased as the links between Vichy and the occupiers strengthened, and as Vichy's repression of the French population increased. When the Germans occupied the entire country in late 1942, Vichy's freedom of action ended and resistance became more acceptable to many people.

Women's role in resisting the Vichy regime was a neglected topic until quite recently. As Françoise Thébaud has pointed out, the image of 'The Resistance' as a paramilitary force camouflages the movement's geographical and chronological diversity. Distinctions between active and passive resistance, and between fighters and auxiliaries, 'mask the equality of risk' and understate the involvement of women in resistance activities.[84] Redefining resistance to incorp-orate a broader range of actions than sabotage and paramilitary activities uncovers a more substantial role for women than has often been recognised.

A catalogue of female resistance 'heroes' can be placed alongside that of men, demonstrating once again women's active participation in the political contests of this period. Such 'heroes' would include Bertie Albrecht and Danièle Casanova, who were prominent figures in the Communist women's resistance network; Lucie Aubrac, who was co-founder of *Libération*, another important resistance organisation; and Marie-Madeleine Fourcade, who oversaw 3000 agents of the British Intelligence Service.[85] A narrow military definition of 'Resistance', and de Gaulle's anti-Communism, nevertheless meant that few women were recognised in the official post-war annals of 'Resistance Heroes'. Jewish women were even less likely to be recognised than other women.[86]

Women's upbringing did not prepare them for resistance in the same way that men's did. Marie-Françoise Brive argues that, since they were not citizens, they had not been raised to play overtly political roles. Nor had they been raised to engage in physical combat. In undertaking resistance activities, therefore, women challenged the accepted ideology of womanhood.[87]

Women's exclusion from citizenship did not mean that they lacked political understanding or political commitment, particularly in the highly polarised context of the Occupation. Nor did cultural assumptions about sexual difference exclude women from resistance activities. But those assumptions, and women's pre-war lives, influenced the forms of their participation. Men's resistance work was justified by cultural norms associating masculinity with protecting their families, fighting for the nation, and defending political principles. Women's resistance work reflected their desire to defend political principles too, but the ways in which they resisted depended on their family position.

Many women who undertook resistance activities were young and single, or at least childless.[88] Such women performed exactly the same tasks as men in resistance groups, although they were less likely to be involved in combat units. As Rita Thalmann has illustrated, women undertook sabotage missions and attacks on German soldiers, worked as spies, transported weapons and manufactured explosives, produced false papers and ration cards, and printed clandestine publications. If caught, they were subject to penalties just as harsh as those suffered by men, although not always the same. Vichy legislation was clear: sheltering, feeding or aiding wanted persons, or assisting the Allied cause in any way, was a capital offence, and many women paid that price. They were likely to be deported

rather than shot, but deportation often meant that they died slowly
or that they were executed in the Reich, out of sight of the French
public.[89]

Women with domestic responsibilities could not readily go underground or undertake life-threatening missions that might leave their
children orphaned, especially since many families were without their
fathers at this time. For these reasons, women with families to care
for generally undertook less 'heroic' roles compatible with their daily
activities in the home and with cultural norms designating them for
caring roles. All resistance organisations, large or small, had auxil-
iary units, often made up of women. These units provided the
support networks without which underground networks could not
have survived. They supplied food, clothing and safe shelters. They
passed on messages, false documents and information. They sheltered young men who were evading compulsory labour service in
Germany. In some ways, these unspectacular activities were more
important for the resistance cause than the particular acts of
'heroes'. One Resistance leader later declared that 'without [women]
half of our work would have been impossible'.[90]

The sexual division within the resistance organisations also reflected
the fact that pre-war political groups and organisations were sexually divided. Women who worked in Communist resistance circles,
for instance, had often been members of the communist JFF in their
youth.[91] Besides, as we noted previously, even the Communist
movement had adopted a maternal image of women, defining that
ideal in ways compatible with women's political engagement. The
Communist resistance therefore appealed to Frenchwomen as
mothers to join the resistance effort. In Reims a poster encouraged
women to protest against food shortages. It attacked 'the traitor
Laval' who requisitioned fabric for Germany. 'Women, that is why
you can get nothing to clothe your kids and your husbands!' It called
on women to prevent their men from going to Germany to work:
'Persuade them to go to the country [that is, to become resisters], to
fight with all their might against the Boches!'[92]

Many women were drawn into resistance work through family
connections, if not directly through motherhood. The bonds of
loyalty could be extremely useful, though they could also be dangerous. Even supporting resisters in this way represented a politicising
of women's domestic role, because it required a political choice, a
deliberate commitment.[93] The family connection also explains why
Jewish women and Communists were particularly likely to engage in

resistance work. These women belonged to persecuted minorities who had less to lose than others from resisting, and more to gain from an Allied victory. Bertie Albrecht observed, for instance, that she had nothing to lose by becoming a resister because, being Jewish, she was already under sentence of death.[94]

Women also used their peace-time skills and resources to aid resistance activities. Nurses with medical training and secretaries with access to official letterhead or official stamps became invaluable resources to resistance groups. The concierges who controlled access to buildings and kept an eye on activities within them provided information and safe houses, while peasant women were critical to the survival of some rural partisans. Individual women across the social spectrum played a part, from nuns concealing documents in their habits, to prostitutes sheltering escapees.[95] While not every purchase on the black market should be taken to be 'resistance', many ordinary French women enabled resistance activities to occur by turning a blind eye, or simply by 'holding on': enduring to the end. This helps explain why women who did not 'hold on' – who eased hunger, fear and desire by taking German lovers, for instance – were so bitterly resented and so severely punished when France was liberated.

Punishing traitors: the 'shorn women'

The Germans were gradually driven out in France between June and August 1944. In the disorder and confusion of these months, as resistance groups jockeyed for power in post-war France and tried to re-establish systems of government, the desire to punish 'traitors' was widespread. Communities, or individuals within those communities, took the law into their own hands in a wave of 'purification' (*épuration*) or purges of collaborators. These purges were generally confined to the weeks following the liberation of an area, beginning in March 1944. A second wave occurred when surviving prisoners and forced labourers returned home in May–June 1945, with horrific stories of their sufferings. The fact that this corresponded with the return of volunteers who had gone to work in Germany highlighted the issues of collaboration and persecution.[96] Estimates put the numbers executed in the purges at about 10,500, of whom 9000 were executed without trial.[97] Only gradually did the courts assume control over the prosecution of collaborators.

Both women and men were punished for crimes of collaboration, but women were over-represented when compared with the numbers who were convicted of offences in peacetime. They comprised about 25 per cent of those tried before special tribunals, and about 21 per cent of those executed, when they normally represented about 10 per cent of the convicted population.[98] In Brittany, 41.5 per cent of those prosecuted were women.[99] The number of accused women varied geographically, and was particularly great in areas where large numbers of German troops had been present. This reflected the particular forms of collaboration of which women were accused, and prevailing norms of gender relations.

Some women were prosecuted (or executed without trial) for political crimes. In the Hérault, in the south of France, almost 38 per cent of women arrested were charged with political offences, such as belonging to collaborationist parties.[100] The political accusation most frequently brought against women was denunciation. In the Paris region, 76 per cent of those prosecuted were accused of this offence.[101] The Vichy government had, however, encouraged the denunciation of enemies, as some women noted in their defence. One woman argued that she was doing her patriotic duty by denouncing 20 people who broke Vichy law by listening to English radio broadcasts, or who were Communists. Another woman, a member of a Fascist organisation and then of the *Milice*, was inspired by devotion to Marshall Pétain:

> I acted from political passion [...] I was as I have said on the side of the Marshall [...] I didn't love the Germans but after Montoire, I had the impression that we could still reach an accord with them to avoid future wars just as Vichy policy proposed. I pursued these politics because they were the politics of Marshall Pétain.[102]

These cases reveal a strong sense of political engagement by such women. They took responsibility for having acted as political agents, although other women blamed their actions on the influence of husbands or lovers. By prosecuting them, too, the courts treated them as fully responsible for their actions. This contrasts with cases where women were prosecuted as the wives of collaborators rather than in their own right.

The most common accusation against women, however, was not political collaboration but 'sentimental' or 'horizontal' collaboration: sleeping with the enemy. Dozens of women were executed for this crime alone,[103] but many more were ritually humiliated by having their heads shaved. Fabrice Virgili puts the number of *femmes tondues* ('shorn women') at about twenty thousand across France. More than half of these were accused of sexual relations with the enemy, the remainder of other forms of collaboration.[104] This punishment was generally carried out by groups of men, often from the local Resistance unit, and was not officially authorised. But the fact of having had intimate relations with German soldiers was widely regarded in the community as 'collaboration', and the crowds who watched this public ritual usually included women as well as men.[105]

Explanations for this short-lived yet violent phenomenon vary. The victims were generally believed to have traded sexual favours for material reward: not insignificant when basic food supplies, not to mention luxuries like chocolate and silk stockings, were in very short supply. The possibility of a romantic attachment between the pair was rarely seen as credible. So the punishment reflected community anger with those who lightened the burden of their war by consorting with the enemy. These women chose pleasure rather than sharing the suffering of the community. In this sense their actions did represent 'betrayal', particularly if their relationship with the soldier was carried out in public.

The limited available evidence suggests that the majority of those who formed relationships with Germans were particularly vulnerable: young, poorly educated, single or divorced, and with one or both parents dead. The complexities of living under occupation, when 'Nazism' often seemed quite separate from a friendly young German man, made the definition of 'collaboration' problematic.[106] The very act of being seen in public in the company of a German soldier was nevertheless a political act in the eyes of many. It denoted acceptance of the occupation and hence of the humiliation of France. Such women thus disrupted the emerging myth that the people had endured; that France was a nation of resisters.[107]

Nevertheless, the fact that, with few exceptions, the shaving of women's heads was a punishment reserved for women and largely carried out by men highlights the sexual politics of the phenomenon. It was shaped by a pattern of gender relations in which men were accustomed to dominating women. Even little boys recognised this pattern: a group playing partisans in rural Charente Maritime (Western France) in 1944 'attacked' a farmyard, liberated the rabbits and then shaved the heads of three small girls.[108] Sometimes there was an element of personal vengeance, or of local petty tyranny, in these ritualised attacks. But the phenomenon was an international one, reported at the Liberation in a number of European countries.[109]

Shaving women's heads was an act of violence against women, and was often associated with other forms of violence: stripping or partially stripping them, tarring their bodies, painting the swastika on their faces or heads, or between their breasts, and parading them semi-naked through the town. A few women were also raped before or after these attacks.[110] The treatment of such women differed markedly from that reserved for men who had sexual relations with German women, which rarely featured in accounts of their 'collaboration' even though it was forbidden.[111]

As some historians point out, the cutting of women's hair was a 'sexual' punishment, because women's hair was regarded as one of their main sexual attractions. This was therefore a 'sexual' punishment for a sexual 'crime'. The sexual 'crime' was not sleeping with the enemy, however, but asserting their sexual autonomy. One accused woman asserted: 'I had a German lover, however I have never held pro-German ideas.'[112] But this distinction was meaningless because women's free disposal of their bodies, rather than their political ideas or even their sexual relations with Germans specifically, was the underlying issue.

Shaving women's heads was a form of re-appropriation of French women by French men. It suggests that enforcing male control was particularly important at this moment. Julian Jackson argues that the focus on female sexual behaviour at the end of hostilities reflected men's sexual anxieties and jealousies, and perhaps their own guilt at having resisted less than they might have.[113] Men had been humiliated by defeat, and by the failure to fulfil the 'masculine' responsibility of protecting the nation, while women had survived, and (in 1944) were becoming citizens.[114] The shaving of women's heads was a symbolic assertion of male power over women, and an attempt to ensure that the post-war distribution of power between the sexes would remain unchanged.

As Fabrice Virgili suggests, then, the phenomenon of shaving women's heads illustrated the contradictions in relations between the sexes at the end of the Second World War. On the one hand, punishing women for their sexual behaviour implied that they were independent agents who had willingly committed a crime against the nation. On the other hand, the punishment of such sexual misdemeanours indicated that women were not seen as independent individuals.[115] Their identity derived from the men to whom they were related.

A woman 'possessed' by a German became 'German', just as a woman who married a foreigner lost her national identity. Some historians suggest further that this concept of women's contingent status gave the issue of sentimental collaboration broader symbolism: the 'soiled woman', defiled by the enemy, also symbolised the nation, abused by invasion and occupation. To 'purify' women who had collaborated in this way was to purify Marianne too.[116]

The Vichy years saw an attempt to halt the processes of social change which were underway in France before the war, not least those affecting women's lives. Vichy's vision emphasised motherhood and domesticity for women, who were to be shaped physically, intellectually and socially for subordination to men in the home and to a paternalist authoritarian state. Nevertheless, despite its 'separate spheres' agenda, the Vichy regime was forced to continue the politicisation of women, well underway by the 1930s. It needed to win women over to its 'revolution' since they were at the heart of its vision. Vichy propaganda therefore addressed women specifically, thus recognising their political identity. Rural women were presented with arguments about 'what has divided France', and 'what will unite France' (brotherhood, almsgiving, service, a 'logical' social doctrine, love for France, fidelity to the decrees of the Marshall, devotion to the Saint of the Fatherland, Jeanne d'Arc).[117] Urban women were addressed through popular magazines which mobilised fashion in the cause of politics.

Despite the hardships of the war, women illustrated that they were far from disinterested in its outcome. Women's ordinary domestic roles were politicised because ordinary daily roles carried political overtones.[118] Women worked for the victory of the collaborationist project, or for the resistance. In both cases they acted politically. As Paula Schwartz argues of women resisters, they assumed the burdens of citizenship before enjoying citizens' rights.[119] They had mounted the scaffold before gaining access to the tribune. As the war ended, then, it was not just women's political choices that were faulted by some, but their political participation and their assumption of autonomy. The Provisional government assumed control in 1944, announcing universal suffrage, but how France would accommodate a female French citizen remained to be seen.

Part IV
Transformations and Continuities,
1945–2003

9 From the Liberation to 'Women's Liberation', 1945–1975

After France was liberated in 1944, the Vichy regime was succeeded by the Fourth Republic (1946–1958). Vichy's authoritarian agenda was overturned in favour of democracy and women became citizens, marking a major shift in French politics. Yet women did not enjoy full equality under the law despite the fact that sexual equality was inscribed in the Constitution.

Both public discourse and social policy after the war focused on returning women to the home. While many women welcomed the opportunity to resume family life, this political agenda was shaped by the policy objectives of the State, not by the desires expressed by women. Women were to be channelled into this role because they were required to reproduce, and because many people found it difficult to imagine a society that was not shaped around sexual difference. Sexual difference meant women as mothers.

If the 1950s were shaped by the desire to re-create the 'mother' who would now double as the 'modern housewife', the 1960s were to reveal the fragility of that project. A new generation of women began to challenge male domination of social and political life. The rise of the 'women's liberation movement' in the early 1970s marked a new stage in the effort to dismantle power structures based on sexual difference, and to allow women's full participation in society as individuals. By 1975, women had overturned the remnants of legal discrimination, and the concept of female autonomy was widely accepted. They nevertheless faced significant challenges in negotiating a path between personal independence and family responsibilities.

Returning to 'normal' life

The end of hostilities in 1944 did not mark the end of hardship. France had suffered 600,000 war casualties, both military and civilian. Infant mortality had skyrocketed, and was higher in 1945–1946 than during the Occupation.[1] Nearly four million prisoners, forced labourers, and refugees had to be brought home, reunited with their families and rehabilitated. Most of the country had been a battleground. The infrastructure lay in ruins. Railways and ports had been devastated, and bridges and roads destroyed. A quarter of all buildings had been reduced to rubble, and nearly two million homes were either completely destroyed or uninhabitable. More than 500,000 families needed rehousing. Coal for fuel and electricity generation was in short supply. In the winter of 1944–1945, coal was limited to less than a kilogramme per day for each family in Lyon, while Paris was completely without fuel.[2]

Malnutrition affected 75 per cent of the population in 1945, and a study showed that 14-year-olds were seven to nine kilogrammes lighter, and seven to eleven centimetres shorter, than those of 1935.[3] Food supplies remained inadequate. Meat was a luxury, and adults were entitled to only 160 grams per week. Bread was rationed until 1948; sugar and dairy products until 1949. Children over six lost their entitlement to a milk ration. The black market still flourished, but prices were beyond the means of ordinary people. Women's problems in feeding their families therefore continued unabated. They continued to queue with their ration books at whatever store happened to have produce to sell. Rural women faced added difficulties in registering for rations and in getting goods delivered, given the lack of transport.[4]

With the return of POWs, families were reunited. Many women were relieved to surrender the additional burdens of supporting their families as single parents. Rural women, in particular, welcomed a reduction in their hard labour on the farm.[5] But reunions were sometimes an occasion for renewed pain. Some men returned physically weakened and psychologically damaged by their experiences. Some were prone to depression; others to fits of rage. Many felt shame at their capture and at the devastating French defeat, and were bitter at inadequate compensation for their captivity. Spouses no longer knew each other, and fathers and children were strangers. Divorce rates rose sharply in 1945 and 1946.[6]

Some wives later reported severe pressure to submit to their husbands' authority in order to help them readjust. But women had developed new skills, self-confidence and independence as a result of their wartime experiences, and some were unwilling to do so. One woman observed:

> The return of the men created serious problems. The women did not want to renounce the rights that they had been forced to acquire in 1940. Those women who, during the war, had grown accustomed to dealing with all the problems left them by their husbands, did not accept that they should suddenly become of negligible importance in the couple once again.[7]

This problem seems to have been greatest amongst younger women who played active roles in resistance organisations. One later explained:

> From my engagement in the Resistance I retained a sort of intellectual independence that I have found in other women. We had become aware of the roles we could play. After that period, the young women who were 21 to 24 years old at the time of the Liberation, wanted to live as independent women.[8]

Women's memories of these events may have been inflected by later experiences and ideas.[9] Nevertheless, some women did not accept that women's wartime experiences had changed nothing.

Citizenship without liberation

Women's post-war situation was different in one key respect from before the war: they were now citizens of the nation for the first time. On 24 March 1944 the Consultative Assembly of the French National Committee of Liberation (CFLN), which had assumed power in Algeria, had decided that 'Women will be electors and eligible for election on the same terms as men.'[10] General de Gaulle, President of the CFLN, signed the ordinance on 21 April. Considerable debate surrounds the origins of this decision by men to grant women the same rights they themselves possessed. Women had been campaigning for citizenship in France for decades. The first debates over the question had been heard during the French Revolution itself, when the idea was roundly defeated. After the measure was passed in 1944, however, when women were eyed warily as voters, all political groups were keen to present themselves as supporters of the change.

The Resistance movement, unified in 1943, claimed the credit for female suffrage, but none of the programmes of the member-groups included such a provision. The parties of the pre-war Left had a stronger record on the question than those of the Right, and the Communists now declared that women had earned the vote by their resistance to the German oppressor. The Radicals tried to redeem their reputation as the intransigent opponents of female suffrage by highlighting interwar legislation benefiting women, for which they claimed the credit. The new Christian Democrat party (the MRP) asserted that de Gaulle had proposed female suffrage in June 1942. He was therefore responsible for liberating women. There is no independent evidence for this claim, although his opposition in 1944 would probably have been fatal.[11]

The vote in the Consultative Assembly was not a ringing endorsement for women's enfranchisement. Fifty-seven men voted for the proposition and sixteen against, but four were absent and ten abstained. If the abstentions are taken to be unsupportive, 26 men – close to 30 per cent – were opposed. The debates also revealed considerable opposition. The question was discussed on at least 10 occasions before the final debate in the Consultative Assembly. No-one suggested, as Claire Duchen points out, that women should vote because they had the same 'inalienable rights' as men.[12] Rather, many objections were raised, not least by Commission president Paul Giacobbi, a Radical from Corsica: was women's vote 'indispensable'? Was it of 'great importance' that they vote? Others raised practical problems: there were no electoral lists for women, and voting would be delayed by drawing them up. If the lists were assembled too hastily they might be inaccurate or even fraudulent.[13]

The debates, both behind the scenes and in the public assembly on 24 March, were acrimonious according to former Resistance leader, Raymond Aubrac.[14] The prospect of female power at the ballot box alarmed many. Many French men were still prisoners and would be unable to vote for some months. Enfranchising women before the men returned would give them an 'unequal' weighting in the results. There was also the risk that women would vote 'impulsively'. One speaker argued that 'twice as many women as men will take part in the vote. Will this give us a true picture of the views of the country?'

Another feared that women might be two and a half times as numerous as men – a worse nightmare! Women's suffrage should be delayed, they suggested, so that women would vote for the first time when 'normal conditions' prevailed.[15]

These arguments, as well as being self-serving, seem ironic from the perspective of women. The complete exclusion of women was not perceived to skew the outcome of elections or prevent a 'true picture' of the national mind. 'Normal conditions' were those in which all men and no women voted, not those in which women might outnumber men (though not by the margins suggested). The motion finally presented for debate was thus a compromise designed to neutralise women's influence without rejecting their citizenship altogether: 'women will be eligible for election on the same terms as men'. But the Communist Fernand Grenier put an amendment: 'women will be electors and eligible for election on the same terms as men'. The reiteration of objections led Louis Vallon, Socialist and friend of de Gaulle, to intervene:

> I hear in this debate all the most detestable traditions of the old French Parliament. The Parliament voted almost unanimously on many occasions for the principle of female suffrage, but each time, procedural arrangements were devised so that the reform should not succeed. These little subterfuges have to end.

After the applause had died down he added less confidently, 'we have to be able to take risks'.[16] On this occasion, the 'risk' was finally taken.

Women first voted in the municipal elections of April 1945. One high school teacher sent an account to a Swiss feminist newspaper describing the joy of her first experience of voting: 'Yes, despite the rain, it was a fine day, amongst all the fine days which now remain for us to live.'[17] The national elections in October that year saw 33 women elected to the Constituent Assembly which was to draw up a new constitution. When the first National Assembly of the Fourth Republic was elected in November 1946, 35 women were elected, 6.48 per cent of the total. The proportion of women deputies was not to reach that level again for 40 years.[18] Indeed, the history of the Fourth Republic was one of women's gradual withdrawal or exclusion from visible positions in the National Assembly and the political parties.

The election of women in 1945–1946 reflected the particular context of the immediate post-war era. Nineteen of the women elected in 1945 had backgrounds in the Resistance. Twelve had been decorated for their achievements. Seven had served prison terms.[19] These women were legitimately seen as Resistance heroes, and their presence reflected the Resistance context in which the Constituent Assembly was established. In addition, the significant number of women echoed the strength of the Left, especially of the Communist Party, which gained more than 25 per cent of the vote in both national elections. Seventeen of the women elected in 1945 represented the Communist Party and another six the Socialists.[20]

The MRP and the PCF made serious efforts to attract women voters from the start. The PCF had developed a Women's Charter that included provision for equal pay and crèches, and had established the Union of French Women (UFF) to reach women outside the Party. The PCF included significant numbers of women on Party lists in this period, including many placed first or second, and hence with a real possibility of being elected. The MRP stood fewer candidates, but claimed to be the Party defending the family. Its links to the Catholic Church and to Free France leader Charles de Gaulle also stood it in good stead with some. The MRP attracted a larger number of women voters than the Communists, who picked up a higher share of the male vote.[21]

Many of the women elected to the Assembly brought a desire to address issues customarily defined as part of women's sphere. Re-ordering the country and feeding the population were presented as problems of good housekeeping. As the Socialist Germaine Degrond argued, 'the question of food [...] concerns women, even *députés*, a good deal more than the rows upon rows of budget figures'.[22] Women representatives focused on measures that would improve family life in the war-affected situation, such as crèches and canteens to assist working mothers. Such measures were part of the Communist platform. But women's perspectives were similar across political lines, and they sometimes supported women from other political parties. Hilary Footitt argues that women in the first Assembly – for whom there were no role models – attempted to create the 'woman representative', skilled on issues of concern to a female constituency.[23]

There is some evidence that their approach did meet the expectations of women voters. Women interviewed prior to the elections of 1945 expected that women representatives would help pass social legislation, and would know more about things affecting mothers and children. One said: 'Women have a much clearer grasp of the needs of a family, of the nightmare of the high cost of living; perhaps they'll have more common sense, clearer solutions and be more persevering in improving the food situation.'[24]

The shared interest amongst the 'parties of resistance' in creating a new state may also account for the degree of unanimity on some questions. Few disagreed that the food problem was an issue of great priority. But unanimity soon gave way to 'party politics' in which women defended their parties rather than pursuing female solidarity. This was perhaps an inevitable result of a 'return to normal' after the euphoria of the liberation. Politics became a contest again and personal ambition was unleashed amongst aspiring politicians. Women faced growing difficulty in being placed on party lists, particularly in the winnable first or second position. Socialist, Radical and MRP women all complained about this problem.[25]

Many women regarded the demands of political office as unmanageable at this time, given their other responsibilities. Hannah Diamond's case study of Toulouse is revealing on this point. Resistance to the enemy during the occupation was defined as 'patriotism' rather than 'politics' by the women she interviewed. They did not necessarily expect to continue their public activities after the war. Political life was difficult enough for women voters, let alone for would-be representatives. Evening meetings were as inconvenient for women in the 1940s as they had been in the nineteenth century. One woman recalled: 'Post-war politics was a very difficult commitment for a woman. Despite everything they had to have children – the husband could only ever be a helper because the greatest part of that always falls to us women.'[26]

Female activists in Toulouse withdrew from politics in the late 1940s because peace brought other priorities. The sociologist Evelyne Sullerot, who was 20 in 1944, reported a similar trend: women began to focus on having families, not because of natalist campaigns insisting that they reproduce, but as 'a reaction against death'.[27] Had there been a genuine desire for women to participate in the legislative process, ways might have been found to make it easier for them to do so. The fact that women always carried the 'greatest part' of the burden of childrearing was perceived as part of the 'problem' only by a few.

The Toulouse example highlights a second factor. Women did not necessarily see a connection between voting (or standing for office) and the problems of their daily lives. Even active Communists who participated in their local cells saw 'women's issues' as separate from 'politics'. One woman explained that, when Communist women got together socially, 'we hadn't been together two minutes, just the women, when two problems were raised. One, relations with the husband, the fact that he let the wife do everything in the house. The second was the fear of getting pregnant.'[28] The 'personal' was not 'political' in 1945 as it would be in the 1970s. And women who were overburdened by the 'personal' had no time or inclination to add the 'political' to their load. This suited the many men who believed that women had no place in politics. The first studies by political scientists in the 1950s were clear that men would not vote for women, and only 14 per cent of men (and 22 per cent of women) could imagine a woman President. Even in the 1960s, 21 per cent of those polled still opposed female suffrage.[29]

Despite complaints over 'women's issues', however, feminism was weak in the post-war years. Feminist organisations had been effectively demobilised by the failures of the 1920s, the focus on antifascism and peace activism in the 1930s, and the war. With suffrage won, the main impetus for feminist activism was lost. The pre-war feminists of the French League for Women's Rights continued to argue for reform of the Civil Code and for women's integration into political life, but few were listening. Paradoxically, then, as Claire Duchen notes, the introduction of female suffrage had the effect of demobilising women as a force or an interest group, divided though that 'group' was.[30]

Domesticity and the 'modern' housewife

Post-war social policy focused on rebuilding the economy and rebuilding the French population. This double-barrelled policy had double-edged implications for women, whose contribution to both objectives was essential. The belief that women were mothers above all else was critical to shaping policies affecting women, and to the model of the 'new France' that was constructed in the immediate post-war years. But juggling work and family roles continued to place enormous pressure on women.

General de Gaulle's oft-quoted phrase that France needed 'twelve million bouncing babies in ten years'[31] set the agenda for a natalist programme after the war that bore a remarkable resemblance to its predecessors. The idea of marrying and having children accorded with the aspirations of many people in 1945. Delayed marriage and childbearing sent indicators soaring as the war ended. The marriage rate in 1945 was higher than it had been for decades, and reached unprecedented heights in the 1946–1950 period. The birth rate rose to 21.3 per thousand for the first time since 1902. The baby boom saw 840,000 live births in 1946, up from 613,000 in 1943. Figures began to drop in 1950, stabilising at about 800,000 for the following decade. French women had on average three children, compared with one child in the interwar period.[32]

Motherhood was the ideal to which French women were encouraged to aspire in this period. The Constitution of 1946 focused on their maternal role even as it declared them citizens. Article 24 stated: 'The Nation guarantees woman the exercise of her functions as female citizen and worker in conditions that allow her to fulfil her role as mother and her social mission.'[33] Citizenship for women was thus construed in terms that emphasised their 'difference' from men. No 'new' version of womanhood for the new Republic was envisaged. This constitutional statement even suggested that citizenship was not automatically compatible with motherhood. The model of 'the citizen' still remained male.

Changes in fashion after the war reflected the ambiguous identity of the 'mother-citizen'. Christian Dior's 1947 spring collection introduced the 'new look' (the English expression was used). Its accentuated bust and hips presented a reproductive female form, while the metres of material in full skirts and draped fabrics contrasted with the simple styles imposed by wartime shortages.[34] But Dior's models were often photographed in the open air, before major French monuments like the Eiffel Tower, or before famous paintings in the Louvre. In this context, the 'new look' was not a statement about demure housewives confined to reproduction. Rather the models became cultural icons, reasserting the position of French *haute couture*, or perhaps of France itself, in a world where America now claimed predominance. Besides, at large in the city, wearing tailored suits and carrying 'masculine' accessories like furled umbrellas, Dior's models inhabited male space. In this respect the 'new look' woman was the antithesis of the Vichy woman, who was ideally rural and domestic. The representation of an idealised female form again conveyed broader cultural and political messages.[35]

The prominent busts, hips and bottoms of 'new look' clothing, and the stiletto heels worn with it, might also be read as provocative and sexualised representations of women, rather than as 'reproductive' insignia. The 'new look' conveyed a sense of fun after the austerities and severity of war. It rejected the rigid Vichy moral code that had demonised female sexuality and desire.[36] The 'new look' was complex and ambiguous in its representation of femininity, then, capturing the ambiguities in the position of women in post-war French society. It also illustrated how 'femininity' both shaped, and was shaped by, the new social and political context.

An attempt was also made in the post-war years to construe domesticity as a new and modern occupation rather than a timeless mission. Popular magazines for women provide an insight into the evolution of the 'ideal' housewife in the post-war period. *Elle* magazine, established in 1945, initially focused on helping women deal with the problems of running a home in a situation of austerity. It gave household hints on reviving that old sweater, making bland foods appetising, and keeping the family warm without proper heating. Being inventive and imaginative was the key in January 1948: '*Elle* is the queen of the Make-Doers.'[37]

By 1955, when one in six French women read *Elle*, its image of the ideal housewife had evolved. Its 'modern' home was a bright and pleasant place. Its 'modern' housewife ran an efficient operation surrounded by new appliances like washing machines, refrigerators and dishwashers. This picture was far from realistic. Most families lived in poor and overcrowded conditions until a massive post-war building programme brought housing supply in line with demand. In 1954, only half of French homes had running water; half of rural homes still had no running water in 1962. A poll in 1951 showed that 39 per cent of *Elle* readers bathed only once a month. Only 10 per cent had a bath or shower in their homes in 1954. The demand for labour-saving devices was real, then, but unrealistic for most. The commercials for domestic appliances shown on French television were filmed in American kitchens.[38] Initially *Elle* also used American models who looked healthier and more glamorous than malnourished French women.[39]

The modern housewife was also presented as 'scientific' and efficient in the 1950s. The 'bible' for the housewife was *The House-keeping Manual* (*La Méthode Ménagère*) by Paulette Bernège, first published in 1938 but reprinted many times. Her ideas dominated domestic science teaching, and were popularised in the women's press. Housework should not be done haphazardly, she argued. Ideally, the layout of the workspace and the organisation of tasks should allow the worker to 'move constantly forward, in a straight line, without coming and going or retracing steps'.[40] The ideal housewife should be efficient and work to a timetable.

How the 'average' French woman with three small children would manage this production line is not immediately apparent. Besides, working-class women's access to appliances initially came through co-operative purchases with other families, and for rural women appliances were slow to come at all. As Claire Duchen notes, only 9 per cent of agricultural workers owned a refrigerator in 1954, compared with 34 per cent of senior managers.[41] For many women, the initial acquisition of these labour-saving devices stood out as one of the most significant changes in their lifetimes.[42] Studies in the 1950s suggested, however, that the time spent on housework did not decline as domestic appliances were acquired.[43]

Women in the workforce

The 1946 Constitution stipulated that 'the law will guarantee to women rights equal to those of men in all spheres'. Nevertheless, many women were dismissed from their jobs as the war ended, employers once again giving priority to men. The State set a poor example: the new Statute on the civil service declared that 'women have access to all public employment insofar as their presence in the administration is justified by the interests of the service' – hardly a rousing affirmation of equality![44]

Despite the emphasis on female domesticity, women comprised a significant proportion of the paid labour force. In particular, the proportion of married women continued to grow, except in the agricultural sector. In 1946, 39 per cent of the non-agricultural female workforce was married, but 50 per cent of that group was married in 1962. Over that period, also, the percentage of married women in the workforce (excluding the agricultural sector) rose from 19.6 to 24.5 per cent. Their numbers had risen more than 10 per cent in every age category except the 35–44 age bracket. Many of these women had two or three children.[45]

This trend reflected the rise of a consumer society. Two wages were often needed if families were to afford domestic appliances, and families often wanted a car as well. The creation of low-rent housing estates (HLMs) on the fringes of the cities eased the housing shortage but increased the need for transport to work. The French car industry therefore expanded rapidly in the 1950s, although only one in seven people owned a car in 1958.[46]

If more married women with children were working, this did not produce a more equitable distribution of domestic labour in the 1950s and 1960s. The idealised family was one in which the husband was the provider and the wife the nurturer, but even where the wife shared the providing, social norms did not require the husband to undertake household duties. Studies of the time allocation of married women in 1947 showed that those in paid employment spent less time on housework than non-employed women. But for a woman with three children, who typically spent more than 70 hours per week on housework, paid employment was an additional hardship rather than a liberating option.[47]

The overall number of women in paid work fell between 1946 and 1954, but this was largely due to their departure from agriculture. This period saw a major transformation of the rural sector, increasing mechanisation of farms, and the migration of many rural-dwellers to the towns: a process that continued into the 1960s. Women were over-represented amongst those who left in this period. Whereas 3.3 million women were paid agricultural workers in 1946 (44 per cent of the total), their numbers had declined to one million (32 per cent) by 1968, and to 628,000 (30 per cent) in 1975.[48] Young rural women envisaged better prospects in the towns, even though the majority became unskilled factory workers. Indeed, women working in industry tended to be young and unqualified, with few occupational choices. White-collar work continued to increase in popularity, and secretarial training remained a desirable qualification for girls.[49]

The more highly qualified a woman, the more likely she was to continue working after marriage, but the numbers of professional women were low. According to *Le Monde*, there were 3000 women doctors and 1102 women lawyers registered to practise their profession in 1955, although the numbers qualified were higher. The great majority of professional women were teachers. This was the career into which the majority of girls who matriculated were steered. Few were encouraged to apply for the elite professional schools, the so-called *Grandes Ecoles*.[50]

Women teachers had had equal pay for several decades, but this remained an exception. Professional women earned a smaller share of the equivalent male income than less qualified women. They earned 63 per cent of male salaries in 1962, whereas factory workers earned 69 per cent of the male rate. In both cases, women's lower incomes reflected ongoing discrimination: the civil service continued to reserve some jobs for men, for example. But the fact that women were clustered at lower echelons throughout the workforce, and often had broken careers, added to their disadvantage. The declaration of June 1946 awarding equal pay to women remained ineffective in practice.[51]

The Cold War and the politics of 'women's place'

The post-war return to 'normal' was extremely short-lived, because new political crises soon unfolded. The Vietnam War erupted in December 1946, initiating a sustained period of colonial conflict for France. Barely had the French extricated themselves from Vietnam in 1954, with 172,000 French casualties, when the Algerian uprising (November 1954) initiated an even more bloody and insoluble conflict that would drag on until 1962. The Algerian War divided the French community. The crisis was so severe in 1958 that the Fourth Republic was overturned. General de Gaulle's promise to end the war brought him to power as the first President of the Fifth Republic (1958-present).

On the broader world stage, meanwhile, the Cold War had been unleashed in March 1947 when American President Truman declared: 'The world is dividing into two camps, the free and the unfree [...] Every nation must choose.' The choice facing France was to expel the Communists from government or lose American reconstruction aid. They chose the American bloc in May 1947.[52] This decision opened further rifts in the community that endured for decades.

Raising questions about women's place in politics became more difficult as the political climate became more threatening. Political parties, after the first flush of enthusiasm when women voters were an unknown quantity, did not work to integrate women into party structures or develop policies designed to attract them. Despite the fact that women were now individuals with equal rights, the prevailing view envisaged them as mothers, subsumed within the family, under the protection and authority of men. Despite the political differences dividing MRP and Leftist politicians, Fourth Republic programmes focused on the family, and favoured families with a single male breadwinner.[53]

Political polarisation strengthened with the onset of the Cold War. The bitter ideological divide had major implications for women.

After the expulsion of the Communists in 1947, the electoral system was changed to limit the electoral strength of the PCF. As a result, the number of Communist women deputies dropped by 11–15 in 1951. Simultaneously, de Gaulle's creation in 1947 of a new political group, the Rally of the French People (RPF), weakened the MRP: the only other party to cultivate women. While the RPF sought women's votes it did not foster women candidates and had no women's organisation, unlike the MRP. The two parties which had had the largest numbers of women deputies in 1945–1946 were both considerably weakened during the 1950s.[54]

The 'threat' posed by Communism, as presented in Vatican pronouncements, mobilised Catholic voters in defence of religion and family. Nevertheless, the Cold War did not create a gulf between Left and Right in their vision for women, or their approach to women voters. Rather, they found common ground – perhaps their only common ground – in defending the 'unchangeability' of womanhood.[55] Right and Left became locked in a contest not only for women's loyalties, but also for defending the most 'maternal' image of women.

French Communists, through the UFF, had previously defended the rights of women as both mothers and workers. From 1947, however, they entered into competition with the Catholic women's organisation, the UFCS, to present themselves as the defenders of motherhood and the family. The Catholic accusation that Communism destroyed the family and collectivised childrearing forced Communist women to outdo them in their adulation and support of motherhood. As in the 1930s, the images of motherhood presented by Right and Left differed. The Catholic UFCS couched its vision in an anti-modernist context which Chaperon describes as 'sacrificial motherhood' (*mères sacrifice*), while the Communists created the heroic image of 'courageous motherhood' (*mères courage*). The ideal Communist mother was still involved in the struggle for a better world beyond the home, whereas the ideal Catholic mother sacrificed herself to the well-being of her family.[56]

Given the maternal focus of both Catholic and Communist organisations, there was little real debate over policies affecting women. The UFF campaigned for revision of the Civil Code until 1947, but then abandoned the struggle. It also abandoned the effort to promote the liberation of women through paid work. This meant that its policies were increasingly similar to those of the Catholic UFCS that defended Family Allowances and promoted the 'mother at home'.[57]

Support across the political spectrum for natalist policies also had important consequences for women. Catholic rejection of contraception and abortion was not surprising. They stepped up their efforts to prevent revision of French laws, and found new arguments against working mothers by citing their lower childbearing rates. But Communist women also rejected contraception as a capitalist conspiracy against workers, campaigning for painless childbirth instead.[58] The strict laws of the 1920s against abortion and contraception were strengthened, therefore, in 1946. In the post-war world, and particularly with the onset of the Cold War, the insistence of the main political groups on the maternal destiny of women remained emphatic, despite women's newfound political rights and their presence in the workforce. The challenge to this view was to be led by the 'baby-boomers' who had a broader view of their own talents and destiny.

Modernity and the generation gap

In the early 1950s, *Elle* magazine began a column for teenagers called 'Us Girls'. It addressed girls as though they were younger versions of their mothers, destined to become housewives and mothers too. When the magazine featured an intellectual like Simone de Beauvoir, or '70 women novelists', it focused on their domestic life, their children, or their cooking skills rather than on their talents or careers.[59] The message conveyed to the girls of the 1950s was that domesticity was the norm for women, whether they were celebrities or not. In retaining domestic science lessons for girls, too, the Fourth Republic aimed, as one teacher noted, to help them 'understand that their true happiness lies in the home'.[60]

By the early 1960s, this 'understanding' was becoming less obvious to adolescent girls, as both *Elle* and its new offshoot for teenagers, *Mademoiselle*, recognised. Having a husband and children was still part of girls' imagined lives as adults, but they also envisaged a career and personal success.[61] The newly-discovered 'female adolescent', therefore, was not a clone of her mother. Not only was she often better educated, she was deeply embroiled (along with adolescent boys) in the consumer revolution. She was acquiring more freedom, and was more influenced by external forces – cinema, radio, her peers – than her mother had been. Her aspirations and expectations were therefore changing as well.

The expansion of education was one of the main factors transforming young people's lives in the post-war years. Adolescents of both sexes began to stay at school longer. Boys still outnumbered girls significantly in the technical stream, giving them useful qualifications when they left school at 16, while girls leaving at this age were qualified only for menial jobs.[62] But parents and their daughters aspired to better opportunities for girls. Parents complained about courses in needlework and childcare that left them employable only as servants, or prepared them for occupations that had disappeared. Young people at Colombelles, in Normandy, complained themselves: 'Girls don't have access to professional training and employment with the same opportunity as boys [...] because people have retained the old idea of "the woman at home".'[63]

Significant social differences remained in access to the higher levels of secondary education. In 1962, only 16 per cent of the children of farmers and workers went on to upper secondary school, against 75 per cent of children of higher civil servants. Rural students who did enter the *lycée* (academic high school) often felt isolated and unwelcome in the urban world, while their education made them outsiders back in the village. One young woman noted: 'life at high school influences our attitudes, our ways of thinking, or dressing'. Rural boys saw them as 'town girls' and stopped asking them to dances. The disorientation expressed by rural girls helps to explain why the exodus to the towns in this period was led by young women. Besides, rural life was coming to be seen as inferior to the lifestyle of the town. In 1966, only one per cent of 15–20-year-olds aspired to be farmers.[64]

University education remained largely the province of the children of the urban middle classes, but girls were participating more equally. Their numbers progressed steadily from under 26,000 in 1945–1946, to nearly 97,000 in 1962–1963. The professional disciplines were still difficult to enter. In law, for instance, women made up only 20 per cent of students in 1945–1946 and less than 28 per cent in 1963. Only a third of medical students were female in 1963–1964. By contrast, women made up more than half those studying for the equivalent of an Arts degree across this period, and almost half of women studying at university in 1962–1963 were enrolled in Arts Faculties.[65]

The expansion of education reflected the fact that families had less need of adolescent labour, and that an educated workforce was necessary to the continued expansion of the economy. It also had social implications. Young people spent the years from 14 to 18, when earlier generations had become workers, in the company of others of their own age. Teenagers began to see themselves as a social entity in their own right and their parents recognised the same trend, with less equanimity.

Differences between girls and boys were often less significant amongst teenagers than their shared desire to express their difference from the older generation. This period saw the unfolding of different lifestyles for young women compared to those of their mothers. The young woman who turned 15 in 1955 was too young to recall the hardships of the war and knew only a world of prosperity. As she moved into adulthood between 1955 and 1960, she did so in an expanding economy and a strengthening consumer culture. This culture of plenty (although not accessible equally to all) differed dramatically from the environment of hardship that surrounded those who grew up in the 1930s.

The consumer revolution of the late 1950s and 1960s targeted young people, rightly perceived as an expanding market. A business journal in 1963 noted that 15–20-year-olds represented 'four million fine consumers', an echo of de Gaulle's 'twelve million bouncing babies' at the end of the war. The introduction of pocket money gave students considerable spending power, estimated in 1966 at five billion francs. Adolescents of both sexes sought transistor radios and record players. In 1966, 46 per cent of 15–20-year-olds had a transistor, and 42 per cent had a record player. Like the mobile phone today, the transistor was almost 'a bodily appendage' of the teenager. Its pervasiveness shocked adults and led the Michelin restaurant guide to indicate establishments that were 'transistor free'. But again, farmers' children lagged behind, only 34 per cent owning a transistor in 1966.[66]

American pop music became available to a wide audience from 1959, when radio station Europe 1 began a daily programme.[67] In the 1960s British pop music made its mark, and French singers began to record versions of British songs, as in Sylvie Vartan's *Twiste et Chante* ('Twist and Shout', 1963).[68]

Both boys and girls aspired to own a car. In 1961, 21 per cent of females aged 24, and 24 per cent of males, had achieved that goal. In 1959, 200,000 women had driving licences, compared with 26,000 in 1949. Socio-economic disparities amongst the young were accentuated by car-ownership, but saving for a car became a common experience.[69] The magical appeal of the car, especially for the young, was portrayed in films such as Jean-Luc Godard's *A Bout de Souffle* ('Breathless', 1959), in which the American convertible is the third star (along with Jean Seberg and Jean-Paul Belmondo). Already 18-year-old Françoise Sagan had placed *la belle américaine* ('the beautiful American' car) at the centre of her bestselling novel, *Bonjour Tristesse* (1954).[70]

Young women's disposable income was spent on a range of consumer goods. Expenditure on clothes increased dramatically, with adolescents' objective being to differentiate themselves from their parents. A variety of different 'looks' emerged, each with a specific hairstyle and makeup. Jeans and miniskirts made their appearance, and Sylvie Vartan popularised the platinum blonde look in 1963. Teenage girls also spent their pocket-money on makeup – not powder and lipstick like their mothers, but eyeliner – along with foundation to hide the newly discovered scourge of youth: pimples. Products for personal hygiene were also marketed to young women, who purchased deodorants, depilatory products and cleansers. The taboo surrounding menstruation began to erode with the advertising of Modess pads, while the promotion of tampons indicated that young women now understood their own anatomy.[71]

The impact of Sylvie Vartan's blonde makeover in 1963 illustrates another factor at work from the 1950s: the increasing impact of media images on young women's self-image and aspirations. The teenage girl singer was 'created' as a media product in the 1960s, Françoise Dorléac and Françoise Hardy rivalling Sylvie Vartan for appeal.[72] Adolescent girls were presented with the idea that 'stardom', or at least the opportunity to lead an exciting life, was not confined to men, just as music and advertising created the illusion that purchasing power was unrelated to social background. Youth culture appeared to override class and sex divisions. Teenage magazines like *Salut les Copains* addressed themselves to all young people, and both working-class apprentices and middle-class adolescents identified with their contents. Similarly, young women were enabled to think of themselves as part of *les jeunes*, the young generation, not as beings limited by their sex.[73]

Adolescent girls found other models at the cinema, where the social norms of femininity were questioned. Most famous was the screen character portrayed by Brigitte Bardot in the film *Et Dieu créa la Femme* ('And God created Woman', 1956). Bardot challenged the construction of femininity as demure and innocent, and especially as submissive and dependent. 'B.B.', as she was known (pronounced in French like the word *bébé*, 'baby'), portrayed an independent-minded woman who used her sexuality not just to reward and punish, but also to assert her own desires. For young women of the 1950s, 'B.B.' was 'the explosion of all that was forbidden'. The ideas she represented brought girls into conflict with their mothers, who chastised signs of 'behaving like B.B.' in their daughters.[74]

Bardot's screen persona suggested the possibilities of freedom for young women, an urge also evident in some female pop songs. Sylvie Vartan's *Je Suis Libre* ('I am free', 1962) is a good example. Though not written by her, its lyrics put into the mouth of a leading female singer a sense of personal independence: 'I am free to live my life.' 'No-one has any rights over me anymore, no-one lays down the law to me anymore.' 'I am furious when someone stops me doing this or that, I am not a child any longer, I have already passed the age of slavery.'[75] These sentiments might also have been expressed by a rebellious adolescent boy but have particular resonance, given the constraints on young women.

Adolescent girls did gain greater freedom in the post-war decades. They 'hung out' with their girlfriends or with boys at cafés or in the streets, or socialised around the juke-box. Young people were the strongest patrons of the cinema, and almost every village had at least one. Dances were still popular, particularly in rural areas, because they were accessible and inexpensive. *La surprise-partie*, on the other hand, required a record player, a spacious room for dancing, and co-operative parents.[76]

Such parties were sometimes occasions for *le flirt*: the other key sign of young women's increasing liberty. *Le flirt* was a teenage ritual that involved close embraces and kissing but generally excluded sexual intercourse. Once young people began to socialise outside the family, adult controls on sexual behaviour weakened. But adolescent sexuality had its own taboos. In 1961 the majority of young people still regarded premarital sex as 'dangerous' for women because of possible pregnancy, or even 'reprehensible' on moral grounds. It was more acceptable for boys. However, by the end of the 1950s half of young women had prenuptial sex (up from one third in the 1930s). By 1970, the overwhelming majority of those aged 16–24 had come to regard it as 'normal'; in 1972, 90 per cent of young women had lost their virginity before the age of 18.[77]

Marriage was still the goal of young women and they married very young. In 1964, the average age at marriage was 22.8 for women and

25.1 for men.[78] For women of this generation, marriage presented decisions that it had presented to few of their mothers. In the 1930s and 1940s, paid work had most often been a necessity, a temporary one perhaps, preceding or intersecting with their central role as wife and mother. By the 1960s, adolescent women were torn between the attractions of a continuing career, and the expectation that they centre their lives on the domestic role. The final verse of Sylvie Vartan's *Je Suis Libre* articulated the dilemma of the young woman for whom marriage was imagined as destiny, but also as a loss of autonomy. The dilemma is resolved in the lyrics by presenting self-surrender as freely chosen out of love, against the wishes of 'the world': 'Marriage doesn't scare me, I will be the servant of my lord and master'; 'I am free, you can shut me away [...] you can chain me up, I don't give a damn, I have given myself, I am free, free to love you.'[79] The conflict between freedom and 'destiny' for young women in the 1950s and 1960s was powerful in real life.

Some young women in the early 1960s objected to the fact that domesticity deprived a married woman of other avenues of fulfilment. High school students at Domérat, in the Allier, argued: 'The woman no longer wants to be the one whose role consists of keeping house [...] Women want to be equal to men in society, they want to have real political power [...] They want access to all situations.' Other students argued that work gave a wife independence as well as personal satisfaction and intellectual enrichment. They suggested radical solutions for the problems of working mothers: childcare institutions, sharing domestic tasks with the husband and taking time out from work (in turn) to care for them. They realised, however, that these solutions were visionary at that time.[80]

But many reasserted the dominant view that the primary role of a married woman was in the home: 'She either sacrifices her family for her career, or she sacrifices her career for her family.' In 1961, 18 per cent of those aged 16–24 believed that a woman should stop work at marriage, and another 49 per cent that she should retire when a child was born. They found it impossible to reconcile their ideas about women's right to professional equality and intellectual development with the dilemma of family life, and opted for the *femme au foyer* as the only solution.[81] Women at the end of the war had often seen the home as a haven. Their daughters – better educated, with the prospect of more rewarding work, and immersed in a consumerist world – were less certain of that, but they were equally uncertain about the alternatives.

Strengthening debates over marriage and sexuality

The constraints of the maternal ideal presented an insoluble dilemma for independent-minded young women of the 1960s, but the restrictiveness of this ideal was bolstered by French law. There were two particular areas where women faced major sex-specific problems: the laws governing marriage and those limiting women's right to control their fertility. Women's activism in the 1950s and 1960s focused on these problems and the second, in particular, also mobilised sympathetic men.

Despite earlier revisions, the Civil Code of the Fourth Republic retained the provision defining the husband as head of the family. This entailed an array of legal and financial penalties for women. Once female equality with men was formally acknowledged in the Constitution of 1946, women expected to see anomalies removed from the legal code, but this was not achieved during the life of the Fourth Republic.

The first reform bill was introduced by the government of the Fifth Republic in 1959, after years of campaigning by women. But de Gaulle's regime was no more favourable to legal equality for women than its predecessor. The bill retained husbands' control of both jointly owned property, and that owned by their wives. Feminist lawyers argued that these provisions were contrary to the Constitution and the Universal Declaration of Human Rights, which France had ratified. The bill also retained male 'headship' of the family. The Minister for Justice argued that this was consistent with 'the most ancient [...] and the most reasonable traditions'. Opposition by Communists, feminists and a variety of women's organisations across France saw the bill become a dead letter when it was debated in 1960.[82]

Another Bill was introduced in 1965. While it proposed more equality (enabling women to control their own property, for instance), it still retained the notion of a 'family head', made the husband administrator of joint property, and enabled him to prevent his wife exercising a profession if it endangered 'the interests of the family'. A wife was nevertheless responsible for half the marital debt. The Attorney-General argued that 'the qualification "head of the family" is not contrary to the idea of the equality between spouses. In fact, whatever one says, whatever one does and whatever one wishes, there will always be a "division of labour" within marriage determined by nature.' This bill again provoked outrage. Despite many amendments by women parliamentarians, the provision enshrining male headship of the family remained in place in the new law.[83]

If most women's organisations were in agreement over marriage law reform, the issue of contraception was more contentious. Strict laws against promoting contraception also made it difficult to debate the issue. Inspired by visits to birth control clinics in other countries, gynaecologist Marie-Andrée Lagroua Weill-Hallé along with other concerned women established the organisation *Maternité heureuse* ('Happy Motherhood') in 1956. It had to be a private organisation to meet legal requirements against public advocacy of birth control. *Maternité heureuse* researched 'problems related to motherhood' and reported its findings in bulletins to members only.[84] This obviously limited its effectiveness. A national poll in 1956 reported that 56 per cent of people had 'never heard anyone talk of limiting births'. It also reported that 45 per cent of people (and 52 per cent of women aged 20–49) would approve the creation of special dispensaries where birth control information could be obtained.[85] These figures indicated, however, that half the population still opposed birth control.

In 1960 *Maternité heureuse* became the French Family Planning Movement (MFPF). It grew rapidly, with doctors (male and female) playing leading roles. The first Family Planning clinic opened at Grenoble in 1961 to great fanfare. It, too, utilised the strategy of private membership to circumvent the prohibition on 'promoting' contraception. By 1966, there were 123 centres in 72 departments of France. The organisation had 83,000 members in 1967.[86]

Demand for such services was evident in enquiries revealing widespread female unhappiness about sex and motherhood. A public survey on 'women and love' in 1960 inadvertently exposed the problem, which was reinforced by a survey of 3000 families conducted by a Catholic newspaper in 1966. These surveys reported that women found motherhood a source of constant anxiety. Sex created tension and conflict in marriages as pregnancy, or the fear of pregnancy, drove spouses apart. Women believed they faced the choice of risking repeated pregnancies or seeing their husbands seek satisfaction elsewhere. They felt like 'baby-making machines', they reported, and resented being reduced to their 'animal' function. This picture confirmed the case studies reported in Lagroua Weill-Hallé's 1961 book, *La Grand'peur d'aimer* ('The great fear of loving'). Evidence of women's resort to illegal abortion to end unwanted pregnancies was also reiterated in these accounts.[87]

Socialist women also campaigned for the legalisation of contraception. This was one of the objectives of the Women's Democratic

Movement (MDF), founded by Marie-Thérèse Eyquem in 1961. Eyquem and her colleague, Yvette Roudy, lobbied the emerging Socialist leader, François Mitterrand, to support 'family planning' (a euphemism for legalising contraception). In the 1965 election campaign Mitterrand undertook in a television interview to support reform. This may have put him ahead of the electorate in 1965: he lost a second round run-off against de Gaulle 55 to 45 per cent.[88]

Opposition to reform of the laws on contraception united Catholics and Communists (though for different reasons). Catholic women's organisations supported 'natural' methods of family planning. They argued that abstinence strengthened marriages as each partner exercised self-control for the other. The Catholic Cardinals reiterated their opposition to contraception in 1961, but with the opening of the Second Vatican Council in 1962 change seemed to be in the air. The Communists, who had continued to argue that contraception was a diversion from the needs of working families, also began to soften their position in the mid-1960s as de-Stalinisation progressed. In 1965 they lodged a bill to overturn the 1920 law, and legalise abortion as well.[89]

Strengthening support for change resulted in the Neuwirth Law, passed in December 1967, which legalised contraception. But it was a disappointment to many. No provision was made for sex education, and the grounds for performing legal abortions were not extended. The sale of contraceptives was legalised under very restrictive conditions. They were to be available only at pharmacies, and all clients purchasing them had to be registered. The sale of contraceptives to minors under 18 was prohibited, and for those aged 18–21 it required written parental consent.[90]

The Neuwirth Law left the problems of young women unresolved. As early as 1960 the MFPF had recognised a 'crisis' of youth sexuality, and had become increasingly concerned about the number of minors (that is, those under 21) requesting contraception. MFPF Bulletins of March and June 1960 had addressed 'The Sexual Problems of Students', which they identified as the 'number of abortions, [and] of forced marriages, of couples whom an undesired child stops in their course of study'.[91] Such students still had no access to contraceptives under the revised law, unless their parents agreed. But many parents still believed that premarital sex was unacceptable. The sexuality of young women, in particular, remained contentious. Young people did not discuss sex with their parents, and it seems likely that many would have baulked at requesting the required signature for a prescription for contraceptives.[92]

The 'Events' of 1968: generation and gender

The question of sexuality was raised very publicly in 1968, when France experienced a major social and political upheaval that many at the time thought was the prelude to revolution. The upheaval was led by the young, reflecting the gap that had opened between the conservative establishment, and a younger generation influenced by consumerism and the counter-culture. The 'Events' of May 1968 began with student protests against the unsatisfactory conditions in which the 'baby boom' generation was being educated. They became a broad-ranging challenge to the fundamental structures and assumptions of French society. Many issues were raised, some affecting young people in daily life: education, the sexual rights of the young, the stifling conformity of bourgeois society. The children of plenty were biting the hand that fed them.

Dissatisfaction with the post-war, Cold War world assumed larger dimensions in the May 1968 revolt, producing a critique of draconian workplaces, the exploitative capitalist system, and Western (especially American) imperialism. Slogans protesting the Vietnam War and demanding Third World liberation jostled for wall space with others caricaturing President de Gaulle as a fascist, or demanding free love. University students and workers were at the centre of protests, which included the occupation of a number of university campuses and factories across the country, and running battles with the police and the Security Service in the streets of Paris. So significant was the challenge that it brought an end to the Presidency of de Gaulle in 1969, and opened a space for political change on both the Right and the Left.[93]

Women participated in these events and were beaten and tear-gassed on the Boulevard Saint-Michel along with men. But Kristin Ross notes that, in documents of the period, women participants identified themselves 'as any number of things – as workers, as members of different *groupuscules* or political tendencies, as German Jews, as the "pègre" [riff-raff], as activists or citizens – rather than as women per se'.[94] The events were formative for young women, not because of their participation but because of their marginality. Despite women's presence on action committees and strike committees, men dominated the political activities while women lent a hand. Men excluded women, but they also excluded themselves given the gendered assumptions that prevailed in youth politics at the time.

Women's issues, if they were raised at all, were ignored or dismissed. Militants of one Leftist splinter group announced: 'In tracing an absurd and impossible war of the sexes over the authentic and historical class struggle, feminism has missed the revolution, deceived its followers and created confusion in language.'[95] Male radicals condemned 'bourgeois' prejudices supporting celibacy and monogamy (although they did not question heterosexuality). From women's perspective, however, the implications of having sex needed consideration, and some women felt pressure to be sexually 'available' rather than fulfilled.[96] As a result of 1968, women activists gradually came to perceive their own marginality to radical politics, and to realise that there were issues they wanted (and needed) to raise for themselves.

The Women's Liberation Movement (MLF)

Women who had responded to the ideas behind the May movement reinterpreted that episode in the years that followed, developing ideas that would produce the Women's Liberation Movement. The 1968 call for a 'revolution in daily life', like the call for sexual freedom, was relevant to women, but it only gradually produced a focus on women's daily life: housework, childcare, sexual fulfilment and reproductive rights. As militants of 1968 later reported, too, the gap between theory and practice in the Revolutionary movement was particularly significant in their political evolution. They became disillusioned with 'egalitarian' groups where women were not treated equally, and where the old division of labour was expected to continue.[97]

Between 1968 and 1970, groups of women began meeting to discuss their ideas. They began to read books focused on women's 'condition' (as it was known), particularly *The Condition of the French Woman Today* by Andrée Michel and Geneviève Tixier, published in 1964, and Betty Friedan's *The Feminine Mystique*, translated in 1964 by Yvette Roudy. Issues about female psychology, first raised by Simone de Beauvoir in her 1949 classic *The Second Sex*, dominated the intellectual approaches of the period. In a sense, they all addressed the observation initially made by de Beauvoir 20 years previously: 'One is not born a woman. One becomes a woman.'[98] They explored the process by which women became submissive to men, focused their lives on men and allowed themselves to be dominated. In 1949, de Beauvoir's work had been slated for its anti-family values and its focus on female individuality. The Catholic Church had placed it on the Index of banned books. Its discussion of female sexuality had created a scandal, and even many feminists (like male intellectuals of Beauvoir's own circle) had maintained their distance. But by the early 1970s, feminists had come to appreciate the importance of the book, and acknowledged its radical effect on their lives and thinking.[99]

The so-called 'second wave' feminist movement differed from its predecessor because it focused, not on equality for women, but on allowing women to discover and realise themselves in their specificity. The world reflected its male creators and power-holders, feminists argued. Rather than taking power or sharing it with men, women wanted to reshape social and political institutions to reflect women's ideas and values. 'Difference' was vaunted as positive and liberating, when it normally served to disadvantage women. This was clearly a utopian project, and reflected the idealism and optimism of the May movement.[100] It also reflected the fact that, while most of the legal barriers to equality had been removed by the efforts of earlier generations of feminists, the movement towards 'equality' had had a limited effect on gender relations. Male power remained entrenched.

'Second wave' feminism also brought into the political struggle a younger generation of women, the 'baby-boomers', who gradually took that struggle in new directions. The MLF was not so much a 'movement' as a diverse current of feminist activity, emerging from the 'grass roots' of the increasingly educated and increasingly urban female population. The MLF was a movement of urban middle-class women, 80 per cent of whom had received tertiary education. They were less likely to be married or have children than other women of similar backgrounds, and more likely to be living with a partner or to have had a homosexual experience. They often came to the women's movement from involvement in other political activities.[101]

The name 'MLF' was coined in August 1970. It was first given by the press to a handful of women who attempted to lay a wreath at the *Arc de Triomphe* on the tomb of the Unknown Soldier. They carried a banner saying: 'There is someone more unknown than the unknown soldier: his wife.' They were arrested, but the headlines served their purpose. This was the first of many demonstrations. Later in 1970 a Leftist periodical, *Partisans*, carried a poem asking 'Where are the Women?' when male activists are changing the world: 'they are shopping/doing the dishes from Saturday night/cleaning the house/ watching the children'. The fact that the much-vaunted Revolution did not necessarily promise a 'revolution' for women was made explicit, as women challenged conventional concepts of 'revolution' and conventional forms of 'revolutionary' action.[102]

The feminist paper, *Le Torchon Brûle*, illustrates the character of the new women's movement in the early 1970s.[103] The title, literally 'the torch is burning', evoked several additional meanings. The word *torchon* referred also to a dish cloth or tea-towel. The expression *le torchon brûle* also meant 'it's war'. The paper appeared irregularly, each time produced by a different collective that put forward its own ideas and concerns. There was no editorial committee, reflecting the anti-hierarchical principle of the women's movement. Articles generally carried only women's first names: something reminiscent of the first feminist paper *La Femme Libre* in 1832, and a political statement in itself. The contents of *Le Torchon Brûle* illustrate the concerns of feminists at this time and the diversity that marked the movement. It condemned Mothers' Day and highlighted issues of domestic violence. It protested against the Vietnam War. It proposed and reported on the establishment of a 'women's house' (another project attempted by feminists in 1832). But many of its articles focused on sexuality: this was perhaps the most important issue for feminists of the early 1970s.

The second issue of *Le Torchon Brûle* published explicit photographs of the female genitals, leading to its prosecution for moral outrage. By celebrating the 'power of the cunt', women sought to reclaim the term used by men to express the worst form of insult, and give positive value to female sexuality. *Le Torchon Brûle* also publicised sexual choice and lesbianism, foreshadowing the development of a specifically lesbian feminist movement which appeared as a distinct current by 1974.[104] The tension between lesbian feminists and heterosexual women was to become intense, since it raised important questions about the nature of women's oppression and about feminist political action. Despite activism by gays of both sexes, however, punitive laws governing homosexuality would not be revised until the 1980s.

The legalisation of abortion

The issue of abortion was central to feminist campaigns in the early 1970s. This issue united feminists from earlier movements with those in the new currents, and divided more radical feminists from others. The MLF's campaign for abortion rights grew directly from earlier activism around reproductive rights for women, and ongoing discontent with the Neuwirth Law. In 1970, Family Planning adopted a contentious policy supporting both freedom of contraception and liberalisation of abortion. The abortion issue became even more contentious in April 1971, when a group of 343 high-profile women signed a Manifesto declaring that they had had an abortion illegally:

> A million women abort every year in France. They do so under dangerous conditions because of the furtiveness to which they are condemned, although, when done under medical supervision, this operation is extremely simple.
> No-one ever mentions these millions of women.
> I declare that I am one of them. I declare that I have had an abortion.
> Just as we demand free access to contraception, we demand freedom of abortion.

This manifesto was the lead story in the prominent weekly, the *Nouvel Observateur*, and was accompanied by articles discussing the abortion issue. The signatories included Simone de Beauvoir, Gisèle Halimi (a lawyer who had risen to prominence during the Algerian war by denouncing French torture of prisoners), the actor Catherine Deneuve and prominent authors like Marguerite Duras and Françoise Sagan.[105]

The campaign to legalise abortion emphasised the class inequalities created under the current law. There was 'inequality of risk' because wealthy women could afford to find a supportive doctor or go to England, while poor women resorted to unqualified help. There was 'inequality of justice' because the women who were prosecuted were almost exclusively poor. But feminists were divided on the matter. More conservative women associated with the ANEA (National Association for the Study of Abortion) sought the legalisation of therapeutic abortion (in cases of rape, incest, or when the pregnant woman's life was at risk). But women associated with the MLF regarded abortion as an issue of personal autonomy. Abortion must be free to women and unconditional. Their posters reiterated this theme: 'Neither the judge, nor the Pope, nor the cops' will decide; 'abortion is our right'; 'our wombs belong to us'.[106] The right of women to control their own bodies was the most fundamental of rights to the MLF, and men should have no say in the matter.

The abortion struggle came to a head in late 1972, with the so-called Bobigny Affair. Seventeen-year-old Marie-Claire Chevalier became pregnant after being raped by a classmate. She asked him for money for an abortion, and he reported her to the police. Marie-Claire and her mother (a single parent and *Métro* worker) were then prosecuted, along with two friends who had arranged the abortion and the abortionist herself. Madame Chevalier knew of the Manifesto and approached the organisation *Choisir* (Choice), established by de Beauvoir and Halimi to support women tried for abortion.

Choisir took up the Chevalier case, and Halimi defended the accused in court. Her tactic was not to deny the actions of the accused women, but to call as witnesses gynaecologists who admitted having performed abortions, and prominent women who declared that they had had abortions. In her summing up Halimi condemned 'class justice', the absence of sex education, the unavailability of contraception, legal discrimination against illegitimate children and the patriarchal legal code: 'But there remains the absolutely fundamental way in which women are still oppressed [...] We do not have the power to determine what happens to our bodies. If slavery still exists it is that of woman: she is a serf.'[107] Marie-Claire and her mother received suspended sentences, the friends were acquitted and the abortionist's fine was overturned on appeal.

The court decision made the abortion law unworkable. It divided the medical profession, particularly when 331 doctors issued their own manifesto, in February 1973, admitting that they had performed abortions. It divided Family Planning, the majority joining the MLAC (Movement for Freedom of Abortion and Contraception) at its founding in April 1973.[108] And it divided the politicians. A group of socialist deputies presented a Private Member's Bill, drawn up by *Choisir*, to appeal the current law and make abortion a matter of conscience.[109] The conservative government responded with a bill that announced women's autonomy, but circumscribed the conditions in which abortion was legal. It was returned to a parliamentary commission in February 1973.[110] The issue remained unresolved.

In the Presidential elections of 1974 both the conservative Valéry Giscard d'Estaing and the Socialist François Mitterrand sought women's vote (women were 53 per cent of the voting population). Mitterrand, who was beginning a rise that would take him to victory at the head of a new *Parti Socialiste* (PS) in 1981, had been actively seeking support amongst women. His colleague, Yvette Roudy, worked with him to develop a policy on 'The Promotion of Women', which included a commitment to repeal the abortion laws. Giscard also promised abortion law reform: a promise he kept following his narrow victory (with 50.8 per cent of the vote). Giscard appointed Simone Veil as Minister of Health, and gave her responsibility for dealing with the vexed question of abortion.

Her Bill transferred decision-making to women, allowing voluntary interruption of pregnancy in the first 10 weeks, but it also incorporated measures to dissuade women from having abortions. The opening debate on the bill was televised live on 26 November 1974, demonstrating the significance of the issue. The measure was subject to a conscience vote, so Veil needed to convince her fellow-MPs to vote yes. In the end, the law passed by 284 to 189. All 75 Communists, and 104 of the 105 Socialists, voted in favour, but only 55 of Veil's conservative colleagues supported the law. It came into effect on 17 January 1975.[111]

The passing of the Veil Law marked a major turning point for French women. Abortion had been the last major barrier to women's legal autonomy. Its legalisation, and the freeing up of contraceptive laws that accompanied it, also addressed critical issues for female health and sexuality. It marked a growing acceptance that women's autonomy required their control over their reproductive function. The personal had become political in the hands of the MLF, but it had also been defined as private and hence as 'apolitical': what a woman chose to do with her own body was recognised as a matter of individual choice.

This law also illustrated the changed environment of the 1970s that distinguished the experiences of younger French women from those of their mothers in the post-war period. For women of the 1950s, domesticity was either a pleasure or a necessity. They accepted the primacy of their maternal role, or found great difficulty in managing its responsibilities alongside other roles. Their daughters profited from the educational expansion of the post-war years. They imbibed cultural messages about individualism and personal achievement, and many resented the impediments to their personal fulfilment in a male-dominated society. The women's movement of the 1970s was the result, marking the arrival of a more confident and assertive generation who wanted to seize their rights with both hands.

10   The Politics of 'Women's Place' since 1975

By 1975, all the major legal hurdles to women's equal citizenship with men had been overcome. They had equal political rights. They had gained major revisions to the Civil Code. Access to contraception and the legalisation of abortion made it possible to control childbearing, ending prohibitions that had seriously impeded women's participation in public life. Women were free to assume their full rights as citizens alongside men. Yet the proportion of women in the National Assembly remained one of the lowest in Europe, and the numbers of women in government ministries and the upper echelons of the bureaucracy also remained small: theoretical equality did not translate readily into 'real' equality of power between the sexes.

The 1980s and 1990s nevertheless saw women's increasing encroachment on the 'male' domain of politics. Their gains were painfully slow and constantly contested. Party structures and ways of 'doing politics' were frequently hostile to women, while the 'double burden' made public life more demanding for women than for men. The perception that 'women's place' lay not in the public domain but in the family also proved tenacious in some sectors of the population. Notions of sexual difference and separate spheres have continued to influence political thinking into the twenty-first century, but as the movement for parity in the 1990s illustrated, public opinion has become more receptive to women in public life and in positions of power.

266

Women's entry into the political structures

The Presidency of Valéry Giscard d'Estaing, from 1974 to 1981, was the first to implement a range of measures to address persistent sex inequalities in French society. Both Giscard and his socialist opponent, François Mitterrand, made a pitch for the women's vote in the 1974 elections, one of the closest Presidential elections of the twentieth century. The victorious Giscard appointed Jacques Chirac Prime Minister, and Chirac's cabinet included six women (one a minister, the others junior ministers). Subsequent governments under Giscard included four to seven women, mostly junior ministers. The significance of this shift is clearer when we note that only nine women became ministers until 1987.[1]

President Giscard took two other initiatives to benefit women. First was the creation of a Secretariat of State for the Condition of Women, headed by Françoise Giroud. She was a Resistance hero, and had been editor of *Elle* magazine for many years. Eighty of the one hundred measures she proposed to the Cabinet to improve women's status were adopted.[2] Nevertheless, Giroud noted Giscard's indifferent reaction when she presented her measures to him: 'This conversation bores him. How quickly men get bored when the condition of women is discussed.' The reaction of the Council of Ministers ranged from surprise to resistance to resignation.[3] The second significant measure of the Giscard presidency was the 1975 Veil Law which, despite strong opposition from within conservative ranks, overturned the 1920 ban on abortion (see Chapter 9).

The Socialists in opposition, meanwhile, continued to re-create themselves as a woman-friendly Party (a process begun in the 1960s) and the Left soon outstripped the Right in its recognition of women's political interests and ambitions. Socialist women had taken the initiative in wooing the ambitious Mitterrand, who was the first male politician to 'put women at the heart of his strategy for gaining power'.[4] The 'Common Programme of the Left', signed with the Communists in 1972, had included a series of measures for 'The Promotion of Women'. It promised 'new laws, concrete measures, material means, so that women may accede to equality in work, society and family'. In addition to the legalisation of abortion, these 'concrete measures' included the elimination of discrimination, the establishment of crèches, school meal facilities, and provision of sixteen weeks of maternity leave.[5] In 1978, the Socialists issued a 'Socialist Party Manifesto on the Rights of Women', and supported the candidacies of feminist militants in a 'common women's programme'. Women's rights were also incorporated into the official Socialist programme for the 1980s, which recognised 'the complementary and indissoluble link that exists between feminism and socialism': a belief held by many nineteenth-century predecessors of the Socialist Party.[6]

The Socialists also took steps to redress the low proportion of women in the legislature. They agreed in 1972 that women candidates should stand in at least 10 per cent of winnable seats in Legislative elections. This was raised to 15 per cent in 1974, and 20 per cent in 1981. Prior to the elections for the European Parliament in 1979, Yvette Roudy campaigned to have women allocated 30 per cent of winnable seats. Twenty-two women candidates were included on the Socialist list, and the twenty Socialist and Left Radicals subsequently elected included six women.[7]

By the time of the 1981 Presidential elections, the Socialists had a strong track record as a party that was attentive to women's issues, and Mitterrand could claim to have supported or initiated a range of measures in favour of women. During the campaign, the Party set out to use women's issues to mark the difference between Mitterrand and Giscard, denouncing the threat posed by a conservative victory to the 'liberty', 'security' and 'dignity' of women. When questioned about his view of feminism during the campaign, Mitterrand described himself as friendly and interested, but declared: 'I have reservations. I am not an adherent.'[8] The programme for government drawn up in January 1981 listed a range of measures on women's rights, and included the promise of at least 30 per cent of women on party lists. On the controversial issue of funding for abortion, however, Mitterrand remained vague, promising only to 'revise' the law.[9] He probably opposed abortion personally, and he had to tread a fine line between attracting Left-leaning women and not alienating more conservative voters.

The elections were close once again, but this time Mitterrand was the winner with 52 per cent of the vote. His appeal to women had paid off: he attracted 49 per cent of the female vote compared with 39 per cent in 1965.[10] One of the first measures of his government was to upgrade the status of women's issues. The 'Secretariat of State for the Condition of Women' became the 'Ministry for the Rights of Woman'. As historians have noted, this formulation tapped into a deeply resonant tradition of respect for 'the rights of man' in Republican politics, although feminists would have preferred reference to 'the rights of women' rather than to the abstract 'woman'.[11]

Mitterrand continued the process of incorporating women into the structures of government. Yvette Roudy was named Minister for the Rights of Woman, and she gave strong leadership to the new Ministry. In a circular to Prefects and government officials, she stated her determination not to be a 'minister for the condition of women', but a 'minister for the de-conditioning of women and men'. Her ambition, she declared, was to transform politics and change mentalities so that relations between the sexes would be altered 'irreversibly'. Yvette Roudy placed great importance on paid work as the primary means to improve the status and opportunities of women. Whereas many of her cabinet colleagues preserved a 'familial' image of women and were sympathetic to their rights as wives and mothers, Roudy promoted the rights of women as citizens and autonomous individuals. 'Autonomy, equality, dignity' were her aspirations for women, and they were central to the programme of the Ministry she led.[12]

The Ministry undertook an ambitious programme, developing and supporting initiatives for women in all situations. It funded many women's organisations, even those not necessarily supportive of the government. One of the Ministry's first acts was to establish a major inquiry into the condition of women in France. It was chaired by the historian Madeleine Rebérioux. The sociologist Madeleine Guilbert was also on the committee. The report, *Women in France in a Society of Inequalities* (1982), provided the basis for many of the Ministry's policies. By 1985 the Ministry had established more than 200 departmental and local information centres for women, and distributed thousands of copies of the *Guide to Women's Rights* produced by the Ministry. It established women's refuges in all large towns, and published guidelines on the representation of women in school texts. Also significant was a publicity campaign to increase knowledge about contraception. Roudy wanted to democratise its use by making information available to all, including young people. The film maker Agnès Varda was engaged to prepare a short film clip, which was shown nightly on national television for two weeks in Autumn 1981.[13]

Roudy's initial programme declared: 'I want to be a centre of power and give the women of our country the means to permit their access to power.'[14] She defined her responsibility broadly, encouraging all ministers to consider the implications for women of policies they developed. In July 1983, Roudy sponsored a law on professional equality between men and women, prohibiting discrimination on the basis of sex in hiring or promotion. It put the onus on the employer to prove that gender was not the measure utilised, rather than requiring the worker to prove that it was: a clause that Roudy saw as particularly significant. The law also required employers to report on the status of women in their businesses, and proposed contracts between employers and government to implement equality programmes. This aspect was not successful, partly because it relied on the goodwill of all parties and contained no sanctions for non-compliance.[15]

Mitterrand was caught in a balancing act in addressing women's issues. He was a long-time friend of Roudy and supported many of her initiatives. But he was subject to considerable pressure from conservative organisations, especially those associated with the Catholic Church which had a view of women different from feminists, and the Ministry for the Rights of Woman. Mitterrand's effort to negotiate the divide was evident on 8 March 1982, when the Socialist government held an official celebration for International Women's Day. This celebration was an initiative of Roudy's Ministry. It made a national event of what had previously been largely a socialist one. The centrepiece of the event was to be a reception at the Elysée Palace for which Roudy had proposed the theme of 'women's work'. But Mitterrand and his staff, concerned about excluding non-employed women, stipulated that the guests had to include women with no profession. Mitterrand's speech also omitted any reference to the new and controversial initiative to refund the costs of abortion through the national health system – an initiative leaked to the press on 3 March and confirmed by Prime Minister Mauroy on 8 March. Mitterrand referred instead to the 'close complementarity' between the politics of the family and the advancement of women's rights.[16]

As Françoise Thébaud's detailed analysis of this episode emphasises, Mitterrand had been rethinking his support for the State funding of abortion. He halted the proposed measure partly, it seems, from personal conviction. But he was also subjected to a deluge of letters and telegrams from opponents of the measure. One letter read:

If the demands of the women's liberation Movement and the supporters of Family Planning are loudly orchestrated by a section of the press, they do not reflect the convictions of the real France (*la France profonde*), the [France] that loves you, Mr President, the [France] of so many families and of all the women who bravely bring into the world any child that comes along, whether hoped for or not. There are some fundamental ethical values.[17]

Mitterrand, the astute politician, could not afford to ignore the views of voters like this one, but he finally agreed to a compromise whereby abortion would be reimbursed from a special fund in the annual budget rather than through the public health system. Feminists like Gisèle Halimi (a member of the National Assembly by this time) condemned the compromise as a sign of the impotence of the Ministry.[18] But since the outcome for women was the same, and since the conservative position was defeated, it should count as one of Roudy's successes.

The anti-sexist law Roudy sponsored in 1983, despite being closely modelled on existing laws against racism, failed to gain party support. By this time, the deteriorating economic situation was changing the mood within the government. In March 1983, a move to achieve greater efficiency saw several ministries excluded from the cabinet, including the Ministry for the Rights of Woman. Roudy was returned to cabinet in 1985 and sponsored several other laws, including one establishing complete equality between the sexes in the control of their joint finances, but was unable to have a measure adopted by which children would receive the names of both their parents.[19] In 1986, the Right won the Legislative elections, initiating a period of 'cohabitation' with the Socialist President. Mitterrand followed precedent by appointing as Prime Minister the conservative leader, Jacques Chirac, who immediately disbanded the Ministry for the Rights of Woman.

The 'problem' of women in politics

The period of the Ministry of the Rights of Woman marked a major step in bringing issues concerning women into the heart of government. A Ministry that represented women's interests was invaluable while women remained a small proportion of deputies, ministers and policy-makers. Yvette Roudy argued that all issues were 'women's issues' and attempted to influence policy across all portfolios. The period of the Ministry also demonstrated, however, that women were not a single constituency who could be treated as a bloc. Nor could 'women's interests' be parked in a political siding while 'real politics' continued without them. The representation of 'women's

interests' ultimately depended upon women's representing themselves as citizens and individuals within the structures of government
and politics. And women's ability to do so depended upon those
structures, and the people who controlled them, being receptive to
women's participation.

Chirac's disestablishment of the Ministry of Woman's Affairs
demonstrated that women's place in the power structures in the
1980s remained fragile. The number of women in key positions, and
the status of 'women's affairs', rose and fell with the interplay of
male-dominated political forces. The return of the Left to power in
1988, when Mitterrand won a second term as President, saw a resurgence in women's presence. A Secretariat of State responsible for
women's issues (but not a Ministry) was established under Prime
Minister Pierre Rocard, and in 1991 Edith Cresson became France's
first woman Prime Minister. But that appointment came at a time
when the Socialist government was in serious difficulty and few
would have welcomed the job. The Bérégovoy government that
followed in 1992 included seven women in the ministry. When the
1995 Presidential elections returned the Right to power under
Jacques Chirac there was no ministry for women's affairs, but Prime
Minister Juppé's first cabinet contained 12 women – a record. They
were referred to patronisingly as 'the Juppettes' ('short skirts' or
'Juppé's skirts': *jupe* is the French word for skirt).

The first Juppé cabinet lasted only five months (the second
contained only four women) but the episode highlighted the fact that
women's accession to power came via male patronage. Moreover,
women appointed to ministries were generally drawn from the
bureaucracy: they came from outside the elected Assemblies rather
than rising through the political ranks. The reproach directed at the
'Juppettes' was that they lacked political 'representativeness' and
personal standing in the parties.[20] They depended on male patronage, the 'protection of the prince'. Even women who succeeded in
winning seats in the Assembly or the Senate were often perceived as
'token men'. The election of widows and, more recently, daughters
of male politicians reflects this perception, although women have
sometimes found it useful to appeal to their fathers' names and
reputations to increase their credibility.[21]

From women's perspective, the problem has been to attain a voice
in government by other means: to establish their own legitimacy.
Women's efforts to institute quotas of female candidates in the
Socialist Party in the 1970s, for instance, indicated their awareness

that the right to vote and the right to stand for election had not enabled women to participate in politics on equal terms with men. While women comprise at least 50 per cent of the population, their representation in the National Assembly rarely rose above three per cent until the 1970s. It reached 11 per cent in the 1997 legislative elections, and 12 per cent in June 2002.[22] Women were six per cent of Senators, eight per cent of mayors, and eight per cent of the membership of general (departmental) councils in 1998. In 2001, France ranked second last in the European Union insofar as the proportion of women in parliament was concerned.[23] In 2003, it ranked 18th out of 25 EU countries.[24]

The reasons for women's low representation are complex. Women have had difficulty in gaining pre-selection, particularly in winnable seats. Each woman pre-selected or elected means one man less, and ambitious men object. The socialist Prime Minister Michel Rocard's decision to present a list with equal numbers of men and women for the European elections of 1994 upset men who had lost in the legislative elections of 1993 and hoped to pick up a seat in the European Parliament instead.[25] The electoral system itself affects the likelihood of women's being elected, the chances increasing significantly where voters choose between party lists, rather than voting for a single candidate from each party.

When elected, women encounter a political environment that is strongly homosocial, where women are marginalised and even perceived as intruders.[26] The press contributes to this view, marginalising and trivialising women in power as either 'queens of hearts' (if they are suitably 'feminine') or 'iron ladies' (if they are too 'masculine').[27] The political 'milieu' (as Françoise Gaspard calls it), where careers are fostered through contacts made in clubs and associations, and even over a game of golf, tends to be very masculine. Even the titles of official positions, until recently, seemed to call into question women's right to hold them. The traditional title 'Monsieur le Ministre' was amended to 'Madame la Ministre' only with difficulty. When it was proposed in 1997 that the Senatorial oath be amended to refer to 'an upright and honest person' rather than 'an upright and honest man', the conservative Attorney General, Jacques Toubon, condemned 'political correctness' and argued that such a linguistic switch was 'not French'.[28] These examples illustrate that the apparatus of politics remained inherently masculine. Women were regarded as outsiders, lacking in legitimacy, in a political sphere that was still perceived as the province of men.

'Women's place' and the rise of the *Front National*

As the economic situation deteriorated in the early 1980s, conservatism was revitalised. The oil crisis of 1979–1980 unleashed a severe recession. The 'thirty glorious years', as the period 1945–1975 was often called, came to an end. Unemployment soared past two million, wages and prices were frozen and the currency was twice devalued. In March 1983 a drastic austerity plan brought large increases in petrol and public transport costs. Massive job losses began in shipping, coal mines and steel works. The reaction was massive strike waves and a backlash against the Left, which was held responsible for these problems.[29]

The *Front National* (FN) burst onto the political stage in 1984, when the support of two million voters gave it 11 per cent in the European elections and 10 deputies in the European parliament. The FN had been in existence for 12 years at that time, but had previously had little impact in electoral politics. In 1981 it had been unable to obtain the 500 signatures necessary to stand a candidate in the Presidential elections. In 1983 it had gained a foothold at the municipal level by taking the town of Dreux from its Socialist mayor, Françoise Gaspard.[30] Its national impact in 1984 reflected the search for a scapegoat for France's economic woes, as well as increasing anxiety about French national identity.[31]

But just as earlier political crises had seen an appeal to a 'traditional' womanhood as part of the solution, so the rise of the FN was associated with a conservative backlash against women in public life. The increasing prominence of women since the 1970s, given official status by the Ministry of the Rights of Woman, alarmed conservatives. Above all, the Ministry's initiatives represented 'feminism' by recognising women as independent individuals with their own rights, rather than simply as wives and mothers. The FN's views on women are strongly antifeminist and reactionary. While they are by no means synonymous with all conservative opinion, they might be seen as the tip of the iceberg, expressing what conservatives have often been reluctant to articulate publicly. If the FN has been seen as an 'alternative' by many voters – its vote has not dropped below 10 per cent since 1986, and has been as high as 15 per cent (4.5 million voters)[32] – the 'alternative' they offer to women, or to men who oppose a 'feminist' politics, warrants serious consideration.

The FN is an amalgam of diverse strands. Its original members included an older generation of former collaborators and a younger generation mobilised in the 1950s by the campaigns to keep Algeria French. The FN leader, Jean-Marie Le Pen, a former paratrooper, began his political career at that time. Ideologically, the FN is also an amalgam of a 'traditionalist' current (essentially monarchist and Catholic) and a 'populist-nationalist' current. This combination has produced a nationalist, anti-immigrant and anti-Semitic political agenda, as well as an emphasis on the values of 'family, army, authority, Catholicism'.[33]

In FN tracts and electoral programmes, women appear only as wives and mothers, generally within discussions of family policies. Women are represented only in their 'natural' reproductive and nurturing functions. The reason for this becomes clear when their doctrine of social crisis is understood. The FN argues that France is in crisis: French women refuse to do their demographic duty (a constant theme in conservative thought), placing the very 'demographic survival of the nation' under threat.[34] The country is simultaneously being 'overrun' by immigrants who reproduce rapidly. Nona Mayer and Mariette Sineau summarise the views of the FN on this matter:

> The main explanation the FN offers for what they see as a 'birth collapse' or 'demographic winter', condemning France to demographic and cultural decay, is the crisis of the family brought about by the rise of individualism and the sexual liberation movement of the 60's, the signs of it being the rising number of couples living together without being married, divorces and children born out of wedlock, and the growing proportion of women who work and do not want to have children or do not have time to bring them up properly.[35]

This diagnosis is a critique of modernity, which has supposedly caused a breakdown of 'traditional morality' and 'traditional family' patterns. According to the FN, the hedonism of modern society has produced unstable and non-reproductive relationships. 'Individualism' has replaced duty and self-sacrifice to the greater good, the nation.

Female 'individualism' is implicated heavily here, too, for 'liberated' women supposedly choose careers over marriage and motherhood. The solutions to the 'crisis' therefore become clear from an FN perspective: women must return to the home, where they will fulfil their 'natural' destiny by bearing at least three children and spend their time raising them in 'French' values. Abortion and its reimbursement from Social Security will be banned as 'anti-French genocide'. Instead, the FN will enact family-friendly laws, including pensions for non-working mothers of three or more children, and extra votes for large families. The expenses will be offset by dismantling the system of crèches and nursery schools, as well as by savings on contraception and abortion expenses. A policy of 'national preference' – that is, excluding immigrants from social benefits – will also save money.[36]

From its inception the FN vented its spleen at feminism, deemed responsible for many of the problems besetting French society. Le Pen is reported as saying in 1984: 'I often ask myself: "Is it necessary for a woman to learn a profession? [...] Liberate woman! When you set the bee free, you get the bumble-bee!"'.[37] He condemned women's 'invasion' of the workplace, and the 'confusion of roles' caused by women's new lifestyles. He also criticised the concept of egalitarianism: 'The egalitarian movement, which consists of levelling out ages, sexes and peoples, must be criticised because it masks reality, which is fundamentally inegalitarian; that is to say, there are inequalities which are just and inequalities which are unjust. We are for justice and not for equality.'[38]

The party's women leaders (who are not simple housewives, as the ideology supposedly demands) are avowedly antifeminist as well. Marie-France Stirbois (a general councillor for the Eure-et-Loire Department, former European deputy, and the party's only representative in the National Assembly between 1989 and 1993) rejects political equality between men and women because it 'humiliates women'. In 1998, she gave a speech to the FN's summer university in Toulon entitled 'Liberate women from feminism'.[39] In an interview on the FN website headed 'Elected, but no less a woman', she nevertheless volunteered that she did not like cooking and had no time for it.[40] Women of the FN elite hold elevated positions within the party and accrue many social advantages by not being merely housewives and mothers. Nevertheless, they continue to promote the idea of natural differences and hierarchy between the sexes. There is no evidence that this 'separate spheres' rhetoric attracts women's votes – quite the opposite – but it does attract male voters. A 1999 study showed that the more men believed in a traditional vision of women's role and opposed their 'emancipation', the more likely they were to vote for the FN.[41]

The race issue is also critical to the FN's ideology and has been particularly significant in attracting support amongst voters. FN support, particularly in the 1980s, was strong in areas where de-industrialisation was underway and where the number of immigrants was large. The link between immigration and the unemployment of French workers was easily made, particularly for workers of French origin with low educational qualifications, who were left behind in the boom years prior to 1980, and were unable to secure a place in the new economic order. The growth of the FN reflected 'a local French society in the throes of disintegration'.[42] It also reflected an anxiety shared more broadly in the electorate that there are 'too many immigrants' and that they threaten to transform French society in undesirable ways.[43]

The 'race question' is also linked to the 'woman question' in ways that are politically useful for the FN. Le Pen's 1984 warning – 'Tomorrow the immigrants will move in with you, eat your soup, and they will sleep with your wife, your daughter or your son' – linked fear of immigrants with an unsubtle sexual threat that has been reiterated in FN responses to rape cases. They describe them as attacks on the nation; as 'a veritable symbolic taking possession of our earth and our people'.[44] The FN taps into an underlying fear of the 'Other' triggered by specific issues, often at the local level.

The gender gap has remained a significant feature of the FN electorate. Men consistently outnumber women amongst its voters, but the picture is more nuanced than the overall figures initially suggest. A study by Nona Mayer and Mariette Sineau, based primarily on data from the 1995 and 1997 elections, revealed that the ratio of men to women supporting the FN was 60:40 for every 100 voters. But certain groups of women are susceptible to the FN message. These are predominantly younger women: the gender gap amongst FN voters is large amongst those over 50, but very small amongst younger age groups. In the 35–49 age group, in particular, 15 per cent of both men and women voted for the FN. Female FN voters are also likely to be women with limited education and poor qualifications who are employed in unstable and low-paid jobs. A quarter of working women (and 24 per cent of working men) voted for the FN in the 1997 parliamentary elections. A vote for the FN may therefore be a 'protest vote' by the socially disadvantaged. Conversely, support for the FN is very low among women with higher education, as well as among female students and women in professional and executive positions.[45]

The low level of support among the female electorate has been one element encouraging the *FN* to 'feminise' its image and tone down its aggressive style. It appeals to iconic symbols of womanhood like Joan of Arc and the Virgin Mary. As early as 1985, Le Pen attempted to link Mary with the submissive but respected woman: 'The French knight is filled with respect for his Lady by a kind of reflection from the Lady of Ladies, that is, Our Lady, the mother of Jesus who combines the myth of Virgin and Mother.'[46]

The FN has also attempted to soften its image by presenting more women candidates. It is paradoxical that this party should try to enlist women for political roles, given its claim that domesticity and reproduction are women's biological destiny: for Le Pen, that is 'just a question of admitting the facts'.[47] Nevertheless, the need to address women and enlist their support illustrates that the FN is ultimately unable to present a model of sexual difference that excludes women from public life. The female voter exists, and her vote matters. Party publicity emphasises the women candidates' 'maternal' qualifications for the job, but significant roles for women within the party appear to be reserved for the widows, wives, daughters and associates of party men.[48]

The FN defends its contradictory stance in presenting women political candidates by claiming a particular family-based view of politics. When Le Pen seemed likely to be pronounced ineligible to stand for the European elections of 1999, due to an ongoing court case, he presented his wife Jany as a replacement, arguing: 'It's true that in the National Front we have a culture of the couple, a family culture, and that in the history of our families it is the women who take the place of men when they are at war or unable to be there.'[49] Le Pen cultivated his three daughters (he regrets that he has no son to carry his name) for political roles. The eldest, Marie-Caroline, 'betrayed' him when she left the party with her partner in 1998 to join the splinter party of Bruno Mégret. The youngest, Marine, is now tipped to become party leader after her father, largely because she is 'the clone of Jean-Marie'.[50]

Women's wariness about the politics of the FN prompted the establishment of a separate women's organisation under the party umbrella, the National Circle of European Women (CNFE). It was founded in 1985 by Martine Lehideux, who was also a founding member of the FN. She described the CNFE as 'a reaction to May 68' and to feminism, which she saw as 'destructive of our family values'. The Circle's aim is 'to defend the French family, women and [the] fundamental values of our society'. As Mayer and Sineau report, the CNFE targets 'women ignored by the feminist movement', the housewives, and 'all those who do not feel modern and liberated'.

It has also tapped a vein of support among conservative Catholic women. Only three per cent of practising Catholic women supported the FN in the 1997 CEVIPOF survey. Yet women on the Catholic extreme right, particularly those associated with the anti-abortionist organisation 'Let them live', have made common ground with the CNFE. Martine Lehideux is a practising Catholic, an anti-abortion campaigner, and a member of a European Catholic fundamentalist group that takes tours to Auschwitz to protest about the 'genocide' of abortion. The CNFE reportedly has about 1000 members in France, so its impact to date appears to have been limited.[51]

The FN has become more circumspect in presenting some of its policies to the public, adopting a more 'politically correct' and less punitive stance. For instance, the 1985 claim that Vichy's Family Code was a model for the present has disappeared. The 1985 policy also presented the 'natural' differences between the sexes in terms that are apparently no longer regarded as politically useful. The 1985 policy described the family as a 'natural' unit being undermined by modern tendencies:

In recent years, official ideology, complacently supported by the media, has systematically tried to devalue motherhood and abolish all differentiation between the functions of men and women. This utopian attitude leads to the negation of the biological and cultural reality which gives women a particular responsibility in procreation and the education of children.[52]

The role of women in the family was presented in a more sanitised way in the 1993 programme, focusing on the 'parental right' to stay home with their children, rather than emphasising women's biological destiny. Nevertheless, the FN emphasises the need for 'French' women (defined in racial terms) to have more children. The suggested slogan for its 1990 conference was: 'Let us make French babies with French women.'[53] Its 2004 programme included a 20-year population campaign, 'children for France', special benefits for mothers, and extra votes for parents of large families.[54]

In the 1980s, the FN campaigned openly to repeal the Veil law legalising abortion and conducted a vicious anti-Semitic campaign against Simone Veil herself. The anti-abortion stance was presented in more subtle terms in the 1997 policy – it referred only to 'discouraging' abortion – perhaps in recognition that the majority of voters are pro-choice.[55] However, by 2004 its policy had abandoned persuasion in favour of a more punitive stance. The FN proposed constitutional recognition of the sacredness of life from conception, and repeal of the abortion laws: a sign, perhaps, of the influence of Catholic 'traditionalists' in its ranks and of the conservative political environment.

Despite some refinements in FN rhetoric, there has been no fundamental shift in the FN's vision of women, which continues to focus on their reproductive and family roles. In the 2004 programme women appear only within discussions of its family policy. Women's centrality to the natalist utopia of a 'born-again' France of hierarchy, ethnic purity and stability militates against any significant shift in the FN representation of women. Besides, the FN's anti-individualist stance rejects the notion of 'rights' in favour of the notion of 'duties'. The 'rights' that women have in the FN vision are the 'rights' to fulfil their biological destiny and perform their duty to the nation. It has paid more attention in recent years to proposals to reward them for doing their duty, by giving them entitlements to pensions (for instance) as a result. Its practice of allowing carefully chosen women to play political roles under the FN banner is also at odds with its rhetoric of sexual difference. But women's family roles, inscribed in the female body rather than freely chosen, continue to dominate the model of womanhood presented to the public. The contrast with a feminist view that women are individuals first, and as such choose to play different social roles in public and private life, could not be more marked.

Towards parity: 1990 to the present

Despite the longevity of the reactionary model of womanhood defended by the FN and its sympathisers, the pace of women's entry into public life has accelerated in recent years. The female politician remained an exception into the 1980s, but women became increasingly impatient with female exclusion. They began to seek constitutional and legal means to increase women's participation in politics.

In 1982, Gisèle Halimi proposed a law requiring at least 25 per cent of each sex on party lists for municipal elections. It passed almost unanimously but was rejected by the Constitutional Council on the grounds that it infringed equality before the law. This decision reflected an abstract and universalist view of citizenship that dated to the French Revolution in which 'the citizen' is defined neither as male or female, nor as belonging to a particular culture, religion or other interest group. 'Citizens' are gender-neutral and freely select other gender-neutral 'citizens' to represent them. According to this definition, to make specific criteria like sex the requirement for election would limit democracy.[56] Nevertheless, just as the French Revolution's 'rights of man', supposedly universal, were denied to women, this interpretation refused to admit that all citizens actually are 'gendered' and that the 'democracy' so vaunted was theoretical rather than real when its sexual dimension was considered.

Women of widely different political backgrounds believed that 'democracy' in its existing form had failed women. Given the decision of the Consitutional Council that quotas create 'inequality', however, they had to find an alternative formulation. The result was the concept of parity. Making the case for 'parity' in politics required redefining the 'universalist' notion of citizenship as it had been understood until then.

This task was undertaken in *Au Pouvoir Citoyennes* (*Women Citizens to Power*) published in 1992. The authors, Françoise Gaspard (a leading Socialist and politician, and a sociologist at the *Ecole des Hautes Etudes en Sciences Sociales*), the journalist Claude Servan-Schreiber, and the lawyer Anne le Gall, challenged the view that the abstract 'citizen' was gender-neutral. They argued instead that the 'citizen' endowed with rights who emerged at the time of the French Revolution was gendered male. His fitness to participate in the public political world was premised on the existence of another private world assigned to women, a distinction carried through into the Civil Code of 1804: 'It was in effect the Code of 1804 that allowed lawyers and male politicians to justify "irrefutably" the legitimacy of the masculine monopoly on public affairs: how could woman, this *relative creature* deprived of all autonomy, this being without civil rights, be allowed to have rights of citizenship?'[57] The study went on to show how the fundamental distinction between the sexes, their rights, and their place in society, had been written into French political life since the French Revolution. Men had 'confiscated' the rights of representation by claiming to represent all; only representation based on parity between the sexes could make real equality prevail.

As Danielle Haase-Dubosc explains, the concept of parity was not 'affirmative action'. It was not about 'adding' women to politics, but about reforming 'democracy' to ensure its universality. Only a parity democracy – with women and men present equally – would be a true democracy. Parity sought to create a 'bi-gendered universal' or a 'pluriversalist universalism' to replace the exclusionary model.[58]

The law suggested in *Au Pouvoir Citoyennes* stated: 'Elected bodies, at both local and national level, shall be composed of equal numbers of men and women.'[59] The proposal raised objections amongst those who believed that 'equality' could not be legislated and that the best representative, man or woman, should be elected. It divided feminists: some rejected the assumptions of 'difference' that underlay it and others favoured a class-based approach to political inequality.[60] But as the lawyer Elizabeth Sledziewski observed: 'A democracy without women is not an imperfect democracy. It is not a democracy at all.'[61] And the proposal was not to admit women to power by bypassing electoral procedures but to prevent those procedures from shutting out women. Women would be elected to represent both men and women, as men had been until that time.

The idea gained momentum quickly, both inside France and in Europe. In November 1993 *Le Monde* published a 'Manifesto of the 577 for a democracy based on gender parity'. The number of signatories was chosen to equal the 577 representatives in the Assembly. The 289 women and 288 men signatories called for an Act ensuring 'equal numbers of men and women' at all levels of government. This had no immediate effect because (according to Yvette Roudy) 'the political class, the parties remained impenetrable, although everything depended on them'. She claimed responsibility for the idea that former ministers from both sides of politics should co-operate to advance the cause of parity. In 1996, 10 women, the most prominent being Simone Veil and Edith Cresson as well as Roudy herself, signed the 'Manifesto of the ten for parity', which was published in *L'Express* in June. They also organised an opinion poll that showed 70 per cent support for the idea.[62] Another 1996 poll indicated that 86 per cent of men and women were favourable to parity representation.[63] In 1999, public support remained at 80 per cent.[64]

Political parties were forced to respond more positively to the issue of gender balance in politics, given the weight of public opinion. In 1994 several lists for the European elections had equal or near-equal numbers of men and women. Again the Left led the way, with women comprising 48 per cent of those on the Socialist list and 57 per cent on the Communist list. The conservative list included 21 per cent women, and the National Front list only 9 per cent. The FN remained the only party to openly reject parity as a desirable goal, but other groups also appeared reluctant. Jacques Chirac, elected President in May 1995, established a 'Parity Observatory' to study the issue. Its official report, in December 1996, raised a variety of problems, tending (in the words of Danielle Haase-Dubosc) 'to legitimate the government's wish to bury the project'.[65] In March 1997, conservative Prime Minister Alain Juppé still spoke only of considering 'temporary measures' to 'encourage women candidates'.[66]

When early elections for the National Assembly were called the following month the Socialist leader, Lionel Jospin, announced his intention to stand 30 per cent female candidates. He also promised to change the constitution to incorporate parity. The socialists won the election, initiating another period of 'cohabitation' with the conservative President. In 1998, Prime Minister Jospin reached an agreement with President Chirac that saw a jointly sponsored Constitutional amendment in June 1998. It added a sentence to Article 3 of the Constitution: 'Statutes shall promote equal access by women and men to elective office and positions.'[67] The wording of the amended constitution thus invited law changes to ensure 'equal access', if not equal outcomes.

In December 1999 the Jospin government introduced a bill providing that, in all elections conducted by party list, all party lists must present equal numbers of male and female candidates, although nothing was included about women's positioning on the lists. The elections for the lower house of the National Assembly were the only significant ones not covered by this clause, because members represent individual seats and parties nominate single candidates for each seat, not lists. For these elections, the bill stated that half of each party's candidates had to be women or the party would face financial penalties. Despite fierce opposition in the Senate, amendments were passed to ensure a fair positioning of men and women on party lists, either by alternating them or having alternating blocks of men and women. The Parity Law was finally passed on 6 June 2000.[68]

To date three sets of elections have been held under the new law. Its impact has been mixed. In the Municipal elections of March 2001, women's representation increased dramatically in larger communes (those with more than 3500 inhabitants), from 26 to 47.5 per cent.[69] Similarly, the elections to replace a third of the Senate in September 2001 showed clear gains for departments where Senators are elected by proportional representation (where the parity law applied). Women were elected to 20 of the 74 seats, whereas they had previously held only 5. In departments without proportional representation, where the parity law did not apply, women remained at 2 of 28 senators.[70]

Those gains were not repeated in the legislative elections of June 2002. The number of women elected rose only from 62 to 68, from 11 to 12 per cent of deputies.[71] These elections saw a record number of candidates and an enormous diversity of parties, making the voters' choice particularly complex. More importantly, they came just a month after the crisis in which Jean-Marie Le Pen, leader of the FN, beat the socialist leader in the first round of the Presidential elections. Le Pen came in second to Jacques Chirac, thus running against Chirac for the presidency of France in the second round. The theoretical possibility of a victory for the extreme right sent shock waves through the community. It produced a vote of more than 80 per cent for Chirac in the second round. But it also set the scene in which the selection of candidates for the Legislative elections, and the elections themselves, took place. No-one knew quite how the FN would fare; whether the first round or second round presidential result was a better indicator. The socialists were traumatised and disorientated by their shock loss. The disarray of the Left and the dismay of the electorate contributed to the highest abstention rate ever witnessed: 39 per cent of people refrained from voting in the second round of the legislative elections.[72]

A large number of women candidates – 38.5 per cent overall – stood in these elections but, as we have seen, this did not translate into a victory for parity. The report of the official government watchdog on parity, the *Parité Observatoire*, attributed the outcome largely to a lack of political will.[73] The struggle for power won out over the commitment to democracy. Perhaps the most illuminating aspect of the exercise was the search by all parties to find ways to use – if not to exploit – the law to their own advantage. The small parties with little chance of gaining power came close to or even exceeded the parity target. The far Left parties (*Lutte ouvrière* and the *Ligue Communiste révolutionnaire*) selected more than 50 per cent of women; the Greens reached 50 per cent; the Communists 44 per cent. These parties had a tradition of support for women whereas the FN, despite being hostile to parity, stood 48 per cent of women candidates. For these parties, the presentation of female candidates was a strategy to capture a higher share of the female vote. It also enabled these parties to maximise their funding under the parity rules.

The shifting position of the FN on parity is particularly interesting in this context. Despite their rejection of the idea of parity, they stood more women candidates than any other party in the 2002 legislative elections. Their 270 women almost matched the combined totals of the Socialists (165) and the Chirac-led coalition, the *Union pour la Majorité présidentielle* or UMP (107). They gave several reasons for selecting female candidates. Le Pen noted that presenting women would help to 'de-diabolise' the image of the party. The emphasis was no longer on women replacing warriors fallen in battle, but on female difference. An FN candidate in Burgundy, Nicole Aureau, reported that 'Women need to be represented by women. Lots of things which concern women are decided by men, that's not acceptable.' Another candidate, Alexandra Hardy (aged 25), stated: 'Our Party has confidence in women when other parties do not – it has welcomed us and encouraged us.'[74] The 'natural' division of labour that destines women for the kitchen apparently does not apply when votes (and electoral funding) are at stake.

The major contenders for control of the Assembly came in well under their parity targets. The PS selected 36 per cent women, while the conservative coalition (UMP) managed only 20 per cent, thus winning the 'machismo award' from the authors of the official report. Party representatives were frank about their reasons for selecting men. Victory in these elections, unlike elections for the Municipalities, brought control of the real power structure in the nation. Where party officials estimated that the prospect of winning conflicted with the goal of parity, the 'old' rules of pre-selection were followed at the expense of parity. As observers noted, the parties chose to pay the financial penalty of falling below the parity target. They preferred to stay with their tried and true male candidates, rather than risk standing women and thereby putting those men out of office.[75]

Discussing this issue, the official report quotes the explanation of Françoise Hostalier, vice-president of the small rightist party *Démocratie libérale*. She argued that in electorates where the political parties hoped to win, they made sure of the victory by standing their *mammouths*, their 'big shots', in the seats. Where they thought there was less chance of winning, they gave priority to women candidates. The tactical bid for power shaped their approach to parity. The main parties apparently did not believe that women candidates were as successful as men. Their lack of confidence may have been exacerbated by concerns about heading off the extreme right, particularly if an inexperienced woman was selected ahead of an experienced man. Nevertheless, the official report suggests that lack of confidence in women 'was used to justify and support a political order based on arrangements allowing a minority to preserve power'.[76] It appears that the masculine political 'milieu' remains alive and well, and that reluctance by men to surrender power to women remains strong.

The 'crisis' conditions of the 2002 elections will not always prevail, and despite the continuing resistance of the masculine political elites, there are grounds for cautious optimism about the future impact of the parity law in increasing women's access to political office. In 2003, the conservative government of Prime Minister Jean-Pierre Raffarin included 10 women in a cabinet of 39. They held a range of portfolios including Defence, the responsibility of Michèle Alliot-Marie. Her career, along with those of Socialist women like Martine Aubry, Ségolène Royal and Elisabeth Guigou, demonstrates that women are beginning to establish themselves within the major parties. They are beginning to build careers that allow them to gain experience and demonstrate their competence in a range of areas. Women are prominent in a number of the 'minor' parties, too, with Dominique Voynet leading the Greens (Les Verts): a growing political force.

The career of Martine Aubry, which probably has still to reach its zenith, illustrates the extent of the change that has occurred in recent years. Being the daughter of Jacques Delors, who was Minister of Economics and Finance in the Mitterrand government of 1981 and later head of the European Commission, she grew up in a political household. She graduated from the prestigious School of Public Administration (ENA) and married Xavier Aubry, an executive of Price Waterhouse: one of the five leading international accounting firms. She was active in the progressive trade union organisation, the CFDT, which had its roots in the Catholic trade union movement. After holding senior posts in the Ministry of Labour she was Assistant Director of Péchiney, one of France's largest private companies, from 1989 to 1991, and worked closely with the head of the Employers' Federation. Aubry is active in a number of powerful organisations that pursue a social justice agenda, and a founder (with several leading Christian employers) of FACE (Foundation for Action Against Exclusion).[77]

In 1991, Martine Aubry was appointed Minister of Labour, Employment and Professional Life in the government of Edith Cresson. She retained her ministerial post under Pierre Bérégovoy and later (1997–2001) held the key post of Minister of Employment and Social Solidarity in the Jospin government. In that capacity she pushed through major pieces of legislation on the 35-hour week and universal health cover.[78] Martine Aubry became Mayor of Lille, and stood for the Socialists in the 2002 Legislative elections. She was narrowly defeated in the second round, when a 40 per cent abstention rate and a high vote for the FN handed the seat to the Right.[79] Her career nevertheless demonstrates a longstanding commitment to removing inequality and injustice, as well as the common French pattern of moving between the public and private sectors. She has been touted as a potential French President by some on the Left.

The contrast between a political career like Aubry's, and the extremely limited role allowed women born into political families in the nineteenth century, shows the distance that has been travelled. While such women are still few in number, their presence shows that 'women's place' in the twenty-first century is beginning to encompass the entire social and political spectrum. As women like Aubry build their power-bases within the major parties, the challenge they face is to help open those party machines to the promise of parity, rather than commit themselves to the struggle for power in the old 'masculine' way.

Conclusion: Equality and 'Difference' – Women's Lives from the Eighteenth to the Twenty-first Century

French society has changed dramatically over the last two centuries. The eighteenth-century world of horse-drawn carts, village isolation and widespread illiteracy is barely recognisable in the current world of the TGV, urban density and the internet. From this perspective, a sense of 'progress' in considering the changes in women's lives over that period is inevitable. Yet this does not mean that the history of French women since 1789 fits a Whiggish model of constant improvement. The dominant impression is instead one of slow and fitful transition, in which change in women's lives has frequently been contested (by women, as well as by men) and often perceived as negative.

Beliefs about women's 'proper' place in society have underpinned reactions to changes affecting women, whatever the sex and whatever the social position or ideological standpoint of the observer. Women's 'place', their 'proper' position and social roles have constantly been debated and contested in a way that has not applied to men's 'place' or roles. 'Woman' has remained 'other' to the norm; concepts of sexual 'difference' – of woman's 'difference' from a normative 'man' – have shaped women's lives, their expectations, their legal and political positions. This history is not unique to France, but it has taken a particular shape in the French context.

In economic terms, the transformation in women's lives has been dramatic, although continuities with the past are also evident. Women's lives at the end of the eighteenth century differed remarkably depending on the social situation into which they were born. A peasant woman in 1789 had little in common with an aristocrat or a *grande bourgeoise*. They did not even speak the same language. While France has not evolved into an egalitarian utopia, the extreme differences in wealth, educational levels and lifestyle that marked the late 1700s have become far less pronounced. A small elite of extremely wealthy people, and a substratum of disadvantaged and marginalised people (particularly unemployed and immigrant women, to whom we shall return) still exist today. But between these two extremes, gradations of wealth and opportunity have become considerably less marked. The majority of French women today can be found amongst the broad band of the small-to-middling bourgeoisie, whereas in 1789 they were overwhelmingly peasants.

While the great majority of French women in 1789 lived rural lives, at the beginning of the twenty-first century France was an overwhelmingly urban society. The rural population reached its peak in 1851, when one in two French people lived from agriculture. A century later (in 1946) that proportion had halved to 25 per cent of the population. The process of urbanisation accelerated rapidly in succeeding decades. In 1990, only six per cent of the population lived in agricultural households.[1] In 1999, when the population of France reached 58.5 million, more than three-quarters of the population lived in municipalities officially classified as 'urban zones'.[2]

The rural exodus after the Second World War was led by young women. The percentage of women in the agricultural workforce peaked in 1946 at 44 per cent (3.2 million women) and then began to decline: in 1991, only 400,000 women worked in agriculture.[3] The number of female heads of family farms has continued to rise, and women increasingly farm their own land. But they are still unlikely to inherit farms unless there is no male heir: a continuity with the past though one that varies by region.[4] Twice as many farming women as men have completed secondary or university education – another significant shift in gender patterns – and rural women increasingly work in nearby towns.[5] Urban employment, the urban schooling of children, better transport, and the impact of mass media (especially television) have ended the cultural isolation that characterised nineteenth-century rural life. Village life has become a museum phenomenon, with French and foreign tourists alike enjoying the brief re-creation of the old world before returning to the attractions of the town.

Women's significant contribution to the paid workforce is another constant feature of the last two centuries. Their shift from the industrial sector into the service sector has also continued across that period. In 2001, 48 per cent of women participated in the labour market.[6] They comprised more than 70 per cent of personnel in clerical work, commerce, and lower-level public sector employment, and 87 per cent of workers in retail sales. Women also congregated in the 'caring' professions like nursing and physiotherapy and were more than half of the workforce in teaching.[7] Women workers are now overwhelmingly employed in the broad tertiary sector. They thus form part of a social category which is neither 'bourgeois' nor 'working class' as these were understood in the nineteenth century.

A key feature of women's employment in recent decades has been the very high participation rate of women aged 25–49 years: the childbearing and childrearing years. In 2001, 80 per cent of women in this age group were in the paid labour force.[8] Even 71 per cent of single mothers were economically active in 1998, and 75 per cent of them worked full-time.[9] This high participation rate reflects the increasing acceptance of women's right to combine career and motherhood, and the policies that the State has put in place since the 1970s to facilitate that choice. The funding of childcare centres and nurseries, as well as financial incentives to encourage employers to adopt 'family-friendly' practices like flexible working hours, have aided women's employment. But women are still predominantly responsible for domestic labour and childcare: a significant continuity with the eighteenth century.[10]

In recent years, the growth of temporary and part-time work has affected women workers more than men. Almost a third of women were in part-time employment in 1998. For some, part-time work is an attractive option given their domestic responsibilities. But the part-time workforce is composed primarily of migrant women in low-skilled and low-paid jobs. More than half of migrant women are unqualified. As a result they are clustered at the lower end of the tertiary sector, especially in cleaning and waiting work.[11] While unemployment has persistently been higher for women than for men since 1990,[12] migrant women are over-represented amongst the unemployed in all employment categories, and tend to be unemployed for longer. They therefore comprise the most disadvantaged sector of the labour force.[13]

The experience of migrant women illustrates the extent to which educational qualifications affect job opportunities, job security and income levels. While many women are still disadvantaged in all these respects, and while parity with men is still far from achieved, the gradual shift of women into high-status and high-paid jobs marks another difference from their nineteenth-century experience. Girls are now slightly more likely than boys to stay at school till age 18 and sit the *baccalauréat* examination. The great majority of girls matriculate in the literary stream (82 per cent in 2000), but women's pass rate exceeds that of men in all streams.[14] They outnumber men in tertiary education, even in law and medicine, and more women than men undertake postgraduate study. While women are still underrepresented in the physical sciences, they have extended their options across almost all fields in recent decades, opening up prestigious and high-paying careers.[15]

On the other hand, women's low rate of entry into the elite educational institutions, the *Grandes Ecoles* (literally, 'Great Schools'), means they are less likely than men to enter top-level positions in the public and private sectors. Universities are open to all who pass their *baccalauréat*, but entry to the *Grandes Ecoles* is highly competitive. It generally requires two years of preparatory study after the *baccalauréat*, at which point candidates sit a public entry examination. Successful candidates pursue a course of study lasting from five to six years, eventually qualifying for leadership positions in public administration, engineering, science and technology, or higher education.[16] Boys are twice as likely as girls to enter the preparatory classes for the *Grandes Ecoles*.[17] In 2000, women comprised only a third of candidates for entry to the ENA, for instance, and made up only 21 per cent of those admitted.[18] The reasons for women's under-representation are unclear. However, the combination of the low likelihood of success with the rigorous seven- to eight-year programme of study may be a disincentive for women who envisage not only pursuing a career, but also having a family.

Women's failure to enter the *Grandes Ecoles* is reflected in the fact that only 8 per cent of the CEOs of large businesses (those employing fifty or more staff) were female in 2001, and they occupied only 14 per cent of the highest positions in the Civil Service. But more than a third of company executives, and more than 20 per cent of heads and deputy-heads of government departments, were women.[19] Sex-based pay disparities are reducing, but a clear division is emerging between low-paid women, often poorly qualified and working part-time, and the highly qualified women who work full-time, earning high salaries.[20] These professional women often rely on the paid labour of less-qualified women to enable them to manage their domestic tasks: a modern makeover of the nineteenth-century bourgeois household. The feminist vision of a more equitable distribution of domestic responsibilities to offset women's participation in the paid labour force has yet to eventuate.[21]

The last two centuries have also seen significant changes in women's civil and political status in French society. At the beginning of the nineteenth century, the Civil Code defined them as legally dependent on and subordinate to men, with little control over their own lives. At marriage, women became non-persons, and even well-to-do women, financially secure and socially privileged, could come up against the legal circumscription of their rights. The legal status of women and the formal relationship between the sexes is now dramatically different. Men no longer have legal authority over their wives, and their authority over their children is shared equally with the mothers of those children. The removal of the major legal hurdles to women's equal citizenship with men has been an important if hard-won gain for women.

The history of women's lives in France over the last two centuries is also a history of their gradual emergence as political subjects, despite intense male opposition and considerable debate. With the French Revolution, women as a category became less equal to men than they had been under the Old Regime. The notion of citizenship developed at that time was male and required women's exclusion. Insofar as women acted politically in the nineteenth century, they did so either indirectly and behind the scenes, or in 'exceptional' circumstances where the rules were temporarily waived. In the mid-twentieth century, women finally became political citizens on the same terms as men, with the right to participate fully in political life. As they came to realise, however, formal equality had its shortcomings. The movement for 'parity' in the 1990s demonstrated women's ongoing attempts to transform formal equality into real equality, and to integrate women fully into the power structures of modern France.

This history illustrates, as Simone de Beauvoir suggested in 1949, women's struggle to become and be recognised as 'free and autonomous' beings in a world where men have allocated them 'the status of the Other' and have had the power to enforce this distinction.[22] Clearly, women are now able to exercise more freedom and autonomy than in the eighteenth century. Nevertheless, they have not yet escaped the status of 'Other' since the power of definition, the act of naming, remains a male privilege. The great struggle of 'second-wave' feminism was not only to remove all forms of 'discrimination' against women, in which feminists had much success, but to challenge male power to define the world and allocate positions within it: to define who is the 'centre' and who is the 'other'. The problem of female 'otherness' has constantly resurfaced as women have sought to claim their rights. Joan Scott argued some years ago that French feminists since the Revolution found themselves grappling with a paradox: seeking the same rights as men on the basis of their common humanity, yet needing to organise as a specific 'female' constituency in order to demand those rights. They thereby invoked difference whilst denying difference.[23] That paradox was still evident in the struggle for parity at the turn of the twenty-first century. Parity required a recognition of female difference and women's right as 'different' beings to control political life on equal terms with men. The law on parity shows the distance travelled since 1789. But the fact that parity has not yet produced a complete acceptance of women's legitimate participation in public life shows the path still to be travelled.

Changes in women's lives, illustrated by their visibility in the workforce and in positions of authority, have constantly provoked debate and hostility. The lives of women act as a barometer of social stability for some, with change evoking the prospect of social dissolution. For extreme conservatives, the insecurity of modern life can only be alleviated by restoring distinct gender roles and attempting to recover the mythical demographic purity of the French nation. In this respect the FN currently articulates views of womanhood that have remained largely unchanged on the far Right since the nineteenth century. The majority of French women, however, continue to find a life of personal autonomy more attractive than one determined by biology. And the FN has had to modify its position in response to public rejection of its stance.

The politics of sexuality and reproduction are good examples of both entrenched conservative resistance to change, and of the strength of public support for change. Repeal of the laws penalising homosexuality in the 1980s, for instance, led to the outlawing of discrimination on the basis of sexual preference. A further (and equally controversial) step by the Socialist government produced the PACS or 'pact of civil solidarity' (1999). The 'pact' is a legal agreement available to both gay and 'straight' couples that confers some of the protections of marriage, particularly in tax and inheritance matters.[24] For conservatives, this law is an attack on marriage and the family, but it was widely welcomed in more progressive circles and has enjoyed general acceptance.

The battle over abortion rights continues, with conservatives (not just the FN) intent on achieving repeal of the Veil Law. 'Pro-life' commando groups disrupt the services of abortion clinics in France, as they do elsewhere. The distribution of RU-486 (the 'morning-after' contraceptive pill) was briefly interrupted in 1988, after a major lobbying campaign made the manufacturer fearful of the consequences. But resistance to reproductive freedom remains a minority view, according to public opinion polls. There was little public objection in 2000 when RU-486 became available to adolescent girls without parental consent.[25] The Veil law remains in place, abortion is reimbursed through the social security system, and women have ready access to contraception.

While reproductive rights are critical to all women, migrant women face additional issues of autonomy and personal freedom. In 1990, women were 48 per cent of the immigrant community, the majority having arrived in France after 1974 when the immigration policy began to emphasise family reunion. While immigrant women increasingly engage in paid labour, they are more likely to be confined to the home, particularly amongst communities where mixing the sexes is unacceptable. Cultural practices like polygamy and clitoral excision spark public debate, pitting the right to cultural diversity against the desire to 'liberate' women from the oppressive traditions of male-dominated cultures. Such debates are exacerbated by the fear that alien practices will become established in France.[26] Migrant women's voices are not often heard in these debates, although African women have been active in the opposition to genital mutilation.[27]

The controversy over the *foulard* – the headscarf (or veil: a less polemical term) worn by Muslim women – has mobilised women on both sides of the debate. The debate began in 1989, when three schoolgirls were excluded from class for wearing the *foulard*, on the grounds that it was contrary to the principle of secularism in the State schooling system. Other schools became involved, and a heated public debate began that continues to divide the political parties, the Muslim community and women.

The *foulard* affair is extremely complex. The controversy is linked with fear of Islam, now the second largest religion in the country. In an international climate marked by September 11, 2002, concerns about Islamic fundamentalism fuel the politics of the Right, while rising anti-Semitism stirs Republican nightmares about Vichy. The controversy is occurring in a context of economic difficulty, cut-backs in government spending on social security, a growing gap between rich and poor, and the social 'exclusion' of impoverished immigrants. In the words of sociologist Farhad Khosrokhavar, targeting the headscarf is a cheap and easy alternative to attacking 'poverty, exclusion, ghettoisation, two-tiered schooling and health services'.[28] Beyond these issues, however, lies the deeply emotional subject of the secular state. The *'foulard* affair' has sparked a major controversy over the principle of *laïcité* (secularism), a founding value of the Republic, and over the rights of the individual (another foundation principle, but potentially in conflict with secularism in this instance). For many French people today, secularism remains intrinsically connected with democracy and the Republic, which were established only after a century-long struggle. This explains the passion evoked by this debate.

In July 2003, President Jacques Chirac established a commission (named the Stasi Commission after its chairman) to make recommendations on the protection of *laïcité*. Its report, in December 2003, rejected practices which bring religion into public life, including 'the wearing of any visible (*ostensible*) religious symbol – large cross, yarmulke, or veil' in schools, law courts or by medical personnel. It also made a number of recommendations to improve intercultural understanding, recognise the feasts sacred to both Islam and Judaism by declaring them public holidays, and redress disadvantage in urban communities.[29]

Feminists who struggled long and hard to gain the 'rights of man' for women, like Yvette Roudy, Simone Veil and Gisèle Halimi, see the veil as a sign of women's oppression. Roudy argued: 'it is a sign of subordination, accepted or imposed, in a fundamentalist Muslim society [...] Accepting the wearing of the veil would amount to consenting to the inequality of women in Muslim society in France'.[30] Gisèle Halimi emphasised the gender politics of the veil in her submission to the Stasi Commission: 'the yarmulke is a symbol as opposed to secularism as the veil, but the veil creates a sexual apartheid'.[31] The Commission held closed hearings in which some women testified to the pressure exerted on them to wear the veil. Its report linked veiling to practices like arranged marriage, sexual mutilation, polygamy and repudiation. The Commission rejected veiling, arguing that it was an attack on women's fundamental rights.[32]

Objections to the veil have thus been framed in terms of the 'Republic of the Rights of Man', in which secularism guarantees the religious freedoms of all in private life, and in which the universal 'citizen' enters society bearing no signs of particularity. In this case, however, women are presented as the beneficiaries of 'universalism' whereas in the past (as the parity debate showed) it had served to disadvantage them. As critics of this position have pointed out, however, wearing the veil in France means something different from doing so in a fundamentalist Islamic state. While some women in France may be pressured to wear the veil, others choose it as an affirmation of their identity in a society that rejects them. It can also be a vehicle to freedom for women. Without the veil, they would be prevented from joining in community activities, and would be forced into the seclusion and cultural isolation that those hostile to the veil claim to oppose.[33]

The controversy over the veil demonstrates that the issues dividing women in France are now quite different from the largely class-based divisions of the nineteenth century. Socio-economic divisions still exist, but today they are strongly inflected by the cultural diversity of French society. The controversy might also be seen as part of a revival of 'identity politics' in Europe in the face of globalisation and 'Europeanisation'. In this context, Leora Auslander suggests, both in-groups and out-groups are anxious to distinguish between 'us' and 'them'.[34]

The channelling of cultural anxieties through the issue of veiling women also reveals that national identity is still bound up with feminine representations of 'the nation', just as it was during the French Revolution. When prominent Socialist deputy, Laurent Fabius, declared at the 2003 Socialist Party congress, 'Marianne is not veiled' (*Marianne n'a pas de voile*), he drew on a repertoire of images of the French Republic dating back to 1789.[35] Ironically, of course, for much of the period since 1789 Marianne, image of a free and autonomous citizen, bore no relationship to unfree and disenfranchised French women. Nevertheless, images of women have been critical to the development of modern nationalism, and to the representation of a nation which its (traditionally male) citizens could love.[36] The female form continues to represent the ideal nation to which the community aspires. The challenge facing France is to create a vision of the nation in which diversity is not incompatible with unity.

French women have made enormous gains since the late eighteenth century. Despite entrenched opposition, they have successfully prised open many doors that remained shut in the past. They have achieved full civic and civil equality and have assumed positions of status in the workplace and in public life. While far from a single-interest group, women have used their votes to force often-reluctant politicians to support policies they desire. They enjoy reproductive rights superior to women in many other Western societies. Not all women share these gains – social inequalities remain in all countries – but women are no longer excluded simply because of their sex.

The problem of accommodating cultural diversity is significant as France enters the twenty-first century. The 'one and indivisible' Republic created by the French Revolution has found in the Parity law a way to reconcile sexual difference with the universal 'citizen'. It now needs to find a way to recognise broad cultural differences amongst men and women as well. Only then will the issue of women's 'place' – indeed, their 'places' – in a nation of diversity be resolved.

Notes

Introduction: the French Revolution and gender politics – creating a World of difference

1. 'Requête des dames à l'Assemblée Nationale [1789]', in *Les femmes dans la Révolution française*, 2 vols (Paris: EDHIS, 1982), document 19.
2. Joan B. Landes, *Women and the Public Sphere in the Age of the French Revolution* (Ithaca: Cornell University Press, 1988), p. 204. For a pathbreaking article arguing that the chronology of women's history frequently diverges from that of men, see Joan Kelly-Gadol, 'Did Women have a Renaissance?', in Renate Bridenthal and Claudia Koonz (eds), *Becoming Visible: women in European history* (Boston: Houghton Mifflin, 1977).
3. The essential study of the functioning of Old Regime aristocratic society remains Norbert Elias, *The Court Society*, trans. Edmund Jephcott (Oxford: Blackwell, 1983). For a fascinating insight into aristocratic politics and women's roles within them, see Thomas E. Kaiser, 'Ambiguous Identities: Marie-Antoinette and the House of Lorraine from the Affair of the Minuet to Lambesc's Charge', in Dena Goodman (ed.), *Marie-Antoinette: writings on the body of a queen* (New York and London: Routledge, 2003).
4. Thomas E. Kaiser, 'Madame de Pompadour and the Theatrics of Power', *French Historical Studies* 19, 4(1996), 1035–6, 1039–41.
5. Lynn Hunt, 'The Many Bodies of Marie Antoinette: political pornography and the problem of the feminine in the French Revolution', in Lynn Hunt (ed.), *Eroticism and the Body Politic* (Baltimore and London: Johns Hopkins University Press, 1991); Sarah Maza, 'The Diamond Necklace Affair Revisited (1785–1786): the case of the missing queen', in Hunt (ed.), *Eroticism and the Body Politic*; Joan B. Landes, *Visualizing the Nation: gender, representation, and revolution in eighteenth-century France* (Ithaca and London: Cornell University Press, 2001), p. 73. Cf. Montesquieu, *Lettres Persanes* [1721], Letter 107, quoted in Joan B. Landes, *Women and the Public Sphere in the Age of the French Revolution* (Ithaca and London: Cornell University Press, 1988), pp. 33–4.

298

6. Dorinda Outram, 'Le langage mâle de la vertu: women and the discourse of the French Revolution', in Peter Burke and Roy Porter (eds), *The Social History of Language* (Cambridge: Cambridge University Press, 1987), p. 125.

7. Lenard R. Berlanstein, *Daughters of Eve: a cultural history of French theater women from the Old Regime to the fin de siècle* (Cambridge, Mass.: Harvard University Press, 2001), Chapter 3.

8. Dena Goodman, 'Enlightenment Salons: the convergence of female and philosophical ambitions', *Eighteenth-Century Studies* 22 (1989). See also her book, *The Republic of Letters: a cultural history of the French Enlightenment* (Ithaca and London: Cornell University Press, 1994).

9. The essential work on the creation of a 'public sphere' remains Jürgen Habermas, *The Structural Transformation of the Public Sphere: an inquiry into a category of bourgeois society*, trans. Thomas Burger (Cambridge, Mass.: MIT Press, 1989).

10. Goodman, 'Enlightenment Salons: the convergence of female and philosophical ambitions', p. 339. See also Dorinda Outram, *The Enlightenment* (Cambridge and New York: Cambridge University Press, 1995).

11. For a good discussion of these debates, see Karen Offen, 'Reclaiming the European Enlightenment for Feminism, or Prolegomena to Any Future History of Eighteenth-Century Europe', in Tjitske Akkerman and Siep Stuurman (eds), *Perspectives on Feminist Political Thought in European History: from the Middle Ages to the present* (London and New York: Routledge, 1998), pp. 85–103; Karen M. Offen, *European Feminisms, 1700–1950: a political history* (Stanford: Stanford University Press, 2000), Chapter 2.

12. Robert A. Nye, 'Forum: Biology, sexuality and morality in eighteenth-century France: introduction', *Eighteenth-Century Studies* 35 (2002).

13. Thomas Walter Laqueur, *Making Sex: body and gender from the Greeks to Freud* (Cambridge, Mass.: Harvard University Press, 1990), pp. 194–207.

14. Carole Pateman, *The Sexual Contract* (Stanford: Stanford University Press, 1988), Chapter 4. My emphasis.

15. Nye, 'Forum: Biology, sexuality and morality in eighteenth-century France: introduction'.

16. Berlanstein, *Daughters of Eve*, p. 61; Offen, *European Feminisms*, Chapter 2.

17. Laqueur, *Making Sex: body and gender from the Greeks to Freud*, pp. 26–8.

18. 'Louise d'Epinay's Letter to Abbé Ferdinando Galiani', in Lisa DiCaprio and Merry E. Wiesner (eds), *Lives and Voices: sources in European women's history* (Boston and New York: Houghton Mifflin, 2001), p. 247.

19. Candice E. Proctor, *Women, Equality and the French Revolution* (New York: Greenwood Press, 1990), p. 26.

20. See Elizabeth Colwill, 'Pass as a Woman, Act Like a Man: Marie-Antoinette as tribade in the pornography of the French Revolution', in *Marie-Antoinette: writings on the body of a queen*, p. 142.

21. Carol Blum, *Rousseau and the Republic of Virtue: the language of politics in the French Revolution* (Ithaca: Cornell University Press, 1986), pp. 47–8, 78.

22. Antoine de Baecque, *The Body Politic: corporeal metaphor in revolutionary France, 1770–1800*, trans. Charlotte Mandell (Stanford: Stanford

University Press, 1997); Chantal Thomas, 'The Heroine of the Crime: Marie-Antoinette in pamphlets', in *Marie-Antoinette: writings on the body of a queen*, pp. 99–116.

23. Landes, *Visualizing the Nation*, p. 76.
24. Quoted in Berlanstein, *Daughters of Eve*, p. 63.
25. Margaret Iversen, 'Imagining the Republic: the sign and sexual politics in France', in Peter Hulme and Ludmilla Jordanova (eds), *The Enlightenment and its Shadows* (London and New York: Routledge, 1990), pp. 131–2.
26. Lynn Avery Hunt, *The Family Romance of the French Revolution* (Berkeley: University of California Press, 1992). For a useful discussion of Hunt's ideas, see the forum in *French Historical Studies* 19, 2 (1995), 261–98.
27. Landes, *Women and the Public Sphere*, pp. 7, 12.
28. Offen, *European Feminisms*, pp. 58–66.
29. Berlanstein, *Daughters of Eve*, Chapter 3.
30. Carla Hesse, *The Other Enlightenment: how French women became modern* (Princeton: Princeton University Press, 2001), Chapter 2.
31. This interpretation is developed at length in Dominique Godineau, *The Women of Paris and their French Revolution*, trans. Katherine Streip (Berkeley: University of California Press, 1998).
32. Hesse, *The Other Enlightenment*, p. 38.
33. Good general studies of the French Revolution include William Doyle, *The Oxford History of the French Revolution* (Oxford and New York: Oxford University Press, 2002); Alan Forrest, *The French Revolution* (Oxford and Cambridge, Mass.: Blackwell, 1995); Peter McPhee, *The French Revolution, 1789–1799* (Oxford: Oxford University Press, 2002).
34. Godineau, *The Women of Paris and their French Revolution*, p. 104.
35. Dominique Godineau, 'Pratiques politiques féminines et masculines et lignes de partage sexuel au sein du mouvement populaire parisien pendant la révolution française (1793-an III)', *History of European Ideas* 10 (1989), 297–9.
36. Godineau, 'Pratiques politiques féminines'.
37. Godineau, *The Women of Paris and their French Revolution*, p. 108.
38. Anne Soprani, *La révolution et les femmes de 1789 à 1796* (Paris: MA Editions, 1988), pp. 16–22.
39. Cited in Joan Wallach Scott, *Only Paradoxes to Offer: French feminists and the rights of man* (Cambridge Mass.: Harvard University Press, 1996), p. 35.
40. Godineau, *The Women of Paris and their French Revolution*, p. 135.
41. Godineau, 'Pratiques politiques féminines', p. 299.
42. Ibid., pp. 300–301; Olwen Hufton, 'Women in Revolution', *French History and Politics* 7 (1989), 70.
43. Hufton, 'Women in Revolution', p. 71.
44. Godineau, 'Pratiques politiques féminines', p. 297.
45. Soprani, *La révolution et les femmes de 1789 à 1796*, pp. 48–50, 67–8.
46. Ibid., p. 135.
47. Ibid., pp. 182–3. Soprani calls Roland the 'great political woman of the Revolution', p. 31.
48. P. McPhee, *A Social History of France 1780–1880* (London and New York: Routledge, 1992), pp. 54–6, 60.

49. Hufton, 'Women in Revolution', pp. 76–7.
50. Ibid., pp. 74–80.
51. Soprani, *La révolution et les femmes de 1789 à 1796*, pp. 138–9.
52. Outram, 'Le langage mâle de la vertu: women and the discourse of the French Revolution', pp. 127–9.
53. Scott, *Only Paradoxes to Offer*, p. 19.
54. Soprani, *La révolution et les femmes de 1789 à 1796*, pp. 48–9, 68–9.
55. Quoted in ibid., p. 67.
56. Olympe de Gouges, *Les droits de la femme*, 14 September 1791, full French (and English) text available at http://www.mdx.ac.uk/www/study/xolyf.htm#Declaration, accessed 15 December 2003.
57. Outram, 'Le langage mâle de la vertu: women and the discourse of the French Revolution', pp. 124–5.
58. Scott, *Only Paradoxes to Offer*, p. 3.
59. Charge of the Revolutionary Tribunal, 2 November 1793, quoted in Soprani, *La révolution et les femmes de 1789 à 1796*, p. 190.
60. Hunt, 'The Many Bodies of Marie Antoinette', pp. 108–30.
61. Chaumette, quoted in Soprani, *La révolution et les femmes de 1789 à 1796*, p. 197.
62. Outram, 'Le langage mâle de la vertu: women and the discourse of the French Revolution', p. 125.
63. Quoted in Soprani, *La révolution et les femmes de 1789 à 1796*, p. 197.
64. Quoted in ibid., pp. 198–9.
65. Landes, *Visualizing the Nation*, pp. 73–6, 82, 99–101.
66. Ibid., p. 133.
67. Quoted in Darline Gay Levy, Harriet Branson Applewhite, Mary Durham Johnson (eds), *Women in Revolutionary Paris 1789–1795: selected documents translated with notes and commentary* (Urbana, Chicago and London: University of Illinois Press, 1979), p. 220.
68. Quoted in Soprani, *La révolution et les femmes de 1789 à 1796*, p. 198.
69. Pateman, *Sexual Contract*, Chapters 4 and 5.
70. On Hercules as a symbol of virility in popular and elite representations, see Lynn Hunt, *Politics, Culture and Class in the French Revolution* (Berkeley: University of California Press, 1984), pp. 104–5.
71. Colwill, 'Pass as a woman, Act like a man', pp. 148–9.
72. Ibid., pp. 152–3.
73. Quoted in Levy (ed.), *Women in Revolutionary Paris*, pp. 215–16.
74. Quoted in ibid., p. 217.
75. Quoted in ibid., p. 219.
76. Quoted in ibid., pp. 215–16.
77. Quoted in Tom Holberg, 'The Civil Code (the Code Napoléon)', available at http://www.napoleonseries.org/articles/government.civilcode.cfm, placed on Napoleonseries.org in August 2002, accessed Sunday, 2 March 2003.
78. Holberg, 'The Civil Code'.
79. Ibid.
80. For discussions of the Civil Code as it pertained to women, see James F. McMillan, *France and Women 1789–1914: gender, politics and society* (London and New York: Routledge, 2000), pp. 36–41; Maïté Albistur and Daniel

Armogathe, *Histoire du féminisme français* (Paris: Editions des femmes, 1977), pp. 359–64.

81. Patrick Kay Bidelman, 'The Feminist Movement in France: the formative years, 1858–1889', PhD diss., Michigan State University, 1995.

1 Elite women

1. Simone de Beauvoir, *Le deuxième sexe*, 2 vols (Paris: Gallimard, 1976), II, p. 13.
2. Jean-Noël Luc, '"A trois ans, l'enfant devient intéressant...": La découverte médicale de la seconde enfance (1750–1900)', *Revue d'histoire moderne et contemporaine* 36 (1989), 83–112.
3. Joseph de Maistre, *Lettres et opuscules inédits* (1851), quoted in Geneviève Fraisse, *Muse de la Raison. La démocratie exclusive et la différence des sexes* (Paris: Alinéa, 1989), p. 57.
4. Barbara Corrado Pope, 'Mothers and Daughters in Early Nineteenth-Century Paris', PhD diss., Columbia University, 1981, p. 284.
5. Laura Strumingher, 'L'Ange de la Maison: mothers and daughters in nineteenth-century France', *International Journal of Women's Studies* 2 (1979), 56.
6. Marie de Flavigny, Comtesse d'Agoult, *Mes souvenirs, 1806–1833*, 3rd edn (Paris: Calmann-Lévy, 1880), pp. 99, 105–6, 114, 157.
7. Lucile le Verrier, *Journal d'une jeune fille, Second Empire, 1866–1878*, ed. Lionel Mirisch (Paris, Cadeilhan: Zulma, Calmann-Lévy, 1994), pp. 20, 91.
8. Pope, 'Mothers and Daughters', pp. 108, 174–5, 350–1.
9. Anne-Marie Sohn, *Chrysalides: femmes dans la vie privée (XIXe-XXe siècles)* (Paris: Publications de la Sorbonne, 1996), p. 68.
10. Anne Martin-Fugier, 'Bourgeois Rituals', in Michelle Perrot (ed.), *A History of Private Life, IV: from the fires of Revolution to the Great War*, trans. Arthur Goldhammer (Cambridge, Mass. and London: Belknap Press, 1990), p. 269.
11. Pope, 'Mothers and Daughters', pp. 244–6.
12. *Le journal intime de Caroline B*, eds Michelle Perrot and Georges Ribeill (Paris: Arthaud-Montalba, 1985), p. 71.
13. Pope, 'Mothers and Daughters', pp. 293–4.
14. Marie-Françoise Lévy, *De mères en filles: l'éducation des françaises 1850–1880* (Paris: Calmann-Lévy, 1984), Chapters 2–3.
15. D'Agoult, *Souvenirs*, pp. 41–3.
16. Quoted in Pope, 'Mothers and Daughters', pp. 222–3.
17. Lévy, *De mères en filles*, pp. 26–32.
18. Yvonne Knibiehler *et al.*, *De la pucelle à la minette: les jeunes filles, de l'âge classique à nos jours*, nouvelle édition (Paris: Messidor, 1989), p. 107; Pope, 'Mothers and Daughters', pp. 211–12.
19. Knibiehler, *De la pucelle*, p. 110; Lévy, *De mères en filles*, pp. 36–46.
20. Gabrielle Houbre, *La discipline de l'amour. L'éducation sentimentale des filles et des garçons à l'âge Romantique* (Paris: Plon, 1997), p. 23; Pope, 'Mothers and Daughters', p. 300.

21. Houbre, *Discipline*, pp. 156–7.
22. Pope, 'Mothers and Daughters', pp. 305–8.
23. Houbre, *Discipline*, pp. 157, 162.
24. Yvonne Knibiehler, 'Les médecins et la "nature féminine" au temps du Code Civil', *Annales E.S.C.* 31, 4 (1976), 831–2; Pope, 'Mothers and Daughters', p. 301.
25. Pope, 'Mothers and Daughters', p. 227; Houbre, *Discipline*, p. 157.
26. Knibiehler, 'Les médecins', pp. 827–36.
27. Houbre, *Discipline*, p. 26.
28. *Journal intime de Caroline B*, pp. 112, 190; Le Verrier, *Journal*, pp. 22–3.
29. Houbre, *Discipline*, pp. 207–10.
30. Quoted in ibid., p. 219.
31. Quoted in Adeline Daumard, 'Affaire, amour, affection: le mariage dans la société bourgeoise au XIXe siècle', *Romantisme* 68 (1990), 36.
32. *Journal intime de Caroline B*, p. 24.
33. Ibid., p. 14.
34. Amélie Weiler, *Journal d'une jeune fille mal dans son siècle, 1840–1859*, ed. Nicolas Stoskopf (Strasbourg: La Nuée bleue, 1994), pp. 25, 60, 76. Lejeune argues that the prison metaphor was apt for the lives of young women, who lived constantly under 'high security'. See Philippe Lejeune, *Le moi des demoiselles. Enquête sur le journal de jeune fille* (Paris: Seuil, 1993), p. 83.
35. Le Verrier, *Journal*, p. 50.
36. Ibid., pp. 102–3.
37. Ibid., pp. 81, 82.
38. Ibid., p. 207.
39. Ibid., pp. 45–6.
40. Ibid., pp. 95–6.
41. Houbre, *Discipline*, pp. 241–2.
42. Lévy, *De mères en filles*, pp. 122–3.
43. D'Agoult, *Souvenirs*, pp. 119–20; Le Verrier, *Journal*, p. 65; Weiler, *Journal*, p. 72.
44. D'Agoult, *Souvenirs*, pp. 119–20.
45. Weiler, *Journal*, pp. 65, 72, 76.
46. Ibid., pp. 59–60.
47. Pope, 'Mothers and Daughters', pp. 322–5.
48. Mme Bourdon, *La vie réelle* (1858), quoted in Strumingher, 'L'Ange de la Maison', p. 53.
49. *Journal intime de Caroline B*, p. 113 (1 Nov. 1865).
50. Le Verrier, *Journal*, pp. 239–40, 248 (9 Sep. and 11 Oct. 1873).
51. Pope, 'Mothers and Daughters', p. 309.
52. Le Verrier, *Journal*, p. 67.
53. Stéphanie Jullien to Marc-Antoine Jullien, 29 Feb. 1836, quoted in Houbre, *Discipline*, pp. 377–80.
54. Weiler, *Journal*, p. 81.
55. David Pemberton, 'Industrialization and the Bourgeoisie in Nineteenth Century France: the experience of Saint-Etienne, 1820–1872', PhD diss., State University of New Jersey, 1984, pp. 344–6; Adeline Daumard, *Les bourgeois et la bourgeoisie en France* (Paris: Flammarion, 1987), pp. 139–40, 176–7.

56. Knibiehler, *La pucelle*, pp. 134–6; Bonnie Smith, *Ladies of the Leisure Class: the bourgeoises of northern France in the nineteenth century* (Princeton: Princeton University Press, 1981), pp. 57–9; Pemberton, 'Industrialization and the Bourgeoisie in Nineteenth-Century France', pp. 417–18; Pope, 'Mothers and Daughters', pp. 342–3.

57. David Higgs, *Nobles in Nineteenth Century France: the practice of inegalitarianism* (Baltimore: Johns Hopkins University Press, 1987), pp. 191–5, 215.

58. Pope, 'Mothers and Daughters', pp. 132–3.

59. D'Agoult, *Souvenirs*, pp. 223–4.

60. Martin-Fugier, 'Bourgeois Rituals', in *A History of Private Life*, vol. 4, p. 310.

61. Daumard, 'Affaire, Amour, Affection', pp. 36–7.

62. One example is discussed in *Journal intime de Caroline B*, p. 210, and another in Smith, *Ladies of the Leisure Class*, p. 59. In both cases the young women were married off quickly to older men.

63. Jules Michelet, *La femme* (Paris: Calmann-Lévy, s.d.), pp. 68–9.

64. Auguste Debay, *Hygiène et physiologie du mariage; histoire naturelle et médicale de l'homme et de la femme mariés*, 16th edn (Paris: E. Dentu, 1859), p. 6. This work was first published in 1848, and republished 73 times to 1888. See Laure Adler, *Secrets d'alcove. Histoire du couple de 1830 à 1930* (Paris: Hachette, 1983), p. 93.

65. *Journal intime de Caroline B*, pp. 14, 56; Le Verrier, *Journal*, pp. 199, 203, 208; Weiler, *Journal*, pp. 24, 195, 225.

66. *Journal intime de Caroline B*, p. 101.

67. Weiler, *Journal*, p. 86.

68. Le Verrier, *Journal*, p. 126.

69. Ibid., p. 208.

70. *Journal intime de Caroline B*, p. 129.

71. Weiler, *Journal*, p. 116.

72. Smith, *Ladies of the Leisure Class*, p. 60.

73. D'Agoult, *Souvenirs*, pp. 245–8.

74. Houbre, *Discipline*, pp. 228–9.

75. Weiler, *Journal*, p. 225.

76. *Journal intime de Caroline B*, pp. 128–32.

77. Le Verrier, *Journal*, p. 222.

78. Stéphanie Jullien to Marc-Antoine Jullien, quoted in Houbre, *Discipline*, p. 379.

79. Weiler, *Journal*, p. 387.

80. Houbre, *Discipline*, p. 171.

81. Alain Corbin, 'Intimate Relations', in *A History of Private Life*, vol. 4, pp. 590–1.

82. Sohn, *Chrysalides*, pp. 374–7.

83. Quoted in Laure Adler, *Secrets d'alcove. Histoire du couple de 1830 à 1930* (Paris: Hachette, 1983), pp. 49–50.

84. See for instance Debay, *Hygiène et physiologie*, pp. 72–3, 139. For other discussions of this problem, see Sohn, *Chrysalides*, pp. 371–93, 781; Daumard, 'Affaire, Amour, Affection', p. 40; Pope, 'Mothers and Daughters', pp. 373–4.

85. Michèle Plott, 'The Rules of the Game: respectability, sexuality, and the *femme mondaine* in late-nineteenth-century Paris', *French Historical Studies* 25, 3 (2002), 531–56.
86. Theodore Zeldin, *France 1848–1945*, vol. 1: *Ambition, Love and Politics* (Oxford: The Clarendon Press, 1973), p. 296. On flagellation, see Debay, *Hygiène et physiologie*, pp. 263–73.
87. Quoted in Zeldin, *France 1848–1945*, vol. 1, p. 295.
88. Daumard, 'Affair, Amour, Affection', p. 43.
89. Daumard, *Les bourgeois*, p. 212; Sohn, *Chrysalides*, pp. 447, 554; Alain Corbin, 'Intimate Relations', in *A History of Private Life*, vol. 4, p. 596.
90. Le Verrier, *Journal*, pp. 265–6 (16 May 1874).
91. Daumard, 'Affaire, Amour, Affection', pp. 40, 44.
92. Plott, 'The Rules of the Game', p. 547.
93. Sohn, *Chrysalides*, p. 745. For the longevity of this view, see Martine Sevegrand, *L'Amour en toutes lettres. Questions à l'abbé Viollet sur la sexualité 1924–1943* (Paris: Albin Michel, 1996).
94. Michelle Perrot, 'The Family Triumphant', in *A History of Private Life*, vol. 4, pp. 162–4; William M. Reddy, 'Marriage, Honor, and the Public Sphere in Postrevolutionary France: *Séparations de Corps*, 1815–1848', *Journal of Modern History* 65 (1993), 437–72.
95. Mme de Rémusat, 'Essai', quoted in Pope, 'Mothers and Daughters', pp. 227–32.
96. See Margaret H. Darrow, 'French Noblewomen and the New Domesticity, 1750–1850', *Feminist Studies* 5 (Spring 1979), 41–65.
97. Struminger, 'L'Ange de la Maison', pp. 51–61; Barbara Corrado Pope, 'Revolution and Retreat: upper-class French women after 1789', in Carol Berkin and Clara Lovett (eds), *Women, War and Revolution* (New York: Holmes and Meier, 1980), pp. 215–35; Darrow, 'French Noblewomen', p. 56.
98. D'Agoult, *Souvenirs*, pp. 25–6.
99. Adler, *Secrets d'alcove*, pp. 112–13; Zeldin, *France 1848–1945*, vol. 1, p. 328.
100. Pope, 'Mothers and Daughters', pp. 156–62, 216; Smith, *Ladies of the Leisure Class*, pp. 63–4.
101. Jo B. Margadant, 'The Duchesse de Berry and Royalist Political Culture in Postrevolutionary France', *History Workshop Journal* 43 (1997), 23–52.
102. Pope, 'Mothers and Daughters', pp. 182–6; Zeldin, *France 1848–1945*, vol. 1, pp. 318–24.
103. Perrot, 'The Family Triumphant', in *A History of Private Life*, vol. 4, pp. 105–6. Zeldin notes that manuals promoting authoritarian child-raising continued to be published into the twentieth century. See *France 1848–1945*, vol. 1, pp. 319–20.
104. Anne Martin-Fugier, *La vie élégante: la formation du Tout-Paris, 1815–1848* (Paris: Fayard, 1990), p. 73.
105. Perrot, 'The Family Triumphant', in *A History of Private Life*, vol. 4, p. 134.
106. *Dictionnaire de la Femme* (1897), quoted in Adler, *Secrets d'alcove*, p. 111; *Revue de l'Enseignement des Femmes* 1, 1 (1845), quoted in Struminger, 'L'Ange de la Maison', p. 51.
107. Pope, 'Mothers and Daughters', pp. 334–5, 350, 393.

108. Smith, *Ladies of the Leisure Class*, p. 62.
109. *Journal intime de Caroline B*, pp. 133, 136. The word 'baby' is written in English in the text.
110. Debay, *Hygiene et physiologie*, p. 158.
111. Le Verrier, *Journal*, p. 276 (11 May 1878).
112. Ibid., pp. 283 (1 Sep. 1878), 274 (6 May 1878).
113. Martin-Fugier, 'Bourgeois Rituals', in *A History of Private Life*, vol. 4, p. 322.
114. Karen Offen, 'Depopulation, nationalism and feminism in fin-de-siècle France', *American Historical Review* 89 (1984), 648–76; Joshua Cole, *The Power of Large Numbers: population, politics, and gender in nineteenth-century France* (Ithaca and London: Cornell University Press, 2000), Chapters 5–6.
115. Plott, 'The Rules of the Game', 537–8.
116. Debay, *Hygiène et physiologie*, pp. 403–18.
117. Ibid., p. 409.
118. Jacques Gélis, Mireille Laget and Marie-France Morel, *Entrer dans la vie: naissances et enfances dans la France traditionelle* (Paris: Gallimard/Julliard, 1978), pp. 170–1; Fanny Faÿ-Sallois, *Les nourrices à Paris au XIXe siècle* (Paris: Payot, 1980), pp. 198–220.
119. Gélis *et al.*, *Entrer dans la vie*, p. 162.
120. Le Verrier, *Journal*, p. 274.
121. Angus McLaren, 'Doctor in the House: medicine and private morality in France, 1800–1850', *Feminist Studies* 2, 2 (1975), 39–54.
122. Quoted in Faÿ-Sallois, *Nourrices*, p. 219.
123. Sohn, *Chrysalides*, pp. 70–1, 323; Gélis *et al.*, *Entrer dans la vie*, pp. 111–12, 225; Debay, *Hygiène et physiologie*, pp. 422–3.
124. Anne Martin-Fugier, 'La Maîtresse de Maison', in Jean-Paul Aron (ed.), *Misérable et glorieuse. La femme du XIXe siècle* (Paris: Fayard, 1980), p. 129.
125. Mme de Rémusat, *Essai sur l'éducation des femmes* (1824), quoted in Higgs, *Nobles in Nineteenth Century France*, p. 178.
126. Martin-Fugier, *La vie élégante*, pp. 155–63.
127. Daumard, *Le Bourgeois*, pp. 227–8.
128. Martin-Fugier, *La vie élégante*, pp. 12–15, 159.
129. On women's charitable activities, see Evelyne Lejeune-Resnick, *Femmes et associations (1830–1880), vraies démocrates ou dames patronnesses?* (Paris: Publisud, 1991); Cathérine Duprat, *Le temps des philanthropes. La philanthropie parisienne des Lumières à la Monarchie de Juillet* (Paris: Editions du CTHS, 1993); Susan Grogan, 'Philanthropic Women and the State: the *Société de Charité maternelle* in Avignon, 1802–1917', *French History* 14, 3 (2000), 295–321.
130. Lévy, *De mères en filles*, pp. 118–19.
131. Le Verrier, *Journal*, p. 47; *Journal intime de Caroline B*, pp. 34–5, 87, 99.
132. Archives nationales, F15 2565, *Règlemens de la Société de Charité maternelle*, p. 7.
133. Lejeune-Resnick, *Femmes et associations*, p. 86.
134. Ibid., pp. 84–90, 186, 192; Marie-Claire Vitoux, *Paupérisme et assistance à Mulhouse au XIXe siècle* (Strasbourg: Association des publications près

les Universités de Strasbourg, 1986), pp. 103, 143, 185–202; Yannick
Marec, *Pauvres et philanthropes à Rouen au XIXe siècle* (Rouen: C. R. D. R.,
1981), pp. 29, 41.
135. Report on the *Oeuvre des Faubourgs*, quoted in Lejeune-Resnick,
Femmes et Associations, p. 88.
136. John H. Weiss, 'Origins of the French Welfare State: poor relief in the
Third Republic, 1871–1914', *French Historical Studies* 13, 1 (1983), 47–78;
Anne Cova, 'French Feminism and Maternity: theories and policies,
1890–1918', in Gisela Bock and Pat Thane (eds), *Maternity and Gender
Policies: women and the rise of the European welfare states 1880s–1950s*
(London: Routledge, 1991), pp. 119–37.
137. Elinor A. Accampo, 'Gender, Social Policy, and the Formation of the
Third Republic: an introduction', in Elinor A. Accampo, Rachel G.
Fuchs and Mary Lynn Stewart (eds), *Gender and the Politics of Social
Reform in France, 1870–1914* (Baltimore: Johns Hopkins University
Press, 1995), p. 20; L. L. Clark, 'Bringing Feminine Qualities into the
Public Sphere: the Third Republic's appointment of women inspectors',
in *Gender and the Politics of Social Reform*, pp. 128–37.
138. Ibid., p. 135.
139. Ibid., p. 136.

2 Urban working women

1. Roger Price, *A Social History of Nineteenth-Century France* (London:
Hutchinson, 1987), pp. 84–7.
2. Ibid., p. 84.
3. Katherine A. Lynch, *Family, Class, and Ideology in Early Industrial
France: social policy and the working class family, 1825–1848* (Madison,
Wisc.: University of Wisconsin Press, 1988), p. 77.
4. René Grosso, 'Le peuplement et l'habitat', in René Grosso (ed.), *Histoire
de Vaucluse, II, Les Vauclusiens, des campagnes à la Ville* (Avignon: Editions
A. Barthélemy, 1993), pp. 170–2; Christopher H. Johnson, *The Life and
Death of Industrial Languedoc 1700–1920: the politics of deindustrialization*
(Oxford: Oxford University Press, 1995), p. 21.
5. Lesley Page Moch, *Paths to the City: regional migration in nineteenth-century France* (Beverly Hills: Sage Publications, 1983), pp. 34–9.
6. Christophe Charle, *A Social History of France in the Nineteenth Century*,
trans. Miriam Kocham (Oxford: Berg, 1994), pp. 128–9.
7. Moch, *Paths to the City*, pp. 68–9.
8. Laura S. Strumingher, *What Were Little Girls and Boys Made of?: primary
education in rural France, 1830–1880* (Albany: State University of
New York Press, 1983), Chapter 4.
9. Patricia Hilden, *Working Women and Socialist Politics in France,
1880–1914: a regional study* (Oxford: Clarendon Press, 1986), p. 26;
Johnson, *Life and Death*, p. 106; Anne-Marie Sohn, *Chrysalides: femmes
dans la vie privée (XIXe-XXe siècles)* (Paris: Publications de la Sorbonne,
1996), p. 110.

10. Johnson, *Life and Death*, pp. 107–8; Hilden, *Working Women and Socialist Politics*, pp. 27–8.
11. Price, *Social History*, pp. 216–17; Sohn, *Chrysalides*, pp. 166, 299–304.
12. Price, *Social History*, pp. 62–4; Elinor A. Accampo, *Industrialization, Family Life, and Class Relations: Saint Chamond, 1815–1914* (Berkeley: University of California Press, 1988), p. 131.
13. Price, *Social History*, p. 219.
14. Ibid., pp. 70–2; Johnson, *Life and Death*, pp. 108–9.
15. See Louis Chevalier, *Labouring Classes and Dangerous Classes in Paris during the First Half of the Nineteenth Century*, trans. Frank Jellinek (London: Routledge Kegan Paul, 1973).
16. For useful summaries of these debates on poverty, see Lynch, *Family, Class, and Ideology*; Joshua Cole, *The Power of Large Numbers: population, politics, and gender in nineteenth-century France* (Ithaca and London: Cornell University Press, 2000), Chapter 4.
17. Louise A. Tilly and Joan W. Scott, *Women, Work and Family*, 2nd edn (New York: Routledge, 1987), pp. 10–60.
18. On Proudhonianism, see K. Steven Vincent, *Pierre-Joseph Proudhon and the Rise of French Republican Socialism* (New York: Oxford University Press, 1984); Claire Goldberg Moses, *French Feminism in the Nineteenth Century* (Albany: State University of New York Press, 1984), pp. 152–8.
19. Gérard Noiriel, *Workers in French Society in the Nineteenth and Twentieth Centuries*, trans. Helen McPhail (New York: Berg, 1990), pp. 14, 26.
20. Johnson, *Life and Death*, pp. 21–2.
21. Judith G. Coffin, *The Politics of Women's Work: the Paris garment trades, 1750–1915* (Princeton: Princeton University Press, 1996), pp. 121–4.
22. Michelle Perrot, 'On the Formation of the French Working Class', in Ira Katznelson and Aristide Zolberg (eds), *Working-Class Formation: nineteenth-century patterns in Western Europe and the United States* (Princeton: Princeton University Press, 1986), p. 72.
23. Ibid., pp. 81, 84.
24. Noiriel, *Workers in French Society*, p. 27.
25. Joan Wallach Scott, 'Work Identities for Men and Women: the politics of work and family in the Parisian garment trades in 1848', in her *Gender and the Politics of History* (New York: Columbia University Press, 1988), pp. 96–102; Coffin, *Politics of Women's Work*, pp. 53–8.
26. Joan Wallach Scott, '"L'Ouvrière! Mot impie, sordide...": women workers in the discourse of French political economy, 1840–1860', in her *Gender and the Politics of History*, pp. 162–3.
27. Ibid., pp. 143–5; Cole, *The Power of Large Numbers*, pp. 126–7.
28. Charles Sowerwine, 'Workers and Women in France before 1914: the debate over the Couriau Affair', *Journal of Modern History* 55, 3 (1983), 411–41.
29. J.-P. Locci, 'De la soie à l'agro-alimentaire, aperçu d'une évolution industrielle', in *Histoire de Vaucluse*, vol. 2, p. 109.
30. Louise A. Tilly, 'The Family Wage Economy of a French Textile City: Roubaix, 1872–1906', *Journal of Family History* 4 (1979), 381–94.
31. Cole, *The Power of Large Numbers*, pp. 126–8.

32. Louis René Villermé, *Tableau de l'état physique et moral des ouvriers employés dans les manufactures de coton, de laine et de soie* [1840] quoted in William H. Sewell, Jr, *Work and Revolution in France: the language of labor from the Old Régime to 1848* (Cambridge: Cambridge University Press, 1980), p. 227.
33. This was a theme of the Left-wing press in the Nord. See Hilden, *Working Women*, pp. 60–1.
34. Scott, ' "L'Ouvrière" ', pp. 148–52.
35. Ibid., pp. 159–62.
36. Coffin, *Politics of Women's Work*, Chapter 5; Marilyn Boxer, 'Women in Industrial Homework: the flowermakers of Paris in the Belle Epoque', *French Historical Studies* 12, 3 (1982), 401–23.
37. Suzanne Voilquin, *Souvenirs d'une fille du peuple ou la Saint-Simonienne en Egypte* (Paris: François Maspero, 1978), pp. 93–9.
38. Jeanne Bouvier, 'My Memoirs; or, fifty-nine years of industrial, social and intellectual activity by a working woman, 1876–1935', in Mark Traugott (ed. and trans.), *The French Worker: autobiographies from the early industrial era* (Berkeley: University of California Press, 1993), pp. 367–74.
39. Rachel G. Fuchs, *Poor and Pregnant in Paris: strategies for survival in the nineteenth century* (New Brunswick, N.J.: Rutgers University Press, 1992), p. 26.
40. Ibid., pp. 48, 86; Scott, 'Work Identities', pp. 108–12.
41. Scott, ' "L'Ouvrière" ', pp. 142–5.
42. Anne Martin-Fugier, *La place des bonnes. La domesticité féminine à Paris en 1900* (Paris: Grasset, 1979), pp. 34–6; Charles Sowerwine, *France since 1870: culture, politics and society* (Houndmills, Basingstoke: Palgrave, 2001), pp. 7–8.
43. Martin-Fugier, *La place des bonnes*, pp. 19–24; Theresa McBride, 'Social Mobility for the Lower Classes: domestic servants in France', *Journal of Social History* 8 (1974), 63–78.
44. Fuchs, *Poor and Pregnant*, p. 25.
45. Ibid., pp. 18–27.
46. Ibid., p. 26; Martin-Fugier, *La place des bonnes*, pp. 326–9.
47. Martin-Fugier, *La place des bonnes*, pp. 102–3, 267.
48. Ibid., pp. 99–101.
49. Amélie Weiler, *Journal d'une jeune fille mal dans son siècle, 1840–1859*, ed. Nicolas Stoskopf (Strasbourg: La Nuée bleue, 1994), pp. 144, 151, 181–2, 195, 221, 229, 293.
50. Tilly and Scott, *Women, Work and Family*, pp. 150–9.
51. Theresa McBride, 'A Woman's World: department stores and the evolution of women's employment, 1870–1920', *French Historical Studies* 10 (1978), 664–83.
52. Tilly and Scott, *Women, Work and Family*, p. 157.
53. Laura S. Strumingher, 'The Artisan Family: traditions and transition in nineteenth-century Lyon', *Journal of Family History* 2, 3 (1977), 211–22.
54. Accampo, *Industrialization*, pp. 50–1.
55. Ibid.; Tilly and Scott, *Women, Work and Family*, pp. 99–101.
56. Hilden, *Working Women and Socialist Politics*, pp. 37–44; Bonnie G. Smith, *Ladies of the Leisure Class: the bourgeoises of northern France in the nineteenth century* (Princeton: Princeton University Press, 1981).

57. Tilly, 'Artisan Family', p. 215.
58. Accampo, *Industrialization*, pp. 54–68.
59. Tilly and Scott, *Women, Work and Family*, pp. 167–72.
60. Quoted in Lynch, *Family, Class*, pp. 77–8.
61. Ibid., pp. 89–90.
62. Edward Shorter, *The Making of the Modern Family* (London: Fontana, 1977).
63. Michel Frey, 'Du mariage et du concubinage dans les classes populaires à Paris (1846–1847), *Annales ESC* (July–Aug. 1978), 803–29.
64. Ibid., p. 814.
65. Lynch, *Family, Class*, pp. 111, 113.
66. Accampo, *Industrialization*, p. 115.
67. Tilly and Scott, *Women, Work and Family*, pp. 96–7; Johnson, *Life and Death*, p. 275, note 2; Lynch, *Family, Class*, pp. 101–2.
68. Lynch, *Family, Class*, p. 110.
69. John H. Weiss, 'Origins of the French Welfare State: poor relief in the Third Republic, 1871–1914', *French Historical Studies* 13, 1 (1983), 49–51; Stuart Woolf, 'The *Société de Charité Maternelle*, 1788–1815', in Jonathan Barry and Colin Jones (eds), *Medicine and Charity before the Welfare State* (London: Routledge, 1991), pp. 105, 109; John H. Merriman, *The Red City: Limoges and the French nineteenth century* (New York: Oxford University Press, 1985), pp. 36, 52.
70. Hilden, *Working Women*, pp. 41, 59; Accampo, *Industrialization*, pp. 152–5, 166–7, 173; Christine Adams, 'Constructing Mothers and Families: the Society for Maternal Charity of Bordeaux, 1805–1860', *French Historical Studies* 22 (1999), 75–6.
71. Tilly and Scott, *Women, Work and Family*, pp. 124–5.
72. Coffin, *Politics of Women's Work*, Chapter 5; Sohn, *Chrysalides*, pp. 650–72.
73. Béatrice Craig, 'La structure de l'emploi féminin dans une ville en voie d'industrialisation: Tourcoing au XIXe siècle', *Canadian Journal of History* 27, 2 (1992), 320.
74. Ibid., p. 318; Tilly and Scott, *Women, Work and Family*, p. 82.
75. Craig, 'La structure de l'emploi', p. 313.
76. Coffin, *Politics of Women's Work*, Chapter 5; Boxer, 'Women in Industrial Homework', pp. 414–22; Sohn, *Chrysalides*, pp. 650–72.
77. Tilly, 'The Family Wage Economy', pp. 381–94.
78. Hilden, *Working Women*, pp. 24–5, 33–4.
79. Ibid., p. 21.
80. Accampo, *Industrialization*, pp. 84–5.
81. Quoted in ibid., p. 85.
82. Blanqui, *Des classes ouvrières*, p. 208.
83. Scott, '"L'Ouvrière"', p. 155.
84. Blanqui, *Des classes ouvrières*, p. 168.
85. Laura S. Strumingher, *Women and the Making of the Working Class: Lyon 1830–1870* (St Alban's VT: Eden Press Women's Publications, 1979), pp. 2–3.
86. Scott, '"L'Ouvrière"', p. 156.
87. Flora Tristan, *Le tour de France, journal 1843–1844*, 2 vols (Paris: François Maspero, 1980), vol. 2, pp. 127–8.

88. On 'depopulation', see Karen Offen, 'Depopulation, Nationalism and Feminism in Fin-de-Siècle France', *American Historical Review* 89 (1984), 648–76; Cole, *The Power of Large Numbers*, Chapters 5–6; Alisa Klaus, 'Depopulation and Race Suicide: maternalism and pronatalist ideologies in France and the United States', in Seth Koven and Sonya Michel (eds), *Mothers of a New World: maternalist politics and the origins of welfare states* (New York: Routledge, 1993), pp. 188–212.

89. See Weiss, 'Origins of the French Welfare State', pp. 47–78; Koven and Michel, *Mothers of a New World*, introduction; Gisela Bock and Pat Thane (eds), *Maternity and Gender Policies: women and the rise of the European welfare states 1880s–1950s* (London: Routledge, 1991); Elinor A. Accampo, Rachel G. Fuchs and Mary Lynn Stewart (eds), *Gender and the Politics of Social Reform in France, 1870–1914* (Baltimore: Johns Hopkins University Press, 1995).

90. Anne Cova, 'French Feminism and Maternity: theories and policies 1890–1918', in Bock and Thane (eds), *Maternity and Gender Policies*, pp. 119–37; Coffin, *Politics of Women's Work*, pp. 125–30; Rachel G. Fuchs, 'The Right to Life: Paul Strauss and the politics of motherhood', in Accampo, Fuchs and Stewart (eds), *Gender and the Politics of Social Reform*, pp. 82–105; Mary Lynn Stewart, *Women, Work and the French State: labour protection and social patriarchy, 1879–1919* (London: McGill-Queen's University Press, 1989).

91. Stewart, *Women, Work and the French State*, pp. 98, 107, 118–19.

92. Accampo, *Industrialization*, pp. 84–5.

93. Rachel G. Fuchs, 'Morality and Poverty: public welfare for mothers in Paris, 1870–1900', *French History* 2, 3 (1988), 288–311.

94. Cova, 'French Feminism and Maternity'; Marilyn J. Boxer, 'French Socialism, Feminism, and the Family', *Third Republic/Troisième République* 3/4 (1977), 128–67. On French socialists' efforts to devise a theory and practice of women's rights in the late nineteenth century, see Charles Sowerwine, *Sisters or Citizens? Women and socialism in France since 1876* (Cambridge: Cambridge University Press, 1982).

95. Mary Lynn Stewart, 'Setting the Standards: labor and family reformers', in Accampo, Fuchs and Stewart (eds), *Gender and the Politics of Social Reform*, pp. 106–27.

3 Peasant women

1. Raw figures from B. R. Mitchell, *International Historical Statistics: Europe, 1750–1993*, 4th edn (London and New York: Macmillan Reference; Stockton Press, 1998), Table B1, 'Economically active population by major industrial groups', p. 149; Charles Sowerwine, *France since 1870: culture, politics and society* (Houndmills, Basingstoke: Palgrave, 2001), p. 9.

2. James R. Lehning, *Peasant and French: cultural contact in rural France during the nineteenth century* (Cambridge: Cambridge University Press, 1995), p. 129.

3. Martine Segalen, *Love and Power in the Peasant Family: rural France in the nineteenth century*, trans. Sarah Matthews (Oxford: Basil Blackwell, 1983), Chapter 6.

4. Emilie Carles, *A Wild Herb Soup: the life of a French countrywoman*, trans. Avriel H. Goldberger (London: Victor Gollancz, 1992), p. 8. Catherine Vallier and Joseph Allais were the parents of Emilie Carles.

5. Rosemary O'Day, *The Family and Family Relationships, 1500–1900, England, France and the USA* (New York: St Martin's Press, 1994), pp. 146–8.

6. Carles, *A Wild Herb Soup*, pp. 48–9.

7. Anne-Marie Sohn, *Chrysalides: femmes dans la vie privée (XIXe-XXe siècles)* (Paris: Publications de la Sorbonne, 1996), p. 510.

8. Segalen, *Love and Power in the Peasant Family*, p. 12.

9. James R. Lehning, 'The Timing and Prevalence of Women's Marriage in the Department of the Loire, 1851–1891', *Journal of Family History* 13, 3 (1988), 307–27.

10. Martin Nadaud, *Mémoires de Léonard, ancien garçon maçon* [1895], in Mark Traugott (ed. and trans.), *The French Worker: autobiographies from the early industrial era* (Berkeley: University of California Press, 1993), pp. 183–249.

11. Emile Guillaumin, *The Life of a Simple Man*, revised trans. and introduction by Eugen Weber (London: Sinclair Browne, 1983), p. 70.

12. Segalen, *Love and Power in the Peasant Family*, p. 125. Lehning, *Peasant and French*, pp. 117–18.

13. Jacques Gélis, *History of Childbirth: fertility, pregnancy and birth in early modern Europe*, trans. Rosemary Morris (Cambridge: Polity Press, 1991), pp. 20–1.

14. 'Invocation which girls who want to marry must make', quoted in Judith Devlin, *The Superstitious Mind. French Peasants and the Supernatural in the Nineteenth Century* (New Haven and London: Yale University Press, 1987), p. 9.

15. Roger Price, *A Social History of France in the Nineteenth Century* (London: Hutchinson, 1987), p. 169.

16. René Grosso, 'Le peuplement et l'habitat', in René Grosso (ed.) *Histoire de Vaucluse, II, Les Vauclusiens, des campagnes à la Ville*, (Avignon: Editions A. Barthélemy, 1993), p. 194.

17. Gérard Boutet, *Ils étaient de leur village* (Paris: Denoël, 1979), p. 82.

18. O'Day, *The Family and Family Relationships*, pp. 146ff.; Segalen, *Love and Power in the Peasant Family*, pp. 20–5; Price, *Social History*, p. 74.

19. Lehning, *Peasant and French*, pp. 114–16.

20. Carles, *A Wild Herb Soup*, pp. 68–9.

21. Nadaud, *Mémoires*, in Traugott, *The French Worker*, pp. 238–9.

22. Guillaumin, *Life of a Simple Man*, pp. 65–8.

23. Ibid., pp. 43–4.

24. The character Etienne Bertin was born in 1823, and the events described above took place when he was 17 or 18.

25. Sohn notes, for instance, that 'I love you' could not easily be expressed in Breton (*Chrysalides*, p. 549).

26. See Lehning, *Peasant and French*, pp. 26–7, for a discussion of Guillaumin's presentation of the peasantry.

27. Segalen, *Love and Power in the Peasant Family*, p. 16.

28. Pierre-Jakez Hélias, *The Horse of Pride: life in a Breton village*, trans. and abridged by June Guicharnaud (New Haven and London: Yale University Press, 1978), p. 287.

NOTES 313

29. See Devlin, *The Superstitious Mind*, p. 9.
30. Quoted in Segalen, *Love and Power in the Peasant Family*, p. 17. The cabbage was also a fertility symbol.
31. Ibid., pp. 16–19.
32. Guillaumin, *Life of a Simple Man*, p. 165.
33. Ibid., p. 128.
34. Hélias, *The Horse of Pride*, p. 292.
35. Sohn, *Chrysalides*, pp. 494–7, 568.
36. Segalen, *Love and Power in the Peasant Family*, pp. 49–50.
37. Ibid., pp. 51, 131; Lehning, *Peasant and French*, pp. 120–1.
38. Carles, *A Wild Herb Soup*, pp. 70–1.
39. Price, *Social History*, pp. 78–9.
40. Segalen, *Love and Power in the Peasant Family*, pp. 129–32. Emilie Carles notes that sexual ignorance was the norm in the Briançonnais until the First World War (*A Wild Herb Soup*, pp. 52, 71).
41. Carles, *A Wild Herb Soup*, pp. 48–9, 69–71.
42. *Mémé Santerre: a French woman of the people*, ed. Serge Grafteaux, trans. and introduction by Louise A. Tilly and Kathryn L. Tilly (New York: Schocken Books, 1985), pp. 44–5.
43. Gélis, *History of Childbirth*, pp. 23–31, 36–7.
44. Auguste Debay, *Hygiène et physiologie du mariage; histoire naturelle et médicale de l'homme et de la femme mariés*, 16th edn (Paris: E. Dentu, 1859), pp. 391, 416.
45. Gélis, *History of Childbirth*, p. 98.
46. Lehning, *Peasant and French*, p. 119.
47. Gélis, *History of Childbirth*, pp. 97–9, 115–19, 121–33, 147.
48. Ibid., pp. 161–71.
49. Ibid., pp. 217–20.
50. Ibid., pp. 223–31, 242–3; Jacques Gélis, Mireille Laget and Marie-France Morel, *Entrer dans la vie: naissances et enfances dans la France traditionnelle* (Paris: Gallimard/Julliard, 1978), pp. 211–2.
51. Price, *Social History*, p. 147.
52. Ibid., p. 82.
53. Sohn, *Chrysalides*, pp. 625–6.
54. See Richard Lalou, 'L'infanticide devant les tribunaux français (1825–1910)', *Communications* 44 (1986), 175–200; James M. Donovan, 'Infanticide and the Juries in France, 1825–1913', *Journal of Family History* 16, 2 (1991), 157–76.
55. Gélis, *Entrer dans la vie*, p. 80.
56. Price, *Social History*, p. 73; Lehning, *Peasant and French*, pp. 122–8.
57. Price, *Social History*, p. 74.
58. Hélias, *Horse of Pride*, pp. 221, 294; Guillaumin, *Life of a Simple Man*, pp. 65–8.
59. Price, *Social History*, p. 74.
60. Louise A. Tilly and Joan W. Scott, *Women, Work and Family*, 2nd edn (New York: Routledge, 1987), pp. 38–9, 122.
61. Elinor A. Accampo, *Industrialization, Family Life, and Class Relations: Saint-Chamond, 1815–1914* (Berkeley: University of California Press, 1989), pp. 74, 210–12; Guillaumin, *Life of a Simple Man*, p. 49.

62. *The Memoirs of Frédéric Mistral*, trans. George Wickes (New York: New Directions, 1986), p. 6.
63. Gélis, *Entrer dans la vie*, pp. 116–18, 128–9; Sohn, *Chrysalides*, p. 294.
64. Gélis, *History of Childbirth*, pp. 194–5.
65. Sohn, *Chrysalides*, pp. 296–310; Gélis, *Entrer dans la vie*, pp. 119–21.
66. Gélis, *History of Childbirth*, pp. 255–6; Sohn, *Chrysalides*, pp. 317–19.
67. Price, *Social History*, pp. 70–1.
68. Ibid., p. 72; Grosso, 'Le peuplement et l'habitat', pp. 167, 197.
69. Boutet, *Ils étaient de leur village*, p. 68.
70. Sohn, *Chrysalides*, pp. 273–87; Gélis, *Entrer dans la vie*, pp. 127–8.
71. Hélias, *Horse of Pride*, p. 38.
72. Sohn, *Chrysalides*, pp. 271–2, 300.
73. O'Day, *The Family and Family Relationships, 1500–1900*, p. 169.
74. Guillaumin, *Life of a Simple Man*, p. 106.
75. Ibid., p. 17.
76. Ibid., pp. 128–9, 145–6, 170–1.
77. Carles, *A Wild Herb Soup*, p. 6.
78. *The Memoirs of Frédéric Mistral*, pp. 13–16.
79. *Mémé Santerre*, p. 13.
80. Gélis, *History of Childbirth*, pp. 193, 203–4.
81. Debay, *Hygiène et physiologie du mariage*, pp. 132–4.
82. Quoted in Gélis, *History of Childbirth*, p. 39.
83. Hélias, *Horse of Pride*, p. 282.
84. Yvonne Knibiehler *et al.*, *De la pucelle à la minette: les jeunes filles, de l'âge classique à nos jours*, nouvelle édition (Paris: Messidor, 1989), p. 145.
85. Guillaumin, *Life of a Simple Man*, p. 7.
86. Hélias, *Horse of Pride*, p. 38.
87. *The Memoirs of Frédéric Mistral*, pp. 111–13.
88. Hélias, *Horse of Pride*, pp. 232–6. See also the description of threshing in the Seine-Inférieure in the 1920s in *Mémé Santerre*, p. 90.
89. Lehning, *Peasant and French*, pp. 113–16.
90. Segalen, *Love and Power in the Peasant Family*, pp. 2, 9.
91. George D. Sussman, 'The End of the Wet-Nursing Business in France, 1874–1914', *Journal of Family History* 2 (1977), 237–58; Gélis, *Entrer dans la vie*, pp. 158–62; Sohn, *Chrysalides*, pp. 257–8; Fanny Faÿ-Sallois, *Les nourrices à Paris au dix-neuvième siècle* (Paris: Payot, 1980), pp. 58–9.
92. Grosso, 'Le peuplement et l'habitat', p. 198.
93. *Mémé Santerre*, Chapter 2; Price, *Social History*, pp. 158–9.
94. Hélias, *Horse of Pride*, p. 268.
95. Quoted in Segalen, *Love and Power in the Peasant Family*, pp. 95, 160, 158.
96. Ibid., p. 137.
97. Ibid., pp. 43–4.

4 Women, politics and citizenship, 1814–1852

1. Anne Verjus, 'Le suffrage universel, le chef de famille et la question de l'exclusion des femmes en 1848', in *Femmes dans la cité 1815–1871*, sous

la direction d'Alain Corbin, Jacqueline Lalouette and Michèle Riot-Sarcey (Grâne: Créaphis, 1997), pp. 401–13.

2. André Jardin and André-Jean Tudesq, *Restoration and Reaction 1815–1848*, trans. Elborg Forster (Cambridge and Paris: Cambridge University Press and Maison des Sciences de l'Homme, 1983), Chapter 1.

3. On the Ultra philosophy, see Pierre Rosanvallon, *Le sacre du citoyen. Histoire du suffrage universel en France* (Paris: Gallimard, 1992), pp. 220–30; Theodore Zeldin, *France 1848–1945*, vol. 1 (Oxford: Clarendon Press, 1973), Chapter 15. On sexual difference, see Geneviève Fraisse, *Muse de la raison. La démocratie exclusive et la différence des sexes* (Paris: Alinéa, 1989).

4. These arguments are outlined above in the introduction.

5. Quoted in Maïté Albistur and Daniel Armogathe, *Histoire du féminisme français du moyen âge à nos jours* (Paris: Editions des Femmes, 1977), p. 243.

6. Quoted in ibid., p. 243.

7. Quoted in Michelle Perrot, 'The Family Triumphant', in Michelle Perrot (ed.), *A History of Private Life, IV: from the fires of Revolution to the Great War*, trans. Arthur Goldhammer (Cambridge Mass. and London: Belknap Press, 1990), pp. 105–6.

8. Fraisse, *Muse de la raison*, p. 57.

9. Quoted in Albistur and Armogathe, *Histoire du féminisme français*, p. 243.

10. Ibid., pp. 244–5; Fraisse, *Muse de la raison*, p. 57.

11. The 'Dauphine' was the title of the wife of the heir to the throne. In this passage it refers to the Duchesse d'Angoulême, wife of the elder son of Charles X.

12. Marie de Flavigny, Comtesse d'Agoult, *Mes souvenirs, 1806–1833*, 3rd edn (Paris: Calman-Lévy, 1880), pp. 272–3.

13. For a detailed argument that the monarchy pursued a politics of 'forgetting' the revolution during the Restoration, see Sheryl Kroen, *Politics and Theater: the crisis of legitimacy in Restoration France, 1815–1830* (Berkeley: University of California Press, 2000).

14. Jo B. Margadant, 'The Duchesse de Berry and Royalist Political Culture in Postrevolutionary France', *History Workshop Journal* 43 (1997), 23–52.

15. Noëlle Dauphin, 'Les salons de la Restauration. Une influence spécifique sur les milieux dirigeants', in *Femmes dans la cité*, pp. 251–9.

16. David Higgs, *Nobles in Nineteenth Century France: the practice of inegalitarianism* (Baltimore and London: Johns Hopkins University Press, 1987), pp. 182–3.

17. Claude-Isabelle Brelot, 'De la tutelle à la collaboration: une femme de la noblesse dans la vie politique (1814–1830)', in *Femmes dans la cité 1815–1871*, pp. 237–50.

18. See Kroen, *Politics and Theater*, Chapter 5.

19. Jardin and Tudesq, *Restoration and Reaction*, pp. 93–9; David Barry, *Women and Political Insurgency: France in the mid-nineteenth century* (Houndmills, Basingstoke: Macmillan, 1996), pp. 23–4.

20. Barry, *Women and Political Insurgency*, pp. 24–6.

21. Jardin and Tudesq, *Restoration and Reaction*, pp. 100–1; Edgar Leon Newman, 'What the Crowd Wanted in the French Revolution of 1830', in John Merriman (ed.), *1830 in France* (New York: New Viewpoints, 1975).

22. Maurice Agulhon, *Marianne into Battle: Republican imagery and symbolism in France, 1789–1880* (Cambridge and Paris: Cambridge University Press and Maison des Sciences de l'Homme, 1980), Chapters 1 and 2. For the debates on Delacroix's painting in 1831, see Marcia Pointon, 'Liberty on the Barricades: woman, politics and sexuality in Delacroix', in Siân Reynolds (ed.), *Women, State and Revolution: essays on power and gender in Europe since 1789* (Brighton: Wheatsheaf, 1986), pp. 25–43.

23. See Barry, *Women and Political Insurgency*, pp. 26–7, for a discussion of this point.

24. François Guizot, speech of 5 October 1831, quoted in Pierre Rosanvallon, *Le moment Guizot* (Paris: Gallimard, 1985), p. 100.

25. Rosanvallon, *Le moment Guizot*, pp. 12–13, 20.

26. Michèle Riot-Sarcey, *La démocratie à l'épreuve des femmes: trois figures critiques du pouvoir 1830–1848* (Paris: Albin Michel, 1994), pp. 94–108.

27. Rosanvallon, *Le moment Guizot*, pp. 138–9, 109.

28. Verjus, 'Le suffrage universel', pp. 403–7; Riot-Sarcey, *La démocratie*, pp. 99–108.

29. Duc de Broglie, 'Discours sur le projet de loi électorale de 1820', quoted in Rosanvallon, *Le Moment Guizot*, p. 121.

30. Anne Martin-Fugier, *La vie élégante: la formation du Tout-Paris, 1815–1848* (Paris: Fayard, 1990), pp. 69, 75–7.

31. D'Agoult, *Souvenirs*, pp. 257, 262, 286.

32. Ibid., pp. 339–40. Sainte-Beuve and Sue were up-and-coming writers, while Liszt was beginning to make his name as a pianist.

33. See William M. Reddy, *The Invisible Code: honor and sentiment in postrevolutionary France, 1814–1848* (Berkeley: University of California Press, 1997), pp. 131–2, 148–54.

34. Dauphin, 'Les salons de la Restauration', in *Femmes dans la cité*, pp. 251–9.

35. Gabrielle Houbre, *La discipline de l'amour: l'éducation sentimentale des filles et des garçons à l'âge du romantisme* (Paris: Plon, 1997), pp. 330–1; Martin-Fugier, *La vie élégante*, pp. 186–9. A Prefect was head of an administrative region.

36. Martin-Fugier, *La vie élégante*, pp. 215–18.

37. Dauphin, 'Les salons de la Restauration', p. 256.

38. Jean Schlumberger (ed.), *Lettres de François Guizot et de la Princesse de Lieven*, vol. 1 (Paris: Mercure de France, 1936), preface, pp. xiii–xv.

39. Elizabeth P. Brush, *Guizot in the Early Years of the Orleanist Monarchy* (New York: Howard Fertig, 1974), pp. 13, 25, 38, 112; Douglas Johnson, *Guizot: aspects of French history 1787–1874* (London: Routledge and Kegan Paul, 1963), pp. 2–7.

40. Quoted in Brush, *Guizot*, p. 66.

41. Schlumberger (ed.), *Lettres*, preface, p. xiv.

42. Gita May, 'Tocqueville on the Role of Women in a Democracy', in Maxine G. Cutler (ed.), *Voltaire, the Enlightenment and the Comic Mode: essays in honor of Jean Sareil* (New York: Peter Lang, 1990), pp. 159–69.

43. Pauline Guizot's writings on girls' education stressed their roles as wives and mothers. See Barbara Corrado Pope, 'Revolution and Retreat: upper-class women after 1789', in Carol Berkin and Clara Lovett (eds), *Women, War and Revolution* (New York: Holmes and Meier, 1980), pp. 226–7.

44. Guizot had a third female assistant in his daughter Henriette while the Princess of Lieven, former wife of the Russian Ambassador to England, undertook his diplomatic apprenticeship when he became Ambassador for France in 1840. See Schlumberger (ed.), *Lettres*, preface, pp. xix, xxxvii.

45. Maurice Agulhon, *The Republican Experiment 1848–1852*, trans. Janet Lloyd (Cambridge and Paris: Cambridge University Press and Maison des Sciences de l'Homme, 1983), p. 14.

46. Agulhon, *The Republican Experiment*, pp. 14–18.

47. This is Riot-Sarcey's description, in *La démocratie*, p. 105.

48. Michèle Riot-Sarcey, 'De l'historicité du genre citoyen', in Hans Ulrich Jost, Monique Pavillon, and François Vallotton (eds), *La politique des droits. Citoyenneté et construction des genres aux 19e et 20e siècles* (Paris: Editions Kimé, 1994), pp. 43–52.

49. Barry, *Women and Political Insurgency*, pp. 28–30.

50. On Madame de Lamartine's role in her husband's political career, see William Fortescue, 'The Role of Women and Charity in the French Revolution of 1848: the case of Marianne de Lamartine', *French History* 11, 1 (1997), 54–78.

51. Quoted in Riot-Sarcey, *La démocratie*, pp. 107–8.

52. Ibid., p. 101.

53. Riot-Sarcey, 'De l'historicité', p. 51. On Republican ideas about the family, see Whitney Walton, 'Republican Women and Republican Families in the Personal Narratives of George Sand, Marie d'Agoult, and Hortense Allart', in Jo B. Margadant (ed.), *The New Biography: performing femininity in nineteenth-century France* (Berkeley: University of California Press, 2000), pp. 99–136.

54. The coining of the term 'socialism' is usually attributed to Pierre Leroux. See A. E. Bestor, Jr, 'The Evolution of the Socialist Vocabulary', *Journal of the History of Ideas* IX, 3 (1948), 259–302; Raymond Williams, *Keywords: a vocabulary of culture and society* (London: Flamingo, 1983).

55. See Marguerite Thibert, *Le féminisme dans le socialisme français de 1830 à 1850* (Paris: Giard, 1926); Susan K. Grogan, *French Socialism and Sexual Difference: women and the new society, 1803–1844* (London: Macmillan, 1992), Chapters 4–7; Claire Goldberg Moses, *French Feminism in the Nineteenth Century* (Albany: State University of New York Press, 1984), Chapters 3–4; Albistur and Armogathe, *Histoire du féminisme français*, Chapter 3.

56. Prosper Enfantin to Charles Duveyrier, August 1829, in *Oeuvres de Saint-Simon et d'Enfantin*, 47 vols (Paris: E. Dentu, E. Leroux, 1865–1878), vol. 26, p. 6.

57. Prosper Enfantin to Philippe Buchez, 2 Oct. 1829, in *Oeuvres*, vol. 26, p. 105.

58. Grogan, *French Socialism*, Chapters 2 and 3; Thibert, *Le féminisme*, pp. 95–121; Moses, *French Feminism*, pp. 90–8; Albistur and Armogathe, *Histoire du féminisme français*, pp. 411–16.

59. For Proudhon's views on women, see Albistur and Armogathe, *Histoire du féminisme français*, pp. 476–81; Thibert, *Le féminisme*, pp. 171–92; Moses, *French Feminism*, pp. 152–8.

60. Diana M. Garno, 'Gender Dilemmas: "Equality" and "Rights" for Icarian Women', *Utopian Studies* 6, 2 (1995), 52–74.

61. On the history of the term 'feminist', see Karen Offen, 'Sur les origines des mots "féminisme" et "féministe"', *Revue d'histoire moderne et contemporaine* 34, 3 (1987), 492–6; 'Defining Feminism: a comparative historical approach', in Gisela Bock and Susan James (eds), *Beyond Equality and Difference: citizenship, feminist politics and female subjectivity* (London and New York: Routledge, 1992), pp. 69–88.

62. Laure Adler, *A l'aube du féminisme. Les premières journalistes (1830–1850)* (Paris: Payot, 1979), pp. 102–5; Moses, *French Feminism*, pp. 98–107.

63. Quoted in Adler, *A l'aube du féminisme*, p. 88.

64. Odile Krakovitch, 'Les pétitions, seul moyen d'expression laissé aux femmes. L'exemple de la Restauration', in *Femmes dans la cité*, pp. 348–70; Michèle Riot-Sarcey, 'Des femmes pétitionnent sous la monarchie de Juillet', in *Femmes dans la cité*, pp. 389–400.

65. Adler, *A l'aube du féminisme*, pp. 85, 93–4.

66. Ibid., pp. 84–5.

67. Jeanne-Désirée, 'Amélioration du sort des femmes et du peuple par une nouvelle organisation du ménage', *Tribune des Femmes*, vol. 1, pp. 36–9; Angélique et Sophie-Caroline, *Tribune des Femmes*, vol. 1, pp. 91–8; Marie-Reine, 'Aux Femmes', *Tribune des Femmes*, vol. 1, pp. 201–5. Most issues of this periodical are undated, but all date from 1832–1834. I have retained the title *Tribune des Femmes* despite the changes it underwent to minimise confusion.

68. Pauline Roland to Aglaé Saint-Hilaire, November 1833, quoted in Edith Thomas, *Pauline Roland. Socialisme et féminisme au XIXe siècle* (Paris: Marcel Rivière, 1956), p. 64.

69. Claire Démar, 'Ma Loi d'Avenir', in Valentin Pelosse (ed.), *Textes sur l'affranchissement des femmes (1832–1833)* (Paris: Payot, 1976), pp. 70–1, 86–7.

70. Marie-Reine, 'Réponse à quelques objections qui nous ont été faites', *Tribune des Femmes*, vol. 1, pp. 114–15.

71. Riot-Sarcey, *La démocratie*, pp. 76–81.

72. Marie G., 'De l'Influence des Femmes en Politique', *La Tribune des Femmes*, vol. 1, pp. 255–60.

73. On Flora Tristan's attempts to deal with this problem, see Susan Grogan, ' "O'Connell in Skirts"? Flora Tristan, Sexual Politics and Self-Representation', in Michael Adcock, Emily Chester and Jeremy Whiteman (eds), *Revolution, Society and the Politics of Memory: the proceedings of the tenth George Rudé seminar on French history and civilisation* (Melbourne: University of Melbourne Department of History Monographs, 1997), pp. 206–13.

74. Marie G., 'De l'Influence des Femmes en Politique', *La Tribune des Femmes*, vol. 1, p. 259.

75. Claire Démar, 'Appel d'une Femme au Peuple sur l'Affranchissement de la Femme', in Pelosse (ed.), *Textes*, pp. 16–17.

76. Ibid., p. 21.

77. H. A. C. Collingham, *The July Monarchy: a political history of France 1830–1848* (London and New York: Longman, 1988), Chapters 25, 27.
78. Barry, *Women and Political Insurgency*, pp. 30–1, 39.
79. Ibid., pp. 25–6; Agulhon, *Marianne into Battle*, pp. 66–7, 94; Maurice Agulhon, *The Republic in the Village: the people of the Var from the French Revolution to the Second Republic*, trans. Janet Lloyd (Cambridge and Paris: Cambridge University Press and Editions de la Maison des Sciences de l'Homme, 1982), Chapters 15–16.
80. Moses, *French Feminism*, pp. 127–30; Edith Thomas, *Les Femmes de 1848* (Paris: Presses Universitaires de France, 1948); Judith de Groat, 'The Public Nature of Women's Work: definitions and debates during the Revolution of 1848', *French Historical Studies* 20, 1 (1997), 31–47.
81. Barry, *Women and Political Insurgency*, pp. 99–100; Laura S. Strumingher, 'The Vésuviennes: images of women warriors in 1848 and their significance for French history', *History of European Ideas* 8, 4–5 (1987), 451–86.
82. Gisèle Roche-Galopini, *Saint-Etienne-les-Orgues et la gloire de la Montagne. Notables et gens du peuple face au coup d'Etat de 1851* (Mane: Les Alpes de Lumière, 1994); Agulhon, *The Republic in the Village*, Chapter 16.
83. Verjus, 'Le suffrage universel', pp. 401–13.
84. *La Voix des Femmes*, 22 March 1848.
85. See articles in *La Voix des Femmes*, 22, 23, 27 and 30 March, 10, 19 and 28 April 1848; *L'Opinion des Femmes*, 28 January, 10 April 1849.
86. 'Faits divers', *La Voix des Femmes*, 20 March 1848; J. D., 'Aux démocrates socialistes', *L'Opinion des Femmes*, 10 April 1849.
87. 'Les femmes à l'oeuvre', *La Voix des Femmes*, 26 March 1848. See also *La Politique des Femmes*, 18–24 June and August 1848, on various societies for the rights of women.
88. 'Organisation du travail des ouvrières. Société pour l'émancipation des femmes. Manifeste', published in Michèle Riot-Sarcey, 'Emancipation des femmes, 1848', *Genèses* 7 (March 1992), 194–200.
89. 'Les femmes au club', *La Voix des Femmes*, 14 April 1848.
90. See Joan Wallach Scott, *Only Paradoxes to Offer: French feminists and the Rights of Man* (Cambridge, Mass.: Harvard University Press, 1996).
91. *La Voix des Femmes*, 18 April 1848.
92. Pauline Roland, 'La Femme a-t-elle droit à la Liberté?', *Almanach des Corporations nouvelles*, 1852, 97.
93. Jeanne Deroin, in *La Voix des Femmes*, 27 March 1848.
94. *La Voix des Femmes*, 19 April 1848; *L'Opinion des Femmes*, 10 April 1849.
95. *La Voix des Femmes*, 23 March 1848.
96. Anon., 'Aux membres du Club lyonnais', *La Voix des Femmes*, 14 April 1848.
97. 'Manifeste', p. 197.
98. *L'Opinion des Femmes*, 28 January and 10 April 1849.
99. *La Voix des Femmes*, 27 March 1848.
100. Ibid., 22 March 1848.
101. Ibid., 19 April 1848.
102. Ibid., 30 March, 14 April 1848.
103. 'Manifeste', p. 198. Popular references to the 'democratic and social republic' frequently likened it to a mother who would nourish all her

children. Daumier's 'Sketch for "The Republic"', exhibited at the Salon of 1848, picks up this theme, portraying the republic as a sturdy woman nourishing a son at each breast. For a reproduction, see *Daumier 1808–1879* (Ottawa: National Gallery of Canada, 1999).

104. *La Voix des Femmes*, 10 April 1849.
105. Ibid., 27 and 28 March 1848.
106. *L'Opinion des Femmes*, 10 April 1849. See also her statements in *La Voix des Femmes*, 27 and 28 March, and 8–10 June 1848.
107. *La Voix des Femmes*, 10 and 19 April 1848.
108. 'Manifeste', introduction, p. 196.
109. *La Voix des Femmes*, 28 March 1848. See also Roland, 'La Femme a-t-elle droit à la Liberté?', pp. 97–8.
110. 'Manifeste', p. 198.
111. Jeanne-Marie, *La Voix des Femmes*, 18 April 1848.
112. Moses, *French Feminism*, p. 146.
113. Roland, 'La Femme a-t-elle droit à la Liberté?', p. 98.
114. Jeanne Deroin, 'Réponse à la lettre de Miss Anne Knight', *Almanach des Femmes*, 1854, 82.
115. Verjus, 'Le Suffrage universel', pp. 408–10.
116. Riot-Sarcey, 'Manifeste', introduction, p. 196.

5   Women and the creation of Republican France, 1852–1914

1. Judith F. Stone, *Sons of the Revolution: Radical Democrats in France, 1862–1914* (Baton Rouge: Louisiana State University Press, 1996), Chapter 1.
2. Claire Goldberg Moses, *French Feminism in the Nineteenth Century* (Albany: State University of New York Press, 1984), pp. 174–7; Maïté Albistur and Daniel Armogathe, *Histoire du féminisme français du moyen âge à nos jours* (Paris: Editions des Femmes, 1977), p. 312.
3. See Susan Grogan, 'Women, Philanthropy and the State: the *Société de Charité maternelle* in Avignon, 1802–1917', *French History* 14, 3 (2000), 295–321.
4. Patrick Lagoueyte, 'Le rôle des femmes dans les élections législatives sous le Second-Empire', in *Femmes dans la cité 1815–1871*, sous la direction d'Alain Corbin, Jacqueline Lalouette and Michèle Riot-Sarcey (Grâne: Créaphis, 1997), pp. 373–88.
5. Moses, *French Feminism*, pp. 173–4, 178–81; Albistur and Armogathe, *Histoire du féminisme français*, pp. 321–3.
6. See Pamela Pilbeam, *Republicanism in Nineteenth-Century France, 1814–1871* (Houndmills, Basingstoke: Macmillan, 1995), Chapter 10.
7. Sylvie Aprile, 'Bourgeoise et républicaine, deux termes inconciliables?', in *Femmes dans la cité*, pp. 211–23.
8. Ibid.
9. Letter of Hortense? Kestner to Hermione Quinet, 27 January 1869, quoted in ibid., p. 215. Aprile attributes the letter to Hortense but this seems to be an error since it was Hortense who married Floquet.

10. Kathleen B. Jones and F. Vergès, 'Women of the Paris Commune', *Women's Studies International Forum* 14 (1991), 491–503; Eugene W. Schulkind, 'Le rôle des femmes dans la Commune de 1871', *Revue des Révolutions contemporaines* 43, 185 (1950), 15–29; David A. Shafer, '*Plus que des Ambulancières*: women in articulation and defence of their ideals during the Paris Commune (1871)', *French History* 7, 1 (1993), 85–101; Martin P. Johnson, 'Citizenship and Gender: the *Légion des Fédérées* in the Paris Commune of 1871', *French History* 8, 3 (1994), 276–95; Moses, *French Feminism*, pp. 189–96.

11. Edith Thomas, *Les pétroleuses* (Paris: Gallimard, 1963); Gaye L. Gullickson, *Unruly Women of Paris: images of the Commune* (Ithaca and London: Cornell University Press, 1996); Gaye L. Gullickson, '*La Pétroleuse*: representing Revolution', *Feminist Studies* 17, 2 (1991), 241–65.

12. *Discours et plaidoyers politiques de M. Gambetta (1881–5)*, cited in Theodore Zeldin, *France 1848–1945*, vol. 1 (Oxford: The Clarendon Press, 1973), p. 613. On the development of republicanism, see Jean-Marie Mayeur and Madeleine Rebérioux, *The Third Republic from its Origins to the Great War, 1871–1914*, trans. J. R. Foster (Cambridge and Paris: Cambridge University Press and Maison des Sciences de l'Homme, 1987), part 1.

13. Zeldin, *France 1848–1945*, vol. 1, pp. 612–14; Christophe Charle, *A Social History of France in the Nineteenth Century*, trans. Miriam Kocham (Oxford and Providence: Berg, 1991), p. 100.

14. Zeldin, *France 1848–1945*, vol. 1, p. 613.

15. Sylvie Aprile, 'La République au salon: vie et mort d'une forme de sociabilité politique (1865–1885)', *Revue d'Histoire Moderne et Contemporaine* 38 (July–Sep. 1991), 473–87; Gordon D. Wright, *Notable or Notorious?: a gallery of Parisians* (Cambridge, Mass.: Harvard University Press, 1991), pp. 62–4.

16. Aprile, 'La République au salon', p. 481; Stone, *Sons of the Revolution*, pp. 250–1. On salaries, see Stone, p. 247.

17. Jean-Michel Gaillard, *Jules Ferry* (Paris: Fayard, 1989), p. 93. Katherine Auspitz attributes the civil marriage to Eugénie's grandmother. See *The Radical Bourgeoisie: the Ligue de l'enseignement and the origins of the Third Republic, 1866–1885* (Cambridge: Cambridge University Press, 1982), p. 189, note 102.

18. See Mary Lynn Stewart, *For Health and Beauty: physical culture for French-women 1880s–1930s* (Baltimore: Johns Hopkins University Press, 2001), Chapters 1 and 2; Charles Sowerwine, 'Woman's Brain, Man's Brain: feminism and anthropology in late nineteenth-century France', *Women's History Review* 12, 2 (2003), 311–29.

19. See Jack D. Ellis, *The Physician-Legislators of France: medicine and politics in the early Third Republic, 1870–1914* (New York: Cambridge University Press, 1990).

20. Robert Nye, *Masculinity and Male Codes of Honor in Modern France* (New York and Oxford: Oxford University Press, 1993), pp. 90–4; Robert Nye, 'Sexuality, Sex Difference and the Cult of Modern Love in Third Republic France', *Historical Reflections/Réflexions Historiques* 20, 1 (1994), 57–76.

21. A. J. E. Fouillée, 'La Psychologie des sexes et ses fondements physiologiques' [1893], quoted in Karen Offen, 'Depopulation, Nationalism

and Feminism in Fin-de-Siècle France', *American Historical Review* 89, 3 (1984), 648–76 (p. 666).
22. Auspitz, *Radical Bourgeoisie*, pp. 18–21, 33–8; Nye, *Masculinity and Male Codes of Honor*, Chapter 8; Judith Stone, 'The Republican Brotherhood: gender and ideology', in Elinor E. Accampo, Rachel G. Fuchs and Mary Lynn Steward (eds), *Gender and the Politics of Social Reform in France, 1870–1914* (Baltimore and London: Johns Hopkins University Press, 1995), p. 39.
23. Philip Nord, 'Republican Politics and the Bourgeois Interior in Mid-nineteenth Century France', in Suzanne Nash (ed.), *Home and its Dislocations in Nineteenth-Century France* (Albany: State University of New York Press, 1993), pp. 193–214.
24. Stone, 'The Republican Brotherhood', pp. 32–8.
25. Stone, *Sons of the Revolution*, p. 58.
26. See Nord, 'Republican Politics and the Bourgeois Interior', *passim*.
27. Quoted in Stone, 'The Republican Brotherhood', pp. 28–9.
28. Quoted in Auspitz, *Radical Bourgeoisie*, p. 43.
29. Stone, 'The Republican Brotherhood', p. 34.
30. Ibid., pp. 56–8.
31. Ibid., p. 46; Aprile, 'La République au salon', p. 485; Nye, *Masculinity*, pp. 154–5.
32. Whitney Walton, 'Republican Women and Republican Families in the Personal Narratives of George Sand, Marie d'Agoult, and Hortense Allart', in Jo B. Margadant (ed.), *The New Biography: performing femininity in nineteenth century France* (Berkeley: University of California Press, 2000), pp. 99–136.
33. André Léo, *La femme et les moeurs. Monarchie ou liberté* [1869], introduction et notes de Monique Biarnais (Tusson, Charente: Editions du Lérot, 1990), p. 104.
34. Madame d'Héricourt, *A Woman's Philosophy of Woman; or Woman Affranchised. An answer to Michelet, Proudhon, Girardin, Legouvé, Comte, and other modern innovators, translated from the last Paris edition* [1860] (New York: Carleton, 1864), p. 30; Moses, *French Feminism*, p. 171.
35. Léo, *La femme et les moeurs*, p. 92. For women's views on the family, see also Moses, *French Feminism*, pp. 165, 181–2.
36. D'Héricourt, *A Woman's Philosophy of Woman*, pp. 17–21.
37. Ibid., p. 25.
38. Léo, *La femme et les moeurs*, pp. 77–8.
39. Joan W. Scott, *Only Paradoxes to Offer: French feminists and the Rights of Man* (Cambridge, Mass.: Harvard University Press, 1996), p. 109.
40. Quoted in Moses, *French Feminism*, pp. 185, 166.
41. See the statement of Jules Ferry, quoted in Gaillard, *Jules Ferry*, pp. 186–7.
42. Moses, *French Feminism*, p. 170; Scott, *Paradoxes*, pp. 100–1; Léo, *La femme et les moeurs*, pp. 77–8.
43. D'Héricourt, *A Woman's Philosophy of Woman*, pp. 21–3; Scott, *Paradoxes*, p. 103.
44. Léo, *La femme et les moeurs*, pp. 75–7; Scott, *Paradoxes*, p. 100.
45. D'Héricourt, *A Woman's Philosophy of Woman*, pp. xii, 24.

46. Léo, *La femme et les moeurs*, p. 109.
47. Ibid., p. 57.
48. Ibid., p. 95.
49. D'Héricourt, *A Woman's Philosophy of Woman*, p. x.
50. Scott, *Paradoxes*, p. 109.
51. Léon Gambetta to La Princesse Lise Troubetzkoï, 26 July 1874 and 15 October 1877; to Marie Meersmans, 9 March 1870; to Mme Juliette Adam, 8 June 1874; to Léonie Léon, 17 January 1879, in *Lettres de Gambetta 1868–1882*, recueillies et annotées par Daniel Halévy and Emile Pillias (Paris: Editions Bernard Grasset, 1938), nos 86, 194, 197, 343, 400.
52. Léon Gambetta to Mme Auguste Scheurer-Kestner, 2 August 1874, ibid., no. 200. See also Léon Gambetta to Mme Clément Laurier, 17 January 1872 (no. 131).
53. See Wright, *Notable or Notorious?*, pp. 59–71.
54. Léon Gambetta to Mme Juliette Adam, 17 October 1876, in *Lettres de Gambetta*, no. 289.
55. The region of Savoy only became part of France in 1860.
56. Léon Gambetta to Mme Juliette Adam, 15 November 1874, in *Lettres de Gambetta*, no. 221.
57. Wright, *Notable or Notorious?*, p. 59.
58. Léon Gambetta to Mme Juliette Adam, 27 January 1877, in *Lettres de Gambetta*, no. 300. See also his letter dated 11 September 1874 (no. 206).
59. Ludmilla Jordanova, *Sexual Visions: images of gender in science and medicine between the eighteenth and twentieth centuries* (Madison: University of Wisconsin Press, 1989), Chapter 4; Nye, 'Sexuality', pp. 57–76.
60. On Léonie Léon, see Emile Pillias, *Léonie Léon amie de Gambetta* (Paris: Librairie Gallimard, 1935). The similarity between their names is purely coincidental.
61. Léon Gambetta to Léonie Léon, 5 June 1875, in *Lettres de Gambetta*, no. 244.
62. Léon Gambetta to Léonie Léon, 13 January 1875, 22 April 1875, 16 May 1877, 24 May 1878, 17 March 1881, in ibid., nos 233, 242, 309, 382, 468.
63. Léon Gambetta to Léonie Léon, 11 December 1881, in ibid., no. 510.
64. Léon Gambetta to Léonie Léon, 17 August 1875, in ibid., no. 247. See also letters dated 22 November 1876 and 24 May 1878 (nos 293, 382).
65. Léon Gambetta to Léonie Léon, 23 February 1878, in ibid., no. 359.
66. See ibid., no. 359, editor's note (a), and Pillias, *Léonie Léon*, pp. 105–7.
67. Léon Gambetta to Léonie Léon, 2 March and 6 March 1878, in *Lettres de Gambetta*, nos 361, 362.
68. Léon Gambetta to Léonie Léon, 7 March 1878, in ibid., no. 363.
69. On this episode see Jacques Chastenet, *Histoire de la Troisième République*, 4 vols (Paris: Hachette, 1952–1963), vol. 1, pp. 246–50.
70. Aprile, 'La République au salon', p. 486.
71. Jules Ferry to Eugénie Ferry, 23 April and 13 January 1876, quoted in Gaillard, *Jules Ferry*, p. 101.
72. Steven C. Hause and Anne R. Kenney, 'The Limits of Suffragist Behaviour: legalism and militancy in France, 1876–1922', *American Historical Review* 86 (1981), 781–806.

73. Steven C. Hause with Anne R. Kenney, *Women's Suffrage and Social Politics in the French Third Republic* (Princeton, N.J.: Princeton University Press, 1984), pp. 40–45, 69. The movement was overwhelmingly urban and Protestant, as well as middle class. See also Charles Sowerwine, *Sisters or Citizens?: women and socialism in France since 1876* (Cambridge and New York: Cambridge University Press, 1982), esp. pp. 88–9, 94–7.

74. Moses, *French Feminism*, pp. 198–212.

75. Mary Lynn Stewart, *Women, Work and the French State: labour protection and social patriarchy, 1879–1919* (Kingston: McGill-Queen's University Press, 1989); Elinor A. Accampo *et al.* (eds), *Gender and the Politics of Social Reform in France, 1870–1914*; Marilyn Boxer, 'Protective Legislation and Home Industry: the marginalisation of women workers in late nineteenth–early twentieth century France', *Journal of Social History* 20, 1 (1986), 45–65; A. Klaus, 'Depopulation and Race Suicide: maternalism and pronatalist ideologies in France and the United States', in Seth Koven and Sonya Michel (eds), *Mothers of a New World: maternalist politics and the origins of welfare states* (New York: Routledge, 1993).

76. Jules Michelet, *Le prêtre, la femme et la famille*, 8th edn (1862), quoted in Ralph Gibson, 'Why Republicans and Catholics Couldn't Stand Each Other in the Nineteenth Century', in Frank Tallett and Nicholas Atkin (eds), *Religion, Society and Politics in France Since 1789* (London and Rio Grande: Hambledon Press, 1991), pp. 107–20 (p. 118).

77. Quoted in Jean Rabaut, *Histoire des féminismes français* (Paris: Stock, 1978), pp. 182–3.

78. Gaillard, *Jules Ferry*, p. 520.

79. Ibid., p. 507.

80. Christopher Thompson, 'Un troisième sexe? Les Bourgeois et la bicyclette dans la France fin de siècle', *Le Mouvement social* 192 (July–Sep. 2000), 11.

81. Quoted in Laurence Klejman and Florence Rochefort, *L'égalité en marche: le féminisme sous la Troisième République* (Paris: Presses de la Fondation Nationale des Sciences Politiques; Des Femmes Antoinette Fouque, 1989), p. 58.

82. Anne Martin-Fugier, *La bourgeoise: femme au temps de Paul Bourget* (Paris: Bernard Grasset, 1983), pp. 17–18; James McMillan, *France and Women, 1789–1914: gender, society and politics* (London: Routledge, 2000), pp. 144–52.

83. Quoted in Gaillard, *Jules Ferry*, pp. 186–7 (undated).

84. Quoted in ibid., pp. 520–1 (undated).

85. Sharif Gemie, *Women and Schooling in France, 1815–1914: gender, authority and identity in the female schooling sector* (Keele: Keele University Press, 1995), p. 80.

86. Speech dated 19 April 1881, quoted in Gaillard, *Jules Ferry*, p. 510.

87. Stewart, *For Health and Beauty*, p. 34.

88. Ibid., p. 52.

89. Camille Pert, *Le livre de la femme. Guide pratique de la vie* (Paris: Editions de femina, 1901), p. 178.

90. Stewart, *For Health and Beauty*, pp. 52–3; Michelle Perrot, 'The New Eve and the Old Adam: changes in French women's condition at the turn

of the century', in Margaret Randolph Higonnet *et al.* (eds), *Behind the Lines: gender and the two World Wars* (New Haven and London: Yale University Press, 1987), pp. 52–3; Debora Silverman, 'The "New Woman", Feminism, and the Decorative Arts in Fin-de-Siècle France', in Lynn Hunt (ed.), *Eroticism and the Body Politic* (Baltimore and London: Johns Hopkins University Press, 1991), p. 149.

91. Mary Louise Roberts, 'Subversive Copy: feminist journalism in fin-de-siècle France', in Dean de la Motte and Jeannene M. Przyblynski (eds), *Making the News: modernity and the mass press in nineteenth-century France* (Boston: University of Massachusetts Press, 1999), pp. 302–50.
92. Sowerwine, *Sisters or Citizens?*, p. 23; Moses, *French Feminism*, pp. 212–15.
93. Hubertine Auclert, *La Citoyenne*, 13 February 1881, quoted in Moses, *French Feminism*, p. 215.
94. Hause with Kenney, *Women's Suffrage*, pp. 86–90.
95. Groupe de Propagande de l'Union Française pour le Suffrage des Femmes [UFSF], *Le suffrage des femmes en France*, 2nd edn (Paris: Marcel Rivière et Cie., 1910), pp. 1–2.
96. Le Groupe Franc-Comptois de l'Union Française pour le Suffrage des Femmes, *Rapport sur la question du vote des femmes présenté au conseil municipal de Besançon* (Besançon: La Solidarité, Imprimerie Coopérative, 1913), pp. 8–9. See also Groupe de Propagande de l'UFSF, *Le suffrage des femmes en France*, pp. 3–4; Ferdinand Buisson, *Le vote des femmes* (Paris: H. Dunot and E. Pinat, 1911), Chapters 2–14, *passim*.
97. Le Groupe Franc-Comptois, *Rapport sur la question du vote des femmes*, p. 21.
98. Buisson, *Le vote des femmes*, p. 309.
99. Le Groupe Franc-Comptois, *Rapport sur la question du vote des femmes*, pp. 17–21.
100. Ibid.
101. Ibid., pp. 15–18; Buisson, *Le vote des femmes*, pp. 309–16; Speech of Deputy Louis Marin, in Mme Oddo Deflou, *Congrès national des droits civils and du suffrage des femmes, les 26, 27 et 28 juin 1908, compte rendu in extenso* (Paris: n.p., 1910), pp. 192–3.
102. Buisson, *Le vote des femmes*, p. 311.
103. Le Groupe Franc-Comptois, *Rapport sur la question du vote des femmes*, p. 21.
104. Buisson, *Le vote des femmes*, p. 317.
105. Georges Clemenceau, *La 'Justice' du sexe fort* (1907), quoted in Hause with Kenney, *Women's Suffrage*, p. 99.
106. Quoted in Moses, *French Feminism*, p. 220.
107. Hause with Kenney, *Women's Suffrage*, pp. 97–100.
108. Le Groupe Franc-Comptois, *Rapport sur la question du vote des femmes*, p. 23.

6 'New Women' in the era of Great War, 1890s–1920s

1. The death of civilisation was a major theme of post-war literature. See Mary Louise Roberts, *Civilization Without Sexes: reconstructing gender*

in postwar France, 1917–1927 (Chicago and London: University of Chicago Press, 1994), pp. 2–4.

2. Stéphane Audoin-Rouzeau, *Cinq deuils de guerre 1914–1918* (Paris: Editions Noesis, 2001); Stéphane Audoin-Rouzeau and Annette Becker, *14–18: retrouver la guerre* (Paris: Gallimard, 2000).

3. Jean-Jacques Becker, *The Great War and the French People*, trans. Arnold Pomerans (Providence and Oxford: Berg, 1983); Charles Sowerwine, *France Since 1870* (Houndmills, Basingstoke: Palgrave, 2001), Chapter 8.

4. See Joan Kelly-Gadol, 'Did Women have a Renaissance?', in Renate Bridenthal and Claudia Koonz (eds), *Becoming Visible: women in European history* (Boston: Houghton Mifflin, 1977), pp. 137–64. Sîan Reynolds considers a similar question for the Belle Epoque in 'Albertine's Bicycle, or, Women and French Identity during the Belle Epoque', *Literature and History* 10, 1 (2001), 28–41.

5. On contemporary perceptions of the *flâneuse*, see Lisa Tiersten, *Marianne in the Market: envisioning consumer society in fin-de-siècle France* (Berkeley: University of California Press, 2001).

6. On changing interpretations of women's roles as consumers, see Leora Auslander, 'The Gendering of Consumer Practices in Nineteenth Century France', in Victoria de Grazia with Ellen Furlough (eds) *The Sex of Things: gender and consumption in historical perspective* (Berkeley: University of California Press, 1996), pp. 79–112; Leora Auslander, *Taste and Power: furnishing modern France* (Berkeley: University of California Press, 1996).

7. Michael Miller, *The Bon Marché: bourgeois culture and the department store, 1869–1920* (Princeton: Princeton University Press, 1981); Rosalind Williams, *Dream Worlds: mass consumption in late nineteenth-century France* (Berkeley: University of California Press, 1982).

8. Rita Felski, *The Gender of Modernity* (Cambridge, Mass. and London: Harvard University Press, 1995), Chapter 3.

9. *La Fronde*, 29 February 1899, p. 5.

10. Editor's introduction to Steven Zdatny (ed.) *Hairstyles and Fashion: a hairdresser's history of Paris, 1910–1920* (Oxford and New York: Berg, 1999), pp. 11–23.

11. Emile Long, Paris correspondent for the English *Hairdressers' Weekly Journal*, in Steven Zdatny (ed.), *Hairstyles and Fashion*, p. 64.

12. Ibid., p. 56.

13. Anne Hollander, 'Women and Fashion', in Kenneth W. Wheeler and Virginia Lee Lussier (eds), *Women, the Arts, and the 1920s in Paris and New York* (New Brunswick and London: Transaction Books, 1982), pp. 111–14.

14. Jane Doria, 'La beauté par les haltères', *La Fronde*, 2 February 1899, p. 5.

15. Anne Martin-Fugier, *La bourgeoise. Femme au temps de Paul Bourget* (Paris: Bernard Grasset, 1983), p. 13; Mary Lynn Stewart, *For Health and Beauty: physical culture for Frenchwomen 1880s–1930s* (Baltimore and London: Johns Hopkins University Press, 2001), p. 168.

16. *La Fronde*, 9 December 1897, p. 3. 'Yachtswomen' is in English in the text.

17. On the range of supplements, see ibid., 7 January 1899.
18. For an example, see Lady Betty, 'Chronique de La mode', ibid., 1 June 1900, p. 3.
19. Reynolds, 'Albertine's Bicyle', p. 32.
20. Stewart, *For Health and Beauty*, p. 163.
21. Christopher Thompson, 'Un troisième sexe? Les bourgeoises et la bicyclette dans la France fin de siècle', *Le Mouvement social* 192 (July–Sep. 2000), 28–38. See also J. Hudry-Menos, 'Les Sports et les Femmes', *La Fronde*, 8 January 1898, p. 1.
22. Marcel Proust, *In Search of Lost Time, II: Within a Budding Grove*, trans. C. K. Scott Moncrieff and Terence Kilmartin, rev. D. J. Enright (London: Chatto and Windus, 1992), p. 431. This passage is also discussed in Reynolds, 'Albertine's Bicycle', p. 38.
23. See, for instance, the front page of *Le Grelot* for 19 April 1896, which shows a woman in bloomers, with her bicycle and cigarette, instructing a henpecked husband to prepare dinner for 8 o'clock sharp as she departs for a feminist congress. Reproduced in Debora Silverman, 'The "New Woman", Feminism, and the Decorative Arts in Fin-de-Siècle France', in Lynn Hunt (ed.), *Eroticism and the Body Politic* (Baltimore and London: Johns Hopkins University Press, 1991), p. 151. This satire may owe its inspiration to those of 1848, which employed similar tropes.
24. Marc Angenot, ' "La fin d'un sexe": le discours sur les femmes en 1889', *Romantisme* 63 (1989), 13.
25. Thompson, 'Un troisième sexe?', pp. 14–16, 26–7, 32–3.
26. Néva, 'Cyclisme', *La Fronde*, 27 January 1898, p. 4. See also 16 May 1898 for a report on women training for a race. The results were published on 1 June (p. 4).
27. Thompson, 'Un troisième sexe?', pp. 30–3.
28. Stewart, *For Health and Beauty*, pp. 151–62.
29. Thompson, 'Un troisième sexe?', pp. 14–16, 37.
30. Néva, 'Régénérés par le Sport', *La Fronde*, 12 January 1899, p. 6.
31. Hollander, 'Women and Fashion', pp. 112–14.
32. Daniel Lesueur, 'La Coquetterie', *La Fronde*, 1 July 1898, p. 1. Daniel Lesueur was the pseudonym of the writer and poet, Mme Jeanne Loiseau. See 'La femme Moderne, par les principales personnalités féminines de France et de l'Etranger', *Revue Encyclopédique Larousse*, 28 November 1896, p. 872.
33. Thompson, 'Un troisième sexe?', pp. 22–4. Conversely, *La Fronde*'s female correspondents emphasised the discomfort of saddles designed for men (9 December 1897, p. 3; 11 December 1897, p. 4).
34. Proust, *In Search of Lost Time*, vol. 2, p. 862.
35. Quoted in Thompson, 'Un troisième sexe?', p. 21.
36. Ibid., pp. 19–20.
37. Quoted in ibid., p. 9.
38. J. Hudry-Menos, 'Les Sports et les Femmes', *La Fronde*, 8 January 1898, p. 1.
39. Néva, 'Régénérés par le Sport', ibid., 12 January 1899, p. 6.
40. Lady Betty, 'Chronique de La mode', ibid., 1 June 1900, p. 3.

41. Serge Grafteaux (ed.), *Mémé Santerre: a French woman of the people*, trans. Louise A. Tilly and Kathryn L. Tilly (New York: Schocken Books, 1985), pp. 75–6.
42. Françoise Thébaud, 'The Great War and the Triumph of Sexual Division', in Georges Duby and Michelle Perrot (general eds) *A History of Women in the West, vol. V: toward a cultural identity in the twentieth century*, ed. Françoise Thébaud (Cambridge Mass. and London: Belknap Press, 1994), pp. 24–5.
43. Becker, *The Great War and the French People*, pp. 3–4.
44. Françoise Thébaud, *La femme au temps de la guerre de 14* (Paris: Stock/ Laurence Pernoud, 1986), pp. 45–7.
45. Ibid., pp. 49–58; Audoin-Rouzeau and Becker, *14–18: retrouver la guerre*, pp. 59–78.
46. See Stéphane Audoin-Rouzeau, *L'enfant de l'ennemi 1914–1918* (Paris: Aubier, 1995); Ruth Harris, 'The "Child of the Barbarian": rape, race and nationalism in France during the First World War', *Past and Present* 141 (1993), 170–206.
47. Quoted in Thébaud, 'The Great War', p. 28.
48. Reports quoted in Becker, *The Great War*, pp. 14–15.
49. Christine Bard, *Les femmes dans la société française au 20e siècle* (Paris: Armand Colin, 2001), p. 21.
50. Emilie Carles, *A Wild Herb Soup: the life of a French countrywoman*, trans. Avriel H. Goldberger (London: Victor Gollancz, 1992), p. 56.
51. Thébaud, *La femme*, p. 150; Becker, *The Great War*, pp. 125–31.
52. James McMillan, *Housewife or Harlot: the place of women in French society, 1870–1940* (Brighton: Harvester Press, 1981), pp. 132–3; Becker, *The Great War*, p. 26.
53. Thébaud, *La femme*, p. 30.
54. McMillan, *Housewife or Harlot*, pp. 132, 134. According to Thébaud, Joffre said the war would have been lost if these women had stopped working for twenty minutes (*La femme*, p. 182).
55. McMillan, *Housewife or Harlot*, pp. 134–8; Bard, *Les femmes*, pp. 20–1.
56. Quoted in Thébaud, *La femme*, p. 177.
57. Charles Sowerwine, *France Since 1870: culture, politics and society* (Houndmills, Basingstoke: Palgrave, 2001), p. 110.
58. Thébaud, *La femme*, pp. 163–5, 169–75; McMillan, *Housewife or Harlot*, pp. 139–40.
59. Thébaud, *La femme*, pp. 158–66.
60. Becker, *The Great War*, pp. 17–21; Bard, *Les femmes*, pp. 29–30.
61. Steven C. Hause, 'More Minerva than Mars: the French Women's Rights Campaign and the First World War', in Margaret Randolph Higonnet *et al.* (eds), *Behind the Lines: gender and the two World Wars* (New Haven and London: Yale University Press, 1987), pp.104–5.
62. Becker, *The Great War*, p. 206.
63. Thébaud, *La femme*, pp. 215–18.
64. Pauline to the Deputy for Maine-et-Loire, July 1917, published in Bard, *Les femmes*, p. 30. Pauline could not work because there was no employment in Denée and her absent husband refused her permission to move into nearby Angers.

65. For an analysis of the strikes see Becker, *The Great War*, Chapter 17; McMillan, *Housewife or Harlot*, pp.145–56.
66. Thébaud, *La femme*, p. 85; Bard, *Les femmes*, p. 18. The remaining 20,000 were nuns (10,000) and visitors.
67. Thébaud, *La femme*, pp. 209–10.
68. Madame H. Cloquié, *La femme après la guerre (ses droits, son rôle, son devoir)* (Paris: Chez Maloine, 1915), p. 30.
69. Thébaud, *La femme*, p. 139.
70. Quoted in ibid., p. 137.
71. See Joan B. Landes, *Visualizing the Nation: gender, representation, and revolution in eighteenth-century France* (Ithaca and London: Cornell University Press, 2001), Chapter 4.
72. Bard, *Les femmes*, p. 28.
73. Thébaud, *La femme*, p. 196.
74. Jacques Flach, introduction to Jules Combarieu, *Les jeunes filles françaises et la guerre* (Paris: Armand Colin, 1916), p. xi.
75. Odile Krakovitch, 'Sous la Patrie, le Patriarcat: la représentation des femmes dans le théâtre de la Grande Guerre', in Odile Krakovitch and Geneviève Sellier (eds) *L'exclusion des femmes: masculinité et politique dans la culture au XXe siècle* (Paris: Editions complexe, 2001), pp. 33–5.
76. Quoted in Thébaud, *La femme*, p. 94.
77. Krakovitch, 'Sous la Patrie', pp. 39–50.
78. Thébaud, 'The Great War', pp. 26–30.
79. Audoin-Rouzeau and Becker, *14–18: retrouver la guerre*, p. 31.
80. Anne Roche and Marie-ClaudeTaranger (eds), *Celles qui n'ont pas écrit: récits de femmes dans la région marseillaise, 1914–1945* (La Calaude, Aix-en-Provence: Edisud, 1995), p. 102. The word 'l'armistice' resembles the word 'larmes'.
81. Quoted in Thébaud, *La femme*, p. 205. For a discussion of this and other cases of post-war grieving see Audoin-Rouzeau, *Cinq deuils*.
82. Audoin-Rouzeau, *Cinq deuils*, pp. 97–141.
83. Bard, *La femme*, pp. 28–9.
84. See McMillan, *Housewife or Harlot*, part II; Thébaud, 'The Great War'; Hause, 'More Minerva than Mars'.
85. Bard, *Les femmes*, pp. 61–2.
86. McMillan, *Housewife or Harlot*, p. 159.
87. Thébaud, 'The Great War', p. 70; Bard, *Les femmes*, pp. 60–1.
88. Bard, *Les femmes*, p. 63; Hause, 'More Minerva than Mars', pp. 105–6.
89. McMillan, *Housewife or Harlot*, p. 159.
90. Ibid., p. 157.
91. Bard, *Les femmes*, p. 64.
92. Before 1924, girls had to study some subjects privately in order to sit the examination whereas boys' schools taught the full curriculum. Siân Reynolds notes the issues that prompted the 1924 change, arguing that it was not put forward specifically to benefit girls. See *France Between the Wars: gender and politics* (London: Routledge, 1996), pp. 48–50.
93. Quoted in Bard, *Les femmes*, p. 76.
94. Bard, *Les femmes*, p. 77.

95. For a debate on the relative merits of social and cultural approaches to the study of the 'new woman' see Steven Zdatny, 'La mode à la garçonne, 1900–1925: une histoire sociale des coupes de cheveux', and Mary-Louise Roberts, 'Prêt-à-déchiffrer: La mode de l'après guerre et la "nouvelle histoire culturelle" ', in *Le Mouvement social* 174 (1996), 23–56 and 57–73.
96. Zdatny, 'La mode', p. 34.
97. Long, in Zdatny (ed.) *Hairstyles and Fashion*, p. 170.
98. Ibid., p. 159; Zdatny, 'La mode', pp. 40, 43–5, and note 71.
99. Hollander, 'Women and Fashion', pp. 111–16.
100. Long, in Zdatny (ed.) *Hairstyles and Fashion*, p. 172.
101. Hollander, 'Women and Fashion', pp. 110, 121; Zdatny, 'La mode', pp. 43, 49.
102. Hollander, ibid., pp. 118–22; Roberts, *Civilisation Without Sexes*, pp. 66–9.
103. Roberts, 'Prêt-à-déchiffrer', pp. 68–71 (quotation 69).
104. Long, in Zdatny (ed.) *Hairstyles and Fashion*, pp. 171–2.
105. Zdatny, 'La mode', p. 35.
106. Hollander, 'Women and Fashion', p. 110.
107. Roberts, *Civilization Without Sexes*, p. 156.
108. Ibid., pp. 131–7, and figure 18.
109. Bard, *La femme*, pp. 52–3.
110. Quoted in ibid., p. 52.
111. Quoted in Reynolds, *France between the Wars*, p. 18.
112. Sowerwine, *France Since 1870*, p. 125.
113. Bard, *La femme*, p. 54.
114. Reynolds, *France between the Wars*, p. 19; Sowerwine, *France Since 1870*, p. 125.
115. Reynolds, ibid., pp. 26–7; Bard, *La femme*, pp. 14, 53.
116. Reynolds, ibid., pp. 29–30.
117. Martine Sevegrand, *L'amour en toutes lettres: questions à l'Abbé Viollet sur la sexualité 1924–1943* (Paris: Albin Michel, 1996), Chapter 6.
118. Anne-Marie Sohn, *Chrysalides: femmes dans la vie privée (XIXe-XXe siècles)* (Paris: Publications de la Sorbonne, 1996), pp. 906–7.
119. Bard, *La femme*, p. 47; Sevegrand, *L'amour en toutes lettres*, pp. 91–9.
120. For a discussion of this anomaly, see Reynolds, *France between the Wars*, pp. 31–7.
121. Quoted in Bard, *La femme*, p. 16.
122. Reynolds, *France between the Wars*, pp. 210–11.
123. Bard, *La femme*, pp. 84–7; Charles Sowerwine, *Sisters or Citizens? Women and socialism in France since 1876* (Cambridge: Cambridge University Press, 1982), Chapter 7.
124. Bard, ibid., pp. 87–8; McMillan, *France and Women*, pp. 226–7.
125. This argument has been made in Pierre Rosanvallon, *Le sacre du citoyen: histoire du suffrage universel en France* (Paris: Gallimard, 1992); and Mona Ozouf, *Les mots des femmes: essai sur la singularité française* (Paris: Fayard, 1995). For useful discussions of the argument see McMillan, *France and Women*, pp. 227–30; Reynolds, *France between the Wars*, pp. 207–12.

126. Reynolds, ibid., pp. 209–11.
127. McMillan, *France and Women*, pp. 218, 221.
128. Sowerwine, *France Since 1870*, pp. 123, 134–7, 141, Chapter 11.
129. Reynolds, *France between the Wars*, p. 25.
130. Ibid., pp. 210–11.
131. Bard, *La femme*, pp. 96–7.
132. Gaston Rageot, *La natalité: ses lois économiques et psychologiques* (1918), quoted in Roberts, 'Prêt-à-déchiffrer', p. 61.
133. Letter from an unnamed female correspondent, quoted in Henry Bordeaux, *Le mariage, hier et aujourd'hui* (1921), quoted in Roberts, *Civilization Without Sexes*, p. 139.

7 Taking sides: women in the 1930s

1. Christine Bard, 'Le Triomphe du Familialisme', in Christine Bard (ed.), *Un Siècle d'antiféminisme* (Paris: Fayard, 1999), pp. 169–92.
2. See Christine Bard, *Les femmes dans la société française au 20e siècle* (Paris: Armand Colin, 2001), pp. 127–8; Christine Bard and Françoise Thébaud, 'Les effets antiféministes de la Grande Guerre', in *Un Siècle d'antiféminisme*, pp. 149–68.
3. Geneviève Sellier, 'Le Cinéma des années 1930', in *Un Siècle d'antiféminisme*, pp. 205–14.
4. A photograph of a meeting of the eminently respectable National Council of French Women (CNFF) in the 1930s shows all the women wearing short hair. See Christine Bard, *Les Filles de Marianne: Histoire des féminismes 1914–1940* (Paris: Fayard, 1995), p. 389.
5. Jean-Yves Mollier and Jocelyne George, *La Plus Longue des Républiques, 1870–1940* (Paris: Fayard, 1994), pp. 605–7; Philippe Bernard and Henri Dubief, *The Decline of the Third Republic 1914–1938*, trans. A. Forster (Cambridge and Paris: Cambridge University Press and Maison des Sciences de l'Homme, 1985), pp. 173–89.
6. Siân Reynolds, *France Between the Wars: gender and politics* (London and New York: Routledge, 1996), pp. 83–108.
7. Ibid., pp. 112, 115–18; Charles Sowerwine, *France since 1870: culture, politics and society* (Houndmills, Basingstoke: Palgrave, 2001), pp. 138–9.
8. Bard, *Les Femmes*, pp. 60–1.
9. Reynolds, *France Between the Wars*, p. 111; Christine Bard, *Les Filles de Marianne: Histoire des féminismes 1914–1940* (Paris: Fayard, 1995), pp. 313–19.
10. Catherine Omnès, *Ouvrières Parisiennes: Marchés du travail et trajectoires professionnelles au 20e siècle* (Paris: Editions de l'Ecole des Hautes Etudes en Sciences Sociales, 1997), p.168; Bard, *Les Filles de Marianne*, pp. 318–19.
11. Alexander Werth, *The Destiny of France* (London: Hamish Hamilton, 1937), p. 295; Bard, *Les Filles de Marianne*, pp. 315–16.
12. Reynolds, *France Between the Wars*, p. 93.
13. Bard, *Les Filles de Marianne*, pp. 323–6.

14. Omnès, *Ouvrières Parisiennes*, p. 183.
15. Ibid., pp. 170–3; Reynolds, *France Between the Wars*, p. 113.
16. Reynolds, ibid., pp. 113–14; Bard, *Les Filles de Marianne*, pp. 319–20.
17. Omnès, *Ouvrières Parisiennes*, pp. 298–309; Bard, *La Femme*, pp. 70–1; Susan B. Whitney, 'Gender, Class and Generation in Interwar French Catholicism: the case of the *Jeunesse ouvrière chrétienne féminine*', *Journal of Family History* 26, 4 (2001), 492–3.
18. Mme Y. G., quoted in Omnès, *Ouvrières Parisiennes*, p. 301.
19. On female friendship and workplace sociability, see the interviews in ibid., pp. 319–29.
20. Sowerwine, *France since 1870*, p. 140.
21. Reynolds, *France Between the Wars*, pp. 116–17.
22. Quoted in Whitney, 'Gender, Class and Generation', p. 494.
23. Simone Weil, 'La Vie et la Grève', in Simone Weil, *La condition ouvrière* (Paris: Gallimard, 1951), p. 221.
24. Interview with Mme G., in Omnès, *Ouvrières Parisiennes*, p. 321 (ellipses original).
25. Werth, *The Destiny of France*, p. 304.
26. Bard, *Les Femmes*, pp. 73–4; Reynolds, *France Between the Wars*, pp. 118–20.
27. Jeanne Bouvier, *Mes Mémoires, ou 59 années d'activité industrielle, sociale et intellectuelle d'une ouvrière 1876–1935*, eds Daniel Armogathe with Maïté Albistur (Paris: La Découverte/Maspero, 1983), pp. 135–6.
28. Joceline Chabot, 'Les syndicats féminins chrétiens et la formation militante de 1913 à 1936: "propagandistes idéales" et "héroïne identitielle" ', *Le Mouvement Social* 165 (Oct.–Dec. 1993), 7–22; Christine Bard, 'L'apôtre social et l'ange du foyer: les femmes et la C.F.T.C. à travers *Le Nord-Social* (1920–1936)', *Le Mouvement Social*, 165 (Oct.–Dec. 1993), 23–42.
29. Sowerwine, *France since 1870*, pp. 122–3, 130–1.
30. Quoted in ibid., p. 149.
31. See Jean-Pierre Rioux, '1936: L'Illusion de Printemps', in Jean-Pierre Rioux and Jean-François Sirinelli (eds), *La France d'un Siècle à l'Autre 1914–2000, Dictionnaire Critique* (Paris: Hachette Littératures, 1999), pp. 32–5.
32. Sowerwine, *France since 1870*, pp. 148–50; Bernard and Dubief, *The Decline of the Third Republic*, pp. 299–306. For a more extended discussion of the Popular Front, see Julian Jackson, *The Popular Front in France: defending democracy, 1934–1938* (Cambridge: Cambridge University Press, 1988).
33. Charles Sowerwine, *Les Femmes et le Socialisme* (Paris: Presses de la fondation nationale des sciences politiques, 1978), pp. 217–27.
34. Christine Bard and Jean-Louis Robert, 'The French Communist Party and Women 1920–1939: from "feminism" to familialism', trans. Nicole Dombrowski, in Helmut Gruber and Pamela Graves (eds), *Women and Socialism, Socialism and Women: Europe between the two World Wars* (New York and Oxford: Berghahn Books, 1998), pp. 321–48.
35. Speech at the Congress of Tours, quoted in ibid., p. 327.
36. Susan B. Whitney, 'Embracing the status quo: French Communists, young women and the Popular Front', *Journal of Social History* 30, 1 (Fall, 1996), 29–53.

37. Ibid., p. 33. Some women nevertheless recalled enthusiastically having participated in such activities.
38. Bard and Robert, 'The French Communist Party and Women', pp. 323, 333–6.
39. Ibid., pp. 338, 340.
40. Danièle Casanova, speech to the first congress of the UJFF, quoted in ibid., p. 331.
41. Whitney, 'Embracing the status quo', p. 43.
42. Ibid., p. 41.
43. Bard and Robert, 'The French Communist Party and Women', p. 343.
44. Reproduced in Gérard Vincent, 'Communism as a Way of Life', in Philippe Ariès and Georges Duby (general editors), *A History of Private Life, V: Riddles of Identity in Modern Times*, Antoine Prost and Gérard Vincent (eds), trans. Arthur Goldhammer (Cambridge and London: The Belknap Press of Harvard University Press, 1991), p. 315.
45. Bard and Robert, 'The French Communist Party and Women', pp. 341, 343.
46. Danièle Casanova, speech to the first congress of the UJFF, quoted in ibid., p. 331.
47. Whitney, 'Embracing the status quo', p. 44.
48. Ibid., p. 42.
49. For an extended analysis of French fascism see Robert Soucy, *French Fascism: the First Wave, 1924–1933* (New Haven: Yale University Press, 1986) and *French Fascism: the Second Wave, 1933–1939* (New Haven: Yale University Press, 1995); Jean-François Sirinelli (ed.), *Histoire des Droites en France: politique, cultures, sensibilités*, 3 vols (Paris: Gallimard, 1992).
50. For an account of the crisis of February 1934 and its impact, see Sowerwine, *France since 1870*, pp. 144–7; Mollier and George, *La Plus Longue des Républiques*, pp. 613–20.
51. Bard, *Les Filles de Marianne*, pp. 404–5.
52. Lucienne Blondel, 'La Solidarité Française et les Femmes', October 1935, reproduced in Lisa Di Caprio and Merry E. Weisner (eds), *Lives and Voices: sources in European women's history* (Boston and New York: Houghton Mifflin, 2001), pp. 490–2.
53. Bard, *Les Femmes*, p. 87.
54. Anne Cova, *'Au service de l'Eglise, de la Patrie et de la Famille': Femmes catholiques et maternité sous la IIIe République* (Paris: L'Harmattan, 2000), pp. 40–4.
55. Ibid., p. 149.
56. Bard, *Les Femmes*, p. 87.
57. James McMillan, *France and women, 1789–1914: gender, society and politics* (London and New York: Routledge, 2000), pp. 226–7.
58. Quoted in Cova, *'Au service de l'Eglise'*, p. 154.
59. Quoted in ibid., pp. 156–7.
60. Quoted in Laurence Klejman and Florence Rochefort, *L'Egalité en Marche: Le féminisme sous la Troisième République* (Paris: Presses de la Fondation nationale des Sciences politiques, Des Femmes Antoinette Fouque, 1989), p. 205.

61. Whitney, 'Gender, Class and Generation', pp. 480–507.
62. Ibid., pp. 482–94.
63. Ibid., p. 500.
64. Mollier and George, *La Plus Longue des Républiques*, pp. 635–6.
65. Weil, 'La Vie et la Grève', pp. 229–30.
66. Mollier and George, *La Plus Longue des Républiques*, p. 635.
67. See Jackson, *The Popular Front in France*, Chapter 3, for an analysis of the spontaneity of the strikes. Oral histories of women also emphasise spontaneity. See Anne Roche and Marie-ClaudeTaranger (eds), *Celles qui n'ont pas écrit: récits de femmes dans la région marseillaise, 1914–1945* (La Calaude, Aix-en-Provence: Edisud, 1995), pp. 117–19.
68. Reynolds, *France Between the Wars*, pp. 120–5; Omnès, *Ouvrières parisiennes*, pp. 319–24.
69. Werth, *The Destiny of France*, pp. 304–5, 309.
70. Reynolds, *France between the Wars*, p. 121.
71. Werth, *The Destiny of France*, pp. 296, 298.
72. Ibid., pp. 303–4.
73. Ibid., p. 312.
74. Reynolds, *France between the Wars*, pp. 126–7; Bard, *Les Filles de Marianne*, pp. 326–9.
75. See Bard, ibid., pp. 342–4. Bard puts the number of women members of the Radical Party at 10 in 1924, and 150 in 1932.
76. On the 'women ministers', see ibid., pp. 341, 352–6; Reynolds, *France between the Wars*, pp. 159–62; Siân Reynolds, 'Women and the Popular Front in France: the case of the three women ministers', *French History* 8, 4 (1994), 196–224; Siân Reynolds, 'Trois dames au gouvernement (1936)', in *Un Siècle d'antiféminisme*, pp. 193–204.
77. Reynolds, *France between the Wars*, pp. 157–61.
78. Sowerwine, *France since 1870*, p. 153.
79. Bard, *Les Filles de Marianne*, pp. 353–4.
80. Reynolds, 'Trois dames', pp. 197–8.
81. Quoted in Reynolds, *France between the Wars*, p. 159.
82. Jackson, *The Popular Front in France*, pp. 256–7.
83. Quoted in Reynolds, *France between the Wars*, p. 162.
84. Reynolds, 'Trois dames', pp. 199–202; Bard, *Les Filles de Marianne*, pp. 356–61.
85. Reynolds, *France between the Wars*, Chapter 7.
86. Bard, *Les Filles de Marianne*, pp. 361–5.
87. Sowerwine, *France since 1870*, pp. 183–4.
88. Susan Pedersen, 'Catholicism, Feminism, and the Politics of the Family during the late Third Republic', in Seth Koven and Sonya Michel (eds), *Mothers of a New World: maternalist politics and the origins of welfare states* (New York: Routledge, 1993), p. 264. See also Susan Pedersen, *Family, Dependence and the Origins of the Welfare State: Britain and France, 1914–1945* (Cambridge: Cambridge University Press, 1993).
89. Bard, *Les Filles de Marianne*, p. 323.
90. Pedersen, 'Catholicism, Feminism, and the Politics of the Family', p. 265.
91. Anne-Marie Sohn, *Chrysalides: Femmes dans la vie privée (XIXe-Xxe siècles)* (Paris: Publications de la Sorbonne, 1996), p. 813.

92. Bard and Robert, 'The French Communist Party and Women', p. 341.
93. Whitney, 'Embracing the status quo', p. 43.
94. Ibid.
95. Françoise Thébaud, *La Femme au Temps de la Guerre de 14* (Paris: Stock, 1986), pp. 250–1.
96. 'Les dissidentes du CNFF', in Maïté Albistur and Daniel Armogathe (eds), *Le Grief des Femmes: anthologie de textes féministes, vol. 2, du Second Empire à nos jours* (Paris: Editions Hier et Demain, 1978), pp. 207–8.
97. Thébaud, *La Femme*, pp. 252–8.
98. Reynolds, *France between the Wars*, p. 192; Bard, *Les Filles de Marianne*, p. 311.
99. Mona Siegel, ' "To the Unknown Mother of the Unknown Soldier": pacifism, feminism, and the politics of sexual difference among French *Institutrices* between the wars', *French Historical Studies* 22, 3 (1999), 421–51 (quotation 429).
100. Bard, *Les Filles de Marianne*, pp. 310–11.
101. 'Pourquoi dois-tu, en tant que femme, combattre la guerre?' (1935), in *Le Grief des Femmes*, pp. 233–6.
102. Madeleine Vernet, *De l'Objection de Conscience au Désarmement* (1930), in ibid., pp. 213–18.
103. Nelly Roussel, 'Guerre à la Guerre', *La Mère Educatrice* (June 1921), in ibid., p. 222.
104. Claire Géniaux, 'Les Femmes et la Paix', *Cahiers bleus pour la république syndicale* (no. 92, 7 February 1931), in ibid., pp. 229–33.
105. Bard, *Les Filles de Marianne*, p. 312.
106. Hélène Brion, *Déclaration lue au 1er Conseil de Guerre le 29 mars 1918*, in *Le Grief des Femmes*, pp. 222–9 (quotation p. 225).
107. Romain Rolland, 'A l'Antigone éternelle', quoted in Thébaud, *La Femme*, p. 248.
108. Madeleine Vernet, 'Appel aux Femmes', *La Mère Educatrice*, January 1921, in *Le Grief des Femmes*, pp. 211–13.
109. Siegel, ' "To the Unknown Mother of the Unknown Soldier" ', pp. 425, 449.
110. Ibid., p. 437.
111. Ibid., pp. 440, 442.
112. Ibid., pp. 441, 447.
113. Blondel, 'La Solidarité Française et les Femmes', in Di Caprio and Weisner, *Lives and Voices*, pp. 491–3.

8 Vichy France: reviving the 'natural woman', 1940–1944

1. The vote was 569 for dissolution, 80 against. The 'no' vote may have been stronger had the Communists and another 27 MPs (who had headed to Algeria hoping to establish a government-in-exile) been able to take part. The yes vote came mostly from conservatives and Radicals, but only 36 socialists voted against.

2. The best analysis of the French defeat is Julian Jackson, *The Fall of France: the Nazi invasion of 1940* (Oxford: Oxford University Press, 2003). For a summary, see Charles Sowerwine, *France since 1870: culture, politics and society* (Houndmills, Basingstoke: Palgrave, 2001), pp. 184–92; Jean-Pierre Azéma, *From Munich to the Liberation 1938–1944*, trans. Janet Lloyd (Cambridge and Paris: Cambridge University Press and Maison des Sciences de l'Homme, 1984), pp. 29–50.

3. Quoted in Sowerwine, ibid., p. 188.

4. Sarah Fishman, *We Will Wait: wives of French prisoners of war, 1940–1945* (New Haven and London: Yale University Press, 1991), p. 25; Sowerwine, *France since 1870*, p. 191.

5. Fishman, ibid., pp. 24–6.

6. Ibid., p. 27.

7. Robert O. Paxton, *Vichy France: old guard and new order 1940–1944*, reprint of 1982 edn (New York: Columbia University Press, 2001), pp. 143–5.

8. Christine Bard, *Les Femmes dans la société française au 20e siècle* (Paris: Armand Colin, 2001), p. 137.

9. Ibid., p. 133.

10. Fishman, *We Will Wait*, pp. 74–5, 134–42.

11. Quoted in Hanna Diamond, 'Libération! Quelle Libération? L'expérience des femmes toulousaines', *Clio, Histoire, Femmes et Sociétés*, 1 (1995), 91.

12. Fishman, *We Will Wait*, pp. 61–2.

13. Ibid., pp. 63–8.

14. Azéma, *From Munich to the Liberation*, pp. 102–3.

15. Sowerwine, *France since 1870*, pp. 204–5; Paxton, *Vichy France*, p. 237.

16. Bard, *Les Femmes*, p. 139.

17. Christiane Germain and C. de Panafieu (eds), *La Mémoire des femmes: sept témoignages de femmes nées avec le siècle* (Paris: Sylvie Messinger, 1982), p. 150.

18. Fishman, *We Will Wait*, pp. 57–60; Bard, *Les Femmes*, p. 138.

19. Quoted in Sowerwine, *France since 1870*, p. 204.

20. Azéma, *From Munich to the Liberation*, pp. 101–2.

21. For a balanced summary, see John F. Sweets, 'Hold that Pendulum! Redefining Fascism, Collaborationism and Resistance in France', *French Historical Studies* 15 (1987–1988), 731–58.

22. Sowerwine provides a clear summary in *France since 1870*, pp. 196–8.

23. Poster reproduced in Miranda Pollard, *Reign of Virtue: mobilizing gender in Vichy France* (Chicago: University of Chicago Press, 1998), p. 4. The 'French Legion of Veterans' was the returned servicemen's association re-organised under Vichy to support the regime.

24. Quoted in Julian Jackson, *France the Dark Years 1940–1944* (Oxford: Oxford University Press, 2001), p. 34.

25. Gustave Thibon, quoted in ibid., p. 328.

26. The images reproduced in Pollard, *Reign of Virtue*, commonly show three to five children. One which advertises benefits for large families shows nine children (figure 10).

27. Francine Muel-Dreyfus, *Vichy and the Eternal Feminine: a contribution to a political sociology of gender*, trans. Kathleen A. Johnson (Durham and London: Duke University Press, 2001), pp. 110–22.

28. Philippe Pétain, 'Allocution du 25 mars 1941', published in *Discours aux Français 17 juin 1940–20 août 1944*, ed. Jean-Claude Barbas (Paris: Albin Michel, 1989), pp. 133–4.
29. Paule Marie Weyd, *Vie Paysanne féminine* (Angers: Ecole supérieure d'agriculture et de viticulture d'Angers, 1942), pp. 19, 153.
30. Quoted in Pollard, *Reign of Virtue*, p. 51.
31. On the repression of 'desire', see particularly ibid., pp. 56–9.
32. Muel-Dreyfus, *Vichy and the Eternal Feminine*, pp. 117, 171–2.
33. Weyd, *Vie Paysanne*, pp. 106–7.
34. Quoted in Pollard, *Reign of Virtue*, p. 57.
35. For a discussion of Vichy's science, see Muel-Dreyfus, *Vichy and the Eternal Feminine*, pp. 286–90; Jackson, *The Dark Years*, pp. 327–30.
36. Dr E. J. Roy, *L'Avortement: Fléau national* (1944), quoted in Pollard, *Reign of Virtue*, p. 59.
37. Pollard, ibid., pp. 66–9.
38. Jackson, *The Dark Years*, p. 330.
39. Bard, *Les Femmes*, pp. 134–5.
40. Jackson, *The Dark Years*, p. 333.
41. Quoted in Pollard, *Reign of Virtue*, p. 13.
42. Bard, *Les Femmes*, p. 136.
43. Quoted in Pollard, *Reign of Virtue*, p. 150.
44. Bard, *Les Femmes*, p. 136.
45. See Pollard, *Reign of Virtue*, p. 159.
46. Catherine Omnès, *Ouvrières Parisiennes: Marchés du travail et trajectoires professionnelles au 20e siècle* (Paris: Editions de l'Ecole des Hautes Etudes en Sciences Sociales, 1997), pp. 233–44.
47. Pollard, *Reign of Virtue*, pp. 153–62; Bard, *Les Femmes*, pp. 136–7.
48. Quoted in Muel-Dreyfus, *Vichy and the Eternal Feminine*, pp. 176, 183–4.
49. Bard, *Les Femmes*, pp. 131–2.
50. Muel-Dreyfus, *Vichy and the Eternal Feminine*, p. 189; Weyd, *Vie Paysanne*, pp. 105–9, 129–30.
51. Weyd, ibid., pp. 34, 109–10; Berthe Bernage, *Brigitte, Femme de France* (1940), quoted in Colette Cosnier, 'Maréchal, nous voilà! Ou *Brigitte* de Berthe Bernage', in *Un Siècle d'antiféminisme*, sous la direction de Christine Bard (Paris: Fayard, 1999), p. 250.
52. 'Discours du 8 juillet 1941', published in *Discours aux Français*, pp. 147–55 (quotation p. 150).
53. Sowerwine, *France since 1870*, p. 200.
54. See the discussion in Muel-Dreyfus, *Vichy and the Eternal Feminine*, pp. 295–309; Rita Thalmann, 'Vichy et l'Antiféminisme', in *Un Siècle d'Antiféminisme*, pp. 229–39.
55. Georgette Varenne, *La Femme dans la France nouvelle* (1940), quoted in Muel-Dreyfus, ibid., p. 186.
56. Muel-Dreyfus, ibid., pp. 176, 240–5; Jackson, *The Dark Years*, p. 332.
57. *Le Temps*, 20 October 1940, quoted in Muel-Dreyfus, ibid., p. 235.
58. Quoted in Margaret Collins Weitz, *Sisters in the Resistance: how women fought to free France, 1940–1945* (New York: John Wiley and Sons, 1995), pp. 53–5.
59. *La Légion*, 15 April 1942, quoted in Muel-Dreyfus, *Vichy and the Eternal Feminine*, p. 187.

60. Ibid., p. 188.
61. *L'Instituteur et son role dans la restauration de la famille française*, quoted in ibid., p. 187.
62. See Jackson, *The Dark Years*, p. 328.
63. Muel-Dreyfus, *Vichy and the Eternal Feminine*, p. 253.
64. Weyd, *Vie Paysanne*, pp. 60, 114–15.
65. Muel-Dreyfus, *Vichy and the Eternal Feminine*, pp. 294–5.
66. See Fishman, *We Will Wait*, p. 38, for examples.
67. The relationship between Vichy and the Catholic Church is also the subject of considerable debate. The Church gave official sanction to the regime. However, some clergy later criticised its anti-Semitic measures and many Catholics broke with the Church when the deportations began. See Paxton, *Vichy France*, pp. 148–53, 268–73. For a more extended discussion, see W. D. Halls, *Politics, Society and Christianity in Vichy France* (Oxford: Berg, 1995).
68. 'Lise', in Anne Roche and Marie-Claude Taranger (eds), *Celles qui n'ont pas écrit: récits de femmes dans la région marseillaise, 1914–1945* (La Calaude, Aix-en-Provence: Edisud, 1995), p. 122.
69. John F. Sweets, *Choices in Vichy France: the French under Nazi occupation* (Oxford: Oxford University Press, 1986).
70. Paula Schwartz, 'Résistance et différence des sexes', in *Clio, Histoire, Femmes et Sociétés* 1 (1995), 76.
71. Weitz, *Sisters in the Resistance*, p. 264.
72. Bard, *Les Femmes*, pp. 132–3.
73. F. Leclerc and M. Weindling, 'La répression des femmes coupables d'avoir collaboré pendant l'Occupation', in *Clio, histoire, femmes et sociétés* 1 (1995), 133, 139, 142.
74. G. D., quoted in ibid., p. 140. The authors point out that the history of women who worked for the Gestapo or the German army remains to be written.
75. Weitz, *Sisters in the Resistance*, p. 269.
76. Jackson, *The Dark Years*, p. 335.
77. Weitz, *Sisters in the Resistance*, pp. 273–85.
78. This is the argument of François Rouquet, in Christine Fauré (dir.), *Encyclopédie politique et historique des femmes* (Paris: PUF, 1997), quoted in Bard, *Les Femmes*, p. 139.
79. For a fuller discussion, see Michael R. Marrus and Robert O. Paxton, *Vichy France and the Jews* (New York: Basic Books, 1981).
80. Rita Thalmann, 'L'Oubli des femmes dans l'historiographie de la Résistance', in *Clio, Histoire, Femmes et Sociétés* 1 (1995), 24.
81. Sowerwine, *France since 1870*, pp. 207–12; Bard, *Les Femmes*, pp. 144–7.
82. Bard, ibid., p. 146.
83. Sowerwine, *France since 1870*, p. 210.
84. Françoise Thébaud, 'Résistances et Libérations', in *Clio, Histoire, Femmes et Sociétés* 1 (1995), 11–19. See also Paula Schwartz, 'Redefining Resistance: women's activism in wartime France', in Margaret Randolph Higonnet *et al.* (eds), *Behind the Lines: gender and the two World Wars* (New Haven and London: Yale University Press, 1987), pp. 141–53.
85. Thalmann, 'L'Oubli des femmes', p. 27.

86. Ibid., pp. 32–3; Schwartz, 'Redefining Resistance', p. 144.
87. Marie-Françoise Brive, 'Les Résistantes et la Résistance', in *Clio, histoire, femmes et sociétés* 1 (1995), 61.
88. Schwartz, 'Redefining Resistance', p. 151; Thalmann, 'L'Oubli des femmes', pp. 22–3.
89. Thalmann, ibid., pp. 27–31; Schwartz, ibid., pp. 147–8.
90. Quoted in Thalmann, ibid., p. 31.
91. Schwartz, 'Résistance et différence des sexes', pp. 81–2.
92. Tract reproduced in Bard, *Les Femmes*, p. 145.
93. Schwartz, 'Redefining Resistance', p. 143.
94. Thalmann, 'L'Oubli des femmes', pp. 23–5.
95. Schwartz, 'Redefining Resistance', pp. 144–6.
96. Fabrice Virgili, 'Les "tondues" à la Libération: le corps des femmes, enjeu d'une réappropriation', in *Clio, histoire, femmes et sociétés* 1 (1995), 114.
97. Claire Duchen, *Women's Rights and Women's Lives in France 1944–1968* (London and New York: Routledge, 1994), p. 13.
98. Luc Capdevila and Fabrice Virgili, 'Epuration et tonte des collaboratrices: un antiféminisme?', in Bard (ed.), *Un Siècle d'antiféminisme*, p. 256; Leclerc and Weindling, 'La répression des femmes', pp. 131–3.
99. Bard, *Les Femmes*, p. 151.
100. Capdevila and Virgili, 'Epuration et tonte des collaboratrices', p. 257.
101. Leclerc and Weindling, 'La répression des femmes', pp. 139, 133.
102. Y. T., quoted in ibid., p. 146. Montoire was the site of a meeting between Hitler and Pétain on 24 October 1940, after which Pétain announced that France would collaborate with Nazi Germany. This brought some concessions in the terms of the occupation. See Jackson, *The Dark Years*, pp. 172–4.
103. Capdevila and Virgili, 'Epuration et tonte des collaboratrices', p. 257.
104. Fabrice Virgili, *La France 'virile': Des femmes tondues à la liberation* (Paris: Payot, 2000), pp. 7, 22–8.
105. Capdevila and Virgili, 'Epuration et tonte des collaboratrices', pp. 259–60.
106. Jackson, *The Dark Years*, pp. 336–8.
107. Virgili, *La France 'virile'*, pp. 44–7, 53–6; Capdevila and Virgili, 'Epuration et tonte des collaboratrices', p. 262.
108. Virgili, 'Les "tondues" à la Libération', p. 113.
109. Capdevila and Virgili, 'Epuration et tonte des collaboratrices', p. 258.
110. Henri Amouroux, *La Grande Histoire des Français sous l'Occupation*, vol. 8: *Joies et douleurs du peuple libéré* (Paris: Editions Robert Laffont, 1988), pp. 527, 530, 532; Virgili, *La France 'virile'*, p. 247.
111. Duchen, *Women's Rights and Women's Lives*, p. 16.
112. Quoted in Capdevila and Virgili, 'Epuration et tonte des collaboratrices', p. 264.
113. Jackson, *The Dark Years*, p. 336.
114. M. Kelly, 'Reconstructing Masculinity at the Liberation', in H. R. Kedward and Nancy Wood (eds), *The Liberation of France: image and event* (Oxford and Washington: Berg, 1995), pp. 117–28.

115. Virgili, *La France 'virile'*, pp. 10, 50, 264–6; Virgili, 'Les "tondues" à la Libération', p. 115.
116. Virgili, 'Les "tondues" à la Libération', p. 126; Capdevila and Virgili, 'Epuration et tonte des collaboratrices', p. 263.
117. Weyd, *Vie Paysanne*, pp. 163–87.
118. Diamond, 'Libération!', p. 93.
119. Schwartz, 'Redefining Resistance, p. 153.

9   From the liberation to 'women's liberation', 1945–1975

1. Hanna Diamond, 'Libération! Quelle Libération? L'Expérience des Femmes Toulousaines', *Clio, Histoire, Femmes et Sociétés* 1 (1985), 99.
2. Claire Duchen, *Women's Rights and Women's Lives in France* (London and New York: Routledge, 1994), pp. 17, 29; Charles Sowerwine, *France since 1870: culture, politics and society* (Houndmills, Basingstoke: Palgrave, 2001), pp. 232–3.
3. Sowerwine, ibid., p. 232.
4. Duchen, *Women's Rights*, pp. 18–21.
5. Diamond, 'Libération!', pp. 100–1.
6. Sarah Fishman, *We Will Wait: wives of French prisoners of war, 1940–1945* (New Haven: Yale University Press, 1991), pp. 147–65.
7. Mme Augot, quoted in Diamond, 'Libération!', p. 99.
8. Mme Rivals, quoted in ibid., p. 98.
9. On this point see Karen Adler, 'No Words to Say It? Women and the Expectation of Liberation', in H. R. Kedward and Nancy Wood (eds), *The Liberation of France: image and event* (Oxford and Washington: Berg, 1995), pp. 77–89.
10. See the official record of the debate, reproduced with commentary by William Guéraiche in 'Documents', *Clio, Histoire, Femmes et Sociétés* 1 (1995), 263–71.
11. William Guéraiche, 'Les femmes politiques de 1944 à 1947: quelle libération?', *Clio, Histoire, Femmes et Sociétés* 1 (1995), 167–8.
12. Duchen, *Women's Rights*, pp. 33–4.
13. Guéraiche, 'Les femmes politiques', pp. 169–76.
14. Sowerwine, *France since 1870*, p. 222.
15. 'Documents', pp. 67–8; Guéraiche, 'Les femmes politiques', pp. 170–3.
16. 'Documents', pp. 265, 268.
17. 'A. H.', quoted in Christine Bard, *Les Filles de Marianne: Histoire des féminismes 1914–1940* (Paris: Fayard, 1995), p. 449.
18. Hilary Footitt, 'The First Women *Députés*: "les 33 Glorieuses"?', in *The Liberation of France*, pp. 129–41.
19. Ibid., p. 132.
20. Duchen, *Women's Rights*, p. 39.
21. Ibid., pp. 38–40; Sowerwine, *France since 1870*, pp. 237–9. Duchen points out that other factors like regional and age differences would need to be studied in order to determine whether the voting difference was actually a 'gender' difference.

22. Quoted in Footitt, 'The First Women *Députés*', p. 134.
23. Footitt, ibid., pp. 129–31.
24. Quoted in ibid., pp. 130–1.
25. Guéraiche, 'Les femmes politiques', p. 185; Duchen, *Women's Rights*, pp. 48–53.
26. Diamond, 'Libération!', pp. 104–9.
27. Interview quoted in Bard, *Les Filles de Marianne*, p. 450.
28. Madame Augot, quoted in Diamond, 'Libération!', p. 108.
29. Christine Bard, *Les Femmes dans la société française au 20e siècle* (Paris: Armand Colin, 2001), pp. 157–60.
30. Duchen, *Women's Rights*, p. 44.
31. See, for instance, Claire Duchen, 'Une femme nouvelle pour une France nouvelle?', *Clio, Histoire, Femmes et Sociétés*, 1 (1985), 162; Jane Jenner, 'The Liberation and New Rights for French Women', in Margaret Randolph Higonnet *et al.* (eds), *Behind the Lines: gender and the two World Wars* (New Haven and London: Yale University Press, 1987), p. 281.
32. Duchen, *Women's Rights*, p. 97; Sowerwine, *France since 1870*, p. 276.
33. Quoted in Susan Weiner, 'Two Modernities: From *Elle* to *Mademoiselle*. Women's Magazines in Post-war France', *Contemporary European History* 8, 3 (1999), 398.
34. See the illustrations in Susan Weiner, *Enfants Terribles: youth and femininity in the mass media in France, 1945–1968* (Baltimore and London: Johns Hopkins University Press, 2001), figures 2, 3 and 5.
35. See Elizabeth Wilson, *Adorned in Dreams: fashion and modernity* (London: Virago, 1985).
36. On the fetishistic elements of fashion, see David Kunzle, *Fashion and Fetishism: a social history of the corset, tight-lacing and other forms of body-sculpture in the West* (Totowa, N.J.: Rowman and Littlefield, 1982); Valerie Steele, *Fashion and Eroticism: ideals of feminine beauty from the Victorian era to the Jazz Age* (New York: Oxford University Press, 1985).
37. Susan Weiner, 'Two Modernities', p. 399.
38. Ibid., p. 398; Sowerwine, *France since 1870*, pp. 276, 278; Duchen, *Women's Rights*, p. 82.
39. Weiner, *Enfants Terribles*, p. 32.
40. Quoted in Duchen, *Women's Rights*, p. 70.
41. Duchen, ibid., p. 74.
42. See the accounts of Olga Varni and Suzanne Lehmann-Lefranc in Christiane Germain and C. de Panafieu (eds), *La mémoire des femmes: sept témoignages de femmes nées avec le siècle* (Paris: Sylvie Messinger, 1982), pp. 70, 171.
43. Duchen, *Women's Rights*, p. 80.
44. Diamond, 'Libération!', p. 101.
45. Duchen, *Women's Rights*, p. 146; Duchen, 'Une femme nouvel', p. 158.
46. Weiner, 'Two Modernities', p. 401.
47. Duchen, *Women's Rights*, pp. 80–1.
48. Raw figures 1911–1991 from B. R. Mitchell, *International historical statistics, Europe, 1750–1993*, 4th edn (London and New York: Macmillan Reference and Stockton Press, 1998), Table B1, 'Economically Active Population by Major Industrial Groups', p. 149.

49. Duchen, *Women's Rights*, pp. 136–7, 140–3, 153.
50. Duchen, 'Une femme nouvel', p. 158.
51. Duchen, *Women's Rights*, pp. 143, 153, 159.
52. Sowerwine, *France since 1870*, pp. 260–1.
53. Jenner, 'The Liberation and New Rights', pp. 274–83.
54. Duchen, *Women's Rights*, p. 58.
55. Lisa Greenwald, 'Not "Undifferentiated Magma": refashioning a female identity in France, 1944–55', *Historical Reflections/Réflexions historiques* 22, 2 (1996), 407–30; Miranda Pollard, 'Sexing the Subject: women and the French right, 1938–58', in Nicholas Atkin and Frank Tallett (eds), *The Right in France, 1789–1997* (London and New York: I. B. Tauris Publishers, 1998), pp. 231–44.
56. Sylvie Chaperon, *Les Années Beauvoir 1945–1970* (Paris: Fayard, 2000), pp. 115–25.
57. Ibid., pp. 116, 120–1.
58. Ibid., pp. 122–5.
59. Weiner, 'Two Modernities', p. 402.
60. Quoted in Duchen, *Women's Rights*, p. 68.
61. Weiner, 'Two Modernities', pp. 404–7.
62. Claire Laubier (ed.), *The Condition of Women in France 1945 to the Present: a documentary anthology* (London: Routledge, 1990), pp. 48, 51.
63. Anne-Marie Sohn, *Age Tendre et Tête de Bois: Histoire des Jeunes des années 1960* (Paris: Hachette Littératures, 2001), pp.13–16, 41–2.
64. Sohn, *Age Tendre*, pp. 28–31; 62–3.
65. Raw figures from Table 1.5, 'L'Evolution du nombre d'étudiantes par discipline', in Laubier (ed.), *The Condition of Women in France*, p. 13.
66. Sohn, *Age Tendre*, pp. 66–8; Weiner, *Enfants Terribles*, p. 144.
67. Weiner, ibid., pp. 145–6.
68. http://fr.music.yahoo.com/biographies/sylvie_vartan.html, accessed Monday, 17 February 2003.
69. Sohn, *Age Tendre*, pp. 67–70; Laubier (ed.), *The Condition of Women in France*, pp. 29, 31.
70. Sowerwine, *France since 1870*, pp. 277–8.
71. Sohn, *Age Tendre*, pp. 72–8. Spending on clothes increased almost as much for boys under 20 (103 per cent) as for girls (131 per cent) between 1953 and 1964–1965 (p. 71).
72. Weiner, *Enfants Terribles*, pp. 148–9.
73. Ibid., pp. 150–3; Sohn, *Age Tendre*, pp. 90–1.
74. Verena Aebischer and Sonia Dayan-Herzbrun, 'Cinéma et destins de femmes', *Cahiers internationaux de sociologie* 80 (1986), extracted in Laubier (ed.), *The Condition of Women in France*, pp. 34–9.
75. http://www.aplmusique.com/vartan/vartan161.htm#libre, accessed Monday, 17 February 2003.
76. Sohn, *Age Tendre*, pp. 102–115.
77. Ibid., pp. 121–7, 149, 152.
78. Laubier (ed.), *The Condition of Women in France*, p. 48.
79. http://www.aplmusique.com/vartan/vartan161.htm#libre, accessed Monday, 17 February 2003.
80. Sohn, *Age Tendre*, pp. 220–2.

81. Ibid., pp. 224–7.
82. Chaperon, *Les Années Beauvoir*, pp. 273–7.
83. Ibid., pp. 324–6.
84. Ibid., pp. 238–43; Claire Duchen, *Women's Rights*, pp. 173–4.
85. Marie-Françoise Lévy, 'Le mouvement français pour le planning familial et les jeunes', *Vingtième siècle: revue d'histoire* 75 (July–Sep. 2002), 77.
86. Ibid., p. 83; Chaperon, *Les Années Beauvoir*, pp. 277–80.
87. Duchen, *Women's Rights*, pp. 119–22.
88. Mitterrand stated his support for legalising contraception in an interview with *La Femme du XXe Siècle*, no. 3 (Oct.–Nov. 1965), p. 4. See C. Sowerwine, 'Roudy, Yvette (née Yvette Saldou)', forthcoming in C. Pennetier (ed.), *Dictionnaire biographique du mouvement ouvrier français*, Part V, 12 vols (Paris: Editions de l'atelier, 2004–2006).
89. Chaperon, *Les Années Beauvoir*, pp. 278–86, 314–22.
90. Ibid., pp. 322–3; Lévy, 'Le mouvement français', p. 83.
91. Quoted in Lévy, ibid., pp. 78–9.
92. Sohn, *Age Tendre*, pp. 316–23.
93. For fuller discussion see David Caute, *Sixty-eight: the year of the barricades* (London: Hamilton, 1988). See also Marc Rohan (ed.), *Paris '68: graffiti, posters, newspapers, and poems of the events of May 1968* (London: Impact Books, 1988). For an international perspective, see Detlef Junker, Philipp Gassert and Carole Fink (eds), *1968, The World Transformed* (Cambridge: Cambridge University Press, 1998).
94. Kristin Ross, *May '68 and its afterlives* (Chicago and London: University of Chicago Press, 2002), p. 155.
95. Quoted in Chaperon, *Les Années Beauvoir*, p. 347.
96. Duchen, *Women's Rights*, pp. 197–8.
97. Françoise Picq, 'The MLF: run for your life', in Claire Duchen (ed. and trans.), *French Connections: voices from the women's liberation movement in France* (Amherst: University of Massachusetts Press, 1987), pp. 24–5.
98. 'On ne naît pas femme, on le devient': literally, 'one is not born woman, one becomes it'. Simone de Beauvoir, *Le Deuxième Sexe*, 2 vols (Paris: Gallimard, 1949), vol. 1, p. 287. See also *The Second Sex*, trans. and ed. H. M. Parshley (London: Jonathan Cape, 1953), p. 295.
99. On the reception and influence of *The Second Sex*, see Chaperon, *Les Années Beauvoir*, pp. 151–201.
100. See Françoise Picq, *Libération des Femmes: Les Années-Mouvement* (Paris: Editions du Seuil, 1993).
101. Chaperon, *Les Années Beauvoir*, p. 361.
102. Poem reproduced in Duchen, *Women's Rights*, p. 202.
103. Picq, *Libération des Femmes*, pp.112–19.
104. Ibid., pp. 115, 118, 187.
105. 'Un Appel de 343 femmes', 'Notre Ventre nous appartient', and 'Dossier sur l'avortement', *Le Nouvel observateur*, 5 April 1971, pp. 5, 6, 40ff.
106. Picq, *Libération des Femmes*, pp. 62–4; *Les Femmes s'Affichent: Affiches du Mouvement de Libération des Femmes en France depuis 1970* (Paris: Syros, 1984), pp. 23–37.

107. 'Speech for the Defence by Learned Counsel Gisèle Halimi', in Association Choisir, *Abortion: the Bobigny affair—a law on trial*, trans. Beryl Henderson (Sydney: Wild & Woolley, 1975), pp. 125–52.
108. Lévy, 'Le mouvement français', p. 84.
109. Reproduced in *Abortion: the Bobigny affair*, pp. 166–75.
110. Picq, *Libération des Femmes*, pp. 153–8.
111. Ibid., pp. 162–71.

10   The politics of 'women's place' since 1975

1. Maíre F. Cross, 'Women and Politics', in Abigail Gregory and Ursula Tidd (eds), *Women in Contemporary France* (Oxford and New York: Berg, 2000), pp. 89–111; Raylene L. Ramsey, *French Women in Politics: writing power, paternal legitimization, and maternal legacies* (New York and Oxford: Berghahn Books, 2003), pp. 276–7.
2. Charles Sowerwine, *France since 1870: culture, politics and society* (Houndmills, Basingstoke: Palgrave, 2001), pp. 375–7.
3. Françoise Gaspard, 'L'Antiféminisme en politique', in Christine Bard (ed.), *Un Siècle d'Antiféminisme* (Paris: Fayard, 1999), p. 352.
4. Jane Jenson and Mariette Sineau, *Mitterrand et les Françaises. Un rendez-vous manqué* (Paris: Presses des Sciences Po, 1995), quoted in Françoise Thébaud, 'Promouvoir les droits des femmes: ambitions, difficultés et résultats', in Serge Bernstein, Pierre Milza and J.-L. Bianco (eds), *Les Années Mitterrand: Les années du changement (1981–1984)* (Paris: Perrin, 2001), p. 570.
5. Parti communiste français and Parti socialiste (France), *Programme commun de gouvernement du Parti communiste français et du Parti socialiste (27 juin 1972)* (Paris: Éditions sociales, 1972) unpaginated; Charles Sowerwine, 'Mitterrand's policies on women', unpublished paper (2000), pp. 2–4.
6. Charles Sowerwine, 'ROUDY, Yvette (née Yvette SALDOU)', forthcoming in Claude Pennetier (ed.), *Dictionnaire biographique du mouvement ouvrier français*, part V, 12 vols (Paris: Editions de l'atelier, 2004–2006); Thébaud, 'Promouvoir les droits des femmes', p. 571.
7. Sowerwine, 'ROUDY, Yvette'; Thébaud, 'Promouvoir les droits des femmes', p. 571.
8. Quoted in Sowerwine, *France since 1870*, p. 386.
9. Thébaud, 'Promouvoir les droits des femmes', pp. 571–2.
10. Sowerwine, *France since 1870*, p. 380.
11. Siân Reynolds, 'The French Ministry of Women's Rights 1981–86: modernisation or marginalisation?', in John Gaffney (ed.), *France and modernisation* (Aldershot: Avebury, 1988), p. 151.
12. Thébaud, 'Promouvoir les droits des femmes', pp. 574–6.
13. Ibid., pp. 578–91; Sowerwine, *France since 1870*, p. 386; Sowerwine, 'ROUDY, Yvette'.
14. Quoted in Thébaud, ibid., p. 576.
15. Thébaud, ibid., pp. 577, 594–5; Yvette Roudy, *Parcours. Entretien avec Delphine Gardey et Jacqueline Laufer* (Paris: Editions du Club Zéro, 2002), p. 38.

16. Thébaud, ibid., pp. 588–9.
17. Letter of Catherine X to François Mitterrand, 1 November 1982, quoted in Thébaud, ibid., p. 583, note 63.
18. Thébaud, ibid., pp. 581–2.
19. Ibid., pp. 594–9.
20. Christine Bard, *Les Femmes dans la société française au 20e siècle* (Paris: Armand Colin, 2001), pp. 180–1.
21. Ramsay, *French Women in Politics*, pp. 87–91. Prominent daughters in politics since the 1990s include Frédérique Bredin and Martine Aubry (Socialist Party), and Michèle Alliot-Marie (RPR).
22. 'Proportion des femmes élues à l'Assemblée Nationale depuis la 1ère assemblée constituante d'octobre 1945', official website of the *Observatoire de la parité entre hommes et femmes*, available at http://www.observatoire-parite.gouv.fr/, accessed Tuesday, 25 February 2003.
23. Janine Mossuz-Lavau, 'Gender Parity in Politics', website of the Embassy of France in the United States, 18 May 2001, available at http://www.info-france-usa.org/atoz/gdr_pol.asp, accessed Tuesday, 25 February 2003.
24. Marie-Jo Zimmermann, 'Elections à venir: faire vivre la parité', appendices, Table 3: 'Femmes dans la Chambre unique ou basse des 25 membres de l'Union européenne, par ordre décroissant en pourcentage', available at http://www.observatoire-parite.gouv.fr/, accessed 6 January 2004.
25. Gaspard, 'L'Antiféminisme en politique', pp. 343–4; Cross, 'Women and Politics', p. 101.
26. Gaspard, ibid., pp. 339–54; Françoise Gaspard, 'Système politique et rareté des femmes élues. Spécificités françaises?', in Armelle Le Bras-Chopard and Janine Mossuz-Lavau (eds), *Les Femmes et la Politique* (Paris: L'Harmattan, 1997), pp. 97–118.
27. Ramsay, *French Women in Politics*, pp. 103–8.
28. Gaspard, 'Système politique', pp. 102–3; Gaspard, 'L'Antiféminisme en politique', pp. 341–2.
29. Sowerwine, *France since 1870*, pp. 388–9.
30. Nona Mayer and Mariette Sineau, 'III: France: The *Front National*,' in H. Ambsberger and B. Halbmayre (eds), *Rechtsextreme Parteien* (forthcoming Leverkusen: Leske & Budrich, 2002), pp. 42–103; available at http://elections2002.sciences-po.fr/Enjeux/enjeux.html, from link 'Women and the National Front/Le Front National et les femmes', accessed Sunday, 2 March 2003. See also Françoise Gaspard, *A Small City in France*, trans. Arthur Goldhammer (Cambridge, Mass.: Harvard University Press, 1995).
31. Jean-François Sirinelli, 'L'Extrême Droite à Répétition', in Jean-Pierre Rioux and Jean-François Sirinelli (eds), *La France d'un siècle à l'autre 1914–2000, Dictionnaire Critique* (Paris: Hachette Littératures, 1999), pp. 891–9.
32. Mayer and Sineau, 'III: France: The *Front National*', pp. 42–103.
33. Ibid., pp. 45–6.
34. Harvey G. Simmons, *The French National Front: the extremist challenge to democracy* (Boulder, Col.: Westview Press, 1996), p. 243. The current FN policy (January 2004) also includes a discussion of the 'French

demographic winter' and expresses alarm at the immigrant birth rate. See 'Le programme du Front National', available at http://www.frontnational.com/prog_famille.php, accessed 8 January 2004.

35. Mayer and Sineau, 'III: France: The *Front National*', p. 73.
36. Ibid., p. 74. See also the current 'programme du Front National'.
37. J. Marcilly, *Le Pen sans Bandeau* (Paris: Grancher, 1984), quoted in ibid., p. 80.
38. Quoted in Simmons, *The French National Front*, p. 244.
39. Mayer and Sineau, 'III: France: The *Front National*', pp. 66, 70.
40. 'Interview de M. F. Stirbois: 4) Elue mais non moins femme: Retrouvez ses passions', available at http://votants.free.fr/UE/stirbois4.htm, accessed 8 January 2004.
41. Nona Mayer, *Ces Français qui votent Front national* (Paris: Flammarion, 1999) cited in Mayer and Sineau, 'III: France: The *Front National*', p. 57, note 5.
42. Emmanuel Todd, *The Making of Modern France: politics, ideology and culture*, trans. A. and B. Forster (London: Basil Blackwell, 1991), pp. 196–8.
43. According to a 1997 survey, 59 per cent of voters held this view. See Mayer and Sineau, 'III: France: The *Front National*', p. 47.
44. Jean-Marie Le Pen, quoted in Simmons, *The French National Front*, p. 240.
45. Mayer and Sineau, 'III: France: The *Front National*', pp. 55–7.
46. Jean-Marie Le Pen, *Les Français d'abord* (Paris: Carrère/Laffon, 1984), quoted in Simmons, *The French National Front*, p. 239.
47. Jean-Marie. Le Pen, *L'Espoir* (Paris: Albatros, 1989), quoted in Simmons, ibid., p. 248, note 21.
48. Mayer and Sineau, 'III: France: The *Front National*', p. 65.
49. Jean-Marie Le Pen, interview with *Agir* (an FN youth publication), 1998, quoted in ibid., p. 59. Jany later left Le Pen. She posed as a 'housewife' for *Playboy* magazine, perhaps in a gesture of revenge.
50. 'Le Pen et Filles', 29 November 2002, in *Le Monde.fr*, available at http://www.lemonde.fr:80/cgi-bin/ACHATS/ARCHIVES/
51. Mayer and Sineau, 'III: France: The *Front National*', pp. 54–5, 68–9, 82–3.
52. Quoted in ibid., p. 75.
53. Ibid.
54. 'Le programme du Front National'.
55. Simmons, *The French National Front*, p. 249, note 34.
56. Mossuz-Lavau, 'Gender Parity in Politics'.
57. Françoise Gaspard, Claude Servan-Schreiber and Anne Le Gall, *Au Pouvoir Citoyennes! Liberté, Egalité, Parité* (Paris: Seuil, 1992), pp. 88–9.
58. Danielle Haase-Dubosc, 'Sexual difference and politics in France today', *Feminist Studies* (Spring, 1999), 3, available at http://www.findarticles.com, accessed 8 January 2004.
59. Mossuz-Lavau, 'Gender Parity in Politics'.
60. For an outline of the arguments for and against parity, see Mossuz-Lavau, 'Gender Parity in Politics'; Haase-Dubosc, 'Sexual Difference and Politics'.
61. Quoted in Bard, *Les Femmes*, p. 182.

62. Roudy, *Parcours*, p. 18; Mossuz-Lavau, 'Gender Parity in Politics'.
63. Haase-Dubosc, 'Sexual Difference and Politics', p. 4.
64. Ramsay, *French Women in Politics*, p. 80.
65. Haase-Dubosc, 'Sexual Difference and Politics', p. 4.
66. *Journal officiel. Débats parlementaires*, 12 March 1997, quoted in Mossuz-Lavau, 'Gender Parity in Politics'.
67. Mossuz-Lavau, 'Gender Parity in Politics'.
68. The provisions of the Parity Law can be viewed on the official website of the *Observatoire de la parité entre les femmes et les hommes*, available at http://www.observatoire-parite.gouv.fr.
69. Ibid.
70. 'Application de la loi du 6 juin 2000 dite sur la parité aux élections législatives de juin 2002', available at http://www.observatoire-parite.gouv.fr/dossier/investiture.html, accessed Tuesday, 25 February 2003.
71. 'En 2002, il n'y aura que six femmes de plus qu'en 1997 dans l'hémicycle', *Le Monde*, 18 June 2002. In January 2004 there were 70 women, still 12 per cent of the total (577).
72. 'Législatives 2002: 3 records?', available at the web site of the *Union Féminine Civique et Sociale*: http://www.ufcs.org/leg02.html, accessed Monday, 24 February 2003.
73. 'Application de la loi du 6 juin 2000 dite sur la parité aux élections législatives de juin 2002'.
74. 'Le Pen and his feminine side', BBC News Online, UK Edition, Tuesday, 28 May 2002, available at: http://news.bbc.co.uk/1/hi/world/europe/2011370.stm, accessed Monday, 24 February 2003.
75. 'Législatives 2002: 3 records?'; 'En 2002, il n'y aura que six femmes de plus qu'en 1997 dans l'hémicycle', *Le Monde*, 18 June 2002.
76. Ibid.
77. 'Martine Aubry, ministre de l'Emploi et de la Solidarité', available at http://decrypt.politique.free.fr/partis/ps/aubry.shtm, accessed Sunday, 23 February 2003.
78. Sowerwine, *France since 1870*, p. 423; Bard, *Les femmes*, p. 179.
79. 'Martine Aubry, la défaite d'un symbole de la gauche', *Le Monde*, 16 June 2002, available at http://www.lemonde.fr/article/0,5987,3224--280729-,00.html, accessed Sunday, 23 February 2003.

Conclusion: equality and 'difference' – 'women's lives from the eighteenth to the twenty-first century

1. S. Rattin, 'L'Agriculture n'est plus un état mais une profession', *INSEE Première* (publication of *L'Institut national de la statistique et des études économiques*), 420 (January 1996), available at http://www.insee.fr/fr/ffc/docs_ffc/femmes_et_hommes.htm, accessed Friday, 13 December 2002.
2. 'Population totale (urbaine et rurale) de la France métropolitaine et densité de la population aux recensements de 1846 à 1999', available at INED (*Institut national d'études démographiques*), http://www.ined.fr/

population-en-chiffres/indexF.html, accessed Friday, 13 December 2002.

3. Raw figures from B. R. Mitchell, *International historical statistics: Europe, 1750–1993*, 4th edn (London and New York: Macmillan Reference; Stockton Press, 1998), Table B1, 'Economically active population by major industrial groups', p. 149.

4. Marion Demossier, 'Women in Rural France', in Abigail Gregory and Ursula Tidd (eds), *Women in Contemporary France* (Oxford and New York: Berg, 2000), pp. 204–5.

5. 'Activité des femmes selon la catégorie socioprofessionnelle du conjoint en 2001', INSEE, *Enquête emploi 2001*; Demossier, 'Women in Rural France', pp. 194–5.

6. Christine Bard, *Les femmes dans la société française au 20e siècle* (Paris: Armand Colin, 2001), p. 216.

7. 'Taux d'activité par tranche d'âge des femmes et des hommes de 1975 à 2001', and 'Actifs occupés selon le sexe et la catégorie professionnelle', in INSEE, *Enquête emploi 2001*; A. Gauvin, 'Emploi des Femmes, tertiarisation de l'emploi et de la société', in *Ephesia, La Place des Femmes: les enjeux de l'identité et de l'égalité au regard des sciences sociales* (Paris: Editions de la Découverte, 1995), pp. 562–8.

8. 'Taux d'activité par tranche d'âge des femmes et des hommes de 1975 à 2001'.

9. Abigail Gregory, 'Women in Paid Work', in *Women in Contemporary France*, p. 23.

10. Ibid., pp. 23–4.

11. C. Borrel and J. Boëldieu, 'De plus en plus de femmes immigrées sur le marché du travail', *INSEE Première*, 791 (July 2001); S. Thave, 'L'Emploi des immigrés en 1999', *INSEE Première*, 717 (May 2000), http://www.insee.fr/fr/ffc/docs_ffc/femmes_et_hommes.htm, accessed Friday, 13 December 2002.

12. Female unemployment peaked at 14.6 per cent in 1994, compared with 10.94 per cent for men. In 2001 the respective rates were 10.9 per cent for women and 7.21 per cent for men. There are significant variations between male and female rates in each age group. See 'Taux de chômage des femmes et des hommes par tranche d'âge de 1990 à 2001', available at http://www.insee.fr/fr/ffc/docs_ffc/ femmes_et_hommes.htm, accessed Friday, 13 December 2002.

13. S. Thave, 'L'Emploi des immigrés en 1999'.

14. 'Taux de réussite au baccalauréat en 2000', available at http:// www.insee.fr/fr/ffc/docs_ffc/femmes_et_hommes.htm, accessed Wednesday, 18 December 2002.

15. 'Effectifs et part des femmes dans les principaux cycles universitaires (rentrée 2000–2001)', available at http://www.insee.fr/fr/ffc/docs_ffc/ femmes_et_hommes.htm, accessed Wednesday, 18 December 2002; Z. Djider, 'Femmes et Hommes: les inégalités subsistent', *INSEE Première*, 834 (March 2002), available at http://www.insee.fr/fr/ffc/docs_ffc/ femmes_et_hommes.htm, accessed Wednesday, 18 December 2002.

16. See the web site 'Conférence des Grandes Ecoles': http://www.cge.asso.fr/ cadre_ecole.html, accessed Wednesday, 18 December 2002.

17. Z. Djider, 'Femmes et Hommes: les inégalités subsistent'.
18. 'Les concours de l'ENA selon le type de concours', available at http://www.insee.fr/fr/ffc/docs_ffc/femmes_et_hommes.htm, accessed Wednesday, 18 December 2002.
19. 'Part des femmes dans l'encadrement des enterprises du secteur privé', and 'Effectifs et part des femmes dans les emplois de direction et d'inspection de la Fonction publique de l'Etat en 2000', both available at http://www.insee.fr/fr/ffc/docs_ffc/femmes_et_hommes.htm, accessed Wednesday, 18 December 2002.
20. Gregory, 'Women in Paid Work', pp. 34–8.
21. Jan Windebank, 'Women's Unpaid Work and Leisure' in *Women in Contemporary France*, pp. 47–64.
22. See Simone de Beauvoir, *Le Deuxième Sexe*, 2 vols (Paris: Gallimard, 1949), vol. 1, pp. 34–5.
23. Joan W. Scott, *Only Paradoxes to Offer: French feminists and the rights of man* (Cambridge, Mass.: Harvard University Press, 1996).
24. Charles Sowerwine, *France since 1870: culture, politics and society* (Houndmills, Basingstoke: Palgrave, 2001), pp. 424–5.
25. Bard, *Les Femmes*, pp. 206–7; Sowerwine, *France since 1870*, p. 426.
26. Bard, ibid., pp. 211–13.
27. Ibid., p. 212.
28. Farhad Khosrokhavar, 'Une laïcité frileuse', *Le Monde*, 20 November 2003.
29. 'Le rapport de la Commission Stasi sur la Laïcité', published in *Le Monde*, 12 December 2003, 17–24 (p. 21).
30. Yvette Roudy, quoted in *Le Monde*, 25 October 1989.
31. Quoted in Philippe Bernard, 'L'Egalité entre les hommes et les femmes au centre de la dernière audience publique de la commission Stasi', *Le Monde*, 16 November 2003.
32. 'Le rapport de la Commission Stasi', p. 22.
33. Michelle Zancarini-Fournel, review of Françoise Gaspard and Fahrad Khosrow-Kharvar, *Le Foulard et la République* (Paris: La Découverte, 1995), in *Clio*, 2 (1995), available at http://clio.revues.org/documents 510.html, accessed 10 January 2004. See also C. Killian, 'The Other Side of the Veil: North African women respond to the headscarf Affair', *Gender and Society*, 17, 4 (2003), 567–91.
34. Leora Auslander, 'Bavarian Crucifixes and French headscarves: religious signs and the postmodern European State', *Cultural Dynamics*, 12, 3 (2000), 283–310.
35. Quoted in Philippe Le Coeur, 'De l'Assemblée nationale au congrès du Parti socialists, onze mois de débat jalonnés de revirements et d'ambiguïtés', *Le Monde*, 12 December 2003.
36. See Joan B. Landes, *Visualizing the Nation: gender, representation, and revolution in eighteenth-century France* (Ithaca and London: Cornell University Press, 2001), Chapter 4.

Suggestions for Further Reading

This list of suggested readings is designed to help the reader pursue themes developed in each chapter. The aim is to provide a list of readily accessible materials in English. Apart from some classic works of special interest, it does not include French titles except in translation.

The list is by chapter. Works relevant to more than one chapter are listed only under the first chapter in which they appear. Thus, for example, Christophe Charle's *Social History of France in the Nineteenth Century* is listed under Chapter 2, but would be relevant for Chapter 3. Readers should therefore scan previous chapters for relevant titles as well as the chapter in which they are particularly interested. In most cases, I have given collections rather than individual essays within them.

Introduction: the French Revolution and gender politics – creating a World of difference

Blum, C. *Rousseau and the Republic of Virtue: The Language of Politics in the French Revolution* (Ithaca: Cornell University Press, 1986).

Elias, N. *The Court Society*, trans. Edmund Jephcott (Oxford: Blackwell, 1983).

Godineau, D. *The Women of Paris and their French Revolution*, trans. Katherine Streip (Berkeley: University of California Press, 1998).

Goodman, D. (ed.) *Marie-Antoinette: Writings on the Body of a Queen* (New York and London: Routledge, 2003).

—— *The Republic of Letters: A Cultural History of the French Enlightenment* (Ithaca and London: Cornell University Press, 1994).

Hesse, C. *The Other Enlightenment: How French Women Became Modern* (Princeton: Princeton University Press, 2001).

Hunt, L. *Politics, Culture and Class in the French Revolution* (Berkeley: University of California Press, 1984).

—— *The Family Romance of the French Revolution* (Berkeley: University of California Press, 1992).

—— (ed.), *Eroticism and the Body Politic* (Baltimore and London: Johns Hopkins University Press, 1991).

Landes, J. B. *Women and the Public Sphere in the Age of the French Revolution* (Ithaca: Cornell University Press, 1988).
—— *Visualizing the Nation: Gender, Representation, and Revolution in Eighteenth-Century France* (Ithaca and London: Cornell University Press, 2001).
Laqueur, T. W. *Making Sex: Body and Gender from the Greeks to Freud* (Cambridge, Mass.: Harvard University Press, 1990).
McMillan, J. F. *France and Women 1789–1914: Gender, Politics and Society* (London and New York: Routledge, 2000).
Offen, K. M. *European Feminisms, 1700–1950: A Political History* (Stanford: Stanford University Press, 2000).
Outram, D. *The Enlightenment* (Cambridge and New York: Cambridge University Press, 1995).
Pateman, C. *The Sexual Contract* (Stanford: Stanford University Press, 1988).
Scott, J. W. *Only Paradoxes to Offer: French Feminists and the Rights of Man* (Cambridge Mass.: Harvard University Press, 1996).

1 Elite women

Bock, G. and P. Thane (eds), *Maternity and Gender Policies: Women and the Rise of the European Welfare States 1880s–1950s* (London: Routledge, 1991).
Darrow, M. 'French Noblewomen and the New Domesticity, 1750–1850', *Feminist Studies*, 5 (1979), 41–65.
Grogan, S. K. 'Women, Philanthropy and the State: The Société de Charité Maternelle in Avignon, 1802–1917', *French History* 14, 3 (2000), 295–321.
Higgs, D. *Nobles in Nineteenth Century France: The Practice of Inegalitarianism* (Baltimore: Johns Hopkins University Press, 1987).
Kale, S. D. 'Women, Salons, and the State in the Aftermath of the French Revolution', *Journal of Women's History* 13, 4 (2002), 54–80.
Margadant, J. B. 'The Duchesse de Berry and Royalist Political Culture in Post-revolutionary France', *History Workshop Journal*, 43 (1997), 23–52.
McLaren, A. 'Doctor in the House: Medicine and Private Morality in France, 1800–1850', *Feminist Studies* 2, 2 (1975), 39–54.
Nord, P. 'Republican Politics and the Bourgeois Interior in Mid-Nineteenth Century France', in S. Nash (ed.), *Home and Its Dislocations in Nineteenth Century France* (New York: State University of New York Press, 1993), pp. 193–214.
Perrot, M. (ed.), *A History of Private Life*, Vol. IV: *From the Fires of Revolution to the Great War*, trans. A. Goldhammer (Cambridge, Mass. and London: Belknap Press, 1990).
Pope, B. C. 'Revolution and Retreat: Upper-Class French Women after 1789', in C. Berkin and C. Lovett (eds), *Women, War and Revolution* (New York: Holmes and Meier, 1980), pp. 215–35.
Reddy, W. H. 'Marriage, Honor, and the Public Sphere in Post-revolutionary France: Séparations de Corps, 1815–1848', *Journal of Modern History* 65 (1993), 437–72.
Smith, B. G. *Ladies of the Leisure Class: The Bourgeoises of Northern France in the Nineteenth Century* (Princeton: Princeton University Press, 1981).

Sohn, A.-M. *Chrysalides: femmes dans la vie privée (XIXe-XXe siècles)* (Paris: Publications de la Sorbonne, 1996).

Strumingher, L. 'L'Ange de la Maison. Mothers and Daughters in Nineteenth Century France', *International Journal of Women's Studies* 2 (1979), 51–61.

Weiss, J. H. 'Origins of the French Welfare State: Poor Relief in the Third Republic, 1871–1914', *French Historical Studies* 13 (1983), 47–78.

2   Urban working women

Accampo, E. *Industrialization, Family Life, and Class Relations. Saint-Chamond, 1815–1914* (Berkeley: University of California Press, 1989).

Accampo, E., R. G. Fuchs and M. L. Stewart (eds), *Gender and the Politics of Social Reform in France, 1870–1914* (Baltimore: Johns Hopkins University Press, 1995).

Charle, C. *A Social History of France in the Nineteenth Century* (Oxford: Berg, 1994).

Chevalier, L. *Labouring Classes and Dangerous Classes in Paris during the First Half of the Nineteenth Century*, trans. Frank Jellinek (London: Routledge Kegan Paul, 1973).

Coffin, J. G. *The Politics of Women's Work: The Paris Garment Trades, 1750–1915* (Princeton: Princeton University Press, 1996).

Fuchs, R. G. *Poor and Pregnant in Paris: Strategies for Survival in the Nineteenth Century* (New Brunswick, N.J.: Rutgers University Press, 1992).

Hilden, P. *Working Women and Socialist Politics in France, 1880–1914: A Regional Study* (Oxford: Clarendon Press, 1986).

Johnson, C. *The Life and Death of Industrial Languedoc 1700–1920: The Politics of Deindustrialization* (Oxford: Oxford University Press, 1995).

Katznelson, I. and A. R. Zolberg (eds), *Working Class Formation: Nineteenth-Century Patterns in Western Europe and the United States* (Princeton: Princeton University Press, 1986).

Lynch, K. A. *Family, Class, and Ideology in Early Industrial France: Social Policy and the Working-Class Family 1825–1848* (Madison: University of Wisconsin Press, 1988).

Merriman, John. *The Red City: Limoges and the French Nineteenth Century* (New York: Oxford University Press, 1985).

Moch, L. P. *Paths to the City: Regional Migration in Nineteenth-Century France* (Beverly Hills: Sage Publications, 1983).

Noiriel, G. *Workers in French Society in the Nineteenth and Twentieth Centuries* (New York: Berg, 1990).

Sewell, W. H., Jr. *Work and Revolution in France: The Language of Labor from the Old Régime to 1848* (Cambridge: Cambridge University Press, 1980).

Stewart, M. L. *Women, Work and the French State: Labour Protection and Social Patriarchy, 1879–1919* (London: McGill-Queen's University Press, 1989).

Traugott, M., ed. and trans. *The French Worker: Autobiographies from the Early Industrial Era* (Berkeley: University of California Press, 1993).

3 Peasant women

Agulhon, M. *The Republic in the Village: The People of the Var from the French Revolution to the Second Republic*, trans. J. Lloyd (Cambridge and Paris: Cambridge University Press and Editions de la Maison des Sciences de l'Homme, 1982).

Darrow, M. *Revolution in the house: Family, Class, and Inheritance in Southern France, 1775–1825* (Princeton: Princeton University Press, 1989).

Debay, A. *Hygiène et physiologie du mariage: histoire naturelle et médicale de l'homme et de la femme mariés* (Paris: E. Dentu, 1859).

Gélis, J. *History of Childbirth: Fertility, Pregnancy and Birth in Early Modern Europe*, trans. R. Morris (Cambridge: Polity Press, 1991).

Hélias, P.-J. *The Horse of Pride: Life in a Breton Village*, trans. June Guicharnaud (New Haven and London: Yale University Press, 1978).

Price, R. *A Social History of Nineteenth-Century France* (London: Hutchinson, 1987).

Scott, J. W. *Gender and the Politics of History* (New York: Columbia University Press, 1988).

Shorter, E. *The Making of the Modern Family* (London: Fontana, 1977).

Strumingher, L. *What Were Little Girls and Boys Made of? Primary Education in Rural France, 1830–1880* (Albany: State University of New York Press, 1983).

Tilly, L. and J. W. Scott. *Women, Work and Family* (New York: Holt, Rinehart and Winston, 1978).

4 Women, politics and citizenship, 1814–1852

Agulhon, M. *Marianne into Battle. Republican Imagery and Symbolism in France, 1789–1880* (Cambridge and Paris: Cambridge University Press and Maison des Sciences de l'Homme, 1980).

Barry, D. *Women and Political Insurgency: France in the Mid-Nineteenth Century* (Houndmills, Basingstoke: Macmillan Press Ltd, 1996).

Faure, C. *Democracy Without Women: Feminism and the Rise of Liberal Individualism in France*, trans. C. Gorbman and J. Berks (Bloomington: Indiana University Press, 1991).

Fraisse, G. *Reason's muse: Sexual Difference and the Birth of Democracy*, trans. Jane Marie Todd (Chicago: University of Chicago Press, 1994).

Grogan, S. K. *French Socialism and Sexual Difference: Women and the New Society, 1803–1844* (London: Macmillan, 1992).

—— *Flora Tristan: Life Stories* (London and New York: Routledge, 1998).

——. '"O'Connell in Skirts"? Flora Tristan, Sexual Politics and Self-Representation', in M. Adcock, E. Chester and J. Whiteman (eds), *Revolution, Society and the Politics of Memory: The Proceedings of the Tenth George Rudé Seminar on French History and Civilisation* (Melbourne: University of Melbourne Department of History Monographs, 1997), pp. 206–13.

Jordanova, L. *Sexual Visions. Images of Gender in Science and Medicine between the Eighteenth and Twentieth Centuries* (Madison: University of Wisconsin Press, 1989).

354 SUGGESTIONS FOR FURTHER READING

Margadant, J. B. (ed.), *The New Biography: Performing Femininity in Nineteenth-Century France* (Berkeley and Los Angeles: University of California Press, 2000).

Maza, S. 'The Diamond Necklace Affair, 1785–1786', in her *Private Lives and Public Affairs: The Causes Célèbres of Prerevolutionary France* (Berkeley: University of California Press, 1993).

McPhee, P. *The Politics of Rural Life: Political Mobilisation in the French Countryside 1846–1852* (Oxford: Clarendon Press, 1992).

Moses, C. G. *French Feminism in the Nineteenth Century* (Albany: State University of New York Press, 1984).

Reynolds, S. (ed.), *Women, State and Revolution. Essays on Power and Gender in Europe since 1789* (Brighton: Wheatsheaf, 1986).

Thomas, C. *The Wicked Queen: The Origins of the Myth of Marie-Antoinette*, trans. J. Rose (New York: Zone Books, 1999).

5 Women and the creation of Republican France, 1852–1914

D'Héricourt, Madame. *A Woman's Philosophy of Woman; or Woman Affranchised. An Answer to Michelet, Proudhon, Girardin, Legouvé, Comte, and Other Modern Innovators, translated from the last Paris edition* [1860] (New York: Carleton, 1864).

Gullickson, *Unruly Women of Paris: Images of the Commune* (Ithaca and London: Cornell University Press, 1996).

——. 'La Pétroleuse: Representing Revolution', *Feminist Studies* 17, 2 (1991), 241–65.

Hause, S. C. and A. R. Kenney, 'The Limits of Suffragist Behaviour: Legalism and Militancy in France, 1876–1922', *American Historical Review* 86 (1981), 781–806.

——, with A. R. Kenney, *Women's Suffrage and Social Politics in the French Third Republic* (Princeton, N.J.: Princeton University Press, 1984).

Johnson, M. P. 'Citizenship and Gender: The Légion des Fédérées in the Paris Commune of 1871', *French History* 8, 3 (1994), 276–95.

Jones, K. B. and F. Vergès, 'Women of the Paris Commune', *Women's Studies International Forum* 14 (1991), 491–503.

Mayeur, J.-M. and M. Rebérioux, *The Third Republic from its Origins to the Great War, 1871–1914*, trans. J. R. Foster (Cambridge: Cambridge University Press; Paris: Editions de la Maison des Sciences de l'Homme, 1987).

Nye, *Masculinity and Male Codes of Honor in Modern France* (New York and Oxford: Oxford University Press, 1993).

——. 'Sexuality, Sex Difference and the Cult of Modern Love in Third Republic France', *Historical Reflections/Réflexions Historiques* 20, 1 (1994), 57–76.

Offen, K. 'Depopulation, Nationalism and Feminism in Fin-de-Siècle France', *American Historical Review* 89 (1984), 648–76.

Pilbeam, P. *Republicanism in Nineteenth-Century France, 1814–1871* (Houndmills, Basingstoke: Macmillan, 1995).

Shafer, D. A. 'Plus que des Ambulancières: Women in articulation and defence of their ideals during the Paris Commune (1871)', *French History* 7, 1 (1993), 85–101.

Sowerwine, C. *France since 1870: Culture, Politics and Society* (Houndmills Basingstoke: Palgrave, 2001).

———. *Sisters or Citizens? Women and Socialism in France since 1876* (Cambridge: Cambridge University Press, 1982).

Stewart, M. L. *For Health and Beauty: Physical Culture for Frenchwomen 1880s–1930s* (Baltimore: Johns Hopkins University Press, 2001).

Stone, J. *Sons of the Revolution: Radical Democrats in France, 1862–1914* (Baton Rouge: Louisiana State University Press, 1996).

Thomas, Edith. *The Women Incendiaries* trans. James and Starr Atkinson (London: Secker & Warburg, 1967).

———. 'The Women of the Commune', *The Massachusetts Review* 12 (1971), 409–17.

6   'New women' in the era of the Great War, 1890s–1920s

Barbusse, Henri. *Under Fire*, trans. W. Fitzwater Wray (London: Dent, 1926).

Becker, J.-J. *The Great War and the French People*, trans. A. Pomerans (Providence and Oxford: Berg, 1983).

Carles, E. *A Wild Herb Soup: The life of a French countrywoman*, trans. A. H. Goldberger (London: Victor Gollancz, 1992).

Cole, J. H. '"There are only good mothers": The Ideological Work of Women's Fertility in France before World War I', *French Historical Studies* 19, 3 (1996), 639–72.

Duby, G. and M. Perrot (general eds), *A History of Women in the West*, Vol. V: *Toward a Cultural Identity in the Twentieth Century*, ed. F. Thébaud (Cambridge Mass. and London: Belknap Press, 1994).

Felski, R. *The Gender of Modernity* (Cambridge, Mass. and London: Harvard University Press, 1995).

Gemie, S. *Women and Schooling in France, 1815–1914: Gender, Authority and Identity in the Female Schooling Sector* (Keele: Keele University Press, 1995).

Grafteaux, S. (ed.), *Mémé Santerre: A French Woman of the People*, trans. L. A. Tilly and K. L. Tilly (New York: Schocken Books, 1985).

Grazia, V. de, with E. Furlough (eds), *The Sex of Things: Gender and Consumption in Historical Perspective* (Berkeley: University of California Press, 1996).

Higonnet, M. R. *et al.* (eds), *Behind the Lines: Gender and the Two World Wars* (New Haven and London: Yale University Press, 1987).

McMillan, J. *Housewife or Harlot: The Place of Women in French Society, 1870–1940* (Brighton: Harvester Press, 1981).

Miller, M. *The Bon Marché: Bourgeois Culture and the Department Store, 1869–1920* (Princeton: Princeton University Press, 1981).

Motte, D. de la, and J. M. Przyblynski (eds), *Making the News: Modernity and the Mass Press in Nineteenth-Century France* (Boston: University of Massachusetts Press, 1999).

Reynolds, S. 'Albertine's bicycle, or, Women and French Identity during the Belle Epoque', *Literature and History* 10, 1 (2001), 28–41.

——. *France Between the Wars: Gender and Politics* (London: Routledge, 1996).

Roberts, M. L. *Civilization Without Sexes: Reconstructing Gender in Postwar France, 1917–1927* (Chicago and London: University of Chicago Press, 1994).

Tiersten, L. *Marianne in the Market: Envisioning Consumer Society in Fin-de-Siècle France* (Berkeley: University of California Press, 2001).

Wheeler, K. W. and V. L. Lussier (eds), *Women, the Arts, and the 1920s in Paris and New York* (New Brunswick and London: Transaction Books, 1982).

Zdatny, S. (ed.), *Hairstyles and Fashion: A Hairdresser's History of Paris, 1910–1920* (Oxford and New York: Berg, 1999).

7 Taking sides: women in the 1930s

Bard, C. and J.-L. Robert, 'The French Communist Party and Women 1920–1939: From "feminism" to familialism', trans. N. Dombrowski, in H. Gruber and P. Graves (eds), *Women and Socialism, Socialism and Women: Europe between the two World Wars* (New York and Oxford: Berghahn Books, 1998).

Bernard, P. and H. Dubief, *The Decline of the Third Republic 1914–1938*, trans. A. Forster (Cambridge: Cambridge University Press; Paris: Editions de la Maison des Sciences de l'Homme, 1985).

Koven, S. and S. Michel. *Mothers of a new world: Maternalist Politics and the Origins of Welfare States* (New York: Routledge, 1993).

Jackson, J. *The Popular Front in France: Defending Democracy, 1934–1938* (Cambridge: Cambridge University Press, 1988).

Pedersen, S. *Family, Dependence and the Origins of the Welfare State: Britain and France, 1914–1945* (Cambridge: Cambridge University Press, 1993).

Prost, A. and G. Vincent (eds), *A History of Private Life*, Vol. V: *Riddles of Identity in Modern Times*, trans. A. Goldhammer (Cambridge and London: The Belknap Press of Harvard University Press, 1991).

Reynolds, R. 'Women and the Popular Front in France: The Case of the Three Women Ministers', *French History* 8, 4 (1994), 196–224.

Siegel, M. ' "To the Unknown Mother of the Unknown Soldier": Pacifism, Feminism, and the Politics of Sexual Difference among French *Institutrices* between the Wars', *French Historical Studies* 22, 3 (1999), 421–51.

Soucy, R. *French Fascism: The First Wave, 1924–1933* (New Haven: Yale University Press, 1986).

——. *French Fascism: The Second Wave, 1933–1939* (New Haven: Yale University Press, 1995).

Whitney, S. B. 'Embracing the status quo: French Communists, Young Women and the Popular Front', *Journal of Social History* 30, 1 (Fall, 1996), 29–53.

——. 'Gender, Class and Generation in Interwar French Catholicism: The Case of the Jeunesse ouvrière chrétienne féminine', *Journal of Family History* 26, 4 (2001), 480–507.

8   Vichy France: reviving the 'natural woman', 1940–1944

Duchen, C. *Women's Rights and Women's Lives in France 1944–1968* (London and New York: Routledge, 1994).
Fishman, S. *We Will Wait: Wives of French Prisoners of War, 1940–1945* (New Haven and London: Yale University Press, 1991).
Kedward, H. R. and Nancy Wood (eds), *The Liberation of France: Image and Event* (Oxford and Washington: Berg, 1995).
Marrus, M. R. and R. O. Paxton, *Vichy France and the Jews* (New York: Basic Books, 1981).
Muel-Dreyfus, F. *Vichy and the Eternal Feminine: A Contribution to a Political Sociology of Gender*, trans. K. A. Johnson (Durham and London: Duke University Press, 2001).
Paxton, R. O. *Vichy France: Old Guard and New Order 1940–1944*, reprint of 1982 edn (New York: Columbia University Press, 2001).
Pollard, M. *Reign of Virtue: Mobilizing Gender in Vichy France* (Chicago: University of Chicago Press, 1998).
Sweets, J. F. 'Hold that Pendulum! Redefining Fascism, Collaborationism and Resistance in France', *French Historical Studies* 15 (1987–1988), 731–58.
Weitz, M. C. *Sisters in the Resistance: How Women Fought to Free France, 1940–1945* (New York: John Wiley & Sons, 1995).

9   From the liberation to 'Women's liberation', 1945–1975

Association Choisir, *Abortion: The Bobigny Affair—A Law on Trial*, trans. Beryl Henderson (Sydney: Wild & Woolley, 1975).
Duchen, C., ed. and trans. *French Connections: Voices from the Women's Liberation Movement in France* (Amherst: University of Massachusetts Press, 1987).
Greenwald, L. 'Not "Undifferentiated Magma": Refashioning a Female Identity in France, 1944–55', *Historical Reflections/Réflexions historiques* 22, 2 (1996), 407–30.
Laubier, C. (ed.), *The Condition of Women in France 1945 to the Present: A Documentary Anthology* (London: Routledge, 1990).
Ross, K. *May '68 and Its Afterlives* (Chicago and London: University of Chicago Press, 2002).
Weiner, S. *Enfants Terribles: Youth and Femininity in the Mass Media in France, 1945–1968* (Baltimore and London: Johns Hopkins University Press, 2001).
——. 'Two Modernities: From *Elle* to *Mademoiselle*. Women's Magazines in Postwar France', *Contemporary European History*, VIII, no. 3 (1999), 395–409.

10   The politics of 'women's place' since 1975

Gregory, A. and U. Tidd (eds) *Women in Contemporary France* (Oxford and New York: Berg, 2000).

Haase-Dubosc, D. 'Sexual Difference and Politics in France Today', *Feminist Studies* (Spring, 1999), available at http://www.findarticles.com, accessed 8 January 2004.

Mayer, N. and M. Sineau, 'III: France: The *Front National*,' in H. Amsberger and B. Halbmayre (eds), *Rechtsextreme Parteien* (forthcoming Leverkusen: Leske & Budrich, 2002), pp. 42–103; http://elections2002.sciences-po.fr/ Enjeux/enjeux.html, from link 'Women and the National Front/Le Front National et les femmes', accessed Sunday, 2 March 2003.

Ramsey, R. L. *French Women in Politics: Writing Power, Paternal Legitimization, and Maternal Legacies* (New York and Oxford: Berghahn Books, 2003).

Reynolds, S. 'The French Ministry of Women's Rights 1981–86: Modernisation or Marginalisation?', in J. Gaffney (ed.) *France and Modernisation* (Aldershot: Avebury, 1988).

Simmons, H. G. *The French National Front: The Extremist Challenge to Democracy* (Boulder, Col.: Westview Press, 1996).

Todd, E. *The Making of Modern France: Politics, Ideology and Culture*, trans. A. and B. Forster (London: Basil Blackwell, 1991).

Index

LaVergne, TN USA
26 November 2010
206352LV00001B/72/P